African Cities in Crisis

African Modernization and Development Series
Paul Lovejoy, Series Editor

Psychoses of Power: African Personal Dictatorships, Samuel Decalo

African Cities in Crisis: Managing Rapid Urban Growth,
edited by Richard E. Stren and Rodney R. White

Patriarchy and Class: African Women in the Home and the Workforce,
edited by Sharon B. Stichter and Jane L. Parpart

The Precarious Balance: State and Society in Africa,
edited by Donald Rothchild and Naomi Chazan

African Population and Capitalism: Historical Perspectives,
edited by Dennis D. Cordell and Joel W. Gregory

Southern African Labor Migration and the South African Gold Mines: 1960-1984, Jonathan Crush, Alan Jeeves, and David Yudelman

African Cities in Crisis

Managing Rapid Urban Growth

EDITED BY

Richard E. Stren
Rodney R. White

Westview Press
BOULDER, SAN FRANCISCO, & LONDON

Published in cooperation with
The International Federation of
Institutes for Advanced Study (IFIAS)

African Modernization and Development Series

This Westview softcover edition is printed on acid-free paper and bound in softcovers that carry the highest rating of the National Association of State Textbook Administrators, in consultation with the Association of American Publishers and the Book Manufacturers' Institute.

All rights reserved. No part of this publication may be reproduced or transmitted in any form or by any means, electronic or mechanical, including photocopy, recording, or any information storage and retrieval system, without permission in writing from the publisher.

Copyright © 1989 by Westview Press, Inc.

Published in 1989 in the United States of America by Westview Press, Inc., 5500 Central Avenue, Boulder, Colorado 80301, and in the United Kingdom by Westview Press, Inc., 13 Brunswick Centre, London WC1N 1AF, England

Library of Congress Cataloging-in-Publication Data
African cities in crisis.
  (African modernization and development series)
  Bibliography: p.
  Includes index.
  1. Urban policy—Africa.   2. Cities and towns—
Africa—Growth.   3. Urbanization—Africa.   I. Stren,
Richard E.   II. White, Rodney R.   III. Series.
HT148.A2A34   1989   307.7'6'096   87-31622
ISBN 0-8133-7466-9

Printed and bound in the United States of America

∞ The paper used in this publication meets the requirements of the American National Standard for Permanence of Paper for Printed Library Materials Z39.48-1984.

10 9 8 7 6 5 4 3 2 1

Contents

List of Tables	vi
List of Figures	ix
List of Currencies	x
Preface	xi
CHAPTER 1. The Influence of Environmental and Economic Factors on the Urban Crisis. Rodney R. White	1
CHAPTER 2. Urban Local Government in Africa. Richard E. Stren	20
CHAPTER 3. The Administration of Urban Services. Richard E. Stren	37
CHAPTER 4. Urban Growth and Urban Management in Nigeria. Adepoju G. Onibokun	69
CHAPTER 5. Côte d'Ivoire: An Evaluation of Urban Management Reforms. Koffi Attahi	113
CHAPTER 6. Kinshasa: Problems of Land Management, Infrastructure, and Food Supply. Kankondé Mbuyi	149
CHAPTER 7. Appropriate Standards for Infrastructure in Dakar. Thiécouta Ngom	177
CHAPTER 8. Local Government and the Management of Urban Services in Tanzania. Saitiel Kulaba	203
CHAPTER 9. Management Problems of Greater Khartoum. Mohamed O. El Sammani, Mohamed El Hadi Abu Sin, M. Talha, B.M. El Hassan, and Ian Haywood	247
CHAPTER 10. Urban Management in Nairobi: A Case Study of the Matatu Mode of Public Transport. Diana Lee-Smith	276
Conclusion	305
Bibliography	313
Contributors	322
About the IFIAS	324
Index	327

List of Tables

CHAPTER 1. The Influence of Environmental and Economic Factors on the Urban Crisis
1.1 Population Growth and Urbanization 3
1.2 Some Indicators of Demographic Change 4
1.3 The Population of the Largest City 5
1.4 Some Economic Indicators 10
1.5 Long-Term External Debt and Service Ratios, 1970-1984 12
1.6 Multilateral Debt Renegotiations, 1976-1984 12
1.7 Some Socio-economic Indicators 16

CHAPTER 4. Urban Growth and Urban Management in Nigeria
4.1 Nigerian Population 1921-1984 70
4.2 Contribution of Migration and Natural Increase to Urban Growth and Average Annual Growth in Selected Cities 70
4.3 Population of Some Nigerian Cities 78
4.4 Urban Household Demographic Characteristics 80
4.5 Number of Primary Schools and Enrollment in the States of Oyo, Anambra, and Kaduna 81
4.6 Water Supply 82
4.7 Proportion of Households with In-house Pipe-borne Water Supply 86
4.8 Degree of Regularity of Household Potable Water Supply 87
4.9 Level of Daily Household Potable Water Consumption Measured in Kerosene Tins 88
4.10 Level of Monthly Household Expenditure on Water 89
4.11 Percentage of Total Solid Waste Generation in Ibadan, Kaduna, and Onitsha 90
4.12 Mean Percentage Composition by Weight of Solid Wastes 93
4.13 Temporal Changes in the Organization of Solid Wastes Management in Ibadan, Kaduna, and Enugu 94
4.14 Storage of Domestic Wastes in Three Nigeria Cities 95
4.15 Ownership of Energy Appliances 96
4.16 Access to Energy Appliances 98
4.17 Residential Energy Appliances and their Energy Requirements 100

4.18	Energy Most Frequently Used	102
4.19	Reason for Using Energy for Cooking by Type of Energy	104
4.20	Grants Distributed to States for Local Governments between 1976 / 1977 and 1980	108

CHAPTER 6. Kinshasa: Problems of Land Management, Infrastructure, and Food Supply

6.1	The Population of Zaire by Province	150
6.2	Distribution of Facilities by Zone	166
6.3	Fresh Produce by Road	168
6.4	Estimate of Consumption in Tons, Kinshasa, 1984	170

CHAPTER 7. Appropriate Standards for Infrastructure in Dakar

7.1	Districts and Neighborhoods of the *Département* of Dakar	184
7.2	Sectors and Neighborhoods of the *Département* of Pikine	184
7.3	Population Distribution in the Dakar and Pikine *Départements*	186
7.4	Pupils per Class, *Département* of Dakar	186
7.5	Responsibility for Services	198
7.6	Personnel with the CUD and the Three Communes	199
7.7	Vehicles Owned by the Dakar, Pikine, and Rufisque-Bargny Communes	199
7.8	Receipts of the Communes	200

CHAPTER 8. Local Government and the Management of Urban Services in Tanzania

8.1	Population Growth Trends in Tanzanian Study Towns, 1948-2000	210
8.2	Target and Actual Cesspit Emptying for Three Weeks, June – July 1985, in Dar es Salaam	222
8.3	Main Sources of Revenue of Tanzanian Urban Councils from Local Taxes, 1985 / 86	222
8.4	Performance in Tax Collection of the Development Levy in Selected Tanzanian Urban Authorities, 1984 / 85 – 1985 / 86	232
8.5	Urban Local Government Authorities Development Budgets, 1978-1987	234
8.6	Refuse Production and Collection, Tanzanian Urban Councils, 1986	236
8.7	Number and Condition of Construction Equipment in Tanzanian Urban Areas as of 31st December 1985	238
8.8	Estimated Cost of Repairing and Reconstructing Roads in Tanzanian Study Towns	238
8.9	Number, Condition, and Carrying Capacity of UDA Buses, Dar es Salaam	240

CHAPTER 9. Management Problems of Greater Khartoum
  9.1 Emigration of Khartoum Household Members and their
       Remittances to Household Budgets, 1985   250
CHAPTER 10. Urban Management in Nairobi
  10.1 Characteristics of Matatu Operators   291

List of Figures

CHAPTER 1. The Influence of Environmental and Economic Factors on the Urban Crisis
1.1. Cities Studied by the African Urban Management Project   xiv
1.2. Gross National Product per capita, World Bank 1976-1984   14

CHAPTER 4. Urban Growth and Urban Management in Nigeria
4.1. Nigeria State Boundaries and Urban Settlements   68
4.2. Nigerian States: Quality of Urban Life   74
4.3. Areal Extent of Ibadan 1935, 1963, 1973, 1985   75
4.4. Areal Extent of Kaduna 1930, 1982, 1985   76
4.5. Areal Extent of Enugu 1975, 1985   77

CHAPTER 5. Côte d'Ivoire: An Evaluation of Urban Management Reforms
5.1. Côte d'Ivoire: Distribution of Urban Population   112
5.2. The Growth of Abidjan   124

CHAPTER 6. Kinshasa: Problems of Land Management, Infrastructure, and Food Supply
6.1. Zaïre: Distribution of the Urban Population, 1984   148
6.2. Kinshasa: Stages of Growth   152

CHAPTER 7. Appropriate Standards for Infrastructure in Dakar
7.1. Senegal: Regions and Principal Towns   176
7.2. The Region of Dakar, 1984   182

CHAPTER 8. Local Government and the Management of Urban Services in Tanzania
8.1. Tanzania: Study Towns and Cities   204
8.2. Dar es Salaam: Areal Extent   205

CHAPTER 9. Management Problems of Greater Khartoum
9.1. Sudan: Distribution of the Urban Population, 1956, 1973   246
9.2. The Growth of Khartoum   252

CHAPTER 10. Urban Management in Nairobi
10.1. Kenya 1979: Towns with Population over 10,000   280
10.2. Nairobi: Land Use   282

List of Currencies

The currencies referred to in this book are listed below with their average (official) exchange rate to the 1985 Annual Supplement of the Quarterly Economic Reviews of The Economist Intelligence Unit. However, it is not always easy to interpret these exchange rates as many of them greatly overvalue the currency compared with the unofficial rates which more closely reflect their purchasing power. The rates are quoted for the period when most of the fieldwork reported in these studies was carried out.

Côte d'Ivoire	CFA franc	437 per $
Kenya	Kenyan shilling	14.414 per $
Nigeria	naira	0.8 per $
Senegal	CFA franc	437 per $
Sudan	Sudanese pound	1.3 per $ (official)
		2.5 per $ (alternative)
Tanzania	Tanz. shilling	18.10 per $
Zaire	zaire	36.1 per $

Preface

The funding of urban projects in Africa in the late 1970s was overshadowed by national and international attempts to establish agriculture as the highest priority for development. Although reality rarely matched rhetoric, this shift in discourse drew attention away from efforts that had begun in such a promising fashion in the early 1970s to reform certain sectors of urban management (Cohen 1983). These attempts at reform included the promotion of aided self-help housing (involving sites and services as well as squatter upgrading schemes), support for administrative decentralization, and a new tolerance for and understanding of the informal sector.

Throughout the 1970s the largest cities in each country grew very rapidly as a result of migration from the rural areas and the high rate of natural increase of the established urban-dwellers. Although comparative data on rural and urban health conditions are difficult to obtain, water supply and basic health care in the cities seem to have been adequate to prevent mortality rates from surpassing those in rural areas. (Whether the spread of AIDS will change this relationship remains to be seen.) The very rapid urban population growth rates that resulted from the conjunction of these demographic trends all but overwhelmed the reform efforts.

Yet under increasingly difficult conditions, urban governments continued to operate, turning to home-made solutions, or at least accepting the grim reality as an inevitability (Stren 1986). Without other alternatives, some governments began to tolerate the survival tactics of the urban poor – squatting on illegally occupied land, using "pirate" taxis and minibuses in competition with the public transport services, and relying on community-based self-help groups to develop water, roads, and educational facilities when none of these appeared in the official Master Plan. The growing gap between the realities of official plans and perspectives, on the one hand, and the mushrooming world of the urban poor, on the other hand, has scarcely been studied in African cities. This book presents the results of the first project which was designed to study comparatively governmental responses to this gap in Africa.

This study (which came to be known as the "African Urban Management" project) was first proposed at a meeting held in Nairobi in April 1982, funded by the International Development Research Centre (IDRC), Ottawa, and by the International Federation of Institutes for Advanced Study (IFIAS), headquartered now at Toronto. Leaders of the seven research teams represented in this volume were present at that first meeting. The African countries in the group were Côte d'Ivoire, Kenya, Nigeria, Senegal, Sudan, Tanzania, and Zaire. These countries together represented Anglophone and Francophone traditions, east and west Africa, "socialism" and "state capitalism" in ideological persuasion, as well as humid and semi-arid climates.

At that first meeting in Nairobi, it was decided that a comparative framework would be essential if the lessons drawn from one country were to be applicable elsewhere. However, since the ultimate purpose of the research was to carry out "policy-relevant" studies and since every country has its own agenda of urban issues, it was decided that each country team would make the decision on the sector or sectors for intensive study. The comparative framework which each team accepted as the basis for its own research was empirical, not highly abstract or theoretical. The reasoning behind this approach was twofold. First, the results of the study had to be understandable to local administrators, politicians, and officials who might not be *au courant* with theories of urban development, however fascinating these might be to the academic researchers themselves. Second, there is very little published work of any kind on the urban problems as discussed in this book. And what has been published – in formal publications or fugitive documents – is quickly outdated by the pace of change. On the premise that good theory needs a firm groundwork of empirical investigation, the case studies in this volume stress the empirical rather than the theoretical.

Following the Nairobi meeting, more discussions were held among the participants until, in 1984, IDRC funded a comparative study to take place over a two-year period. Workshops to develop the comparative framework and to compare results were held in Abidjan in March 1985 as well as in Toronto in September 1985 and October 1986. A bilingual, annotated bibliography assembled to aid the research was published later by the Centre for Developing-Area Studies of McGill University (Stren and Letemendia 1986). At the end of the project in 1986 and 1987, each country team produced a separate final report, from which a shorter (approximately fifty-page) version was written for this volume. These shorter versions provide the country case studies in Chapters 4 through 10 of this volume. We wrote the three opening chapters and the concluding chapter to provide a comparative overview. In these overview chapters, many of the ideas expressed are the result of the original research reports and stimulating comments and insights provided by our African colleagues. While we are the editors of this book, its contents are truly a joint effort.

On behalf of all the researchers involved, we would like to register our appreciation to IFIAS which through Project Ecoville in Toronto provided constant support, encouragement, and a timely contribution to the production of this volume. We are also grateful for generous and imaginative research funding from IDRC (and in particular the early support for the project given by Yue-man Yeung), from the Social Sciences and Humanities Research Council of Canada, and from the various African institutions where the research teams were based. We greatly benefitted from all the help given by the Institute for Environmental Studies of the University of Toronto, which provided a home for the coordinating unit. A great many individuals contributed to the work; some are thanked individually in particular chapters. Michael Cohen helped us to get the project underway, and provided invaluable advice in the early stages. We would particularly like to thank Claire Letemendia for some French-English translations and for the preparation of the index; Robbie Barnum-Carty, Susan Roberts, and Michelle Carr for producing the English manuscript; Claude Stren for the French translation; and Roger Riendeau for his meticulous work in managing the editorial production of this volume. The efforts of so many people will have been worthwhile if some support is gained for the improved management of African cities.

Richard Stren and Rodney White
Institute for Environmental Studies
University of Toronto
September 1988

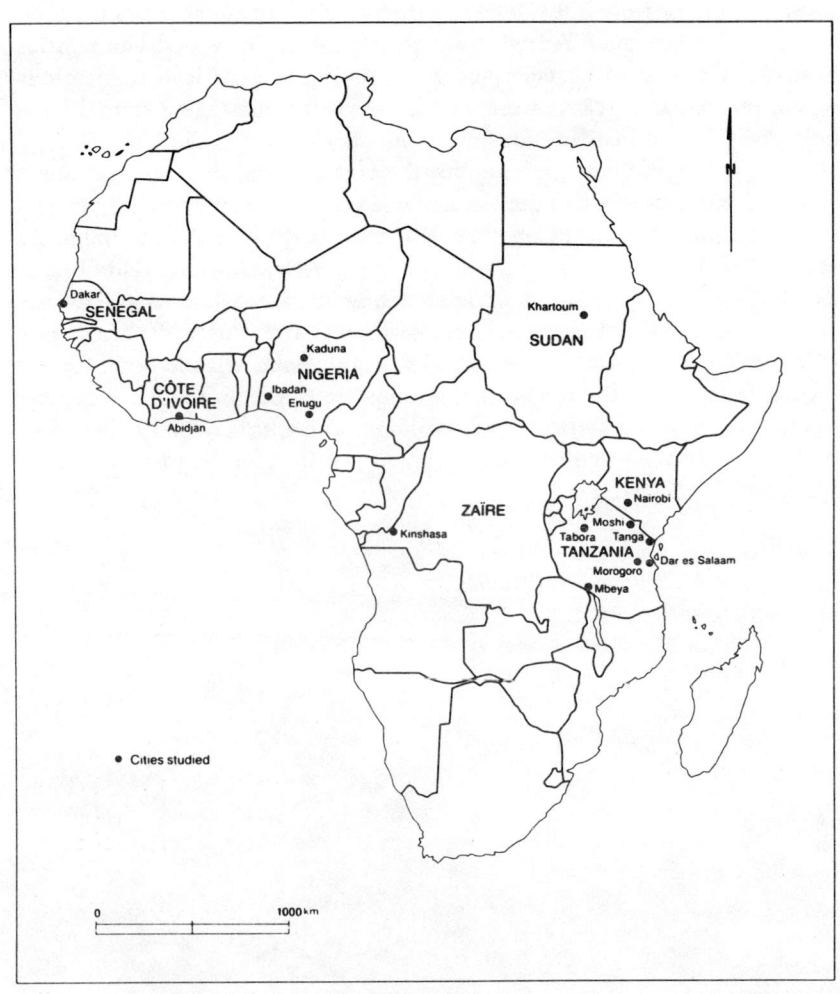

**Figure 1.1
Cities Studied by the African Urban Management Project**

CHAPTER 1
The Influence of Environmental and Economic Factors on the Urban Crisis
Rodney R. White

The economic plight of sub-Saharan Africa is a problem of growing concern. Economic stagnation coupled with rapid population growth has produced a grave crisis on which there is widespread agreement as to the condition but little agreement as to the best mix of policies. Indeed, so much has been written recently on policy proposals for Africa that the critique of these proposals has itself become a growth industry for academics (Ravenhill 1986).

The following statement from a World Bank report is a typical appraisal of the symptoms of the problem:

> Africa's economic and social conditions began to deteriorate in the 1970's, and continue to do so. GDP grew at an average 3.6 percent a year between 1970 and 1980, but has fallen every year since then. With population rising at over 3 percent a year, income per capita in 1983 is estimated to be 4 percent below its 1979 level. Agricultural output per capita has continued to decline, so food imports have increased; they now provide a fifth of the region's cereal requirements. Much industrial capacity stands idle.... Many institutions are deteriorating, both in physical capacity and in their technical and financial ability to perform (World Bank 1984a, 1).

The purpose of this chapter is to provide an overview of the process of urbanization at this difficult time. The manner in which urban policy options are constrained by current conditions needs to be understood, and the effects of past urban policy need to be examined.

Since the "urban bias" in national policies was identified (Lipton 1977; Dumont and Mottin 1983), the tendency has been to assume that if the bias could be reversed then conditions would improve; answers have included "integrated rural development," "true market prices," and many more. Yet as each incorrect policy has been identified and a new watchword proposed, the problems have grown deeper. To any informed observer over the past fifteen years, the process has resembled the peeling of an infinite number of layers of the onion skin.

Clearly, no single cause explains the population growth and economic decline syndrome from which sub-Saharan Africa is suffering. Rapid societal change on a continental scale is a complex process, and many variables must be considered simultaneously. It is not a question of determining whether the rural sector or the urban sector is the most important; an understanding of their symbiotic relationship is required. Neither "integrated rural development" nor "privatization" nor "letting the market operate" is going to solve the problem. The fact is that the economy and society suffer simultaneously from a lack of foreign exchange and from a shortage of clean drinking water among many other needs.

In this sort of situation, it is foolish to champion tourism (for example) as the best foreign-exchange earner, without first considering whether the urban system is salubrious enough to support a tourist industry and whether the water demands of tourism can be met from available supplies. One cannot let the urban system crumble to the point that it cannot support rural development, while channeling all available funds into the rural sector. Unfortunately, the solution is much more complex than the simple either / or alternatives that have so often been considered in the last fifteen years.

Through a set of case studies, this study attempts to examine the interplay of many factors – domestic policies as well as exogenous events such as changes in the price of oil and severe fluctuations in rainfall. The remainder of this chapter looks at population growth, environmental stress, and the economic trends. The two subsequent chapters examine the political and administrative framework in which urban management takes place. These are followed by seven case studies and a concluding chapter.

Population Growth and Urbanization

For sub-Saharan Africa, the two key demographic events of the period 1950 to 1985 are steady population growth and increasing urbanization (see Tables 1.1 and 1.2). Although the region is not highly urbanized by global standards, the trend in that direction has been extremely rapid. Also notable is that, in conformity with world trends, the largest cities have generally been growing fastest. In this case, one would expect the largest city within the national urban hierarchy to become increasingly dominant. Table 1.3 shows the degree of dominance of the major cities in 1980 – the latest date for which comparable data were available.

In only two of the countries covered in this study – Nigeria and Zaire – is any regional manufacturing complex large enough to counter-balance the attractiveness of the largest major city to migrants. (See Table 1.3, column 5 for an indication of this tendency.) Because of this dominance, the majority of import-substitution activities are drawn to the major city, thus reinforcing its demographic weight. Although no less than three of the seven countries have re-located their national capitals to interior locations, none of these new foci has emerged to challenge the former capital (Attahi 1984).[1]

Since the 1960s studies have emphasized the economic rationality of the

Table 1.1
Population Growth and Urbanization
(millions)

	1	2	3	4[1]	5
	Total present population 1984	Population in the year 2000	Projected rate of natural increase to the year 2000	Hypothetical stationary population[2]	% of population that is urban 1984
Côte d'Ivoire	10	17	3.7%	46	46%
Kenya	20	35	3.9	111	18
Nigeria	97	163	3.4	528	30
Senegal	6	10	2.9	30	35
Sudan	21	34	2.9	101	21
Tanzania	22	37	3.5	123	14
Zaire	30	47	3.0	130	39

Source: World Bank 1986a, Table 1 (180-81), Table 25 (228-29), Table 131 (240-1).

[1] In column 4 the dates for stationarity are 2030 for Zaire and Kenya, 2035 for the remainder.

[2] It goes without saying that all these figures (and those that follow) must be treated with extreme reservation. Most of them are taken from the World Bank's *World Development Report*, the most comprehensive annual publication in the field. Many of these figures are taken from United Nations sources, which themselves are taken from member countries, many of which have great difficulty in keeping up-to-date records. As a major example, Nigeria, by far the most populous country in Black Africa, has had no official census since 1963.

Table 1.2

Some Indicators of Demographic Change

Country	Crude Birth Rate per 1000 people		Crude Death Rate per 1000 people		Infant Mortality (0-1 years) per 1000 live births		Child Death Rate (1-4 years) per 1000 children	
	1965	1984	1965	1984	1965	1984	1965	1984
Côte d'Ivoire	44	45	22	14	176	106	37	15
Kenya	51	53	21	13	113	92	25	16
Nigeria	51	50	23	16	179	110	33	21
Senegal	47	46	23	19	172	138	42	27
Sudan	47	45	24	17	161	113	37	18
Tanzania	49	50	22	16	138	111	29	22
Zaire	48	45	21	15	142	103	30	20

For comparison, the figures for Japan and the U.S.A. are:

Japan	19	13	7	7	21	6	1	-0.5
U.S.A.	19	16	9	9	25	11	1	-0.5

Source: World Bank, 1986a, Table 26 (230-31) and Table 27 (232-33).

migrant's move to the big city (Todaro 1976); other studies have emphasized the agglomeration economies that the large cities would produce (Linn 1982). There was no immediate concern that the cities were growing too fast or would become too large, as it was believed that a deterioration in the urban quality of life would produce a decline (perhaps even a reversal) of rural-urban migration. It was also believed that rapid urbanization would stimulate the demand for goods from the domestic rural economy. Eventually, rural wages would rise, and a tendency towards equilibrium would appear, thus encouraging an orderly transition to a Western-style, urban-industrial economy in Africa.

That nothing of the kind has occurred may be attributable to the omission of some exogenous variables from the macro-economic models on which such beliefs were based. (See next section for further elaboration.) A number of important endogenous processes were also under-estimated by the same models. The most important for understanding the urban trajectory is what became known as the "urban bias," as mentioned above. Under this type of policy, governments established price controls to protect urban consumers from inflation. Some simultaneously kept a fixed rate of exchange at above market level. The combination of these two factors encouraged the growing reliance on cheap, imported food with which the

Table 1.3
The Population of the Largest City

Country	% of the urban population in the largest city 1980	% of the total population in the largest city 1980	Population of the largest city (millions) 1980	Annual growth of the largest city (%) 1984	Number of cities with population over 500,000 1980
Côte d'Ivoire	34	16	1.3	10	1
Kenya	57	9	1.5	8	1
Nigeria	17	5	4.2	12	14
Senegal	65	23	1.3	6	1
Sudan	31	8	1.4	7	1
Tanzania	50	8	1.5	13	1
Zaire	28	9	2.6	6	2

Source: World Bank, 1986a, Table 31 (240-41). Various estimates from the country research teams were used for column 4.

domestic farmer could not compete – especially in the provision of grains. This is now believed to have contributed substantially to the decline of the rural economy.

Thus, the redistribution process which began with a strong movement to the cities in search of newly-created jobs in industry and services became entrenched by the steady decline of the domestic rural-urban terms of trade and the decline of agricultural export markets. Since 1985 some governments (under strong pressure from the IMF) have tried to reverse this trend by raising farmgate prices, adopting more realistic foreign exchange rates, and reducing heavily subsidized urban services.

Despite all the uncertainty surrounding economic and demographic trends, the World Bank and other international agencies produce projections of stationary populations. (At stationarity, births equal deaths.) These projections must resemble a nightmare to urban planners (see Table 1.1, column 4). If the percentage of the total population in the largest city (Table 1.3, column 2) were to remain at the 1980 level, then the following city populations would be recorded by the time stationarity occurred (estimated for between the year 2030 and the year 2035):

		(estimated population in 1980)
Abidjan	7 million	(1.3 million)
Dakar	7 million	(1.3 million)
Dar es Salaam	10 million	(1.5 million)
Khartoum	8 million	(1.4 million)
Kinshasa	12 million	(2.6 million)
Lagos	26 million	(4.2 million)
Nairobi	10 million	(1.5 million)

If this growth should seem improbable, it is instructive to remember that Mexico City is estimated to have a population of 18 million and is projected to grow to 26 million by the year 2000 (Salas 1986, 20). (There too, the engine of growth is not the expansion of the urban economic base, but demographic inertia and the perceived lack of economic opportunity in the rural areas.) The World Bank estimates: "by [the year] 2000 ... Dakar and Nairobi are likely to have more than 5 million inhabitants each, compared with between 1 million and 2 million today" (1986b, 10).

It would seem that the best that can be hoped for is a higher level of urbanization which, if living standards can at least be maintained, will encourage a rapid fall in infant mortality and a fall in fertility. Under this scenario, the biggest cities will continue to grow (perhaps even to the size indicated above). Although the links among mortality, fertility, and population change are disputed, there is general agreement that "most programs and policies undertaken to reduce mortality will, in most settings and over the long run, produce even greater fertility declines and thus slower growth" (Gwatkin 1984, Abstract).

The question for urban planners and other policy-makers is: How can urban growth be managed in such a way that it does not occur to the detriment of the rural economy, the surrounding environment, and the urban system itself? The next section will consider some of the key environmental variables on which the sustainability of the urban systems directly depends.

Environmental Stress

Economies do not develop within an unchanging "environment." Economists used to designate certain inputs like air and water as "free goods." Now that clean air, water, woodfuel, untilled land, and wild game are no longer so plentiful, the "value" of the environment is being recognized. Nowhere is this realization more apparent than in Africa. The seven countries examined in this book have similarities and differences not only in their economic context but also in their environmental situation. The commonalities are presented in order of importance.

In an urban environment, the water supply is the most crucial element. As cities expand, they incorporate the neighboring villages, in which the people followed a rural way of life and drew water from local wells. Gradually, the population density outstrips the capacity of the wells. The groundwater, which drains into the wells, becomes more subject to pollution. Also, as Oumar Wane (1983) has pointed out about Dakar, the extension of the asphalted area reduces the amount of rainwater that can seep through to recharge the local aquifer.

As local water sources are outstripped by demand and by pollution (or as in the case of Dakar, by over-pumping and salt-water intrusion), the search for piped urban water extends gradually into the surrounding region. This extension has three negative implications. First, it will draw water from areas in which other (smaller) communities already have established demands. Second, the urban demand may overpump the aquifer, in comparison with the known re-charge rate. Third, the further the water must be transported, the more it will cost.

Another major element of the urban environment is waste disposal. This issue is only just becoming important in highly industrialized countries (at the regional scale). Until recently, waste disposal was a small-scale issue that could be taken care of within the municipal boundaries. In Africa, traditionally, as villages grow into towns, the authorities simply pick up the rubbish and dump it on the roadside at the edge of the built-up area. However, as cities pass the million mark in population, this is no longer a local issue. Space for large, sanitized waste disposal is required on a regional scale, planned over a twenty-year period. If such plans cannot be made, then two problems build up. First, the level of conflict between the municipality and the surrounding jurisdictions heightens. Second, pollution of the groundwater from the seepage from overfilled (and under-designed) waste disposal sites increases.

The situation in Ibadan is perhaps typical. A dump established in the early 1960s near what was then the city's "by-pass" road is now completely surrounded by housing. Not only is the dump still being used but also the waste is not covered over. The "new site" five kilometers further from the center is also surrounded by housing. A search is now under way for a site twenty kilometers from the city center. However, this will sharply increase capital costs for more vehicles and running costs for fuel, personnel, and the like. In Dakar, the same phenomenon is evident. The municipal dump is located fifteen kilometers from the city center, yet it will soon be surrounded by housing. The waste is not covered or managed in any way. It lies between two shallow freshwater lakes the borders of which are used for intensive market-gardening. Drinking water is still drawn from wells in the vicinity of the dump.

Two other examples of the environmental impact of rapid urban growth will be considered by way of illustration. In many African cities, the major domestic fuel is charcoal. Certainly, this is the case in Dakar, where sixty percent of households still rely exclusively on charcoal (Tibesar and White 1985, 10). Charcoal is used in urban environments, as opposed to fuelwood in rural areas, because it is lighter to transport and hence cheaper. Also, it is more compact for burning. However, in terms of wood volume used it is forty percent less efficient than fuelwood. Hence, urban dwellers exert a greater demand per capita on forest resources than do rural dwellers. Thus, the continuing urbanization trend has a major impact on forest reserves. In no country (including Canada) is reforestation keeping up with the demand for forest products. René Dumont estimates that for every tree being planted in Senegal, fifty are cut down (Dumont and Mottin 1982, 19). In Senegal, Sudan, Kenya, and Tanzania, the situation is already critical. In Côte d'Ivoire, Nigeria, and Zaire, the existence of large tracts of forest near the major urban centers may give the impression that they do not share the problem. However, detailed study would reveal the same process at work.

The switch from fuelwood to charcoal is not the only important shift in consumption habits brought about by urbanization. Tastes also change from eating traditional crops such as millet, sorghum, and cassava to wheat and rice. Wheat (except in Tanzania and Kenya) is almost entirely imported; rice is becoming more and more prominent in the national "food gap" – the difference between what is produced and what is consumed. The environmental impact of this shift is to encourage governments to invest in large-scale irrigation schemes to produce more rice. The unfortunate side-effects on human health and on the salinization of the soil of these projects are now well-known.

The above environmental factors – the consumption of water, energy and food, and waste disposal – have large-scale, regional consequences. At the level of the micro-environmental effects on the household, other important processes are in operation. Although the urban-dweller usually has better access to health facilities than does the rural-dweller, he is also exposed to additional risks. These urban risks appear in both chronic and acute forms. The former includes exposure to urban pollution in the home, in the workplace, and on the street. Given the more immediate priorities of finding food and shelter, these risks generally receive even less attention in Africa than they do in wealthy, industrialized countries. The acute risks include motor vehicle and industrial accidents.

Urbanization thus entails a complex interaction between people and their environment. In the past, the benefits of urbanization have been emphasized, both at the level of the national economy and at the level of the individual. More recent studies have begun to assess some of the negative impacts as well (White and Burton 1983).

Apart from the impacts of large scale urbanization on the environment, there is also the major exogenous fact of the deterioration of the climate over much of Africa. In November 1984 the Food and Agriculture Organization of the United Nations (FAO) identified twenty-four African countries which "are facing ... food and agricultural emergencies in the current 1983 / 84 or 1984 season because of drought or other calamities" (FAO 1984, 1). The list includes Kenya, Senegal, and Tanzania. There is now convincing evidence that climatic change has been more extreme and more rapid over the last twelve thousand years than was previously thought to be the case (Petit-Maire and Riser 1983). Against this record, it can be appreciated that the period since independence has been significantly drier than the twenty years before independence (Glantz and Katz 1985). The dry period has both undermined the economic position of the countries affected (by reducing food production) and has accelerated migration from the countryside to the city.

The management of rapidly growing cities must therefore continue on the assumption of increasing dessication and reduced soil productivity as long as present policies continue. One season of "good rains" appears to push this salient fact into the background. But as Rolando Garcia (1982) and Michael Glantz and Robert W. Katz (1985) point out, as long as one cannot predict the trends in climate, one must plan for uncertainty. In addition, some countries have suffered even more from the drought because of the influx of refugees from other countries, some the victims of drought, some of political disturbances, and some of both. Two countries in the study

Table 1.4
Some Economic Indicators

Country	% Average Annual Growth of GDP 1973-1984	% Growth of Agriculture per capita 1970-1982	% of Labor Force in Agriculture 1980	% Average Annual Growth of Terms of Trade 1970-1982	Balance of Payments Current Account (millions of $US) 1984
Côte d'Ivoire	3.7	0.1	65	0.6	-190
Kenya	4.6	-1.2	81	-0.4	-135
Nigeria	0.7	-0.2	68	15.7	346
Senegal	2.6	-1.4	81	-0.3	-274
Sudan	5.5	-1.6	71	-0.6	25
Tanzania	3.6	-2.3	86	-1.3	-354
Zaire	-1.0	-1.7	72	-5.9	-310

Source: Columns 1, 3, and 5 are taken from the World Bank, 1986a, from Table 2 (182-83), Table 30 (238-39) and Table 14 (206-7) respectively. Columns 2 and 4 are taken from the World Bank, 1984, from Table 21 (77) and Table 11 (67) respectively.

group which have received a great many refugees (in proportion to their own populations) are Sudan (with refugees from Chad, Ethiopia, and Uganda) and Senegal (from Cape Verde, Mauritania, Mali, and Guinea).

One last aspect of the conflict between rapid urban growth and the quality of the environment needs to be mentioned. Several major African cities were located by European traders for ease of access to the sea and a good defensive position with regard to attack from the land. Thus, islands and promontories were favored sites. Lagos, Abidjan, and Dakar are examples of this phenomenon. These sites are now a major problem for rapidly expanding cities, intensifying the problems associated with congestion – traffic, waste disposal, saltwater intrusion into the aquifer, and so on. From this point of view, the decision to relocate the capital at a more internally accessible site is very sound.

Economic Trends

The major factors influencing the course of urbanization in Africa today may be summarized as (1) population growth and the rural exodus; (2) the drought; (3) the price of petroleum (and the price of the US dollars); (4) the slowdown of the global economy; (5) the adverse trend in the terms of trade for exporters of primary goods; (6) domestic policies which favor the urban-dweller over the rural-dweller. These factors have combined to produce a situation in which the following conditions are widespread:(1) an increase in the national debt; (2) a negative balance of payments; (3) a decline in per capita agricultural production; (4) a dependence on food aid and concessionary capital. Some of these factors and their consequences are illustrated by Table 1.4. The particular country situations vary and therefore the detailed consequences will be made clear in Chapters 4 through 10 which analyze the seven country case studies.

The rapid increase of petroleum prices in the 1970s and the appreciation of the American dollar as the price began to soften later in the decade are commonly viewed as the principal causes of the current economic crisis. African countries which remained dependent on the export of minerals and agricultural products for foreign exchange saw their balance of payments reduced to a negative level (see Table 1.4). The industrialization drive of the early post-colonial era was based very heavily on the importation of "cheap" oil. Nigeria used some coal, and Zaire and Nigeria some hydro-electric power; but oil was the ubiquitous source of energy for the expanding urban-industrial system.

The rapid rise of the price of crude petroleum from 1973 to 1978 brought boom conditions to Nigeria and severe balance of payments pressures elsewhere. A partial exception is Côte d'Ivoire where about 1.3 million tons of crude oil were pumped in 1984, which met sixty percent of demand,

Table 1.5
Long-Term External Debt and Service Ratios, 1970-84

	1	2	3	4	5
	Long-term debt: GNP ratio		Debt service: export earnings		Total debt million $US
	1970	1984	1970	1984	1984
Côte d'Ivoire	19	108	1	31	4,824
Kenya	26	53	5[1]	21[1]	3,062
Nigeria	6	17	7	28	12,710
Senegal	16	69	4	n/a	1,659
Sudan	15	78	11	14	5,659
Tanzania	21	70	5	n/a	2,654
Zaire	18	92[1]	4	n/a	4,022[1]

Source: World Bank, 1986a, Table 17 (212-13). n/a = not available.
[1]For 1983.

Table 1.6
Multilateral Debt Renegotiations, 1976-1984, in millions of $US

	1976	1977	1978	1979	1980	1981	1982	1983	1984
Côte d'Ivoire									153
Kenya					(none)				
Nigeria								1,923	
Senegal						77	84	64	97
Sudan				373		638	174	502	245
Tanzania					(none)				
Zaire	211	236		1,147	402	574		1,317	
TOTAL	211	236		1,520	402	1,289	258	4,064	495

Source: Based on the World Bank, 1985, Box Figure 2.4A, 28.

including exports to Mali and Burkina Faso (Economist Intelligence Unit 1985a, 19). Also, production in Zaire appears to have levelled off after coming close to self-sufficiency (EIU 1985f, 20). However, exploration has not yet produced paying wells in Senegal, Sudan, Kenya, or Tanzania (EIU 1985d, 22; 1985c, 24; 1985d, 16; 1985e, 14).

The softening of the oil price brought no relief to the oil-importers as the 1981-85 period coincided with the steady appreciation of the American dollar in which oil is priced. The end of the boom brought disaster to Nigeria, which had moved almost overnight from being an exporter of agricultural products to being ninety percent dependent on oil exports for earning its foreign exchange.

While it is true that several countries had persistent balance of payments problems even before the oil price rise, the rise pushed them into a state of deepening debt and the absorption of an increasing proportion of scarce foreign exchange for debt servicing (see Table 1.5). During the third quarter of 1986, the non-gold financial reserves of all of Africa were less than one-third those of France, and "in the view of most authorities the situation in the sub-Saharan countries will deteriorate further over the next two years, unless a 'debt-forgiveness' policy is adopted" ("Africa's Reserves Go On Dwindling" 1987, 1). Although the debt burden is not on the Latin American scale, it has proved increasingly difficult to manage (see Table 1.6).

Domestic economic problems were not entirely the result of exogenous events. The policies adopted by many African countries in the 1960s and 1970s were ill-suited to the stress they had to undergo. For example, five of the seven countries in the study group maintained fixed currency exchange rates, which generally tended to overvalue the domestic currency. Whereas there are sometimes good reasons for maintaining fixed exchange rates, in the circumstances of this period, the stress of the exogenous events was, in a sense, postponed. Hence, the pressure built up around the national economy and the currency was no longer acceptable for most international exchanges. The market reaction to this development was twofold. First, all external trade had to be met in a hard currency, such as the US dollar. The second effect was domestic in that a clandestine market developed to reflect the "true value" of the currency. This process tends to undermine the coherence of the domestic economy and the relevance of government attempts to manage it.

The shortage of foreign exchange has had several impacts on urban management. In particular, it has made the maintenance of services based on imported materials very difficult. In cities such as Dakar and Ibadan, water supply may be cut, not because of the unavailability of raw water but because of the lack of foreign exchange to buy the chemicals to treat it. The sums involved are very small compared to other demands for foreign

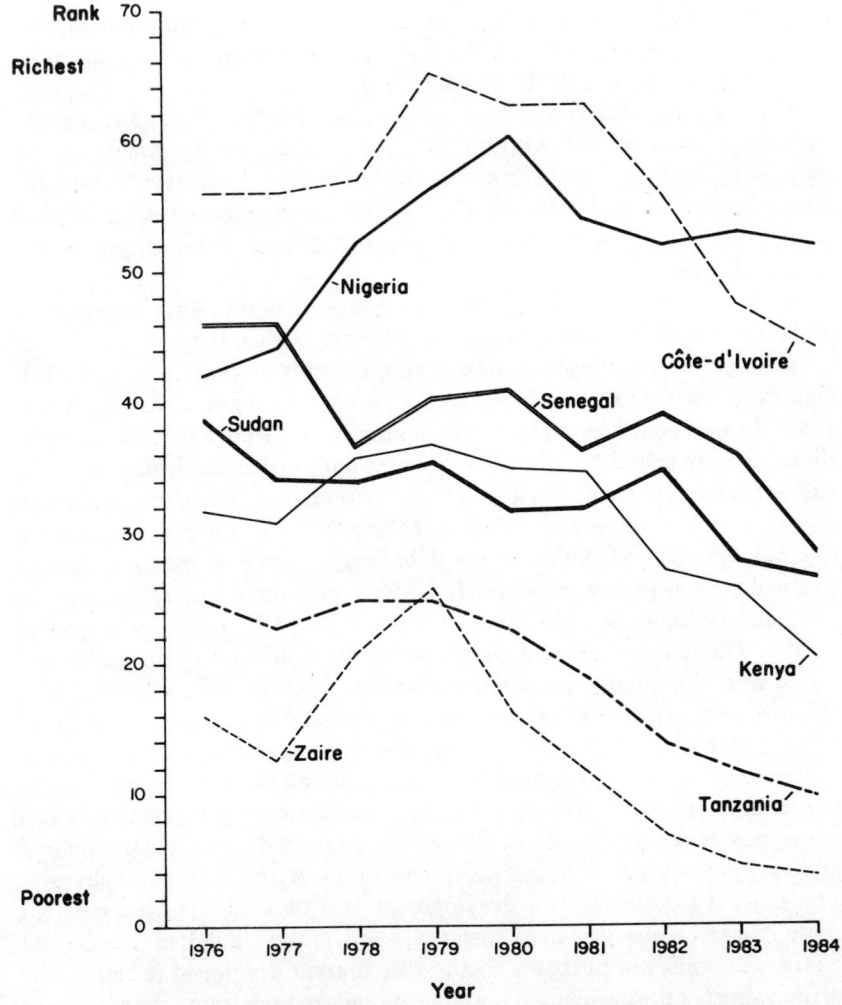

Figure 1.2
Gross National Product per capita, World Bank 1976-1984

exchange; but there appears to be no currency management system which takes care of the vital details.

For the recent history of urbanization the key policy decision in many African countries was an attempt to provide a decent level of urban services and to control domestic prices, especially the price of domestic agricultural products, in order to reduce the impact of inflation on the urban cost of living. Although this policy took different forms in different countries, there is a pattern throughout sub-Saharan Africa.

In Senegal, for example, twenty-nine key prices are fixed by an interministerial committee (Sénégal 1984). The commodity prices are so low in comparison to the input costs to the farmer that the profit margin is too small to encourage investment, even in a good year. Under such circumstances, a two hectare family plot (with an annual rainfall of one thousand millimeters) is simply insufficient to support a traditional farming family at a reasonable standard of living. Even in years with good rains it is a very marginal proposition.

It is fair to say that the price policies adopted by most African governments were designed to control rapidly escalating prices in the cities. They did not anticipate the crisis of the 1970s, nor did they really consider the impact on the rural economy. If the urban economic base had developed as was originally anticipated, then the urban areas may have begun to generate a surplus to pay for the goods they consumed. As this did not happen, the problem was passed on to the rural areas in the form of fixed prices. In this situation, the young people in the rural areas went to the city where they believed better opportunities were available.

An examination of Table 1.4 provides a quick summary of the implications of some of the events described above. Even if a large margin of error is ascribed to these figures, the story they tell is interesting. Six of these seven economies actually performed quite well, in macro-economic terms, in the period from 1973-84 (see column 1), although this time range obscures a downturn after 1976. However, in each case, the expansion of the economy has been less than the growth of the population. Since 1980 all seven countries have slipped on the world table of GNP per capita. (See Figure 1.2.) Column 2 of Table 1.4 shows the negative effects on agriculture of the "urban bias" of fixed currency exchange rates and fixed prices for agricultural products. Although there were some increases in agricultural output, this failed to keep pace with the growth of population. It might be possible to conclude that these trends are acceptable for a modernizing society (that is becoming more urban-industrial). Yet the fact remains that the great majority of the people are still working in the agricultural sector (see Table 1.4, column 3).

The per capita decline of agricultural production is the most salient fact in the recent evolution of the economies of sub-Saharan Africa. The test case is rice. As urban populations seem to prefer rice to millet and sorghum, the question is: "How is it to be produced?" In Senegal, more rainfed rice could be produced in the southern part of the country to meet the deficit; yet the deficit is currently being met by imports from Thailand and Pakistan. The government's plan is to control the flow of the Senegal River (in the drought-afflicted north) to produce an additional 240,000 tons of irrigated rice per year by 1990 (World Bank 1979, 11: 27). The construction of the dams alone will cost nearly one billion dollars. For a fraction of this investment, a substantial increase in the rice harvest could be produced under rainfed conditions in the south. Why has this decision been taken?

The answer is partly that concessionary capital is available to build the two big dams on the Senegal River. The country is in serious trouble, with a rapidly growing population and a limited physical resource base. As in Nigeria, the "food gap" has a very immediate meaning. In Senegal, the temptation is to go for the technological fix in the hope of avoiding a permanent situation of food-aid dependency. To "control the river" would invariably cost a billion dollars. This kind of policy ignores the reasons behind the imbalance that has developed between the urban and the rural economies.

Table 1.7
Some Socio-Economic Indicators

Country	Life Expectancy at birth 1982	Number enrolled in Primary School as % of age group 1983	Adult Literacy (%) 1980	GNP per capita ($US) 1984	GDP Total (billion $US) 1984
Côte d'Ivoire	47	79	35	610	6.7
Kenya	57	100	47	310	5.1
Nigeria	50	98	34	730	73.5
Senegal	44	53	10[1]	380	2.4
Sudan	47	50	32	360	6.7
Tanzania	52	87	79	210	4.4
Zaire	50	90	55	140	4.7

Source: Column 1, World Bank, 1984a, Table (57); Column 2, World Bank, 1986a, Table 29 (236-37); Column 3, World Bank, 1984b, Columns 4 and 5, World Bank, 1986a, Table 1 (180-81) and Table 3 (184-85) respectively.

[1]Data for 1977.

The present trajectory for some of the poorer African countries appears to be the accumulation of an unmanageable debt (see Tables 1.5 and 1.6) and the drift into deeper and deeper food-aid dependency. For the seven countries under study, the situations are quite diverse, although none are in the extreme situation of the landlocked countries of the Sahel or those of the Horn of Africa. What follows is a brief introduction to the overall economic situation of the seven countries in this study.

Senegal, while not the poorest of the seven in per capita income terms (see Table 1.7, column 4), is the one with the most limited physical resource base. The 1,500 millimeters isohyet (line of equal rainfall) covers only a small portion of the extreme southwest of the country. Other than fuelwood, it has no exploited, domestic sources of energy. Part of its strength comes from membership of the CFA franc zone which provides it with a freely convertible currency, while at the same time gives some flexibility in cushioning the direct impact of a negative balance of payments on the value of the currency (EIU 1985b, 29, 32, 34; Bourdin 1984).

Of the seven countries, Côte d'Ivoire weathered the storm of the late 1970s the best. Its apparent "miracle" was based on the diversity of its export crops – timber, coffee, and cocoa, all being roughly of equal importance. It also benefitted from becoming the pre-eminent regional service center for West Africa. For foreign businesses, it offered a stronger domestic market than could Dakar and less congestion and price escalation than could Lagos. Also, offshore oil is being developed and may soon be sufficient for domestic needs. In the meantime, here too the debt burden has sharply increased in order to finance costly capital development projects and food imports (EIU 1985a).

Nigeria is the most singular of the seven, as it has a population about as great as the other six and is one of the world's major exporters of oil. However, it could be argued that Nigeria would be better off today if the oil had never been discovered. The extremely rapid pace of the development of the Nigerian oilfields in the 1970s completely overshadowed other productive sectors. From being a major exporter of agricultural produce, Nigeria became a net importer. By 1977 the "food gap" (between production and consumption) resulted in such a high level of food imports that the balance of payments became negative, despite continual expansion of petroleum exports. The country embarked on a massive investment in infrastructure – highways, a new capital, airports, and administrative headquarters. However, the fall of the oil price from 1979 onwards has undermined this expansionary phase (EIU 1985g).

Of all the countries in the group Zaire probably has the most favorable population / resource balance. Much of the country has abundant rainfall, and it supports a variety of crops for export and for domestic consumption (EIU 1985f). Its mining base in the Katanga provided the bulk of the export earnings until the long slump in the price of copper which began in the late 1960s. However, the size and topography of the country have perhaps inhibited its effective administration. Despite its vast potential, it has, according to the World Bank figures, the lowest per capita income of the seven under study.

The Sudan is the largest country in Africa at 2.5 million square kilometers. As in the case of Zaire, its sheer size and physical diversity have proved difficult to unify and to develop to make the most of its complementary regions. Although oil was discovered in the 1970s, it has not yet been developed; as a result, the balance of payments is drained by the cost of imported fuel as well as by the ever-present "food gap" (EIU 1985c). To its domestic problems, Sudan must add the burden of refugees from three of its neighbors – Chad, Uganda, and Ethiopia.

In Kenya, the search for oil has proved negative so far. As in Senegal, the burden of the demand for fuel falls on its rapidly diminishing forests. Although Kenya has productive agricultural regions more than half of the country is semi-arid or arid. The rate of population increase (at four percent) is said to be the highest in the world. The rapid population growth together with the shortage of cultivable land has forced the rapid expansion of Nairobi. In the 1970s its strong export base (reliant on coffee, tea, and tourism) encouraged the expansion of the industrial sector (EIU 1985d). However, as is seen elsewhere, the rise of the oil price and the unreliability of the rainfall have undermined its capacity to support its growing population.

In Tanzania, the area capable of supporting intensive cropping for export was more limited than in Kenya, and the government's policy was, in any case, to reduce dependence on export crops. It pursued the goals of decentralization and self-sufficiency by moving the seat of government to Dodoma in the center of the country and by integrating villages into larger productive units (EIU 1985e). But having no oil and a very small manufacturing base, Tanzania was entirely reliant on agriculture. Drought and the increasing cost of imported energy had the same impact as in other countries.

Although differences can be noted among the economic structure of these seven countries, the common factors are clearly important. All are under great pressure, including oil-rich Nigeria and land-rich Zaire. (See Figure 2.) Different policies have been pursued, with Senegal concentrating on the development of manufacturing in the capital region around Dakar, and Tanzania pursuing villagization. Some have promoted prosperous regional service centers like Abidjan and Nairobi; others, like Sudan, export specialists to work in the Middle East from which they remit their earnings. The solutions available for the present predicament will vary from country to country. The purpose of this chapter is to emphasize the commonalities, before the particularities are examined in the country chapters.

Conclusion

The management of large African cities today is taking place in very difficult circumstances. The population is still growing quickly, and the rate of urbanization is increasing. The economies – even those of oil-rich Nigeria and the Ivorian "miracle" – are under great stress, with a negative balance of payments and increasing debt. As the central government is less and less able to maintain services, the obligation falls on the urban population itself (Stren 1985). The rate of urban growth has outstripped management capacity, financial resources, and even information on the urbanization process itself. Perhaps most critically of all, the physical environment is suffering from gross misuse and an absence of long-term planning.

It might be argued that the "urban bias" in government policy has itself contributed to today's urban crisis. But that does not mean that the cities should now be neglected because that will only intensify the national problems. Sustainable policies are urgently needed. Although the details vary from country to country, in all of the major cities there has been an increasingly frantic search for local solutions. Some of these are decisions at the national scale, such as the relocation of the national capital. Some decisions involve municipal reform, such as the decentralization undertaken in Dakar and Abidjan. Most governments have moved away from the provision of free services to the poor (such as standpipes) and the middle-class (subsidized rental housing), leaving individuals and communities to meet their own needs through private water connections, self-help housing, the digging of private boreholes, and the use of individual household generators. But such "solutions" are available only to the relatively wealthy, and some are clearly against the public interest.

In this book, the various research teams examine the different paths pursued in nearly twenty urban communities broadly representative of conditions in sub-Saharan Africa. These case studies are preceded by an analysis of the political and administrative framework within which these changes have taken place.

Note

1. These re-locations are Tanzania, to Dodoma; Côte d'Ivoire, to Yamassoukro; Nigeria, to Abuja.

CHAPTER 2
Urban Local Government in Africa

Richard E. Stren

As Africa's urban areas grow in population and in land area at historically unprecedented rates, governments face increasing pressures to provide efficient services and effective infrastructure, and to coordinate and "manage" a wide range of public and private sector activities at the local level. These pressures are becoming even more compelling in the 1980s, as all across the continent, basic urban services and infrastructure – housing, water supply, garbage removal, road repair, public transportation, health, and educational facilities – are inadequate and in a deteriorating state.

In the 1970s the international response to these service and infrastructural problems was to finance large projects (such as housing and water), to improve urban policies, and to press for reforms of colonially-inspired standards of urban planning and construction (World Bank 1972; Cohen 1983). Since the early 1980s, however, the focus of reform efforts has shifted to the institutional arena. This new focus is evident in a new generation of World Bank urban projects, which include support for "improvements in national housing finance systems, urban management and planning, local government revenue generation and budget procedures, and decentralization of national government authority over cities" ("New Directions in Bank Urban Projects," 1). But if the experience with international development projects over the last decade points to a more important role for local government in the management and coordination of urban services, how much more successful can this new approach be than the approach which it has superceded?

To arrive at a preliminary evaluation of the "management" approach to urban reform for Africa, one must first consider the experiences of the 1970s and early 1980s. These experiences, for convenience, can be classified into two major areas: local government and urban services. While the two clearly overlap, they tend to be treated separately in the literature, and in practice to be delineated by distinctive organizational forms. Thus, agencies of "local government" tend to be multi-purpose organizations, legitimized at some level by a conciliar structure, with a responsibility for a delimited local geographical unit. The administration (or "management") of urban services, on the other hand, tends to be vested in more narrowly conceived, technically specific agencies, either attached to a conciliar organization or operating more autonomously (as private or parastatal corporations), with a responsibility for a specific function within a (not always local) geographical area. This chapter looks specifically at "local government" in urban areas in Africa, paying particular attention to the differences in approach and experience between Francophone and Anglophone cities. The next chapter will focus on the administration of urban services and infrastructure, and the issue of the appropriate balance between the public and private provision of urban amenities.

Local Government in Urban Areas: The Convergence of Two Traditions

In the large and rapidly growing literature on public administration in modern Africa, little attention has been paid to local administration, and even less to "local government." For Francophone Africa,[1] this is perhaps not surprising, since the metropolitan administrative system on which the colonial structure was originally based was consistently centralist dating back to the formative period of the *ancien régime*. Many years after *"les indépendances"* of the early 1960s, the centralization of African administrations remained "a dominant characteristic" (Prats 1979, 132). Even Côte d'Ivoire, which had undergone such spectacular economic growth until the late 1970s, was in the early 1980s still closely

> ... tied to what the colonial system left us, and to the extent that such arrangements suited certain sections of the population, nothing had changed. Even if the prefectures and the sub-prefectures have replaced the circles and the subdivisions of the past, the manner of public administration of our local communities has hardly changed in respect to giving the base more responsibility relative to the highest levels.
>
> The legacy of a centralizing and omnipresent colonizer has been maintained without change and even reinforced, the people having no influence over the structures which administer them (Nguessan-Zoukou 1983, 1-2).

And in Cameroon, a country which had to absorb a large area in which the Anglophone tradition of representative local government had been sustained during the late colonial period, the same pattern of extensive central control over local communes still obtains. As one observer comments,

> The arrival of West Cameroon to form part of the unified state has done little to modify Cameroon's centralist tendencies ... One may speculate that the trend to centralization will, sooner or later, have to go into reverse ... [But such a] change, when it comes in Cameroon, can be expected to occur as the result of a radical shift in the regime, rather than incrementally (Mawhood 1983, 198-99).

The pattern in Anglophone Africa was historically more adventuresome and, by the 1980s, more diverse. Whatever the balance between "direct" and "indirect" rule at the local level during the first three decades of the century, almost all Britain's African colonies were brought to a new level of local involvement with the Colonial Office decision in 1947 to introduce an "efficient and democratic system of local government" in each dependency (Humes 1973, 23). Politically, the 1947 decision was more congruent with the British concern to bypass nationalist political movements in the colonies than it was a reflection of the reality of central-local relations in the United Kingdom. (In the Anglophone West, for example, central administrative and political controls over British local councils have been much closer and more restrictive than in Canada or the United States.) In any case, the strengthening of local institutions which this reform entailed was neutralized in the years immediately following independence, as state after state found it both politically expedient and financially necessary to constrain the growth of local governments and to restrict their powers and functions. It is no coincidence that the two major public administration texts on Anglophone Africa, *The Civil Service in Commonwealth Africa*, by A.L.Adu (1969) and *A Decade of Public Administration in Africa*, edited by Anthony Rweyemamu and Goran Hyden (1975), contain only the briefest and most passing references to local government.

While there were important variations both among and within countries (generally between more effective urban and less effective rural institutions), Africa by the 1980s – in both Anglophone and Francophone areas – had weak and poorly functioning local governments. A survey conducted in 1982 by the IMF showed that, while in the industrial countries some fifty-seven percent of all government jobs were accounted for by "local" rather than "central" government, the figure was only fifteen percent for the developing countries. Of the three main regions of the Third World, Africa averaged a mere six percent, as compared to twenty-one percent for Latin America and thirty-seven percent for Asia (World Bank 1983, 102). While the magnitude of the difference between Africa and the rest of the world may be somewhat exaggerated by these figures which count all sub-national government employment as "local" (there are few state or provincial governments in Africa), the impression of extreme centralization is nevertheless valid.

By the 1970s there was concern in some quarters that African public administrations were too centralized. Julius Nyerere eloquently expressed this concern in a major policy paper, *Decentralisation*, written in 1972. He argued that physical and bureaucratic distance between local areas and the center were frustrating the development needs of the country. In justifying his proposals for a strengthened system of local and regional administration,

Nyerere said:

> Our nation is too large for the people at the centre in Dar es Salaam always to understand local problems or to sense their urgency. When all the power remains at the centre, therefore, local problems can remain, and fester, while local people who are aware of them are prevented from using their initiative in finding solutions ... at present [local] officials have, in reality, very little local power. They have to consult the Ministries in Dar es Salaam for almost everything they wish to do, and certainly about every cent they wish to spend (1972, 1).

At the end of the document, Nyerere argued that the new "decentralised system" the country was going to implement "should increase the reality of democracy in our society because it brings power closer to the people ... local democracy will become more real, even as the institutions of development will become more efficient (12).

Ironically, the pursuit of this "local democracy" involved the abolition of all local government councils in both rural and urban Tanzania and their replacement by regional and district committees dominated by central government officials. In Dar es Salaam, for example, the City Council was dissolved, and its functions were divided among the three District Development Councils of Ilala, Temeke, and Kinondoni. These Councils, which comprised the Dar es Salaam Region, had both rural and urban components. As a former chief officer of one of these Councils argues:

> The decentralization structure ... was really not local. It was an organ of the central government which incorporated the councillors and members of Parliament as local representatives. The decentralization structure facilitated civil service domination in the decisions. The civil bureaucrats monopolized and controlled the planning process. The local representatives played a very marginal role (Sendaro 1985, 41).

Aside from the alienation of ordinary people from government which these structures produced all over the country (Kulaba 1986b, 24), decentralization led in Dar es Salaam to severe problems of administrative coordination and (indirectly) to extreme levels of underfunding and staff shortages with respect to most areas of infrastructure and services. The government did not begin to reconstitute the local councils until 1978, by which time it was clear that the "decentralization" exercise had been a failure.

The Tanzanian case was an extreme example of a general African tendency during the 1970s and early 1980s to proclaim the value of decentralization as a general principle, but to hedge and even to undercut its implementation in practice. In the Sudan, for example, an important range of functions was transferred to the provinces in the 1970s, and a "People's Local Government system" was set up. Nevertheless, arbitrary and inadequate finance from the center, resistance by civil servants to taking up postings in remote areas, the inability to collect taxes in the rural areas, the resistance of traditional authorities in some areas, and unclear lines of authority between upper and lower tiers of local government all combined to undermine the effectiveness of these ambitious arrangements (Norris 1983). With the Local Government Act of 1981, a new system was established. As the chapter on Khartoum in this volume shows, the elaborate three-tiered system of urban government in the capital has floundered in the 1980s as a result of arbitrary central government decisions, a corresponding low level of popular participation, a chronic deficit in the municipal budget, and "a general inefficiency and incompetence of urban management personnel" (see Chapter 9, below).

Nigeria during the 1970s likewise followed a path similar to what Philip Mawhood has called the "pendulum model," according to which periods of high centralization and ineffective local government are followed by attempts to redress the balance through decentralization (Mawhood 1983, 8). Until the advent of military government in 1966, Nigeria had two distinct patterns of local government. In the southern areas, representative local councils had been operating since 1950 (in the East) and 1953 (in the West) to perform a wide range of local functions and development activities. In the north, the councils were much less representative of the local populations, carried out fewer development-related and welfare functions, and were less able to collect local taxes (Oyediran and Gboyega 1979). After 1966, reforms were instituted all over the country, with the effect of considerably restricting the decisional autonomy of local government councils, both in urban and rural areas. But for various reasons, by 1975 (when the government of General Gowon was removed) "there was no part of the country that had a satisfactory local government system" (Gboyega 1983, 229), and there was no national system of local government. In 1976, the federal government published its *Guidelines for Local Government Reform*, intended to ensure through devolution of functions to local representative councils "that local initiative and response to local needs and conditions are maximised" (Gboyega 1983, 230). Following publication and widespread discussion of these guidelines (Adamolekun and Rowland 1979), the local council system was streamlined (with many small-scale authorities becoming absorbed into larger ones), and provision was made for the revenue needs of the local government authorities (LGAs) by various arrangements between the states and the federal government. At the same time, the number of states was increased from twelve to nineteen.

Later, under the Shagari civilian government, an Act passed in 1981 provided for ten percent of all national revenue to be paid to the states for the support of local governments, to be supplemented by an additional ten percent of the revenues collected by the states themselves (Gboyega 1983, 238). In spite of all these supportive legal measures, Nigerian LGAs were in serious administrative and financial difficulties by the early 1980s.One knowledgeable student of Nigerian local government has argued that the Mohammed / Abasanjo military government, which took power in July of 1975 in Nigeria, "allowed local governments relative autonomy between 1976 and 1979 while the successor democratically elected civilian government which existed between 1979 and 1983 restricted this local government autonomy and stifled local democracy" (Adetoyi 1987, 4). As a general statement about the whole country, this interpretation almost certainly exaggerates the degree to which local autonomy was promoted by state government officials in the north during the 1976-79 period (Aliyu and Koehn 1982). For Oyo and perhaps other western states, the evidence is stronger. The argument runs that the key factors in support for local government within the Nigerian military were the military's need to gain the support of the populace in order to prepare for a return to civilian government; and the hierarchical command structure of the military, which reduced confrontation between the states and the federal government, thus ensuring state implementation of federal policies for local government reform. Indeed, the Federal Military Government which seized power in Nigeria in 1984 took measures very early in its rule to strengthen the financial position of local governments throughout the country. Decentralization and some measure of institutional autonomy at the local level, then, is not necessarily incompatible with the centralization of power at the national level in Africa.

Urban Government and Finance

By the 1980s most large African cities had one of two modal structures of urban government. In the representative council structure – typical in various degrees of Anglophone Africa – a mix of elected and centrally-nominated councillors controls a local bureaucracy with a wide range of local functions and an extensive base of local taxation. Most functions that are considered to be genuinely "local" (refuse collection; the regulation of trade and building; transportation; preventative public health; the building and maintenance of roads; sewerage; elementary education) are administered by departments of the council through the agency of a chief executive officer. Budgetary controls and administrative support are the responsibility of the central government. Versions of this structure are operative in large cities in Zimbabwe, Zambia, Tanzania, Kenya, Sudan, and Nigeria. Supplementing this structure in the provision of urban services are state (as in Nigeria) or central government agencies such as housing corporations, water and electricity boards, and town planning agencies.

The second modal structure is the communal pattern, common to the Francophone states. Typically, the commune is a direct creation of the central government, being composed of elected representatives, an executive mayor (responsible to the Ministry of the Interior), and a number of small administrative departments. While it may be almost unlimited in principle, in practice the functional scope of the commune is much more restricted than the representative council pattern, as local bodies in large Francophone cities may only be responsible for such services as garbage removal and street cleaning, the regulation and licensing of markets and public transport, cemeteries and funerals, marriage licenses, and the regulation of animals and butcheries. Many important local services are undertaken by central government agencies, parastatals, or even contracted out to private companies.

A brief statistical comparison between the two capital cities of Nairobi, Kenya and Abidjan, Côte d'Ivoire will more clearly illustrate some of the salient differences between the representative council and the commune system. (Unfortunately, comparable figures are not available for exactly the same years, but the relative proportions are still revealing.) In 1982 Nairobi had a population of approximately one million or six percent of the total population of Kenya. The city was administered by the City Council of Nairobi, with a gross expenditure budget of some (US) $68 million[2] and a work force (including higher level technical staff and management) of 16,908 (City Council of Nairobi, Establishment Section, Computer printouts for May, 1982). To put the work force figure in perspective, Nairobi's share of the total public and parastatal sector in Kenya was 3.1 percent. By contrast, Abidjan was estimated in 1985 to have a population of some 1.7 million or about twenty-two percent of the population of Côte d'Ivoire (Attahi 1985a, 9). It was administered by the Council of the City of Abidjan, with some 1,150 employees, and by ten individual "communes" with a total wage force of approximately one thousand. All in all, the City and its constituent elements employed about 1.7 percent of total public sector employees in Côte d'Ivoire (Attahi 1985b). Budgetary figures for 1984 show that the City Council and its ten constituent communes spent 19.7 billion CFA francs or about (US) $49,250,000 (Attahi 1985b, 107). Thus, while the Nairobi City Council spent on the average approximately $68 per year on services for each inhabitant of the city, the Abidjan Council and its communes spent only about $31 per person.[3]

Yet while the range of services provided by the Nairobi City Council is much broader than the range undertaken by the Abidjan municipal government agencies, the quality of overall urban services and infrastructure in

Abidjan is superior. Some of this difference is explained by the much higher level of per capita income in Côte d'Ivoire, since many local services in Abidjan are provided by outside agencies and billed directly to consumers, who have more disposable income than their counterparts in Kenya. Thus, while in Nairobi both the water supply and garbage removal services are provided directly by the City Council and primary school teachers are part of the City's Education Department, in Abidjan the water supply company is a private company (of which the majority of shareholders are Ivorians), garbage removal services are contracted out to another private firm, and primary education is dealt with by the central government. In 1982 there were about 1,235 full time staff in Nairobi's water department, 1,930 staff in the public cleansing (refuse removal) section of the public health department, 3,332 primary teachers and 998 other staff in the education department (City Council of Nairobi, Establishment Section, Computer Print-outs for May, 1982). These four services accounted for forty-four percent of the Nairobi Council's total staff complement and a roughly equivalent proportion of its recurrent budget. In Abidjan, by contrast, payments to the refuse removal contractor alone represented forty-eight percent of the total budget of the City Council in 1984 (Attahi 1985a, 116).

This brief comparison between Nairobi and Abidjan underscores the considerably wider array of functions and such greater level of staff complement in the Anglophone cities of Africa. This difference began to change in the 1980s. On the one hand, such countries as Côte d'Ivoire (beginning in 1978) and Senegal (beginning in 1983) have been putting into place important administrative changes designed to co-ordinate local decision-making and to give more power to local elected officials in the capital cities. Along with this *de facto* shift in power from the national to the local political systems, governments at both levels have been paying more attention to developing new local sources of revenue and to improving local collection mechanisms. The dynamics of these changes for Côte d'Ivoire are discussed at length by Koffi Attahi in Chapter 5 of this volume. Meanwhile, in the Anglophone cities, a much more robust tradition of local tax collection and support for urban services at the local level is being curtailed under the pressure of politics and the exigencies of the current economic crisis. While at least some of the large Francophone cities actively work toward a more decentralized approach to urban management, the Anglophone cities, more constrained by political and economic forces, fall increasingly under central control.

The financial situation of many African urban governments was, by the mid 1980s, tenuous at best. In general, the Anglophone cities experienced the more serious shortfalls. There were three main reasons for this state of affairs: (l) in an overall context of falling or stagnating government revenues, their extensive responsibilities for rapidly expanding urban populations were much less likely to be supported by either the local tax base or by central government support; (2) administrative controls over the budgets of many Anglophone cities in the representative council systems were much weaker than were comparable controls in the communal systems; and (3) for historical and institutional reasons, they were more of a focus for political pressures, a factor which was incompatible with financial integrity and balanced budgets. Each of these factors will be discussed in turn.

Sources of Local Finance: By the late 1970s most African economies were stagnating or even declining in absolute terms. The reasons for this downturn included a combination of inappropriate government policies, the dramatic increase in the price of imported oil, and falling world prices for primary exports. The Zambian case is typical. In 1981 an International Labour Organisation (ILO) mission reported as follows:

> The situation for most of the urban population has for many years been significantly better than that for most of the rural population. But in the last few years, rising prices, declining formal sector employment, shortages of basic commodities and overstrained and underprovided government services have also hit the urban population very hard. Average real consumption levels throughout the country are estimated to have fallen by a third from 1975 to 1977 and since then there has been only a modest increase and a subsequent decline. Wage increases from 1973 to 1977 fell short of price increases, leading to a decrease in recorded average wages by about a tenth – a decrease which has probably continued since.... It is hardly surprising that most Zambians, urban as well as rural, have suffered very severe reductions in their standard of living. For those at the bottom, the impact on nutrition, health and welfare has been acute (29).

While urban services and infrastructure were deteriorating in the 1970s, economic pressures forced the central government to cut back on its grants to the urban councils, at the same time preventing them from increasing charges on their main local sources of revenue such as property taxes. And in public housing, a field in which Zambian local authorities have a large fixed investment, the government gave in to political pressure not to allow local authorities to raise rents or even to evict the large numbers of tenants who continually practise "rent-dodging" (Greenwood and Howell 1980, 172, 175).

Even in Nigeria, which as a national economy was to some extent insulated from the effects of the economic downturn by buoyant oil exports (at least until the early 1980s) and which had both constitutional and legislative arrangements to ensure a reasonable share of national and state revenue for local authorities, local government finances began seriously to deteriorate in the 1980s. This was partly due to lower national oil revenues (a result of a combination of lower international prices and less oil being produced) available for distribution to the states; but it was also due to unproductive spending by the states themselves (some of whom were obliged to start from scratch in building new state capitals), to the abolition between 1980 and 1982 of the head (community) tax and cattle tax in most states, and to the further subdivision of the original 299 local government authorities by the addition of 475 more by the end of 1982. Furthermore, while local authority revenues did in fact increase during the late 1970s and early 1980s, their responsibilities increased even more, and they become increasingly dependent on state as opposed to local sources of revenue. A study of local authority finances in six states from 1976-79 showed an average of only 18.5 percent was derived from local sources (Gboyega 1983, 241). And an unpublished study by the World Bank showed that in 1982, a year when federal grants to the states began falling steeply, local governments in three state capitals were collecting only from twenty to twenty-five percent of all their revenue from local sources. For those taxes still being applied locally, collection rates were often very low, a function of the reduced administrative support the financially-strapped local governments could give to tax collection, the lower propensity to pay on the part of local people who could not see development projects, and an "increase in embezzlement of the little revenue collected by the rate / revenue collectors some of whom could count on political protection from the higher levels of government" (Adetoyi 1987, 245).

The situation in large Francophone cities in the 1980s was also deteriorating, but the consequences in terms of services and infrastructure were not so serious. The Francophone countries' economies (with the major exception of Zaire) were tied to the French franc, as a result of which there was little foreign exchange constraint on the purchase of essential equipment and infrastructure. Thus, new buses and spare parts could be purchased for the public transport system; sophisticated equipment was available for water, sewerage, and electrical systems; and office equipment and supplies could easily be obtained. Moreover, the Francophone cities were able successfully to collect a tax on professionals and businessmen ("la patente," a tax that originated at the time of the French Revolution) which formed a substantial proportion of their local tax base. In the mid 1980s, for example, returns from this single tax were equivalent to 41.9 percent of total receipts in the district of Dakar, 37.6 percent in the district of Rufisque, 71.5 percent in the district of Pikine, 75.1 percent in the city of Ouagadougou, and 67.0 percent in the city of Bobodioulasso (Chomentowski 1986, 17). In spite of the inequities of this tax and the difficulties of applying it efficiently to informal sector businesses, it will be some time before large urban administrations are in a position either substantially to revise it or to abolish it.

While both Dakar and Abidjan were running deficits by the early 1980s (Communication to author, World Bank 1985), the size of this deficit was relatively modest (about $10 million in Dakar and $2.6 million in Abidjan) in comparison to the level of central government support forthcoming in most large Anglophone cities. And cities such as Dakar were prepared to take exceptional measures to collect tax arrears. In 1985, for example, the commune of Dakar employed only eleven tax collectors. Only fifty-three percent of potential taxes were being collected and back taxes amounted to about $25 million. For the fiscal year 1985-86, nineteen supplementary staff were recruited from the Treasury, along with one hundred collectors. While this raised the city's salary bill somewhat, it had a most salutary effect on tax collection: the level of recovery rose to eighty-one percent for the financial year, and the tax backlog was reduced by almost $16 million (Ndiaye 1987, 39-40; Mazurelle et You 1987, 16-19).

Financial Controls: There are also major differences with respect to financial controls. Because both the assessment and collection of the bulk of local taxes are still the responsibility of agencies of the central government (most local taxes in Anglophone countries are collected by local governments themselves), financial probity is less of a concern. Generally, even in countries where some degree of decentralization has taken place, Francophone states still consider local councils to be "under the close supervision" (*sous la tutelle*) of central government ministries. In Côte d'Ivoire, for instance, the powerful Ministries of the Interior, and of Finance and the Economy, exercise strict controls over, respectively, a wide range of the administrative and financial activities of all local councils (Attahi 1985b, Part IV). And in Dakar, the governor of the Cap Vert region, who is appointed by cabinet decree, must approve all major decisions of the Urban Community of Dakar, can dismiss one or more of its members, and can dissolve the council and appoint new members for a period of six months. At the level of the constituent communes which make up the Urban Community, the Prefect has equivalent power.

Moreover, there are elaborate checks and controls over accounting procedures. For example, it is still a general rule (Campbell, Brierly and Blitz 1965, 84) that the individual who authorizes payments (the *ordonnateur*) cannot be the same person who receives and keeps the cash, and makes the payments (the *receveur*). While the first individual, at least in Côte d'Ivoire and Senegal, is generally the mayor, the second individual is an official of the Treasury. A current and comprehensive manual on local finance in Senegal states that the principal activity of the *receveur* is the verification of receipts and of the payments authorized by the *ordonnateur*. "In fact," the manual says, "such controls permit this officer to carry out a very high level of surveillance over the management activities of local *ordonnateurs*" (Bouat et Fouilland 1983, 188). As an additional control in Côte d'Ivoire, all purchases over $12,500 (5 million CFA francs) must in principle be made through the device of public tender (Attahi 1985a, Part IV). While this requirement seems to have been honored more in the breach than in the observance (the mayors complain that the limit is too low, and that the tender procedure is too time consuming), even the "irregular" purchases have become the subject of negotiations between the mayors and the Local Government Division of the Ministry of the Interior (Attahi 1986, 63). An important control in the case of Senegal seems to be the watchful eye of the Prefect, who tries to ensure that only those items previously passed in the budget are purchased (Personal interview with Prefect of Pikine, 18 July 1986). Finally, there is throughout the Francophone states the widespread single account system or *unicité de caisse*, according to which all revenues at both the local and national levels are credited to a unified budget; debits from this budget must be based on the actual availability of cash.

Financial controls over local councils in most of the Anglophone countries appear to have been much less effective. One of the reasons is certainly a shortage of qualified accounting staff, both at the local level and at the level of the central ministries. Until the mid 1980s many of the Francophone states could count on French *coopérants* to fill a wide range of technical postings. In the Anglophone states, not only were substantially fewer expatriates available for technical positions but also the turnover of qualified local accountants in the public service was extremely high — the result of high demand and high salaries in the private sector. Thus, even when controls existed on paper, they could not be effectively carried out in practice. In comparison with the Francophone states, the problem was exacerbated because of the larger flow of funds and wider range of tax collection vehicles at the local level.

A second difference with the Francophone states is the location of control mechanisms. In the Francophone states, powerful central government ministries maintain supervisory controls. Among the most important of these mechanisms is the presence of a Treasury official, the *receveur*, in the offices of every major urban commune. In Nigeria, most higher level controls over the LGAs are exercised through the state ministries of local government; in Kenya, the Ministry of Local Government is the major controlling agency. As a general rule, ministers of local government are far from the most powerful in the cabinet,[4] and their ministries are often seriously short of experienced staff and other necessary resources for the exercise of effective controls. In Kenya, a major report on the finances of local authorities for the three years ending 31 December 1981 came to the following conclusion:

The Ministry of Local Government has provincial local government officers stationed in all provinces in the country to supervise and advise the councils in their administration. However, financial mal-administration and misuse of councils' funds continues to be widely prevalent in most councils and the role these officers and the ministry play in the administration of the councils therefore, appears to be very ineffective (Kenya 1983, 4).

An analysis of the operation of the Nairobi City Council – which took place after the Council was dissolved by the Minister for Local Government in March 1983 – showed, *inter alia* that the Council's budgets were invariably submitted late to the Ministry, and that the Ministry, in turn, was even later to approve them. A major recommendation of the study was drastically to increase the professional capability of the supervisory Ministry.

Councils as a Focus for Political Conflict

The very size of urban council budgets in some Anglophone states, combined with the range of functions which they control and the relative looseness of central government supervision, has given rise to robust political battles over the control of resources. The case of Kenya is illustrative. In 1983 Nairobi and the other large municipal councils in the country spent a total of KShs. 2,095.8 million or about $199.6 million. This represented 8.8 percent of the total capital and recurrent budget of the Kenyan government for the 1982 / 83 financial year (Kenya 1985). In 1983 Nairobi alone was estimated to have spent (in both capital and recurrent categories) some KShs. 1,304.4 million or about $124.2 million – or 5.5 percent of all public expenditures at the national level. While there were controls over the expenditure of all this money, they were obviously insufficient. The Minister for Local Government announced early in March 1983 that, as a result of activities "which have led to the current gross mismanagement of council funds and poor services to the residents [of the city]" (*The Weekly Review* 11 March 1983, 4), he was suspending the Nairobi City Council (by dismissing the councillors) and replacing it with a Commission appointed by the central government. At the same time, he appointed a "high powered" Task Force to report on the operations of the City Council, and he sent the Council's heads of department on compulsory leave. While the Task Force report was never made public, it was common knowledge in Nairobi that the Council had become insolvent and that evidence of financial mismanagement and peculation on the part of some of the officers and the elected councillors was abundant. One of the results of the suspension of the City Council was the curtailing of the political career of Nairobi's powerful mayor, Nathan Kahara. Kahara, whose style of operation within the City Council was arguably similar to the "machine" model of politics in early twentieth century American cities, was destroyed by the removal of his organizational base (*The Weekly Review* 8 April 1983, 4-7). He hardly contested the September 1983 parliamentary elections.

By March 1986, three years after it took control over the Nairobi City Council, the Kenya government passed a motion through Parliament extending the life of the City Commission two more years (*The Weekly Review* 28 March 1986, 8). Unless the Ministry of Local Government could be made a much more effective control instrument and unless urban government could be rendered more effective and financially responsible, it was not clear how a retreat into the past could be a solution to Nairobi's massive problems. The dilemma is illustrated by the Council's serious rate arrears problem. At the end of 1983, for example, the Council (now Commission) was owed a total of KShs. 356,171,940 in land rates. This figure was almost equal to the total recurrent expenditures for the year by the Commission of KShs. 381,226,120. While sixty-one percent of these rate arrears were owed by private individuals (many of them powerful politicians and senior bureaucrats), the remaining thirty-nine percent were owed by agencies of the Kenya government, most notably Kenya Railways (twenty-two percent of the arrears) and the Commissioner of Lands (seventeen percent of the arrears). The figure at the end of 1983, by which time the Commission had been in operation for nine months, was thirty percent higher than the figure for the previous year, before the government had moved to control the Council (Nairobi City Commission 1985). By the end of 1986, the amount owed to the Commission in arrears was considerably in excess of the yearly annual expenditure figure, though exact details were not available because of an extensive fire in the Commission's offices which had destroyed many important records (Personal communication to author, June 1987). In the opinion of many knowledgeable insiders, the financial problems of the Commission could not be solved unless the government decided to pay its own bills.

It is instructive to note that immediately following his initial moves against the Nairobi City Council, the Minister for Local Government appointed a team to probe the financial management of the Mombasa Municipal Council (Kenya's second largest local council), which sent all heads of administrative departments on compulsory leave, and suspended Mombasa's town clerk (*The Weekly Review* 25 March and 8 April 1983). Mombasa's council had been closed down once before, in 1976,[5] and the municipal council of Kisumu – Kenya's third largest town – was under suspension during most of the early 1980s.

The rash of central government probes and suspensions in Kenya's urban councils during the 1980s underlined the close connection between politics and finance at the local level. Since independence, this connection has been firmly established by numerous government commissions examining the irregularities of councillors and local council officials, although few of these reports have been published.[6] But the wide latitude in the administration of local finance permitted by the system, in addition to a relatively broad definition of functions carried out by councils in Kenya, has tended to create attractive opportunities for discretionary financial dealings. In a study of the Thika Municipal Council during the 1970s, Patricia Stamp focuses on the struggles for control over a sites and services housing scheme between the Ministry of Local Government and the Commissioner for Lands, on the one side, and local councillors on the other. Discretionary control over the allocation of plots in the scheme meant (indirectly, at least) both money and political support to the local councillors; for central government, on the other hand, the allocation process had to operate neutrally, according to established rules and procedures. In 1969 and 1970 the state land comprising three small sites and services schemes was allocated to individuals by an *ad hoc* Plot Allocations Sub-Committee of the Thika Municipal Council's Town Planning and Development Committee. When it was revealed to the central government Commissioner of Lands that many of the allocations of the sub-committee had been irregularly carried out in favor of upper-income individuals, he removed the allocation function from the Council and cancelled parts of some schemes which had already been fully allocated. Following this move, many Thika municipal councillors – deprived of an important patronage resource – lost all interest in the proceedings of the council. Stamp argues that the basis of the conflict here is the difference in perception and behavior between a predominantly petty-bourgeois council and a central government whose interests coincided (on this issue at least) with those of the national bourgeoisie. Efficient and honest administration at the local level was consistent with the needs of the national bourgeoisie, whose business activities in any case rarely extended to the small discretionary transfers of property and licenses which were the basis of petty-bourgeois involvement in council activities (Stamp 1981).

In a study of Nairobi's public housing program covering approximately the same time period, Frederick and Nelle Temple account for the increasing bias in the construction of public housing units toward middle and upper-income groups. Their explanation for the bias in the program away from publicly-expressed goals of support for the poor involves the relatively "closed" nature of the Nairobi political system – consisting of irregular and sometimes even manipulated local elections, a moribund single political party, and effective discouragement of public criticism of the government. In this context, which approximated "machine politics," middle- and upper-income groups were able covertly to influence both the implementation and the allocation of housing schemes to their own advantage (Temple and Temple 1980). The "capturing" of local council functions by local upper-income groups (designated as petty-bourgeois or bourgeois depending on the scale of their involvement) typically focused on public housing allocations because of the potential profits involved in this area. But it has extended to market stall allocations, the allocation of public land, construction or redevelopment permits, the allocation of public tenders for construction of infrastructure, and the like. The "divisible benefits" being allocated at the local level are particularly attractive for the less educated and more entrepreneurial members of the petty bourgeoisie who tend also to be the major source of recruitment into the ranks of local elected councillors. A particularly revealing section of the Kenyan *Miller Commission Report* on the activities of the former Attorney-General, Charles Njonjo, shows the close links established between one faction of the national bourgeoisie and a network of Mombasa councillors and MPs. By funnelling money through a trusted local MP directly to a selected group of local councillors, Njonjo was able to influence the election of the Mayor and Deputy Mayor of Mombasa. But when one of "his" councillors would apparently not comply with a request from Njonjo to remove coastal squatters from a beachfront property, the councillor was expelled from the party (*The Weekly Review* 21 December 1984, 19-20).

The investigation of Charles Njonjo may be interpreted as an attempt by the national political leadership in Kenya seriously to discredit their opponents in the public eye.[7] Seen from this angle, the government move to keep Nairobi City Council under a Commission directly appointed by the Minister of Local Government (and presumably on the advice of the President[8]) is another, related effort at bringing about a new "national balance" by taking control of a substantial political base away from Central Province leaders. More generally, it points up some of the more visible contours of the central-local struggle that is endemic within political systems in which substantial institutional resources have been developed at the local level. If the political pendulum in Francophone cities is moving toward the gradual strengthening of local institutional capacity, it is faltering at the other extreme in Nairobi and many Anglophone cities. But for a fuller understanding of the actual effectiveness of African cities in dealing with their many functional responsibilities, one must look more directly at the administration of urban services. This will be the subject of the next chapter.

Notes

1. Unless otherwise specified, "Francophone Africa" in this analysis does not include Zaire. French is the official language in Zaire, but its Belgian colonial past sets it off from other Francophone countries with a French colonial past. Unlike most of the ex-French colonies whose currency is tied to the French franc and convertible, Zaire's currency is independent and unconvertible.

2. In 1982 the exchange rate of the Kenya shilling was approximately 10.5 shillings to one American dollar. In that year, the gross revenue of the City Council of Nairobi

was KShs. 710 million. Converting, the approximate foreign exchange value of the total revenue figure would have been (US) $68 million. (Source for revenue figures: Nairobi City Council, *Abstract of Accounts For the Year Ended 31st December, 1982*, 53).

3. That the Nairobi figures are not unusually high for large anglophone cities in Africa is suggested by a comparative study of local government finance carried out by the IMF during the 1970s. Local government expenditure per capita in Nairobi was $60.77 in 1976; in 1972 in Zambia (a slightly wealthier country in per capita terms), the Lusaka City Council was spending $183.70 per person, and Ndola was spending $195.30 per person (International Monetary Fund. 1976, Appendix 1: 4).

4. An interesting exception to this rule was the Minister for Local Government and Cooperative Development in Tanzania, Kingunge Ngombale Mwiru, who held this office from 1985 through the end of 1987. An important spokesperson for the ideological left in the CCM party in Tanzania, Ngombale Mwiru was a member of the powerful Central Committee of the party, and head of one of the five major party secretariats – Ideology and Mass Mobilization. In December 1987, however, in a major cabinet shuffle undertaken by President Ali Hassan Mwinyi, Ngombale Mwiru was stripped of his cabinet post and left with only his party position. Under a new minister (Paul Bomani, a long-time supporter of the previous President, Julius Nyerere), the "local government" portfolio was seen by many Tanzanians to have been downgraded.

5. Giving his reasons for the dissolution of the Mombasa Municipal Council in August 1976, the Minister for Local Government spoke of "general slackness, inefficiency, irresponsibility, corruption and financial mismanagement in the Council," arguing that the Council was "completely incapable of meeting its obligations to its residents" (*The Weekly Review* 16 August 1976, 6).

6. Among the published reports on urban councils are: Federal Republic of Nigeria. 1966. *Report of the Tribunal of Inquiry into the Affairs of the Lagos City Council*. Lagos: Ministry of Information Printing Division; Republic of Ghana. 1969. *Interim and Final Reports of the Commission of Enquiry into the Accra-Tema City Council*. Accra: Ghana Publishing Corporation; and Republic of Ghana. 1970. *Report of the Commission of Enquiry into the Affairs of the Kumasi City Council*. Accra: Ghana Publishing Corporation.

7. For an excellent analysis of the fall of Njonjo, based largely on published sources, see Jean-François Médard (1987). Médard ascribes Njonjo's fall to the suspicion of the President that Njonjo was attempting to replace him, a hypothesis supported by the report of the Miller Commission.

8. That the appointed Chairman of the Nairobi City Commission feels directly responsible to Kenya's President has never been in doubt since 1983 when the post was first created. In a public address given in Ottawa on 22 November 1987 on the occasion of the "Capitals of the World" Conference, the Chairman of the Nairobi City Commission – Mr.Eliud Ngala-Mwendwa (a former Minister of Labour under Kenyatta, representing Eastern Province) – spoke of the beauty of his distant city. When in Kenya, he said, he never forgets the words of the President: " "Peace, love and unity' ... We say these words every morning when we wake up."

CHAPTER 3
The Administration of Urban Services

Richard E. Stren

Local councils in large African cities are not the sole locus of decision-making which bears on the quality of urban life. Much more important in Francophone cities, and of at least equal importance in most Anglophone cities, are central government and parastatal agencies responsible for a whole host of urban services and regulations. Among the services typically performed by such agencies are water and electricity supply, refuse removal and public transport, public housing, land allocation, and land-use planning. A central theme of this chapter is the "privatization of services." Privatization here does not imply the wholesale transfer of whole government agencies to either individuals or large firms in the private sector, but rather the gradual taking over of urban services by small-scale enterprise, as a result of the failure of public sector agencies to provide the necessary level of performance. In some cases, large enterprises have profited from this transfer; but in the majority of cases cited, small entrepreneurs have provided services – mostly to the urban poor – because existing public sector enterprises are either unwilling or unable to deal with the massive increase in demand which African city growth has entailed.

The private provision of local public services through "contracting out" has become increasingly common in the United States and Western Europe over the last decade. The reasons have been largely economic, as hard-pressed councils have attempted to obtain more efficient services at a lower overall cost. In Britain, an estimated £3 billion of local authority expenditure was awarded to private firms through some form of competitive tendering during 1985-86; the most visible area of work for private contractors was in refuse collection and street cleaning. Still, by the end of 1985, only about two dozen local authorities had privatized street cleaning or refuse collection, out of a total of well over a thousand in the country, and the trend toward increased contracting out in all areas seemed to have reached at least a temporary plateau (Ascher 1987, Chapter 7).

In the Third World, there are many examples of the private provision of public services, and the trend is probably towards an increase. An extensive examination of this phenomenon by Gabriel Roth (1987) shows that effective services have been provided privately in the areas of education, health, telecommunications, urban transport, water, and sewerage. Many of these services are provided locally, in combination with services offered by local authorities, or by agreements with them.

The trade-off between the public and private sectors varies among countries and with the service area in question. But in Africa, where such a large proportion of the urban population is extremely poor, there is always a danger that the distributional consequences for the weakest groups will be, on balance, negative when a public service becomes privatized. The gradual shift toward private supply of urban services that seems to be taking place (with some exceptions) across the continent is also a response to an array of urban market forces on the one hand, and to the failure of governments, on the other. Under these circumstances, many urban residents (except the poorest) are not only willing, but even anxious to pay a market rate for what they perceive to be necessary services, delivered efficiently and regularly. In the remainder of this chapter, a number of urban services are examined, with special emphasis on how they are delivered and administered and on the fluctuating balance between public provision and private need.

Water Supply

Most water supply agencies and virtually all electricity supply agencies in African cities are either central government parastatals or are directly attached to central government ministries. The situation in Nairobi, in which the Water and Sewerage Department (which supplies water to all consumers) is a constituent part of the City Council (now Commission), is unusual, and is possible only because Nairobi is permitted by the central government to borrow offshore for capital works. Subverting this arrangement, however, was the Council's substantial internal transferring of funds from its water account in order to pay for general purposes. This reduction of water account funds had the effect of reducing the Council's ability to renew its water supply infrastructure, while it was in contravention of an agreement with the World Bank (which had lent the Council a large sum in 1978). While the World Bank contract specified that the Council could not borrow more than KSh. 8,000,000 from the water fund, the actual figure was in excess of KSh. 200,000,000 by the end of 1982 (Kenya 1983, 109). This unwarranted borrowing from the surplus generated from the water supply was one of the main reasons for the government's suspension of the Council in March 1983. But under the Nairobi City Commission, the water supply function remained within the overall structure of the local authority.

The effective provision of water to urban consumers in Nairobi has, in any case, come under severe public criticism in the 1980s. For several years, shortages of piped water were considered a result of the inadequacy in overall supply relative to the city's expanding population. In principle, however, the problem should have been solved by the coming on-line in early 1984 of a large new water supply project, funded by the World Bank. But when the Chania II scheme came on line, water pressure throughout the system increased substantially, and there were pipe-bursts everywhere. (When I visited the Assistant General Manager of the Water and Sewerage Department in January 1985, I was informed that there were some nine hundred unrepaired bursts.) Many of the pipes were old; the equipment to control pressure and to monitor the bursts was insufficient; staff was inadequately trained; and the Department did not have enough vehicles to patrol and maintain the extensive system (Mitullah 1985, 65-71).

Water supply is an even more serious problem in most Nigerian cities. In a comprehensive household survey of Makurdi and Idah (in Benue State, with populations of 144,000 and 47,200 respectively) in 1982, residents identified the poor water supply as their single most serious neighborhood problem. At the time of the survey (which covered 1,525 households in both towns), only 49.8 percent of Makurdi residents and 30.4 percent of Idah residents had access to piped water in their own houses or compounds (Stren 1985). Although there were various other means of obtaining water, 11.4 percent of the Makurdi respondents and 25.3 percent of the Idah respondents said they purchased water from the private sector, using either itinerant water sellers or tanker lorries owned by local firms. Another more elaborate survey of the distribution of piped water and the perceptions of water users was carried out by the Nigerian Institute of Social and Economic Research (NISER) in 1985. Some of the results of this survey are reported in Chapter 4 of this study. Based on a stratified random sample of 2,007 households in Ibadan, Enugu and Kaduna, the NISER researchers found that on the average close to one-third of those interviewed had no pipe-borne water connections to their homes. And of those households which did have water connections, twenty-seven percent of the Ibadan households, forty percent of the Enugu households, and thirty-nine percent of the Kaduna households reported having only a single tap in their premises. Again, most of those with water connections reported various degrees of interuption in their water supply. While from one-fifth to one-third of the connected households reported water availability "every time of day," thirty-four percent of the Ibadan households, twenty-seven percent of the Kaduna households, and twenty-six percent of the Enugu households reported that their pipes were always dry. In general, both the availability of piped connections and the regularity of water supply in the three surveyed towns varied according to the area of residence. The situation was worst in the old core areas of the town (particularly in the old core of Ibadan); it improved slightly in the "intermediate areas" away from the core; and it was best in the newer suburbs.

Explanations for the low and irregular level of urban water supplies cannot be attributed to the shortcomings of LGAs in Nigeria. In the late 1960s the urban water supply function was, in almost all states, transferred from local authorities to state government parastatals. Currently, the Chairman and members of these state water boards or corporations are appointed by the state governments, and both capital and recurrent expenditures are underwritten by the states. Among the reasons that have been advanced for the unsatisfactory services rendered by these parastatals all over Nigeria are the long delays in getting expenditure approval from higher levels of state government, a shortage of spare parts and chemicals (a result of scarce foreign exchange), the low level of rate collection (itself a function of poor service), inadequate coordination with other relevant agencies (such as local planning authorities, contractors, or ministries of works and housing), and the irregularity of electricity supply which shuts down the pumps and reduces water pressure. In particular, the unreliable supply of electricity from the National Electric Power Authority (NEPA)

> ... has led to the various corporations buying generating sets which are always very expensive and ineffective substitutes. This automatically increases the overhead costs, thus draining the already meager finance and increases the need for spare parts, as these generators break down often (Onibokun 1985, 88).

The Nigerian case dramatically illustrates the systemic interaction between different levels of government with respect to urban services. Here, the irregularity of supply of the national electricity parastatal reinforces the ineffectiveness of state water supply boards; but no effective mechanisms of coordination are available to assure delivery where it matters most – at the local urban level. More generally, the Nigerian case illustrates the possibility of a "vicious circle" in the deterioration of services. Because of regular power "outages" in Nigeria, large firms and wealthy individuals purchase imported generators, which provide power to their factories and compounds when the power goes off. Similarly, wealthier Nigerians may also purchase large water storage tanks for their houses as insurance against water shortages. And finally, it is also possible in some cities for individual houseowners to contract with private waste removal firms for the disposal of household rubbish. In all three cases, wealthy (and presumably more powerful) individuals are able to "buy themselves out" of the system, thereby reducing drastically their personal incentive to try to improve the system through political pressure. To use Albert Hirschman's (1970) terminology, ease of "exit" in this case diminishes the likelihood of "voice," the latter being probably a necessary condition for improved efficiency in Nigerian public service agencies.

Water supply agencies in most other African countries are private companies or national parastatals. In Côte d'Ivoire, the Société de Distribution d'Eau de la Côte d'Ivoire (SODECI) was established as a private company in 1959. At that time, the government entrusted the management of the country's urban water supplies to a French company, Société d'Aménagement Urbain et Rural (SAUR), which was the majority shareholder in SODECI. Then, in 1980 the paid-in capital of SODECI was dramatically increased at the same time as SAUR slipped from being the majority shareholder to a 46.5 percent share of SODECI, while Ivorian nationals took over 47.8 percent of the shares. (By 1983 they had 52 percent.) SODECI has a concessionary contract with Abidjan and a fixed price contract with the other towns in the country (Saint-Vil 1983, 476-77).

Jean Saint-Vil, the leading academic authority on urban water supplies in Côte d'Ivoire, argues that the level of water connections in proportion to the population of Abidjan fell from fifty-seven percent in 1977 to forty-seven percent in 1983. The reason for this decline in service is the rapid growth in spontaneous housing, where "in principle" the level of connections is zero (Saint-Vil 1983, 480-81). In these spontaneous settlement areas, water is supplied by private vendors at a unit cost approximately five times the price to consumers with regular connections. Another factor relates to what the Ivorians call *la conjoncture* – the economic downturn of the late 1970s and afterwards. During the 1970s the state was prepared to subsidize water connections to houseowners in poorer areas of the city. But the program fell off in the early 1980s because of a shortage of public funds, and the rate of added connections fell from 8,000 per year in 1977 to 2,300 in 1982 (Saint-Vil 1983, 478). What criticism exists of SODECI in Côte d'Ivoire relates more to the distributional aspects of water connections than to the quality and efficiency of the service which the company provides.

A World Bank evaluation of SODECI, which notes that the agency is allowed to charge a fee adequate to the compensation of staff, equipment, energy, and other inputs plus a margin based on agreed overheads and profits, indexed against inflation, claims that the Côte d'Ivoire company "offers one of the highest standards in West Africa. The systems are well designed, equipped, maintained, and operated. Water quality and pressure are uniformally [sic] good." Among the factors which contribute to this success, argues the Bank, are SODECI's freedom to deal with its own staff, a strong emphasis on training, and the "setting of water tariffs to reflect costs fully ... which means that consumers, rather than taxpayers, pay for the service they receive" (World Bank 1983, 53). While Saint-Vil suggests that some conflict exists between efficiency and distributional equity in SODECI, the World Bank account argues that the very efficiency and profitability of the service permits the company to charge low rates for smaller users, "so the poor can afford the service."

The lowering of the rate of urban connections in Côte d'Ivoire reflects a pattern much more deeply entrenched elsewhere, according to which piped water is generally not available in many newly-developed areas, and in almost all "spontaneous housing" areas. In such circumstances, residents of these areas – among the poorest in the city – are obliged to purchase water from water-sellers. In Dar es Salaam in the early 1970s, public standpipes were installed in "squatter" areas, where water was available free of charge. But because of the distance people would have to walk to obtain water at the few water points, most people needed to purchase water regularly from water-sellers. I calculated that the cost in "squatter" areas of purchasing water in this manner was ten times higher (for equivalent quantities) than in areas where piped connections had been installed for individual houses (Stren 1975, 49). Since the early 1970s more standpipes have been installed, with the result that few Dar es Salaam residents are obliged to purchase from water sellers any more. But an account of the water problems of Nouakchott and Rosso in Mauritania notes that more than sixty-five percent of the inhabitants have no direct access to water.

> In the shanty towns, the Government is supposed to distribute water by lorry on a regular basis. Often, however, the rounds are cancelled because the lorries are needed for emergency deliveries in the bush. In recently parcelled areas, taps are few and far between; only one in a self-help built area of Njourbel in Rosso, and that serves part of the 6,000 inhabitants in addition to the 11,500 people living in Satara [a shanty-town which began in 1968]. The latter have access to no other water point, except one tap in the city and a few wells, whose waters are polluted and in any case dry up during the dry season.
>
> A highly adapted, door-to-door trade in water has developed spontaneously since 1978. The water is contained in one or two drums transported by donkey or horse and cart. Since it is controlled neither by the Government nor by the unorganized inhabitants, this intermediate trade in water has led to highly profitable speculation. Thus, in Nouakchott, the price of a 10-litre bucket sells at 3 ouguiyas and a 30-litre jerrycan at 15 ouguiyas, whereas a household in the well-established urban area connected to the mains pays 15 UM per m^3 (Noukchott price), i.e. thirty times cheaper than do people living in the 5th arrondissement.
>
> The situation is even worse during the dry season in Rosso, which depends for its water on a reservoir filled once a year during the rainy season. The first water cart made its appearance there in 1979. The owner sold his water in the Satara shanty town at 1UM per litre, or one hundred times dearer than the price paid by people connected to the SONELEC system (Theunynck and Dia 1980, 224).

The irony of this situation is that, while they earn little in wages and other income, residents of these peripheral squatter areas pay considerably more for water and for transport than do more affluent residents of the "official" urban neighborhoods.

Waste Removal

Waste removal is one of the most pressing questions in contemporary African cities. Comparative experience shows that the trade-off between equity and efficiency cannot always be evaluated using existing data. While most Anglophone countries rely on a public cleansing service which is integrated with some regular department of the local authority, alternative approaches are to sub-contract the work to local entrepreneurs for specific areas or specific aspects (as is the case in some large Nigerian cities now), or to contract all the work to a single private company (as is still the case in Abidjan, and was formerly the case in Dakar). But a judgement as to which approach is more appropriate for a particular city or country must go beyond pure cost-benefit calculations of price and quantity to consider foreign exchange implications and consistency with the government's overall development strategy, politics, and equity. Thus, for example, a government which is experiencing severe foreign exchange shortages and maintains a statist / redistributional approach to development would be hard pressed to turn its refuse collection service over to the private sector. This is the situation in which Tanzania finds itself today. It would be politically difficult to allocate substantial sums of scarce foreign exchange to private firms for the purchase of new machinery and spare parts, and the higher user fees that a private system would entail could exclude the bulk of the low-income urban population from the service.

The removal of both liquid and solid waste in Dar es Salaam has been a problem since the early 1970s. According to a knowledgeable estimate, "less than 10-15%" of Dar es Salaam's population (estimated at 1.5 million in 1985) have connections to a central sewerage system (Hayuma 1983, 328). Most middle and upper-income areas depend on individual or grouped septic tanks for liquid waste, and most lower-income areas use pit latrines. To empty the septic tanks on a regular basis, a large fleet of cesspit emptying trucks is needed. But in 1983 / 84 only two out of thirty-two cesspit emptiers at the disposal of the Dar es Salaam City Council were in working condition, and only eight percent of the estimated daily production of six million liters of liquid waste could be removed (Kulaba 1985c, 23, 47-48). By 1985 the situation was even worse, with only one of the emptying trucks in operating condition. As Saitiel Kulaba shows in his chapter on Tanzania later in this volume, according to Dar es Salaam City Council records for a typical three-week period in June and July 1985, the cesspit emptying vehicle was able to complete only 332 out of 1,110 planned trips in the whole city or thirty percent of its target. In any case, central government records indicate that in 1986 only 0.3 percent of all the "foul water" being produced in Dar es Salaam was being collected. The figure for all urban areas in the country was 13.09 percent (Kulaba 1986b, 40). Some additional capacity in Dar es Salaam is provided by a number of public institutions which have their own cesspit emptiers; there is even a private citizen with his own. But for individuals to hire the services of these private or semi-public vehicles, costs an average of Shs. 400 to Shs. 600 per trip, compared to Shs. 60 charged by the City Council. As a result of the poor service, concludes Kulaba in Chapter 8, "people live with flooded water closets and latrines for many years."

Refuse removal, also a service provided directly by the Dar es Salaam City Council, is plagued by the same difficulties. In early 1986 the City Council would have needed fifty vehicles to remove all the household refuse produced in the city. But only twenty were available, and of these, only six were in condition to go on the roads every day. The government estimated that only about twenty-two percent of the total estimated daily production of solid waste could be removed. The situation in Tanzania's other major towns was equally bad. Thus, Tanga had only two vehicles regularly operating (it needed twenty), Arusha had two in good condition (it needed seventeen), and Mbeya had four regularly operating (it needed fifteen) (Kulaba 1986b, 39). For all of Tanzania's nineteen major towns, the government itself estimated that only twenty-four percent of the solid waste being produced on a daily basis was actually collected by the local councils. A substantial injection of foreign exchange was necessary to purchase spare parts and new vehicles. But for various reasons, Tanzania's overall financial situation was too precarious for the government to risk diverting such scarce resources to Dar es Salaam, let alone to the other large towns in the country. Full or partial privatization of the refuse removal service would have substantially raised the costs to householders, and put further and unacceptable pressure on the country's limited foreign reserves.

Countries with less of a foreign exchange constraint than Tanzania have a wider range of options in the management of urban refuse removal. Until the early 1980s, refuse removal in most large Nigerian cities was the responsibility of the local governments. Under the 1979 Nigerian Constitution, "provision and maintenance of public conveniences and refuse disposal" is a local government function. But the spectacular failure of the refuse removal service in so many localities has led to the shifting of responsibility among agencies and to some degree of privatization. Ibadan, with an estimated population of 2.2 million in 1982, had severe refuse disposal problems. The 1985 NISER field survey found that thirty-five percent of Ibadan households, thirty-three percent of Kaduna households, and forty-four percent of Enugu households were unaware of any refuse collection service for their premises. Given the unavailability of service for so many, it may not be surprising to learn that seventeen percent of the Ibadan households surveyed, thirty-five percent of the Kaduna households, and eighteen percent of the Enugu households "stored" their refuse outside in "open spaces" (Onibokun, Chapter 4, below).

During the 1970s household refuse removal was the responsibility of an Ibadan Wastes Disposal Board, a creation of the Oyo State Government (1972-78); after this time, the function reverted to the Ibadan Municipal Government. The takeover of the national government by the military on 31 December 1983 led to a renewed effort all over the country "to clear Nigerian settlements of filth" (Onibokun 1986, 174). In Ibadan, this effort resulted in the creation of the Oyo State Environmental Sanitation Task Force, which, in collaboration with the Ibadan Municipal Government, is now responsible for solid waste disposal and collection in the city. The Task Force works closely with the Sewerage and Refuse Matters Department, established by the new military government at the state level in 1984. At the same time, Ibadan had permitted, from the early 1980s, private contractors to operate in this field. These operators could contract with the government for removal in certain areas, or they could contract directly with individuals and institutions or businesses. For individuals, the normal user charge in 1985 was ₦10 per month, and the frequency of collection was once a week. The NISER survey results showed that twenty-six percent of Ibadan households had refuse contracts directly with private firms, and another seven percent were served by private firms employed by the government (Onibokun 1986, 188). A parallel study of six of these private firms demonstrated that their business (which included residences, institutions, industrial and commercial establishments) had expanded substantially from the early 1980s up to 1985 (Onibokun 1986, 192-99).

Some idea of the effectiveness of this policy of limited privatization may be inferred from the responses to the 1985 NISER survey in Ibadan. Of those respondents who answered a fixed-choice question on what they considered the most important environmental problem in their locality, fully sixty-four percent answered "solid wastes." The second highest response, at eight percent, was "liquid wastes." When the same respondents were asked whether they thought the situation had improved over the last ten years, a slightly higher proportion (forty-six percent) answered in the affirmative, rather than in the negative (forty percent). Finally, of those with an opinion on whether the situation was likely to improve over the next ten years, almost twice as many expected it to improve. The Ibadan population thus seems to be cautiously positive about recent changes in solid waste management, and moderately optimistic about the future. The response pattern in the other two cities sampled, Kaduna and Enugu, is similar (Onibokun 1986, 206-10).

Two other cities on which some data is available on solid waste disposal are Abidjan and Nairobi. In Abidjan and Bouaké (the country's second largest city), both the street cleaning and solid waste removal functions are entrusted to a private company, Société industrielle de transports automobiles africaines (SITAF). The company began in 1953 as a branch of the French company SITA and has since benefitted by the tax provisions of the Loi No.59-134 of 3 September 1959. For Abidjan in 1983, the company employed a staff of 1,336 and maintained an operating fleet of 205 vehicles. In estate housing areas and in areas of medium and higher-cost housing, SITAF has collection points every thirty meters; in spontaneous housing areas, the collection points are distributed every one hundred meters. The company is paid by contract by the City of Abidjan. When the City attempted to reduce its payments to the company in 1984 (having paid fifty-eight percent of its operating budget to SITAF in 1983), the company cut back on its refuse removal service and eliminated street sweeping entirely (Attahi 1985a, 66). A study of the distribution of SITAF services compared the disposition of cleaning workers between two communes within the city of Abidjan in 1983: a low-income, densely-populated area (Koumassi); and a high-income, low-density area (Cocody). Koumassi, with an estimated 20.6 percent of the population (based on projections from the 1975 census), was allocated 10.1 percent of all the 626 cleaning workers employed by SITAF. Cocody, the upper-income area with only 10.1 percent of the population of the city, was allocated 14.5 percent of the cleaning workers. On a per capita basis, the high-income area had three times the number of cleaning staff (Banyombo 1983). As SITAF cuts back on services in response to lower payments from the financially-strapped Abidjan council, this difference in treatment between the rapidly-growing low-income (and squatter) areas and the more stable, high-income areas can be expected to increase.

Refuse removal in Nairobi is entirely a local government concern. Under the City Council (from March 1983 through to the present, the Nairobi City Commission), the service has been performed by the Public Cleansing Section of the Public Health Department. Residents who have water connections are invoiced on their monthly water bills for refuse collection; those who do not pay regular water bills receive the service by paying cash in advance. In spite of this elaborate, computerized billing procedure, the cleansing service is "highly subsidised by the Commission from other financial sources" (Nairobi City Commission 1983, 1). By May of 1984, the Public Cleansing Section was employing a total of 1,816 staff, of whom 58 were office and supervisory staff, 101 were skilled workers, and 1,657 were permanently employed laborers. The largest single group of laborers (about twelve hundred) worked as street sweepers; the second largest group (about three hundred) worked in the loading and unloading of refuse removal vehicles.[1] Public criticism of the cleansing service reached a peak in early 1985 when the prestigious *The Weekly Review* featured a large cover photograph of a pile of uncollected garbage, entitling the collection of lead articles

"City in a Mess" – a humorous take-off on Nairobi's official slogan "City in the Sun." As the magazine described the situation,

> It has always been proudly referred to as the Green City in the Sun. But today, Nairobi presents a picture of a city rotting from the inside. Over the past 18 months, the main city news in the local press has been about mounting piles of stinking refuse, dry water taps, gaping pot-holes and unlit streets.
>
> Nairobi residents have watched helplessly their once beautiful city turn into one stinking mess. In the less fashionable but heavily populated areas such as Mathare, Kibera and Kangemi, the refuse piles mount for months before the Nairobi City Commission makes feeble attempts at clearing the mess. In Eastlands, it often takes weeks. At Soko Mjinga in Kariobangi, a refuse heap a whole quarter of an acre or more in size continued to spread between houses before it was finally arrested. Even the more fashionable residential estates have not been spared. In Buru Buru, Kilimani, Plainsview and Golden Gate estates, housewives dumped domestic refuse in unattended public lots as they waited for the city trucks to empty dustbins that filled weeks ago. City health inspectors turned a blind eye (*The Weekly Review* 25 January 1985, 3).

Journalistic hyperbole notwithstanding, Nairobi did indeed have a serious problem with refuse collection. While the population of the city was increasing at an estimated annual rate of at least six percent, the amount of refuse collected fell from a high of 202,229 tonnes in 1977 to 159,974 tonnes in 1983 – a decline of twenty-one percent over six years. Thus, over the late 1970s and early 1980s, the Council was collecting, on average, almost ten percent less refuse per capita every year.

The most important reason for this inadequacy, according to officials operating within the system, was the deterioration of equipment. For instance, the City Council had a total of eighty-three operational heavy vehicles in 1977 and eighty-six in 1978. After that, the number of heavy vehicles that could be used declined to seventy-one by 1983. As the City Council's finances deteriorated during this period, there was a corresponding shortage of foreign exchange available. Spare parts could not easily be obtained and new imported vehicles were much too expensive. The problem of spare-parts "cannibalism" in the Council's transport depot became serious in the 1980s, to say nothing of the gradual attrition of skilled Council mechanics as a result of higher salaries in the private sector. The deterioration of the cleansing vehicles reinforced a bias in the collection system whereby central parts of Nairobi were visited on a regular basis, and more distant parts of the city (where most of the low-income population is located) were served whenever there was "slack" in the system.

A second reason given by some officials for the inadequate collection of household refuse had to do with the supervision of the labor force. Most of the supervisory staff in the Cleansing Section are inadequately trained as public health officers; but because of a Ministry-initiated embargo on new hirings and even internal promotions, they have little incentive to improve their quality of work. As for the laborers, most are unskilled and poorly paid, and many were hired during the early 1980s as a result of the "machine" politics of the City Council. Because they are poorly paid and the job has a low status, workers leave the cleansing section at a high rate (it is difficult to replace them because of the embargo) and often book off sick. As individuals, they cannot easily be dismissed by management because of contract conditions defended by the powerful Kenya Local Government Workers' Union and because they are part of a politically important group within the Council. Although there has been some talk of limited privatization of the cleansing service in Nairobi, the close integration of the Cleansing Section with the Public Health Department (traditionally a powerful force in urban planning in Kenya) and the large numbers of laborers involved would be important constraints on any major change in the existing system. Privatization is more likely to be expressed at the level of neighborhoods burning or disposing of their own refuse than in any wholesale change in the collection system.

Another option, which has appeared in many major African cities but which has hardly been studied, is small-scale scavenging – either at the refuse collection points in town or at the large garbage dumps on the outskirts. In Khartoum, many low-income families keep goats, which scavenge through piles of uncollected refuse, in the process feeding themselves, reducing the level of organic waste, and supplying milk to families that otherwise would not have the means to obtain it. One study carried out in 1982 estimated that of all the solid waste deposited outside by households in Khartoum, thirty-five percent was removed by municipal garbage lorries, twenty-one percent was eaten by domestic animals (especially goats and cattle), twenty percent was removed by people (pickers or scavengers), seventeen percent was eaten by wildlife (including dogs), and eight percent remained as accumulation (Personal communication to the author from Joseph Whitney 5 September 1986). While the recycling of manufactured or semi-manufactured materials by the "informal sector" has often been noted in the literature, it has not been studied systematically. But a wide variety of products (bottles, cartons, scrap metal, newspapers) are regularly recuperated from industrial sites or wealthy households and resold to the poor (with or without conversion) for household use. Scavenging at municipal garbage dumps also takes place – although the only major study of this phenomenon (which is undoubtedly widespread) is based on a field study in Tananarive, Madagascar from 1982 through 1984. Carried out by sociologists, the study focused on a number of small villages, with a total population of from 300 to 350, all located on or beside the site of a fifty hectare municipal garbage dump, some ten kilometers from the capital city. Two major economic activities are worth mentioning here: the keeping of pigs by the majority of the garbage heap residents (to be eaten or sold for a variety of purposes); and the systematic collection of certain "raw" materials from the dump, sold on the "outside" to regular purchasers. Among the products recuperated and sold are charcoal, rags, bottles, animal bones, aluminum, and rubber (Camacho 1986).

Public Transport

Public transport is a service area which, for large cities in most countries, involves some mix of public sector management and private enterprise. As the most important unit of demand is the trip to or from work taken by an individual, a wide range of transport supply mechanisms has developed to respond to the ever-growing needs of an increasingly differentiated workforce. The trend in the 1980s in Africa is for a large public bus company to be supplemented by an informal system of minibuses and/or private cars which provide a more accessible service (particularly to peripheral low-income areas) at a slightly higher price. Behind this shift from monopoly provision of public transport to a mixed system are two major factors. First, experience has shown that large bus companies do not benefit from economies of scale, as had previously been believed. And second, for various political and administrative reasons, public bus companies are costly to run. A comprehensive study by the World Bank concludes:

> With few exceptions, publicly owned transport costs more to run (in many cases, much more) than comparable transport systems run by the private sector. Without the profit motive and the staff accountability that exist in the private sector, publicly owned systems have little incentive to strive for cost-effectiveness, to compete for revenues, or to sustain the high degree of effort necessary to overcome the numerous day-to-day problems. Furthermore, government agencies and publicly owned corporations often lack the flexibility of organization, the ability to hire and fire staff, or the financial discretion needed to adapt speedily to changing conditions (1986c, 21).

In the same vein, Gabriel Roth states flatly: "a monopoly on urban transport cannot be envisaged under any circumstances ... urban transport is not inherently suitable for provision by the public sector" (1987, 199).

A comparative study of Brazzaville and its neighbor Kinshasa is instructive. The system of public transport in Brazzaville, in place since 1963, is described by Xavier Godard (1985) as a "model of a public service monopoly." From 1963, with the exception of a four year period at the end of the 1970s when its fleet was hardly operating (and most of the service was taken over by small private vans, the *foulas-foulas*), the Société des transports de Brazzaville (STB) has enjoyed a legal monopoly within the city proper. The STB is, in effect, run by the Municipality of Brazzaville, although it operates under the close supervision of the Ministry of the Interior. In spite of continual problems of the inadequacy of spare parts, frequent breakdowns, pilferage of receipts, and chronic absenteeism in the STB, the central government has maintained it in operation through large *ad hoc* grants which permit the occasional purchase of large numbers of new vehicles even when the fare structure has been heavily controlled. Since 1981 the privately-owned *foulas-foulas* have been banned from operating in the central parts of the city. At the same time, the efficiency of the STB is low. In 1983, out of a hypothetical fleet of 130 buses, a daily average of only sixty left the garages every day, half of which broke down en route (Godard 1985, 44).

Kinshasa, by contrast, is described by Godard as a "model of the cohabitation of public and private sectors." Since the early 1950s various bus companies (from public to private in ownership) have shared the daily passenger load with smaller, privately owned carriers called *fulas-fulas* and *kimalus-malus*. The former are Mercedes or Toyota eight to ten tonne trucks, organized for about sixty passengers (though the load is often in excess of one hundred passengers); the latter are converted vans which hold up to thirty passengers (Mbuyi 1985, 26). These vehicles are generally owned by individuals, and are rented out on a daily basis. The system, as it operated in the late 1970s, is described by Marc Pain:

> The vehicle is hired by the day by a driver and his team of conductors, who generally number two. A fixed fee is paid each evening to the "boss": everything collected above that amount is kept by the conductors, the "driver's assistants" and by the driver himself. In 1973, the fee was 40-50 zaïres for a fula-fula and 10 zaïres for a taxi. In 1978, "the daily amount for a fula-fula was 160 Z, but a conductor stated that the total received by drivers and conductors was 350 Z." One can only imagine the speed and overload the vehicles are subjected to in order to obtain the maximum profit. "For citizens to find themselves packed in like sardines does not even raise the eyebrows of the drivers and conductors, whose refrain is always the same: 'Move to the back, there! If you don't like it, take a taxi!'" [Quotation from the local newspaper *Elima*].
>
> In fact, in most cases conditions of travel are dangerous. Elementary standards of safety are not respected, but these vehicles remain indispensable for the functioning of the city. And they have, in addition, the advantage of being fast (1984, 174).

In early 1979, according to one estimate, the private transport system (comprising *fulas-fulas*, *kimalus-malus*, and *taxis-bus*) supplied about forty thousand passenger seats while the large public transport companies supplied only twelve thousand (France 1982, 59). Later that year, the Société des transports zaïrois (SOTRAZ) was formed as a "mixed" private company, with twenty percent of its capital held by a French subsidiary of Renault, and another seventy percent held by SOZACOM, a mining parastatal. SOTRAZ began with a fleet of 150 new Renault buses, and two years later added 250 new buses, 80 mini buses, and 60 taxis. But by 1984 SOTRAZ was able to put only about 150 buses on the road daily. Still, in spite of such operating problems as having to give free passage to civil servants (a service compensated for only irregularly by government grants), SOTRAZ was carrying almost as many passengers as the private system (Godard 1985, 48).

One advantage which SOTRAZ had over the private owners was its ability to mobilize scarce foreign exchange, through the resources of its majority owner SOZACOM, in order to purchase spare parts and even new buses from Renault. By the mid 1980s, as fares were raised in response to "galloping" inflation, the company was gradually creating a market niche for itself that was relatively independent of the private transport market. Comparing the Kinshasa and Brazzaville cases, Godard argues that the Kinshasa system of "cohabitation," although uncoordinated at the top, involves more local inputs and is a better adaptation to the needs of the country than is the Brazzaville "monopoly" system, which depends completely on externally purchased products and heavy government grants and may ultimately fail when petroleum-based central government revenues falter (1985, 52-53).

Two other major cities whose public transport systems can usefully be compared are Dar es Salaam and Nairobi in East Africa. From 1949 to 1970 public transport in Dar es Salaam was monopolized by a private British company, DMT. By 1967, the year of the Arusha Declaration in Tanzania, DMT had 107 buses in operation, of which twenty-four were used for long-distance routes. In 1966, DMT carried over thirty million passengers in Dar es Salaam. In 1970 the company was nationalized and put under a national parastatal; and in 1974 it was divided into two companies – KAMATA (which operated up-country) and UDA (which operated within Dar es Salaam). After 1975 UDA's fleet strength and thus its overall performance began to deteriorate. While it was able to carry 137 million passengers in 1983, this was achieved in the face of frequent breakdowns and constant overloading. From a fleet size of 374 buses of which an average of 257 were serviceable every day in 1975, UDA's fleet size fell in 1984 to 205, of which an average of only 131 were operational. (In August 1986 there were 211 buses in the fleet, of which 148 were in working order – a slight improvement over the 1984 position.)

The shortfall is reflected in the fact that, during the 6 *a.m.* to 9 *a.m.* peak period, twenty-one percent of all waiting passengers on Dar es Salaam routes are left behind because of overcrowding on the buses (Kulaba 1986b, 49). At the same time, some twenty-nine staff buses were owned by central government ministries and departments, and 438 vehicles of various kinds (some of which were medium-sized buses) were owned by parastatals for their own employees. The total carrying capacity of the parastatal vehicles, assuming seventy percent of them were roadworthy, was ninety-one percent of the daily capacity of UDA. But for the most part, these vehicles were used once or twice a day, at peak periods. For 1984, a consultant's study estimated that UDA would need 305 serviceable buses to meet the demand; based on a serviceability ratio of seventy percent, this would mean a total fleet of 436 buses (Tanzania 1984, 46). Given UDA's poor record in obtaining foreign exchange from the government (from 1975 through 1983 it obtained 35.33 percent of what it asked for) and the serious problems of pot-holes in Dar es Salaam's very extensive road system, the prospects were not good for an improvement in either the capacity or the running efficiency of the publicly-owned transport service. A study of the maintenance of Dar es Salaam's road system shows that for the 1986 / 87 financial year, the City Council was able to allocate only 0.32 percent and 9.6 percent of the funds necessary for adequate maintenance of its tarred and murram roads, respectively. While the technical staff in the City Engineer's Department has gone up from one or two persons during the decentralization years to sixteen in 1985 and thirteen in 1986, there is a serious shortage of road tar and of lorries and heavy construction equipment in Dar es Salaam (Kulaba 1986b, 41-45).

One response to the shortfall in public transport facilities has been to permit the private sector to take up some of the slack. For many years, private sector public transport was anathema to the socialist beliefs of Tanzania's ruling elite. For a brief period from 1972 through 1974, *sumni-sumni* vehicles were allowed to operate in order to supplement DMT services. The *sumni-sumni* were so named because they charged a flat fare of Shs. = / 50 (called a *sumuni*) per trip. However, they were mainly old micro- and minibuses in poor condition and were driven rapidly and dangerously. They were legally banned in 1975. While various kinds of "pirate" operators took up some of the slack, not until 1983 did the government, under Prime Minister Sokoine, permit private enterprise again in Dar es Salaam. On 1 April private vehicles were permitted to operate in compliance with certain regulations, which included an acceptable standard of mechanical fitness for the vehicle and a license to operate on stipulated routes. By July 1983, 197 of these large minibuses had been registered, with a carrying capacity of 7,134 seats. These buses, which could be purchased by individuals using their own sources of foreign exchange, were called *dala dala* after their Shs. 5 flat fare (a large silver coin called a *dala* in Swahili). The *dala dalas* were generally smaller than the UDA buses and operated on a smaller number of intra-city routes; but they were faster and more expensive for passengers (in 1985 UDA charged a flat adult fare of Shs. 3 for normal routes and Shs. 4 for express routes) (Banyikwa 1985). Assuming both UDA buses and the *dala dala* operators had the same level of serviceability and assuming a passenger "seat" in each would carry the same number of passengers daily, UDA buses were carrying roughly seventy-two percent of the public in 1983, as against twenty-eight percent for the *dala dalas*. (The proportion carried by UDA decreased by 1986, by which year the *dala dalas* numbered three hundred.) But since the *dala dala* operators were more resourceful in keeping their vehicles on the road, and since they carried their passengers more quickly, the proportion was likely less favorable to UDA than this calculation suggests.

While the overall level of service has improved in Dar es Salaam with the regularization of *dala dalas*, transport costs are heavy for ordinary workers. Assuming a worker earned the legal minimum wage of Shs. 810 in 1985 and worked a normal six-day week (including Saturday mornings), he would have had to pay a minimum of Shs. 300 or thirty-seven percent of his gross wage, just for public transport. Workers who lived on the outskirts of the city and needed to take more than one bus or workers who took *dala dalas* paid proportionately more.

The public transport system in Nairobi is also a mix of public and private systems. The public system – in this case Kenya Bus Services Ltd. (KBS) – is seventy-five percent owned by the large British multinational United Transport Overseas Services Ltd. (the owner of the Dar es Salaam bus system before it was nationalized in 1970) and twenty-five percent owned by the City Council of Nairobi. In 1983 KBS had a fleet of 295 buses (most of which were Leyland Victory with a total capacity of 97 passengers), putting on an average eighty-four percent of them (248) on the road per day. In 1983 KBS had a full-time staff of 2,400 and estimated that it carried 131 million passengers. Directly competitive with KBS on many intra-city routes are the *matatus*, privately-owned minibuses or converted vans, which since November 1984 have been legalized by the government. The story of the *matatus* is told in detail by Diana Lee-Smith in her chapter in this volume. At the time of Mazingira Institute's original survey of *matatus* in the early 1980s (when they were only quasi-legal), 1,000 full-time vehicles were operating in Nairobi, carrying forty-two percent (compared to fifty-eight percent for KBS) of the passenger market (Kapila, Manundu and Lamba 1982, 318). Following the complete legalization of *matatus* through the Traffic (Amendment) Act of 1984, many large, new buses (assembled in Kenya by General Motors / Isuzu or by British Leyland and clearly owned by wealthy individuals) were added to the *matatu* ranks. At the same time, stringent licensing procedures for existing vehicles and controls over the age and experience of *matatu* drivers strengthened a tendency toward *rapprochement* in terms of style and quality of service between KBS and its competitors.

Housing

A final service area with important implications for the overall quality of life in African cities is housing. Until the early 1970s in East Africa, and the late 1970s in the more buoyant West African countries, large public housing programs in the major cities supplemented the efforts of individuals to build for themselves and of governments and some large corporations to build for their employees. A.A. Laquian's overview of "basic housing" programs in the Third World is also accurate for Africa:

> The main housing programs prevalent before the 1970s were urban renewal, low-cost housing, and housing finance. They were based on the assumption that if enough housing units were built there would be no housing shortage. Solutions to the housing problem involved providing enough capital for housing, introducing modern technologies in housing construction, finding better and cheaper building materials, and designing more efficient dwellings. A prerequisite for the success of these solutions was control over land use, illegal squatting, population movements, and substandard structures. Housing was a rational, predictable, and regularized activity; it should have been responsive to efficient and effective management. It was not, however, and, one by one, housing policies and programs failed in developing countries (1983, 13).

The main agencies for these conventional housing programs in Africa were national housing corporations. The National Housing Corporation in Kenya, which completed an average of close to two thousand units of conventional (mostly rental) housing all over Kenya per year until the mid-1970s, saw its production rise slightly after that to a high of 4,085 units in 1979, with a falling off to around three thousand units per year through 1982. Although the Corporation (which funnelled low-cost public funds to tendered private contractors) experienced problems of inefficiency in the early 1980s, a new General Manager was appointed in 1983, and by late 1984 the Corporation was planning for an output of five thousand units per year. Still, in 1984 Kenya's Central Bureau of Statistics estimated that only twelve percent of the country's new urban households were being accommodated in new legally-built housing completed by both the public and private sectors. The response to this shortfall was overcrowding in existing dwellings and illegal construction. And because of the high cost of building housing within the by-laws, less than ten percent of the completed legal housing was built by the private sector (Kenya 1985, 38).

The relatively high output maintained by Kenya's National Housing

Corporation through the early 1980s bears comparison with the situation in Côte d'Ivoire. A study by the Centre de recherches architecturales et urbaines (CRAU) analyzes the production in Abidjan of the two major public housing agencies – Société ivoirienne de construction et de gestion immobilière (SICOGI), and Société de gestion financiére de l'habitat (SOGEFIHA). By 1980, these two parastatals had constructed 41,667 units of "low-cost housing" (*logement social*) in the capital, almost all of it built during the decade 1970-80.[3] According to a CRAU survey, ninety-three percent of those living in these "low-cost" units were Ivorians; this contrasts with an approximate proportion of about one-half of all Abidjan residents who were Ivorians (CRAU 1983, 109). Assuming that each public housing unit accommodated eight persons on the average (CRAU 1983, 110) and that the total population of Abidjan in 1980 was about 1.5 million, as many as twenty-two percent of the whole population or fully forty-one percent of the Ivorians in Abidjan lived in this category of state-built housing. And since twenty-seven percent of SICOGI's and thirty-nine percent of SOGEFIHA's units were intended for middle or upper income groups ("Bilan et Perspectives" 1980) the total must have approached one-half of the Ivorian population of the city. But because of financial problems, linked to high debts and a precipitous decline in central government revenues, the state stopped SOGEFIHA in 1978, and SICOGI in 1979, from undertaking any new construction. In 1980, SOGEFIHA was placed under the close supervision (*sous la tutelle*) of the Ministry of Construction and ordered to confine its activities to the administration of its housing stock. Partly because the state had never permitted SOGEFIHA to raise rents (they had been reduced by twenty percent in 1970), the corporation's debt servicing costs – which included a large component of debt in American dollars – were much too high for its income. From 1981 through 1983, the central government subsidized the corporation by 29.3 billion CFA francs – an amount equivalent to about $75 million (Coopers and Lybrand 1984, 13).

The fall-off in parastatal housing construction during the 1980s (SOGEFIHA has ceased construction entirely; SICOGI operates again, but at a very low level) has created pressures in other areas. For example, most of the housing built by the state in the 1970s consisted of rental units; the rents were largely fixed for the lowest-cost units and were offset by "administrative leases" (according to which the state paid the rents) for middle- and upper-middle-income occupants who were teachers or civil servants. But in the 1980s salaries were frozen, "administrative leases" were terminated and rents were allowed to rise. In the higher-cost units, teachers and middle-level civil servants who could no longer afford housing left the premises and found lodging in low-cost rental housing as sub-tenants. On the one hand, this left many of the higher-cost units unoccupied; on the other hand, it put even more pressure on the lower-cost units, as the city continued to grow by an average of from four to five percent per year.

This pressure was reflected in three main ways according to the CRAU survey. First, the level of sub-letting was very high, involving 20.9 percent of all the 982 households interviewed in 1982. These households paid higher rents than the original renters and had very little security. Second, there was more and more overcrowding in the already constrained quarters of from two to four rooms. Third, and partly as a result of the increasing size of households, renters were forced to undertake physical modifications to their rental units, modifications which were not sanctioned by the owning agencies. A full forty-one percent of the households surveyed had undertaken such modifications at their own expense. The three most common modifications were covering the courtyard, changing the internal use of the rooms (i.e. from a kitchen or parlor to a bedroom), and adding one or more rooms to the outside of the dwelling (Djamat-Dubois, N'Guessan, and N'Guessan 1983, 121-23).

The cutback of the subsidized public housing program in Côte d'Ivoire left most of the responsibility for the provision of new housing in Abidjan with a single agency, la Société d'équipement du terrain urbain (SETU). Established in 1971, SETU's mandate is to plan and equip urban land for commercial, industrial, and residential purposes. Once the land is developed, it is leased to an individual or a company at a rate calculated to recover all the costs. By 1980 it had developed 11,272 lots (of which 8,690 were residential) and a further 180 hectares of industrial land in Abidjan. Based on these totals, it was estimated that 350,000 low-income newcomers were living on land originally developed by SETU ("Bilan et Perspectives" 1980, 227-28). Although there were some questions about SETU's management in the 1980s, the agency's plans called for the development of 36,000 more residential plots during the period 1986-90 at a level of infrastructure that would meet the needs of eight percent of the new lower-income households, forty-four percent of the new middle-income households, and thirty-eight percent of the new upper-income households, which were projected to be added to Abidjan's population. In spite of the major effort which these figures reflect, the bulk of newly arriving low-income households would have to find accommodation in areas of spontaneous housing on the outskirts of Abidjan. While it may be the case, as Philippe Haeringer argues, that "the recognition by the state that its housing policy was pure vanity is profound and total" (1985, 40) the lowest income groups – particularly the Ivorians among them – will clearly bear the brunt of the new policy directions.

In comparison with Kenya and Côte d'Ivoire, where the public construction of urban housing has produced a significant quantity of accommodation over the last two decades, some countries (such as Zaire after independence, Uganda, Sudan, and Nigeria until the mid 1970s) have relied almost completely on private construction. In a new departure, in 1973 the Nigerian federal government announced a program to build 54,000 units for low and middle-income groups, establishing a Federal Housing Authority to implement the scheme. And in 1975 the Third Plan announced a public housing target of 200,000 units to be completed by 1980. After 1977, and the creation of new states for a total of nineteen, responsibility for the National Housing Programme shifted essentially to the state governments; each state was to receive federal assistance to build eight thousand units. In addition, the Federal Housing Authority was to construct fifty thousand units in Lagos alone (Hardoy and Satterthwaite 1981, 180). While a start was made on these projects, the level of public spending on housing and other aspects of urban infrastructure during the 1970s (particularly highways and, in the new states, new government buildings) drove up the price of construction materials "and helped create endemic inflation. This inflation – especially the increasing cost of food and transport – ... hit the poor the hardest" (Hardoy and Satterthwaite 1981, 169). In any event, the Nigerian public housing program languished by the early 1980s when oil revenues began seriously to diminish. Overcrowding in the larger centers and increasing unregulated housing development on the outskirts of towns was the response to continued high levels of rural-urban migration all over the country.

The limits of public resources to support large-scale housing construction is also illustrated by the case of Tanzania. In 1961 the government established a National Housing Corporation; its first major program involved the clearing of central city "slums," replacing them with new, single-storey rental houses. From 1964 to 1969 seventy percent of the 5,705 low-cost houses built by the Corporation fell under the Dar es Salaam slum clearance scheme. Slum clearance, which was ultimately unproductive to the extent that no new houses were added to the housing stock, was replaced by a policy of direct construction of rental housing estates. But by the early 1970s, as public funds were dwindling, and the Corporation and other public bodies were able to produce little more than two thousand new units per year all over the country, Tanzania shifted its strategy to aided self-help. In 1973 the Tanzania Housing Bank was set up to provide low-interest loans to lower-income urban and rural builders; and in 1974 the government signed an agreement with the World Bank to provide 8,932 new serviced plots and to improve eight thousand existing squatter dwellings; most of this work was to be carried out in Dar es Salaam. By the late 1970s Tanzania's largest city had an estimated population of 794,000, of which approximately sixty percent lived in squatter areas (Marshall Macklin Monaghan 1979, 26). But as the policy of public housing construction ceded to aided self-help, the upper-income biases of the Housing Bank (Kulaba 1981) and of the urban development bureaucracy (Stren 1982) became crucial in the process of implementation. Other administrative problems in the housing program include the poor coordination of infrastructure in the new sites and services areas (different parastatals do not have the same priorities for the installation of water, electricity, and roads as does the Sites and Services Directorate) and the maintenance of the areas themselves by the City Council of Dar es Salaam. In any case, in spite of the massive and lumpy expenditure of capital and human resources on the program of sites and services and squatter upgrading in the late 1970s and early 1980s, the program is now finished, and most of the new housing in Tanzania's large towns continues to consist of privately-built, unplanned units on public land.

Urban Planning: Structures and Standards

The problem of urban housing in Africa is intimately linked to the whole question of the processes and standards of urban planning. At the most general level, the physical planning of Africa's cities must encounter many of the same problems as the planning of Africa's economies. In the first decade after independence, "planning" in most African countries meant producing a bulky public document (usually the five-year "Plan") which surveyed the growth of the economy by sectors and proposed objectives to be aimed at. The inadequacies of this mode of planning all over the Third World produced what Dudley Seers and his colleagues called a "crisis in planning" by the early 1970s (Faber and Seers 1972). This "crisis" was a result of the unreality of the plans, both in terms of their strictly economic terms of reference (their failure to capture and to predict the economies they were dealing with) and in terms of the non-economic questions – politics and participation, social impact, the environment – which they did not deal with. While it could be argued that economic planning has responded to many of these criticisms (Agarwala 1983), African urban planning still faces many serious disabilities.

One disability that is closely related to the earlier problems of economic planning is a tendency to depend for guidance on a large-scale, expensively produced plan document – the "Master Plan." In many ways, the Master Plan was ideally suited for colonial administration. The expense and technology involved in master plans is appropriate in slowly-growing centers for which tight administrative control over development is possible. In the late 1940s Sir Alexander Gibb drew up a master plan for Dar es Salaam and a comprehensive plan for Mtwara (expected to be the major port for the multi-million pound Groundnut Scheme in southeastern Tanzania). Linda Alexander (1983) has shown how the Mtwara plan was based on Western assumptions of full motorized transport and neighborhoods separated by wide green-belts, low-density and low-rise buildings with wide streets, and the perpetuation of residential standards according to race. Hartmut Schmetzer, discussing Gibb's 1949 Master Plan for Dar es Salaam, emphasizes the attention which was given to the allocation of stratified services in high-density (for Africans), medium-density (for Asians), and low-density (for Europeans) residential areas. When Mtwara's economy collapsed in the 1950s, and that of Dar es Salaam in the 1970s, the cost of services and infrastructure was prohibitive, given the spread-out physical development which these plans left behind. The level of building and infrastructural standards embodied in the colonial plans has still not been adjusted to take account of the realities of post-independent African urbanization.

Because of the elaborate technology involved in producing master plans, these documents have, since independence, generally been drawn up by foreign consulting firms, paid out of either bilateral or multilateral aid funds. Dar es Salaam's first post-colonial master plan was produced by a Canadian consultant firm, paid for entirely out of funds provided by the Canadian International Development Agency (CIDA). While the plan was being developed by the Canadian team resident in Dar, the Tanzanian government passed the famous Arusha Declaration, declaring the primacy of rural over urban development and socialist self-reliance. The technical language of the plan, published in 1968, was at variance with the new participatory ideology of Tanzanian politics; and the plan's proposals for the physical development of Dar es Salaam were largely ignored by a government which had few spare resources for what was now considered a privileged urban center. During the 1970s, the plan's value as a guide for day to day planning decisions lay largely in the zoning map it contained – in particular, the separation between residential and other uses. The government's decision in 1974 to select Mikocheni and Sinza as sites for the first sites and services project to be financed by the World Bank was based largely on a "future land use" plan contained in the 1968 Master Plan. In spite of difficulties with the master plan idea, the Tanzanian government pushed ahead with master planning for all its large towns during the 1970s. In 1975, for example, Finnish town planners attached to the Town Planning Department completed master plans for Tabora, Tanga, Moshi, and Mbeya (Hayuma 1984, 75).

In 1976 another major plan was published – this time for the new capital city of Dodoma. This time, the consultants were much more attuned to local attitudes and worked closely with Tanzanian officials in preparing the plan. One of the planners later said:

> A very real effort was made to understand the aspirations and ideology of the Tanzanian government, and to translate these into urban terms.... One of the

predominant themes in the master plan was the extent to which the population depended on agriculture for their subsistence. This was also the major preoccupation of the Freedom Regional Village program, which led to the creation of "ujamaa" or collectivized villages. The master plan devised a city that would reflect the Ujamaa village idea; a series of small towns of about 20,000 people were located on a ring principle and separated by space that could be used for agriculture, so that the residents could maintain contact with their *shambas* (vegetable gardens). The towns were to be linked together with a fairly simple transportation system of buses (Quoted in Stamp 1980, 252).

In his introduction to the National Capital Master Plan, produced by the same Canadian consultant company, President Nyerere noted the plan's promotion of locally produced, low-cost materials; the building of an efficient and low-cost public transport service; and the planning of the town around a series of small connecting communities within which cooperative activities would be easily organized. President Nyerere concluded that the new plan was "consistent with the ideology of Tanzania" (Tanzania 1976, viii). But by 1983 the Tanzanian government had been able to spend only about one-quarter of the funds it originally estimated it would need for the development of Dodoma; when inflation was taken into account, this amounted to only about ten percent of the total (Communication to author, Dar es Salaam 12 July 1983). Now, in 1988, no major government ministry (with the exception of the Prime Minister's Office) has moved to the new capital; and urban planners are having severe problems controlling the growth of squatting on government land. The irrelevance of master planning in Tanzania is underlined by A.M. Hayuma, who stresses the unrealistic costs involved in these plans, the plans' inherently incremental and "blueprint-oriented" nature, their stress on control mechanisms to regulate development, and the weakness of implementing agencies – particularly at the local level (Hayuma 1984).

The problem of implementation of plans at the local level is particularly worrisome in many African cities. In most of the large cities referred to in this volume, urban land is either entirely or largely vested in the public domain. Planning must thus be concerned not only with the allocation of public land according to zoning regulations but also with the proper standards of building and infrastructure to be applied to all urban land. Under conditions of unprecedented rapid growth, the proper exercise of the urban planning function implies adequate authority and enforcement power for planning agencies as well as adequate manpower to carry out technical functions properly. In poor cities, both prerequisites are often lacking. For new urban residents the number of new plots of land available in "official" subdivisions is minuscule, and few can afford to build housing according to official standards. A rigorous comparative study of (largely urban) land allocations in Nigeria's Bauchi and Kano states over the period 1976-1979 shows that the authorities "have applied official regulations in a manner that prevents the urban and rural poor from securing statutory rights of occupancy" (Koehn 1983, 467). The same study shows that preference was given to higher civil-servants, self-employed businessmen and traders, and managers of large private corporations. The formal nationalization of all urban land in Nigeria under the Land Use Decree of 1978 – intended to open the land market to ordinary Nigerians – had the paradoxical result of conveying even further advantages on middle and senior-level civil servants (Koehn 1983, 481).

The gradual restriction of the formal urban land market to the wealthy and the well-connected is a feature of almost all large African cities. An interesting exception, described in detail by Yves Marguerat, is Lomé, where most of the urban land has been owned privately since the founding of the city in the last quarter of the nineteenth century. But even in this setting, in which only two percent of all urban lots were originally obtained from the state and in which the state plays essentially the role of referee in the land market, only forty-five percent of a large sample of plots were vested with legal title (Marguerat 1984, 40). But perhaps the most extreme case is Kinshasa. According to a recent and well-informed estimate, only about one-quarter of the city's approximately 350,000 plots are legally registered. "These are concentrated in the city centre and in the old residential areas. The peripheral extension zones escape regulation almost totally, and are often given to the most complete anarchy" (Mbuyi 1985, 47).

Not only are few new official titles granted but also colonial-originated building codes and complex procedures required to obtain formal rights to housing further restrict activity. In Dar es Salaam, where the procedures involved in obtaining land, building permission, and government loans for construction are particularly complex (Stren 1982), the bulk of the new accommodation constructed is "squatter" housing – unapproved units on unsurveyed and unserviced land. Although exact figures are hard to obtain, one study showed that an average of seven hundred units per year of legal housing was constructed from 1973 through 1977, while the average annual increase in total units of housing from 1975 through 1979 was 2,200 units (Marshall Macklin Monaghan 1979, 23-24). To the extent these two time series are comparable, at least sixty-eight percent of all new housing per year was in the squatter areas.

A more general argument is made by Donatus Okpala, a Nigerian planner. Okpala estimates that only about twenty to forty percent of all physical development in major Nigerian cities is directly regulated by the government; and the regulation that does take place occurs indirectly as a result of state decisions about large infrastructural projects (such as highways and large institutions) rather than directly through planning regulations and formal enforcement powers (Okpala 1984). The same general failure to implement plans is observed in Khartoum, where Ian Haywood finds the planning system in a state of paralysis:

> Although a new administrative structure has been established for Khartoum, the lack of approved plans, skilled staff and appropriate administrative systems means that there is no systematic control of development and little immediate prospect of a forward planning system being developed. What planning control does operate is through general land-use zoning supported by a rudimentary system of building bylaws, both of which are applied in an arbitrary manner often reflecting the status of the applicant. Land-use control is not enforced at the local level and new development or changes of use may be permitted which create considerable conflict with existing uses. The situation is exacerbated by the failure to control either the height or density of development....
>
> The resultant picture is of an administrative system unable to control the growth of the Three Towns or maintain an adequate level of services. At the perimeter the urban area is increasing, absorbing villages and consuming the agricultural land which supports it. People are having to travel longer and longer distances on an inadequate transportation system to the centre. The centre itself is deteriorating as the natural processes of growth and change come under increasing economic and demographic pressures, and uncontrolled and uncoordinated development overloads services and erodes environmental standards (1985, 192, 194).

In another publication, Haywood expands on what he means by a "rudimentary system of building bylaws":

> Vague, obsolete, and highly ineffective, [the bylaws] are confined to issues such as the minimum distances between the building and the boundary wall (thus practically eliminating the option of row and terrace housing layouts), minimum ceiling heights in habitable rooms (fixed at three meters), and location of soakaway wells. They do not specify building heights in the different urban zones or dictate the provision of parking lots, especially in business areas. So much subjectivity – and corruption – exists in applying these laws that what is readily granted one applicant can be adamantly denied his neighbor. Shops can spread at random all over the neighborhood; four-story walk-up apartment blocks with inadequate accommodation can crop up in the yard of an existing villa overlooking neighbors; introducing offices in residential areas creates parking problems and overloads the sewage disposal system. This state of affairs has recently reached alarming stages; 1982 will be remembered as the year in which architect-designed houses started to collapse because of the cor-

ruption and incompetence of architects and builders (Haywood and Ahmad 1986, 176-77).

This deterioration in the planned fabric of African cities, which has become especially visible in the 1980s as a result of the economic downturn, has elicited a variety of responses. Some governments have attempted the physical removal of beggars, illegal hawkers, slum dwellers, and other undesirables from central city areas. In the early 1970s the Senegalese government undertook a systematic campaign to destroy squatter areas in the city center of Dakar, culminating in the destruction of Nimzatt and Angle-Mousse in 1975. Legal, surveyed plots were laid out on the city's periphery to receive everyone who was removed (Dieng 1977). The government followed up the exercise against squatters with a large-scale effort to rid Dakar's streets of beggars ("human refuse") and small traders. In 1977 the distinguished Minister of State for Justice presented a thirty-eight-page paper to the National Council of the Parti Socialiste Sénégalais in which he denounced "the proliferation on public streets of small hawkers and of beggars and vagabonds, who may be physically fit or handicapped, blind or lepers, adults or children, who have abandoned themselves to reprehensible activities" (Collignon 1984, 574). Echoes of the Senegalese initiatives (both before and after) were the Nairobi "clean-up" campaign of 1970 which demolished ten thousand squatter dwellings and left fifty thousand homeless (Stren 1984, 241), the Ivorian government's destruction of the homes of twenty percent of the Abidjan population from 1969 to 1973 (Joshi, Lubell and Mouly 1976, 66), and the Nigerian government's massive "clean-up" of small urban traders in 1983.

An extreme institutionalization of this "removal" approach to unplanned urban populations is the Tanzanian government's Human Resources Deployment Act of 1983. The purpose of the Act, as described by the Prime Minister, was to force all urban residents into "productive" jobs, including food production, if they could not show proof of regular, wage employment (Miti 1985, 90). An elaborate administrative machinery for the "transfer, training and rehabilitation of unemployed [urban] residents" (Tanzania 1983, 103) was established, leading to thousands of arrests in Dar es Salaam. The government has now given up strong-arm tactics, but the Dar es Salaam City Council still has a large budgetary item for the development of farms on the outskirts of the city to absorb "redundant" urban workers.

These campaigns to arrest or repatriate urban marginals, or to eradicate slums and squatter areas, have had little long-term effect on either the form of African cities or on the quality of life of the majority low-income populations. If anything, these actions have strengthened market forces which tend to peripheralize the housing areas of the poor and to further marginalize the long-term employment prospects of the uneducated, the unskilled, and women. For African cities effectively to incorporate at least significant numbers of their swelling low-income populations, planning decisions will have to be based on criteria and standards which much more closely reflect the culture and the economic situation of the bulk of the population. To the extent that this does not happen, squatter settlements on the periphery of large African cities will continue to proliferate, and ordinary people will take planning decisions into their own hands. The failure to design and apply appropriate planning bylaws in Khartoum, for example, has led to an elaborate network of more than ninety spontaneous residential areas, in which local people look after their own needs. Extensive evidence of self-help in Khartoum's squatter settlements is ascribed to "indigenous culture" as well as to the lack of local resources. "Local communities seem to be predominantly inclined to contribute substantially to education and health projects, but also to financing water projects and local roads. The amount of funds generated by self-help projects ... reached, in 1985, several million Sudanese Pounds in Greater Khartoum" (El Sammani et al. 1986, 20-21).

Important pressures in the direction of adaptation to low-income needs have come from international agencies, in particular the World Bank. Thus, if one extreme of government responses to the ineffectiveness of urban planning has been the coercive removal of structures or of groups of people who give offense, at the other extreme is a whole range of adaptive responses. These adaptive responses consist generally of the institutionalization, in some specific way, of new standards of urban services and infrastructure. Perhaps most well-documented are the costly sites and services and squatter upgrading schemes originally sponsored by the Urban Development Department of the World Bank. By the time of writing, five of the countries covered in this volume (Senegal, Côte d'Ivoire, Nigeria, Kenya, and Tanzania) had completed one or more project of this nature, and a feasibility study has been undertaken for a sixth – Zaire. Over the period from 1972 (when the first project was started in Senegal) through 1981, $449.3 million was spent on fifteen Bank projects in black Africa (Cohen 1983). While the first projects tended to stress the development of infrastructure for the "target population" to build housing on its own, more recent shelter projects sponsored by the Bank have stressed the improvement of existing "slum" or "squatter" housing by the owners themselves. Most of these projects have been able to make only a small dent in the total supply of shelter in African cities. And their final impact on the designated low-income "target populations" has usually fallen short of their original objectives.

But the World Bank projects (and similar ones now being promoted by

German and American aid agencies) represent a progressive technology for the design and production of lower cost infrastructure that has had signficant demonstration effects among urban planners. As the "thin edge of the wedge," these shelter projects have also been used by the World Bank to induce participating countries to accept other reforms (such as local tax reform, the revision of old building codes, the establishment of new urban lending and planning institutions) as part of the credit agreement. Thus, Kenya's various agreements with the World Bank for sites and services and upgrading projects in the 1970s carried with them commitments (*inter alia*) to undertake a full-length study of the country's outdated housing by-laws, to revise Nairobi's valuation rolls (which indirectly account for eighty-five percent of the city's revenue), and to manage the City Council's accounts responsibly. By the 1980s the Bank's urban lending program in Africa was shifting away from a concentration on shelter to a combination of different components. As stated at the outset of Chapter 2, there is now a growing recognition that institutional and city-wide management problems must more seriously be addressed if individual components (transport, shelter, health, water) are to be effectively delivered ("New Directions in Bank Urban Projects," 1-5). In the conclusions which follow, some of the parameters and constraints of such an approach for African cities will be discussed.

Conclusion

Until very recently, little attention has been paid, either by scholars or by governments and international agencies, to the related problems of governing African cities and of managing urban services and infrastructure. But the exorbitant growth of most of the largest cities, combined with a palpable deterioration in the quality of urban life across the continent, has led to a re-evaluation of the importance of institution-building. In spite of large sums having been spent on shelter projects and on numerous consultant contracts for studies of urban transport, roads, water, and other infrastructural needs, there is little hard evidence that projects will be, in the end, replicable. Nor is there much evidence that mistakes in one country will be avoided in others.

Under the circumstances, the locus of thinking about and planning for the future of African cities must shift from the international arena and from central government offices in the capital cities across Africa to the institutions and people who actually deal with African urban problems. This is part of the logic behind the movement toward decentralization in the administration of Dakar and Abidjan and behind the training schemes for local government administrators and finance officers undertaken under World Bank auspices. But in spite of the array of forces behind this new direction in development strategy, there are a number of major dilemmas which cannot easily be overcome. These dilemmas reflect the structural problems of African underdevelopment.

One major difficulty with any attempt to improve the "management" of local institutions in African cities is the level of financial support required. Failure of urban governments and other public agencies to provide adequate services is a function of both manpower inadequacy (including lack of experience) and the lack of financial means. While more attention certainly needs to be given to the questions of training and local finance, a thorough solution for even a single capital city in Africa would require resources well beyond the capacity of the national state in question. And even if the resources could be found to be spent in the capital, the regional imbalances created would be disastrous for the country's economic and political stability.

It could well be argued, on the other hand, that institutional development is a lengthy and complex process; only cautious and judicious programs to improve revenue sources, to train the right people over a long period of time, and to develop local experience and competence in a number of different infrastructure and service areas can ultimately succeed. While this argument is cogent, it counsels incremental change in a continent where urban problems are compounding almost geometrically and where central governments may not be prepared to share power for long with decentralized institutions.

In the end, there is no simple answer, and perhaps no single complex answer either, for all countries. But better comparative knowledge of how urban governments are seeking to solve many of the problems which they have in common must be a beginning. The proper balance between public and private sector initiatives, between local responsibility and central control, between international standards and indigenous requirements, and between the needs of the poor and the requirements of the community as a whole will all have to be worked out through struggles and bitter experience. Ultimately, solutions to problems of urban finance, housing, public transport, the siting and standards of urban infrastructure, public health and public cleansing services, water, electricity, and numerous other urban amenities must be formulated locally, by local people, on the basis of local experience and information. That these local problems are beginning to be taken seriously all over the continent is a hopeful sign. Their solutions will require both imagination and enormous dedication.

Notes

1. Calculation of the figures for different categories of laborers is based on ascertaining the proportion of that category to the total number employed in 1983 (a year

for which an exact breakdown is available) and applying that proportion to the total number employed in 1984. As a result of staff cuts imposed by the City Commission after it took over in March 1983, the total number of laborers employed in the section was cut by about 170 from 1983 to 1984.

2. The following figures are derived from Annual Reports of the Nairobi City Council and Commission and from an unpublished document obtained from the Public Cleansing Section entitled, "Nairobi City Commission / UNICEF Seminar on the Mother and Child Programme for Nairobi" (delivered at the Seminar in Nairobi, December 1984).

3. According to the statistics given to the CRAU team, the SICOGI built 4,770 of its total of 23,755 units in the 1960-70 period; by contrast, the SOGEFIHA built all its 17,912 units in the 1970-80 period (Centre de recherches architecturales et urbaines 1983).

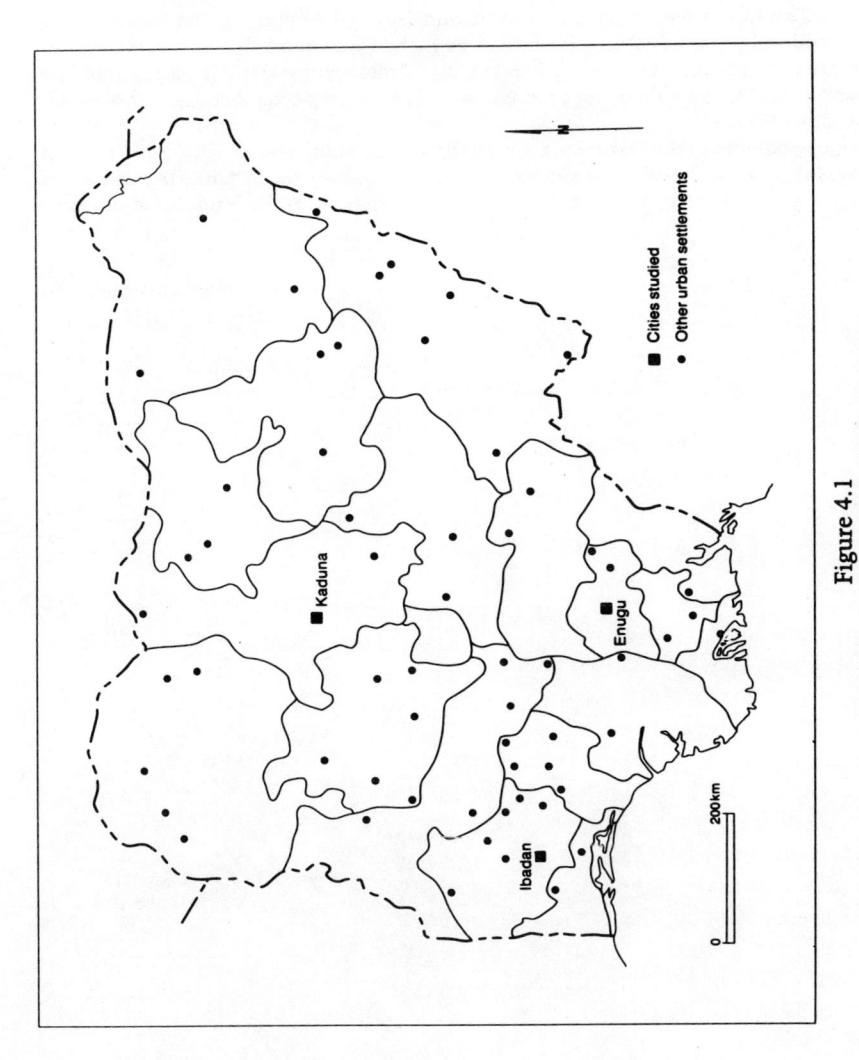

Figure 4.1
Nigeria State Boundaries and Urban Settlements

CHAPTER 4
Urban Growth and Urban Management in Nigeria

Adepoju G. Onibokun

Introduction

Nigeria, the most populous country in Africa, is a classic example of a country in the developing world with a high rate of urban growth. While data on the Nigerian population are grossly deficient and should be interpreted with caution because of the absence of reliable and current census data, available data and studies estimate the country's population to have been about 19 million in 1921, about 30 million in 1952, 55.7 million in 1963, and from 80 to 100 million in 1985 (see Table 4.1). From 1952 to 1963 a compounded growth rate of 1.9 percent was recorded. Official records put the average annual growth of the urban areas at five percent and that of the rural areas at 2.5 percent. At the current rate, the population of Nigeria will probably reach 160 million by the year 2000.

The components of urban growth are natural growth, migration, and reclassification of boundaries. Available evidence suggests that in most of the largest and fastest growing cities in Nigeria, as in most developing countries, migration has accounted for up to two-thirds of urban growth (see Table 4.2). International migration has never played a significant role in the urban growth process in Nigeria. P. O. Olusanya and D. E. Pursell (1981), for example, observe that in the 1963 census only 101,461 non-Nigerians (or 0.2 percent) were part of the 56 million counted in the 1963 census, out of which about 52,809 lived in urban centers.

The urbanization process described for Nigeria is not unique. Most, if not all the developing nations, have been experiencing similar, and in some cases, higher rates of uncontrolled urbanization. Thus, while Nigeria's average annual rate of growth of urban population was 3.6 percent from 1965 to 1970, Upper Volta had 10.8 percent, Sierra Leone 10.1 percent, and Niger 12.5 percent.

This paper draws upon the research conducted with my colleagues in the Nigerian Institute of Social and Economic Research (NISER), University of Ibadan, and in the University of Lagos. They are Kunle Adeniji, Lai Egunjobi, Tunde Agbola, Oye Oyediran, and Sesan Ayodele. I, however, accept resonsibility for the interpretation provided here.

Table 4.1
Nigerian Population 1921-1984

Year	Total Population (000s)	Urban Population Number	Urban Population as % of Total Population	Number of Cities whose Population is: 20,000 or more	Number of Cities whose Population is: 100,000 or more	Number of Cities whose Population is: 500,000 or more
1921	18,720	890	4.8	10	–	–
1931	20,056	1,343	6.7	24	2	–
1952 / 54	30,402	3,701	10.2	54	7	–
1963	55,670	10,702	19.2	183	24	2
1972	78,924	19,832	25.1	302	38	3
1984	96,684	31,906	33.0	356	62	14

Source: Population census of Nigeria, 1952, 1963 and projections of same based on 5% annual growth rate for urban areas, 2.5% for rural areas, and 10% for state capitals.

Table 4.2
Contribution of Migration and Natural Increase to Urban Growth and Average Annual Growth Rate in Selected Cities

	Years	Average Annual Growth Rate (%)	% due to Natural Increase	% due to Net Migration
Lagos	1960-1975	8.6	41	59
Yaoundé	1964-1969	8.7	38	62
Dar es Salaam	1967-1975	6.8	36	63
Jakarta	1971-1976	4.0	66	34
Manila	1960-1970	4.1	55	42
Seoul	1960-1970	7.8	22	73
Bogota	1964-1973	5.4	44	56
Mexico City	1960-1970	5.4	57	43
Baghdad	1965-1970	7.5	54	46

Source: United Nations Department of International Economic and Social Affairs. Estimates and projections of urban, rural, and city populations, 1950-2025; the 1980 assessment, New York, U.N., 1982.

The Problem

The rapid rate of uncontrolled and unplanned urbanization has brought with it complex urban problems in the form of stiff competition for land, long journeys to work, traffic difficulties (congestion), acute shortage of housing, rapid growth of slums and accompanying health hazards, qualitative and quantitative depopulation of the rural areas, the high incidence of crimes of all types, to mention a few (Onibokun 1973). The high rate of population increase and the uncontrolled rural-urban migration lead to the explosive growth of the cities but unfortunately, there is no corresponding change in the rate of economic development, social change, and technological advancement. As has been pointed out:

> rural-urban migration is a menace and overcrowding within the cities is a common problem. Today, the hearts of our cities are like islands of poverty in seas of relative affluence as it does not require professional skill in environmental perception to note the differences between the residential, environmental and the overall physical structure of the central parts of Lagos and Ibadan for example, and their suburbs. The majority of the urban dwellers live in the unkempt and often squalid hearts of the cities, under conditions that are at times subhuman, sharing substandard houses in areas, which, by any standard, are slums (Onibokun 1973, 52).

In 1985 the Nigerian Institute of Social and Economic Research (NISER) carried out a housing survey in every state of Nigeria at the request of the Federal Government.[1] Results show that inadequate accommodation appears to be one of the most serious problems arising from the high rate of urbanization. A substantial proportion of urban houses (as high as 30.9 percent and above in some states) are either dilapidated or are in need of major repair (see Figure 4.2). Overcrowding is pervasive and high rents are a major indicator of urban housing problems. Rent control measures introduced by the State governments have not succeeded in reducing the rents paid by urban families, especially the urban poor who are increasingly exploited by slumlords.

Unemployment and underemployment are other indicators of the urban crisis. In 1983 the Central Bank of Nigeria estimated urban unemployment at twenty to thirty percent. Among the evils which have become associated with the employment situation in Nigerian urban centers are increased rates of armed robbery, burglary, arson, prostitution, and juvenile delinquency. Few urban centers in Nigeria have a viable economic base.

Perhaps the most noticeable and enduring problem is the absence or inadequacy of necessary supporting infrastructure and social amenities in most of the urban areas. Water supply, sewers, roads, electricity, health facilities, and social services are heavily overloaded and unreliable. The environment is dangerously polluted – each increment of urban growth leads to further deterioration of the environment. A high proportion of the roads are in a state of disrepair; garbage is irregularly collected and poorly disposed of; pipe-borne water is generally a scarce commodity as over twenty-five percent of urban dwellers still depend on wells and streams. A very significant portion of urban dwellers use crude and unhygienic methods for the disposal of their liquid waste (see Figure 4.2). Electricity remains a luxury in many homes as even those homes connected to the network cannot predict its regularity.

Case Studies

This chapter focuses on three cities as case studies. Each case relates city growth to the quality of urban life, emphasizing in particular infrastructural facilities such as water supply, electricity supply, and solid waste management, with a view toward determining how their adequacy affects the functioning of the urban system and how the state of efficiency of one utility affects the efficiency of another. The case studies are based on a research project funded by the International Development Research Centre (IDRC) in Ottawa and executed by my associates and me in 1984 and 1985 (Onibokun et al. 1986). The three cities selected as case studies are Ibadan in the west, Enugu in the east, and Kaduna in the north. The three cities were the headquarters of the former political and administrative regions of Nigeria, each of which represented certain distinct ethnic groups. It should be noted from Figure 4.2 that the housing conditions in the states in which these cities are located are better than the national average. Sample household surveys, using structured questionnaires, were conducted in the three cities to probe issues of effectiveness of electricity, water supply, and solid waste management. Also, unstructured interviews were conducted with government / agency officials with a view to eliciting their views and suggestions for improving the delivery of these services.

Of the three cities chosen as case studies, Ibadan is the oldest, the most populous and the fastest growing. (Ibadan was founded in 1829, Enugu in 1909, and Kaduna in 1917.) While Kaduna had a population of 30,000 in 1919, Ibadan already had a population of 100,000 in 1851. At the time of the last official census (1963), the population of Ibadan was four times that of Kaduna and over three times that of Enugu. By 1984 the population of Ibadan had risen to 4,230,278, Enugu 933,585, and Kaduna 1,010,811. Thus, in terms of population growth, Kaduna overtook Enugu according to the 1963 census, but Ibadan maintains its lead in terms of the size of the population and its growth rate.

The three cities were divided into a core area, the intermediate areas, and the newer suburbs. The core is inhabited principally by the indigenous population who are relatively poor, when compared with those in the other zones. The intermediate areas are usually heterogeneous in terms of the socio-economic status of the inhabitants, age of buildings, quality of environment, and quality and quantity of social amenities, public utilities, and social infrastructure. The newer suburbs, on the other hand, represent the modern, most recently developed, and predominantly high class neighborhoods among which are the government reservations (GRAs), public agencies' housing estates, and residential quarters. In most cases, the housing estates were purposely developed as upper and upper middle class neighborhoods. In the survey, 728 of the total households come from the core area, 742 from the intermediate area, and 537 from the newer suburbs.

The demographic variables presented in Table 4.4 describe the households surveyed. The average household size ranged from 4.4 in Kaduna to 4.9 in Enugu and 6.2 in Ibadan. Several households had a very large number of residents. The maximum recorded was forty-one for Ibadan, forty-two for Kaduna, and fifty-one for Enugu.

The survey confirms that urbanization in Nigeria is characterized by a high rate of population growth, a fairly equitable distribution of the sexes, a high dependency ratio because of the very high proportion of youths and unemployed people, relatively stable families characterized by a low rate of divorce, a very high illiteracy rate, and a large proportion of the population in need of education and employment. The demographic patterns are similar for all the zones of the cities; however, greater problems characterize the core area and intermediate areas, as compared with the newer suburbs.

Rapid population growth in these cities has a significant negative impact on the lives of the people in terms of the quality of available urban services. The available services are poor, having become inadequate almost as soon as they were commissioned. Education started late in Kaduna (1909) in comparison with Ibadan and Enugu where formal education had been introduced since the 1840s. One area where all the three towns and their respective states seem to have excelled and, ironically, the area where the inadequacies in the educational system now seem apparent was primary school education. As shown in Table 4.5, since education started early in the south (especially in Oyo State where free primary education had been introduced since 1955), high enrolment figures were recorded. Thus, while Oyo State had 1,755 primary schools and 368,765 pupils in 1970, the corresponding figures for Enugu were 1,628 and 383,023 and those for Kaduna were 624 and 116,383. With the introduction of the Universal Primary Education (UPE) in the 1976/77 session, the number of primary schools and enrolment increased significantly in Kaduna State. In the three cities studied, the average number of pupils per teacher, was high. The average was thirty-three to thirty-five in Ibadan thirty-four to forty in Enugu. Generally, the quality of education and the quality of educational services in Nigeria has declined.

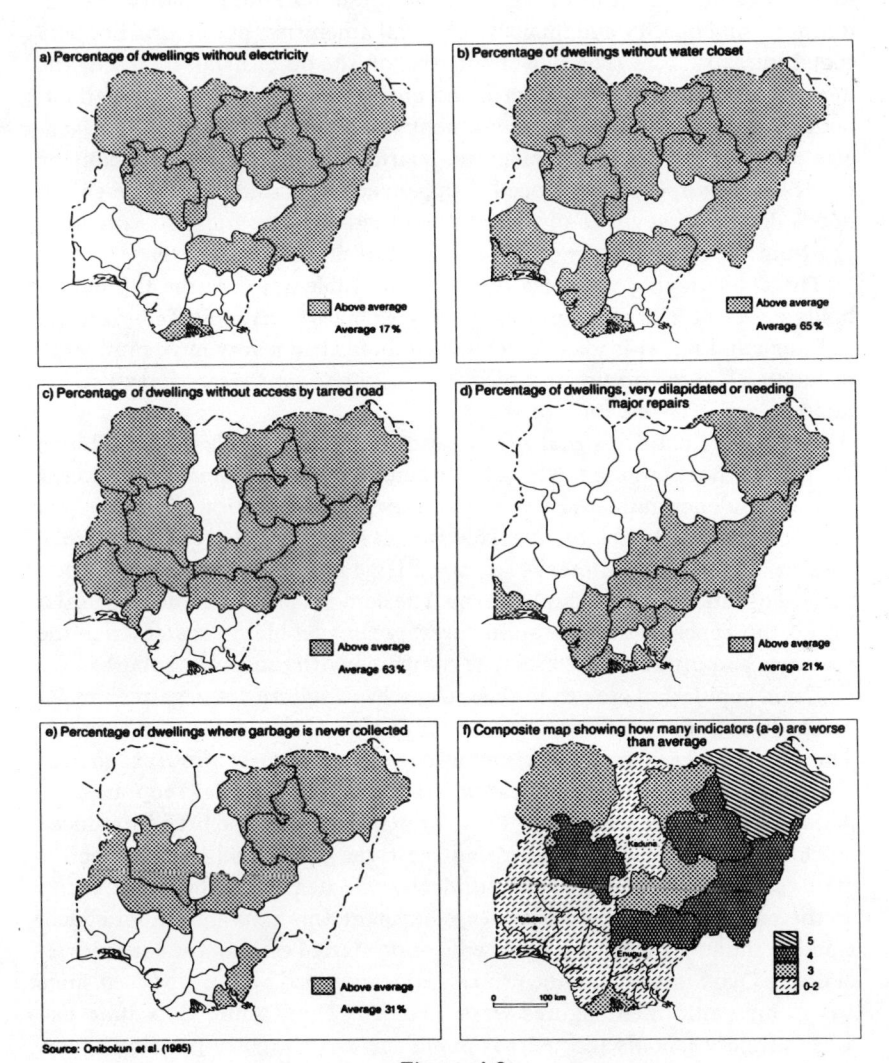

Figure 4.2
Nigerian States: Quality of Urban Life

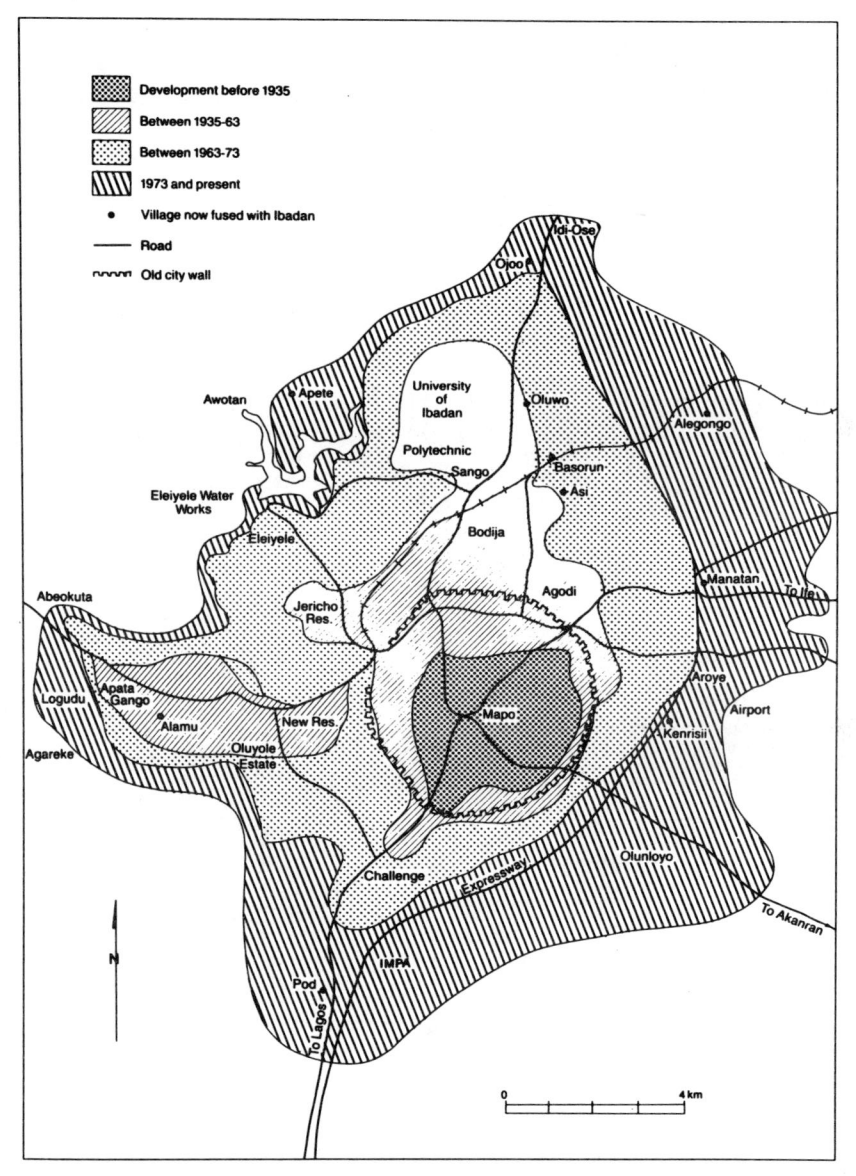

Figure 4.3
Areal Extent of Ibadan 1935, 1963, 1973, 1985

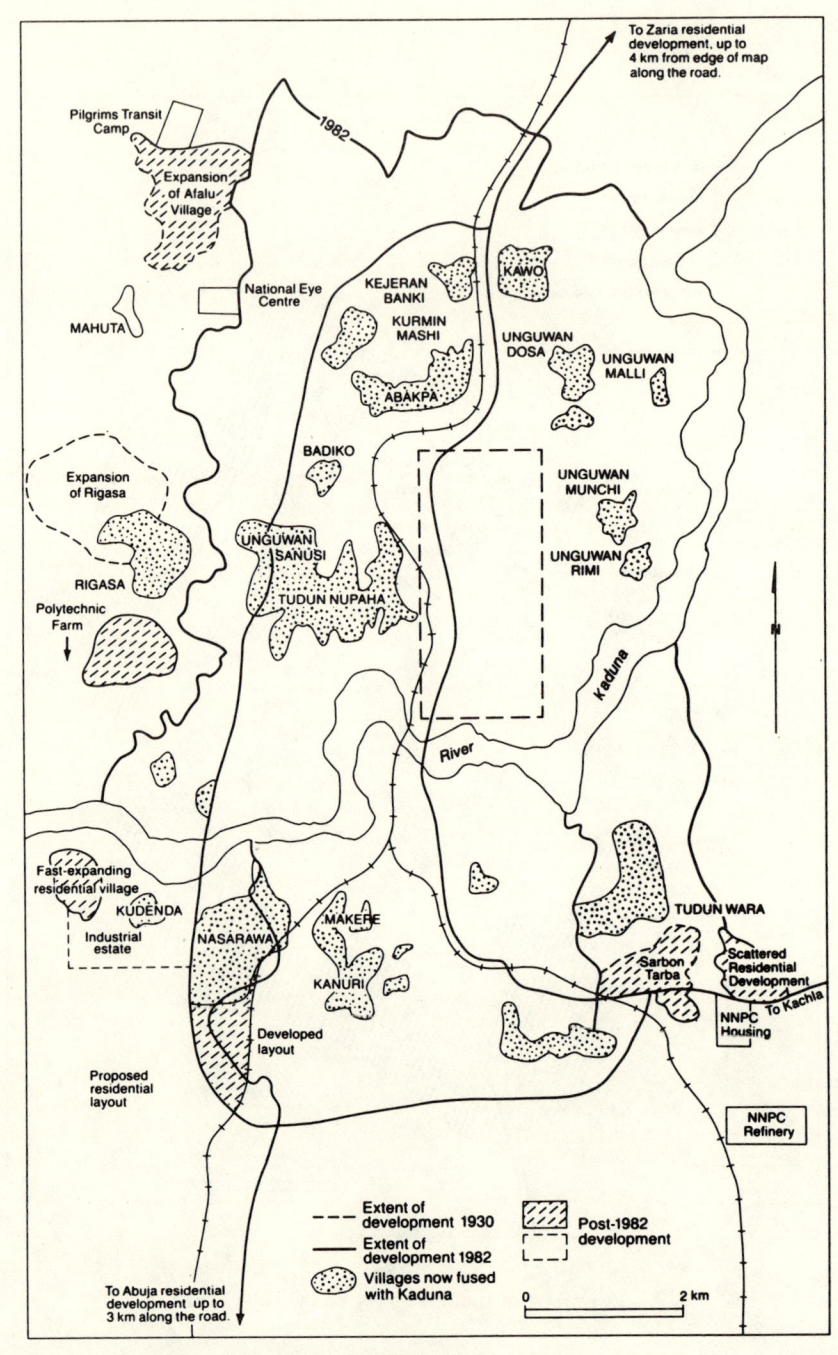

Figure 4.4
Areal Extent of Kaduna 1930, 1982, 1985

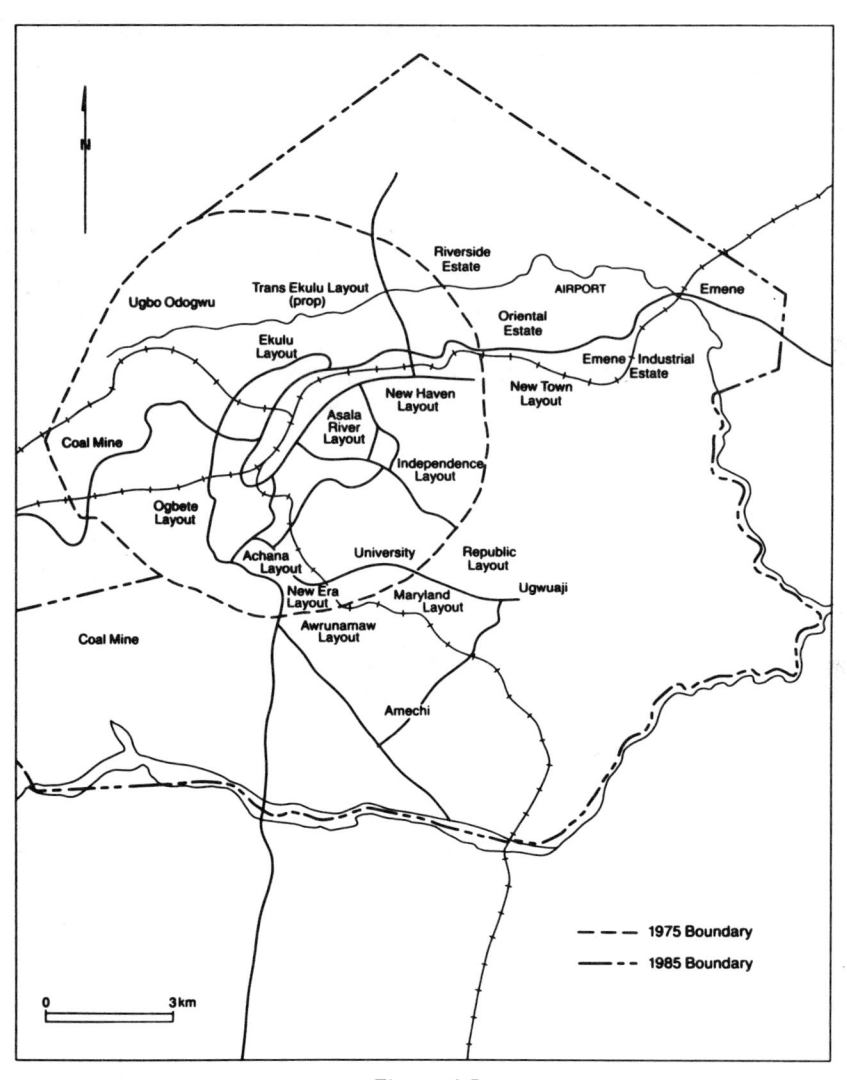

Figure 4.5
Areal Extent of Enugu 1975, 1985

Table 4.3
Population Of Some Nigerian Cities
1952-1982

City	1952	1963	1972[1]	1982[1]	1984[1]
Lagos	267,407	665,246	1,568,650	4,068,578	4,485,607
Ibadan[2]	459,158	627,379	1,479,359	3,836,987	4,230,278
Ogbomosho	139,535	319,881	496,231	808,339	891,194
Kano	127,204	295,432	578,338	1,500,056	1,653,812
Oshogbo	122,728	208,966	324,169	528,057	582,185
Ile-Ife	110,790	130,850	201,747	328,636	362,321
Iwo	100,006	158,583	246,010	400,729	441,815
Abeokuta	84,451	187,292	290,546	623,686	689,819
Onitsha	76,921	163,032	252,912	111,982	454,210
Oyo	72,133	112,349	174,287	283,906	313,006
Ilesha	72,029	105,822	257,240	419,032	461,983
Port-Harcourt	71,634	179,563	351,513	911,731	1,005,183
Enugu[2]	62,764	138,459	326,482	846,789	933,585
Aba	57,787	131,965	203,225	331,045	364,977
Maiduguri	56,740	139,965	273,995	710,672	783,201
Zaria	53,974	166,170	257,780	419,912	462,953
Benin City	53,753	100,694	197,119	511,274	563,680
Katsina	52,672	98,538	140,452	228,790	252,241
Sokoto	51,986	89,817	175,826	455,046	502,791
Iseyin	49,220	95,220	147,715	240,621	265,285
Calabar	46,905	76,418	149,596	388,012	427,783
Ede	44,808	134,440	208,727	340,008	374,859
Kaduna[2]	44,540	149,910	353,488	916,488	1,010,811
Ilorin	44,994	208,546	408,250	1,058,892	1,167,428
Akure	38,853	71,106	110,307	237,544	261,892
Jos	38,527	90,402	176,971	459,016	506,065
Ikere-Ekiti	35,584	107,214	166,824	289,817	319,523
Ila	25,745	157,579	244,359	398,051	438,851
Ado-Ekiti	24,646	157,579	244,359	398,051	438,851
Minna	21,636	27,130	93,059	200,402	220,943

Source: Nigerian Census Reports, 1952 and 1963.
[1]Estimated.
[2]City studied by NISER, 1986.

The same situation was observed for health services where most of the best that the state could offer were concentrated in each of these cities. One very significant difference is that while private practitioners are common in Enugu, in Kaduna and Ibadan government health facilities predominate. In addition, while Enugu and Ibadan had the largest share of health facilities in their respective states, Kaduna was not particularly favored in the location of health facilities. Thus, the health institutions are more evenly distributed in Kaduna state than in the other two states of Oyo and Anambra. Nonetheless, most of the medical personnel in each state were concentrated in the capital cities. Ibadan, for example, had over one-third of all the number of hospitals in the state and over eighty percent of all doctors. The same situation existed in Enugu and Kaduna. Even so, the quality of health services in the three cities was poor. The population per hospital bed was 576 in Ibadan, 256 in Kaduna, and 188 in Enugu. Similarly low standards apply with respect to housing and employment.

Water Supply

The country is blessed with abundant water resources, both underground and surface, though the spatial distribution of these resources varies widely between the southern and northern parts of the country. While the southern parts are better endowed with numerous rivers, streams, and other sources of surface water which flow throughout the year, such surface water sources in the northern parts shrink considerably or disappear during the dry season. In the north, the higher incidence of drought has seriously compounded the problems of potable water supply. Successive governments have made bold attempts to tackle the problem of potable water supply, but with apparently little success.

In Nigeria, each state has set up a water agency. In the states surveyed, the present government agencies – Anambra State Water Corporation, Kaduna State Water Board, and the Oyo State Water Corporation – were established by edicts in 1976, 1971, and 1976 respectively. Their functions are defined in their enabling legislation which also lay down the main financial and administrative guidelines and objectives of the agencies.

State water agencies are parastatals subject to the supervision of a state Ministry or the Office of the Governor of the State. The Commissioners and top civil servants in the parent ministries of their water agencies interfere unduly in the day-to-day running of the agencies. For example, the agencies cannot award contracts for major projects without the consent of the Governor's office. This, according to senior officials of all three water agencies, constitutes a major constraint on the performance of the Corporations because of the tedious bureaucratic procedures that characterize government ministries.

Table 4.4
Urban Household Demographic Characteristics

	All Cases		Core Area			Intermediate Areas			Newer Suburbs		
	Ibadan	Kaduna	Enugu	Ibadan	Kaduna	Enugu	Ibadan	Kaduna	Enugu	Ibadan	Kaduna	Enugu
Population	4495	2769	3178	1793	833	1157	1617	1075	1224	1085	838	787
Households	728	635	644	277	189	262	244	259	239	207	187	143
Household size	6.2	4.4	4.9	6.5	4.4	4.4	6.6	4.1	5.1	5.2	4.5	5.5
Males in household	2166	1490	1673	897	468	614	751	548	623	518	474	436
%	48	54	52	50	56	53	57	57	51	48	56	55
Aged 17 or less	2047	1310	1333	839	377	491	779	511	502	429	422	340
%	45	47	41	47	45	42	48	50	41	39	50	43
Unemployed	2708	1860	1962	1068	529	702	1012	735	753	628	596	507
%	60	41	61	60	63	60	63	68	62	58	71	64
Married	1573	1061	1006	698	307	393	479	441	360	396	313	253
%	35	38	31	40	37	34	30	41	30	36	37	32
Education:												
None	985	796	306	616	236	141	293	330	131	76	230	34
%	22	29	9	35	28	12	31	31	11	7	27	4
Secondary or												
Post-secondary	2144	962	1879	582	316	580	750	346	720	812	300	579
%	47	35	58	55	38	20	47	32	59	75	30	74

Source: Onibokun et al. 1986.
The total number of questionnaires was 2007.

Table 4.5

Number of Primary Schools and Enrollment in the States of Oyo, Anambra, and Kaduna

Year	Oyo (including Ibadan)				Anambra (including Enugu)				Kaduna			
	Primary Schools		Enrollment		Primary Schools		Enrollment		Primary Schools		Enrollment	
	No.	% change	No.	% change	No.	% change	No.	% change	No.	% change	No.	% change
1970	1755	–	368,765	–	1628	–	283,023	–	624	–	116,383	–
1971	1760	0.3	416,816	13.0	1595	-2.0	469,663	65.7	642	2.9	134,092	15.5
1972	1789	1.6	448,866	7.7	1010	-36.7	502,430	7.1	646	0.6	146,615	9.0
1973	1798	0.5	463,608	3.3	1017	0.7	533,336	6.2	n/a	–	n/a	–
1973/74	1798	0	479,042	3.5	1034	1.6	568,920	6.6	650	0.6	158,473	8.2
1974/75	1828	1.7	513,922	7.1	1046	1.2	595,441	4.8	700	7.7	176,228	10.7
1975/76	1995	9.1	532,452	3.7	1739	66.3	638,142	7.2	831	18.7	218,202	24.6
1976/77	2268	13.7	734,832	38.0	1836	5.6	873,826	36.8	2609	313.9	435,861	99.5
1977/78	2318	2.2	886,840	20.7	1914	4.2	899,778	3.0	2647	1.5	638,768	46.7
1978/79	2389	3.1	996,362	12.4	1922	0.0	911,377	1.2				
1979/80	2455	2.8	1,281,744	28.6	1956	1.7	919,964	0.9				
1980/81	2829	15.2	1,463,516	14.2	1976	1.0	948,181	3.2				
1981/82	2701	-4.5	1,877,380	28.3	2033	2.9	969,625	2.2				
1982/83	n/a		1,971,774	5.0	2033	1.5	846,555	12.7				
1983/84	2907	7.6	2,070,362	5.0								

Source: Ministries of Finance and Economic Planning in Oyo, Kaduna and Anambra States.

82 African Cities in Crisis

In some cases, engineers and administrators are seconded from the parent ministries to the water agencies. In theory, such secondments are meant to assist the agencies, but in practice conflict of interests and internal bickering often result among those seconded and their counter-parts in full-time employment of these agencies. In such situations, the efficiency of state water agencies is affected. Four other major problems confront the Water Agencies and hamper their performance: finance, inadequacy and unreliability of electricity supply, shortage of skilled manpower, and absence or scarcity of the needed equipment and materials.

As shown in Table 4.6, the average daily output and the average per capita output for Ibadan are ridiculously low when compared with those of Enugu and Kaduna. Unlike the situation in Ibadan, there has been considerable investment in water supply in Enugu and Kaduna since the early 1970s. For example, a ₦49 million Greater Enugu Water expansion scheme is almost completed. When completed, it is expected to pump 77 million liters daily to Enugu and surrounding settlements. Similarly, a contract has been awarded for the expansion of the Kaduna South water scheme in order to double its present daily output of 36 million liters.

In contrast, the Asejire scheme which supplies the bulk of potable water to Ibadan city has a design capacity of 108 million liters per day; however, it manages to pump only 36 million liters per day. It is designed to have six pumps with each pumping 18 million liters per day. Presently, three pumps are installed, one of which has broken down. Investigation revealed that as a

Table 4.6
Water Supply

Cities	Water Scheme	Population Served	Average Daily output	Average per capita output
Enugu	Enugu Municipality schemes	239,000	83.5 mld[1]	288.9 litres
Ibadan	Eleiyele scheme	1,600,000	2.5	
	Asejire scheme		36.0	24.06
Kaduna	Kaduna North	575,000	89.0	
	Kaduna South		36.0	217.4

Source: Onibokun et al. 1986 (from the three State Water Agencies).
[1]mld = million litres per day.

result of financial constraints, the remaining three pumps could not be installed and repairs on the one that had broken down could not be made. The same story applies for the Eleiyele scheme, where the narrow water mains installed in 1942 could not be replaced owing to financial constraints. As a result, burst pipes are common as the old water mains cannot absorb increased pressure from both water works. Occasionally, in order not to overwork the two functioning pumps at Asejire Scheme, one is closed so that only 18 million liters of potable water is pumped for several days. This leads to water rationing in the city, and many areas do not get water for several weeks.

Although the enabling legislation establishing these state water agencies empowers them to levy rates and charges that would enable them to cover their operating costs, as at the end of 1984, revenue accruing from consumers accounts for 45 percent, 68.5 percent, and 73.4 percent of the operating costs in Ibadan, Kaduna, and Enugu respectively. The rates are not systematically and efficiently collected as a result of a very poor billing and accounting machinery. Furthermore, the present rates are too low and nonprogressive. The quantity of water used in homes is not metered, and the rate is fixed at ₦6 per flat / housing unit and at ₦12 per duplex, irrespective of the number or the socio-economic status of the inhabitants. In many homes, potable water charged at the household rate is being used for small-scale industrial and commercial activities like bakeries, printing presses, or laundries. In some industrial / commercial establishments, the use of water is metered. However, in many cases the meters are not serviced regularly because of institutional problems confronting the water agencies. As a result, some water meters are either malfunctioning or not functioning at all. In either case, the major consumers concerned are not charged for the actual quantity of potable water consumed.

Another problem is the widespread incidence of illegal water connections by people working in collusion with the junior technical workers of the water agencies. Investigations reveal that apart from using potable water free of charge, illegal consumers also increase the maintenance costs of water agencies because of damages done to water mains while making illegal connections. Treated water is contaminated through leakages, and this affects the quality of potable water that ultimately gets to the consumers. For example, stagnant water resulting from seepage caused by illegal connections to water mains breeds mosquitoes. The larvae of mosquitoes escape into the water mains together with muddy water, thereby polluting potable water.

Frequent power failure is another major handicap to the water supply. Power failure is endemic in the country, and this disrupts the water supply and leads to extensive damage to the water pumps and to the treatment plants. The water agencies install stand-by electric generating plants at the water schemes, but these have also proved unreliable as these plants often break down because of over-usage and lack of proper maintenance.

The problem is further compounded by a shortage of skilled manpower and a perennial shortage of water-pumping equipment, fittings, and their spare parts. Usually, the long procedure for import license procurement, coupled with the long delivery dates quoted by contractors and manufacturers, creates bottlenecks for the importation of equipment. Their problems are further compounded by the high incidence of pilferage at Nigerian ports. As a result, equipment and materials are stolen from the ports before they are cleared.

Officials also complained about the unpatriotic practices of some of the contractors to the water agencies. The contractors are in the habit of hoarding imported materials in order to create artificial scarcity and to force the water agencies to pay prohibitive prices.

Prior to the late 1960s, public standpipes were very common features in Nigerian urban centers, and they served the majority of urban households. However, the number of such standpipes has steadily decreased partly because of the cost-recovery strategy being adopted by state water agencies. As shown in Table 4.7, about two-thirds of all the households in those cities now have in-house potable water connections. The rest depend on the remaining standpipes, wells, streams and ponds.

Among the households with a water connection with water, 27 percent, 38.7 percent, and 39.7 percent had a single tap within their premises, while 73 percent, 61.3 percent, and 60.3 percent of them had multiple-tap facilities in Ibadan, Kaduna, and Enugu respectively. A majority of the households within the core and intermediate areas of the three cities had single-tap facilities within their premises.

In-house water connection is no guarantee of regular water supply. As evident from Table 4.8, 34.3 percent, 26.8 percent, and 25.8 percent of the households with in-house potable water connections in Ibadan, Kaduna, and Enugu, respectively, have their taps dry always. In Nigerian urban centers generally, few households receive regular potable water supply from their in-house water connections. Moreover, the quality of the water is not guaranteed because, occasionally, the water is either not clear, has sediments, or has a bad taste. The incidence of cholera, typhoid fever, and dysentery were recorded in the case studies. Apart from showing the variations in the reliability of water supply to households in the three cities, Table 8 shows the remarkable differences in the reliability of water supply within each city. On the whole, the reliability of water supply to households improves as one moves from the core areas through the intermediate areas to the newer suburban areas of the three cities. This picture however, should not hide the fact that some households living in the rapidly emerging suburban slums in Ibadan and Kaduna seldom have water from their taps whether they are legally or illegally connected to the water mains.

The average daily potable water consumption pattern by households surveyed in the three cities is shown in Table 4.9. There is a direct statistical relationship between the daily potable water consumption, on the one hand, and the socio-economic characteristics of households, on the other hand. Such characteristics include: the size of households, level of education, average household income, and the type of house. Low income households generally consume less potable water daily than do middle and high income households, irrespective of what part of the cities they inhabit. This is not unexpected because of the differences in living standard and lifestyles of these types of households. Again, as pointed out earlier, households in the newer suburbs, with the exception of the pockets of suburban slums, get more regular potable water supply than do households in the core and intermediate areas of the three cities.

Apart from the rates paid to the water agencies for pipe-borne water, a substantial proportion of the households spend from ₦10 to ₦30 per month on water from vendors and on procuring water from other sources (see Table 4.10). If finance is a constraint on the performance of the state water agencies, one solution is to ask people to pay more for better water supply services. A question that arises from such a proposition is whether consumers are willing to pay more. Responses to the survey showed that 58.2, 56.3, and 52.1 percent are prepared to pay more for better potable water supply services in Ibadan, Kaduna, and Enugu respectively. Taking into consideration how much they currently spend (Table 4.10), it is little wonder that the majority of households interviewed in Ibadan are willing to pay more for better potable water supply services.

One point that needs to be emphasized is that the problem of water shortage cuts across social classes in Ibadan. A substantial amount of productive man-hours are lost daily as a result of workers searching for potable water in the city. Even within the University of Ibadan campus, lecturers and students alike have come to regard potable water as a scarce commodity to be sought after, even at the expense of their official duties.

Solid Waste Management
Some highlights of urban waste management problems that emerged from this study include indiscriminate dumping of refuse, inaccessibility of the traditional core areas of cities which hampers effective transportation of waste, inadequate quantities of equipment, hazardous modes of disposal, defective institutional arrangements, and limited governmental control over industrial waste. The study reveals that residential and commercial

Table 4.7

Proportion of Households with In-house Pipe-borne Water Supply
(as % of Households in the Case Studies)

	All Cases			Core Area			Intermediate Areas			Newer Suburbs		
	Ibadan	Kaduna	Enugu	Ibadan	Kaduna	Enugu	Ibadan	Kaduna	Enugu	Ibadan	Kaduna	Enugu
Households with potable water supply	68.6	64.7	69.2	38.7	78.8	57.8	79.8	60.7	65.4	95.1	54.4	95.8
Households without potable water supply	31.4	35.3	30.8	61.3	21.2	42.2	20.2	39.3	34.6	4.9	45.6	4.2

Source: Onibokun et al. 1986.

Table 4.8
Degree of Regularity of Household Potable Water Supply
(as % of Total Households in the Case Studies)

Water Availability	All Cases			Core Area			Intermediate Areas			Newer Suburbs		
	Ibadan	Kaduna	Enugu	Ibadan	Kaduna	Enugu	Ibadan	Kaduna	Enugu	Ibadan	Kaduna	Enugu
Every time of day	21.5	28.7	31.3	12.0	26.6	16.3	12.3	27.3	19.3	40.7	50.5	47.1
A few hours in a day	17.6	25.6	24.5	15.8	34.0	28.4	11.4	24.6	26.2	30.2	29.3	21.4
Every other day	9.8	5.3	8.0	8.0	12.2	4.0	12.3	1.6	1.9	9.5	5.2	24.3
Once a week	7.4	11.6	3.4	1.8	2.1	2.6	15.9	1.2	5.6	5.5	2.6	1.4
Fortnightly	1.2	0.9	1.5	0.0	2.7	2.2	3.2	0.4	1.9	0.5	2.0	0.4
Monthly	3.6	0.6	3.1	1.5	0.5	3.1	7.3	0.8	4.6	3.5	0.6	0.2
Bi-annually	2.7	0.2	1.4	1.5	0.6	3.1	3.6	0.4	0.5	2.5	2.4	0.2
Yearly	1.9	0.6	1.0	0.0	1.1	0.9	3.6	0.0	1.9	2.6	2.5	0.2
Never	34.3	26.8	25.8	59.5	20.7	39.5	30.5	43.7	38.3	5.0	4.9	5.0

Source: Onibokun et al. 1986.

Table 4.9

Level of Daily Household Potable Water Consumption Measured in Kerosene Tins[1]

(as % of Total Households in the Case Studies)

	All Cases		Core Area			Intermediate Area			Newer Suburbs		
	Ibadan	Kaduna	Enugu	Ibadan	Kaduna	Enugu	Ibadan	Kaduna	Enugu	Ibadan	Kaduna	Enugu
Less than 2	1.3	7.2	2.7	2.0	7.5	2.3	0.9	8.0	2.6	0.7	6.3	2.8
2–5	17.1	44.3	26.6	22.8	32.7	32.2	16.0	46.0	27.7	8.7	32.8	14.0
5–8	25.0	22.0	31.0	25.6	23.3	26.4	25.5	19.3	30.3	23.2	22.7	34.6
8–10	20.5	12.3	15.4	11.8	15.7	15.0	24.7	10.7	14.9	29.0	11.4	17.8
10–12	14.5	9.7	15.6	11.4	15.0	14.8	14.3	8.0	16.4	20.3	14.5	17.3
12–15	9.3	2.5	3.9	9.3	1.9	3.3	11.3	3.7	4.6	5.8	1.7	3.7
15–18	6.0	0.9	1.5	9.8	1.3	2.3	4.3	2.1	1.5	6.5	0.6	1.9
18–20	6.3	1.1	3.3	2.0	2.6	3.7	3.0	2.1	2.1	5.8	10.0	7.5
Total	100.0	100.0	100.0	94.7	100.0	100.0	100.0	99.9	100.1	100.0	100.0	99.6

Source: Onibokun et al. 1986.

[1] One kerosene tin of water is about 16 liters when full.

Table 4.10

Level of Monthly Household Expenditure on Water

(as % of Total Households in Case Studies)

(naira)

	All Cases			Core Area			Intermediate Area			Newer Suburbs		
	Ibadan	Kaduna	Enugu	Ibadan	Kaduna	Enugu	Ibadan	Kaduna	Enugu	Ibadan	Kaduna	Enugu
Nothing	0.5	0.2	1.4	0.7	0.5	0.8	0.0	0.0	1.3	1.0	0.0	2.8
1.00–10.00	79.7	39.3	27.7	79.1	37.6	30.7	78.8	32.6	18.1	81.6	55.3	38.8
11.00–20.00	8.0	31.3	25.7	19.9	31.7	34.5	7.3	38.8	19.3	3.4	20.3	19.6
21.00–30.00	6.6	20.7	17.5	7.2	20.6	11.5	6.1	22.9	25.2	6.3	16.7	15.2
31.00–50.00	1.8	2.2	14.2	0.4	6.3	7.7	5.3	4.7	18.9	5.4	3.7	16.1
51.00–75.00	0.5	0.9	2.2	0.7	2.1	13.0	1.6	0.8	14.7	2.0	1.6	4.1
76.00–100.00	0.5	0.2	1.4	0.0	1.1	1.9	0.8	0.4	2.5	0.3	2.4	3.2

Source: Onibokun et al.

land uses account for the highest proportion of the volume of waste generated in the cities (Table 4.11). By comparison, waste is mainly organic, although inorganic waste is also important.

Table 4.12 shows variations in the proportion of the components between the traditional core areas of the cities and the new suburbs. While leaves, ashes, and paper constitute the highest proportion of waste in the old areas, the proportion is not substantial in the new areas. Rather, these new areas are characterized by such wastes as food remnants and paper. Again there are inter-city variations in the compositions of wastes. For example, leaves are more dominant in the cites located in the southern part of the country than those in the north.

Traditionally, the responsibility for collection, transporting, and disposing solid wastes has been a local government function. The 1976 Guidelines for Local Government Reform lists as part of the functions of local governments "sanitary inspection, refuse and nightsoil disposal" (Nigeria 1976, 2-3). In the same vein, section 7 of the Fourth Schedule of the Nigerian Constitution (1979) assigns the "Provision and maintenance of public conveniences and refuse disposal" as a local government function. However, experience from all parts of the country, confirmed by the case-studies, has shown that local governments are ill-equipped to deliver these services.

Table 4.11
Percentage of Total Solid Waste Generation
In Ibadan, Kaduna, and Onitsha
By Land-use Types, 1982

	Ibadan	Kaduna	Onitsha[1]
Residential	70.1	57.3	82.7
Commercial	18.8	33.5	6.3
Industrial	9.7	7.7	1.1
Institutional	0.7	–	9.9
Others	0.7	1.5	–
Total	100.00	100.00	100.00

Source: PAI Associates (1982). Extracts from Table 4.

[1]Data from Onitsha have been included as representative of eastern Nigeria, data for Enugu not being available.

This is particularly true of urban local governments. As a consequence, state governments have become involved. Hitherto, the relationship among the three tiers of government (Federal, State, and Local) with regard to solid waste has not been adequately defined. Aspects of the responsibility have therefore been shifted back and forth from one agency to another and from one level of government to another, as shown in Table 4.13. No permanent solution has been found for solid waste management in Nigerian urban centers. In Ibadan, for example, the responsibility has changed hands six times within the last ten years. This attests to the failure or inefficiency of local government administration in Nigeria.

With reference to collection, two methods are generally employed. The first is the depot method which utilizes a concrete or steel structure about four meters in length, three meters in breadth, and one meter in depth. These structures are meant to serve a group of dwellings, and they are emptied periodically. The depot method obviously has a number of disadvantages. First, the structures collect water during the rains since they are not covered. Second, almost invariably, children are sent to dump wastes carried in baskets or other open containers, and these leak part of the wastes on the path even before getting to the depots. Where depots are situated near major streets, collection adds to traffic congestion.

The second method employed is door-to-door collection from dustbins. Less than forty percent of the refuse collected is amenable to this method as some parts of the city are not accessible to vehicular traffic. Individual dustbins are used in those areas with adequate access roads.

The data presented in Table 4.14 give some insight into the type of storage facilities being used by people in Ibadan, Kaduna and Enugu. In all the three cities, the highest percentages (70.5 percent, 46.9 percent, and 73.6 percent respectively) of the populace use household dustbins in storing the wastes generated in their homes. The remaining proportion either use communal collection depots or just dump in open spaces. This represents the proportion of the populace that needs to be catered to either by encouraging them to use household dustbins (where these can be collected) or by providing communal depots at strategic locations. However, these proportions vary according to the three cities studied. Enugu, for example, recorded the highest percentage of dustbin users (73.6) while Kaduna recorded the lowest figure (46.9). Kaduna also appears to have greater problems of indiscriminate dumping than the two other cities.

One other observation that can be made from the table is the degree of variation among the different zones of the cities. In general, it can be inferred that the proportion of dustbin users tends to be progressively higher as one moves from the intermediate zones to the newer suburbs. Conversely, the proportion of the population that uses communal collecting depots and incidental open spaces tends to be higher in the city core zones and decreases to lower levels in the intermediate zones and the newer suburbs.

These two methods – depot and dustbin – are officially recognized in the three cities studied. However, there is the problem of indiscriminate dumping in open spaces, along streets and in the streams. This practice is resorted to either when wastes in depots are uncollected and are overfilled or when they are not easily accessible. In response to the question "who collects your refuse?" thirty-five percent in Ibadan, thirty-three percent in Kaduna, and nearly forty-four percent in Enugu claimed that nobody was responsible – neither direct government agency services nor government-employed private firms. Even when the refuse collection machinery is in operation the equipment and personnel are grossly inadequate to meet the tasks. Although no information about the financing of waste collection management was forthcoming, officials indicated in their discussions during the field survey that their authorities were not adequately funded.

With regard to the disposal of wastes, the system adopted in most Nigerian cities is sanitary landfill. In Ibadan, two major sites are in operation – one in the south-western part of the city and the other in the southeast. Both are already engulfed by residential and road development. The actual method of operation is end-dumping with little or no cover. The use of a bull-dozer is occasionally adopted to spread the loads and to improve accessibility for tipping lorries; burning is resorted to in the dry season. Although the official method of disposal is sanitary landfill, precautions are rarely taken to ensure sanitary conditions. Consequently, the sites have degenerated into open dumps which breed flies and harbor rodents.

Industrial establishments are responsible for the management of the waste they generate within their premises. However, a number of them have selected their disposal sites without official approval. In spite of the laws governing the nature, volume, and disposal of wastes generated by industrial establishments, most industrialists interviewed were ignorant of the existence of such laws. Even where claims of the knowledge of the laws were made, there was neither evidence of compliance nor of enforcement. A survey of people's perception shows that solid waste ranks highest on their scale of urban environmental problems. However, more people perceive that the situation has been improving and will continue to improve. Although a relatively large proportion of the public appears to have an optimistic view other evidence seems to point to the fact that the problem is likely to continue unless determined efforts are now made to remedy the defects identified in the country's urban waste management systems.

Table 4.12
Mean Percentage Composition by Weight of Solid Wastes
in Ibadan, Onitsha, and Jos

Components	Ibadan		Onitsha[1]		Jos[2]	
	Bodija New Estate	Traditional Core (Agugu)	New Onitsha	Old Onitsha	New Jos	Old Jos
Leaves	4.3	50.1	3.0	5.6	—	—
Food Remnants	19.2	6.4	37.0	32.6	11.0	8.6
Paper	26.2	15.2	7.5	5.3	11.1	8.6
Rags	1.5	4.5	2.4	3.6	—	—
Plastics and Polythene	8.9	4.8	2.7	4.7	5.6	4.3
Tins and Metals	11.4	7.7	6.1	8.3	4.2	5.7
Bottles and Glasses	11.8	6.1	6.0	11.3	5.6	6.4
Bones	—	—	—	—	5.6	7.1
Ash, Dust, and Stone	16.7	29.8	35.4	13.3	47.2	32.9
Miscellaneous	—	—	—	—	9.6	26.4

Source: PAI Associates, 1982, pp. 12, 24, and 15.

[1] Onitsha is in eastern Nigeria.
[2] Jos is in the north.

Editor's note: Not all of the columns add to 100%.

Table 4.13
Temporal Changes in the Organization of Solid Wastes Management
in Ibadan, Kaduna, and Enugu

City	Period	Management Agency
Ibadan	Prior to 1972	Ibadan Municipal Government
	1973-1978	Ibadan Wastes Disposal Board
	1978-1983	Ibadan Municipal Government; Ministry of Housing and Environment
	1984-Dec. 1985	Sewerage and Refuse Matters Department; Environmental Sanitation Task Force; Ibadan Municipal Government
Kaduna	1940-1967	Kaduna Native Authority
	1967-1971	Kaduna Local Government
	1971-1985	Kaduna Capital Development Board
	1985-Dec. 1985	Kaduna State Urban Planning and Development Board
Enugu	Prior to 1977	Enugu Urban Council
	1977-1984	Enugu Local Government
	1984-1985	Anambra State Task Force
	1985-Dec. 1985	Anambra State Environmental Sanitation Authority

Source: Onibokun et al. 1986.

Table 4.14
Storage of Domestic Wastes in Three Nigeria Cities (%)

Facilities	All Cases			Core Areas			Intermediate Areas			Newer Suburbs		
	Ibadan	Kaduna	Enugu	Ibadan	Kaduna	Enugu	Ibadan	Kaduna	Enugu	Ibadan	Kaduna	Enugu
Dustbins	70.5	46.9	73.6	56.1	51.0	71.9	64.1	60.9	70.9	91.3	29.0	78.0
Communal Depots	12.1	18.2	8.5	17.9	29.8	13.6	15.0	12.7	9.7	3.4	12.0	2.1
Open Spaces	17.4	34.8	17.9	25.9	19.1	14.4	20.9	26.3	19.4	5.3	59.0	19.9
Total	100.0	99.9	100.0	99.9	99.9	99.9	100.0	99.9	100.0	100.0	100.0	100.0
Sample size	688	622	635	262	188	257	220	251	237	206	183	141

Source: Onibokun et al. 1986.

Table 4.15
Ownership of Energy Appliances
(in percentages)

Item	1 Ibadan	2 Kaduna	3 Enugu
Water heater	17.8	15.1	7.7
Washing machine	1.1	7.8	2.9
Air conditioner	6.5	12.8	12.3
Fan	12.9	60.5	47.4
Refrigerator	29.3	45.6	38.3
Freezer	4.5	16.0	3.9
Electric iron	44.5	50.3	42.3
Charcoal iron	11.0	14.4	3.7
Television	46.3	56.1	45.5
Radio	61.4	58.5	47.8
Gas cooker	8.8	23.2	16.6
Electric cooker	3.0	9.2	2.5
Electric stove	1.3	2.0	1.2
Kerosene stove	62.3	56.8	43.4
Cars or trucks	17.3	34.7	19.8
Number of respondents	463	534	598

Source: Onibokun et al. 1986.

Energy Development and Utilization

Nigeria is well endowed with energy resources – crude oil, natural gas, coal, lignite, wind, ocean tide, and geothermal. Others include nuclear, hydro, wood fuel, and plant wastes. Nigeria has been described as one of the few African countries endowed with energy resources which are well above their domestic energy requirements. The supply and demand position of these resources in Nigeria have been adequately discussed in an earlier work (see Onibokun et al. 1986). Prominent among the commercial energy sources are coal, gas, electricity (from hydro, steam, gas, and private generating plants), and other energy forms from petroleum products (e.g., kerosene). The major component of the non-commercial energy source is firewood and charcoal from woodfuel. The case studies provide a fair statistical picture of the pattern of energy consumption in Nigerian urban areas.

Tables 4.15 and 4.16 show the stock of various energy appliances within the three cities and among the various categories of urban dwellers. (Table 4.15 describes ownership of appliances, while Table 4.16 describes "access," including ability to borrow from a friend or neighbor.) As would be expected, ownership is higher in the newer suburbs. Energy appliances commonly acquired by about fifty percent of the respondents in the three cities are electric fans, electric irons, electric stoves, television sets, radios, and kerosene stoves. Most of these appliances are not really a luxury in the urban centers as they are essential for cooking, fashion, and information within the complex urban living system.

Other energy appliances acquired by twenty to forty-nine percent of respondents include refrigerators, gas cookers, and cars / lorries (irrespective of their capacities). These are prestige appliances and are acquired by energy consumers beyond the low income group. Appliances acquired by one to nineteen percent of the respondents are water heaters, washing machines, air conditioners, freezers, electric cookers, and stoves. All of these constitute luxury goods used by the highest income group of the city dwellers, specifically, those residing in the newer suburbs. Table 4.17 describes the energy requirements of these appliances with their capacities in Nigeria in 1985. All, except for irons, table and standing fans, and radios, are very expensive.

Table 4.18 gives the analysis of energy forms most frequently used for the various residential activities (in percentages) by all respondents in the three cities. About ninety-four percent of the respondents rely on electricity from the public sources for lighting purposes. Others use gas (0.3 percent), kerosene (5.1 percent), and candle or traditional sources (0.4 percent). It may be inferred from these statistics that almost every city dweller in Nigeria relies heavily on publicly supplied electricity for lighting. This heavy

Table 4.16
Access to Energy Appliances:
Absolute Figures and Percentages by Households

	All Cases			Core Area			Intermediate Area			Newer Suburbs		
	Ibadan	Kaduna	Enugu	Ibadan	Kaduna	Enugu	Ibadan	Kaduna	Enugu	Ibadan	Kaduna	Enugu
1 Water heater	142	134	114	10	47	11	17	57	9	115	34	83
%	19.5	20.9	17.2	3.6	24.8	4.2	6.9	22.0	3.7	55.5	18.1	58.0
2 Washing machine	64	16	38	4	4	0	8	4	2	52	5	36
%	8.8	2.5	5.4	1.4	2.1	0	3.2	1.5	0.8	25.1	2.6	25.1
3 Air conditioner	117	53	161	10	14	14	18	20	36	91	20	108
%	16.0	8.3	24.9	3.6	7.4	5.3	7.3	7.7	15.1	43.9	10.6	75.5
4 Fan	595	453	590	187	157	235	218	158	221	192	129	136
%	82.1	70.0	91.3	67.5	82.5	90.3	90.0	61.2	92.8	93.6	68.9	95.1
5 Refrigerator	468	237	472	105	87	155	169	71	183	194	78	131
%	64.1	36.9	72.9	37.9	46.0	59.3	68.9	27.5	76.8	93.7	41.7	91.6
6 Freezer	161	38	126	14	7	24	37	20	23	110	9	79
%	22.0	5.9	19.4	5.0	3.7	9.1	15.1	7.7	9.6	53.4	4.8	55.2
7 Electric iron	511	356	522	134	121	184	178	114	200	199	114	128
%	70.0	55.4	80.6	48.3	64.0	70.4	72.6	44.1	84.0	96.1	60.9	93.7

Source: Onibokun et al. 1986.

Table 4.16 continued

		All Cases			Core Area			Intermediate Area			Newer Suburbs		
		Ibadan	Kaduna	Enugu	Ibadan	Kaduna	Enugu	Ibadan	Kaduna	Enugu	Ibadan	Kaduna	Enugu
8	Television	562	385	566	157	129	219	204	130	205	201	120	139
	%	77.0	59.9	87.4	56.6	68.2	83.9	83.2	50.3	86.1	97.1	64.1	97.2
9	Radio	601	499	582	207	156	222	215	197	219	179	139	138
	%	82.4	77.8	89.9	74.7	82.9	86.9	87.7	76.3	92.0	86.4	74.3	96.5
10	Gas cooker	233	77	198	12	23	24	55	26	58	166	24	104
	%	31.9	11.9	30.6	4.3	12.1	9.1	22.4	10.0	24.3	80.0	12.8	72.7
11	Electric cooker	91	25	32	8	5	4	9	4	4	74	10	23
	%	12.4	3.8	4.9	2.8	2.6	1.5	3.6	1.5	1.6	35.7	5.3	16.1
12	Kerosene stove	566	523	520	234	155	240	220	211	145	112	145	86
	%	77.6	81.4	80.4	84.4	82.0	92.3	89.7	83.3	60.9	59.8	77.5	60.1
13	Cars & lorries	330	144	244	60	57	54	105	49	74	165	35	113
	%	45.2	22.4	37.7	21.6	42.8	19.3	31.0	79.7	18.7	79.0		
14	Charcoal iron	148	85	59	78	21	37	56	33	15	14	31	7
	%	20.3	13.2	9.1	28.1	11.1	14.1	22.8	12.7	6.3	6.7	16.6	4.8
15	Electric stove	22	15	14	9	3	7	5	3	4	8	7	3
	%	3.0	2.3	2.1	3.2	1.5	2.6	2.0	1.6	1.6	3.8	3.7	2.0

Table 4.17

Residential Energy Appliances and their Energy Requirements

Item and Type	Rating	Price (naira)	Power Demand (kWh)	Rated Current (amps)	Average Daily Usage (hrs) in Nigeria	No. of hours to use 1 kWh	Total Daily Consumption (kWh)
Water heater							
– 50-litre	1,200 watt	180	1.2	5.2	1	0.8	1.25
– 100-litre	2,500 watt	320	2.5	11	1	0.4	2.50
Washing machine							
– non-automatic	300 watt	n/a	0.3	1.29	2	3	0.66
– automatic	600 watt		0.6	2.5	2	2	1.00
– automatic with heater	3,000 watt		3.0	13.0	2	0.3	6.67
Air conditioner							
– small	1.5 HP	1,600	1.1	4.7	8	0	8.00
– medium	2.0 HP	2,500	1.5	6.5	8	0.7	11.43
Fan							
– table	0.08 HP	230	0.06	0.25	8	17	0.47
– standing	0.0 HP	420	0.7	0.3	8	14	0.57
– ceiling	0.3 HP	180	0.22	0.9	8	45	0.18

Table 4.17 continued

Item and Type	Rating	Price (naira)	Power Demand (kWh)	Rated Current (amps)	Average Daily Usage (hrs) in Nigeria	No. of hours to use 1 kWh	Total Daily Consumption (kWh)
Refrigerator							
– small	0.2 HP	600	0.15	0.6	24	7	3.43
– medium	0.25 HP	950	0.19	0.8	24	5	4.80
– large	0.3 HP	1,400	0.22	0.9	24	4.5	5.35
Iron							
– small	750 watt	80	0.75	3.2	2	1.3	1.54
– medium	850 watt	125	0.85	3.6	2	1.2	1.67
Television							
– black & white	200 watt	500	0.2	0.9	8	5	1.60
– colour	300 watt	2,500	0.3	1.3	8	3	2.67
Radio							
– transistor	5 watt	100	0.005	0.02	8	200	0.04
– radiogram / stereo system	100 watt	250+	0.1	0.4	8	10	0.80
Cooker							
– regular	8,000 watt	1,200	8.0	34	6	1.2	5.0
– large	10,500 watt	1,800	10.5	45	6	0.1	60.0

Source: Onibokun et al. 1986.

reliance reflects the fact that Nigerian cities have gone through a transition from the traditional palm oil lamps through kerosene lamps to electric light bulbs.

For cooking, about thirty-nine percent of all respondents use kerosene while about twenty-nine percent rely on firewood and nineteen percent on electricity (Table 4.18). However, a few of the affluent use gas (nine percent), and a few of the poor use charcoal (four percent). In the case of cooking for important parties (e.g. burial ceremonies, marriages, child naming ceremonies), more than ninety percent of the respondents opt for firewood while about six percent rely on gas. On the whole, the greatest percentage of the respondents rely on kerosene. This reflects the current wave of change in terms of fashion, convenience, and advertisement which indicate that kerosene will displace firewood as a source of energy for domestic cooking in the cities in Nigeria.

Energy use for cooking in the three cities is very similar. Kerosene is most widely used, followed by gas, firewood, and electricity in that order, except for Kaduna where firewood follows kerosene. There appears to be a keen competition between firewood and gas as energy sources for cooking within the core and intermediate zones. However, at the newer suburbs, the competition is between electricity and gas after kerosene. For ironing, more

Table 4.18
Energy Most Frequently Used

	Lighting	Cooking	Cooking for Major Parties	Ironing	Heating
Electricity	94.2	19.3		86.4	15.7
Gas	0.3	8.7	5.8	8.3	–
Firewood	29.0	94.2	–	46.8	–
Coal	0.1	–	–	–	–
Charcoal	3.9	–	13.5	–	–
Kerosene	5.1	39.0	–	29.3	–
Candle or traditional lamp	0.4	–	–	–	–
Gasoline	–	–	–	–	–
Total	100	99.8	100	99.9	100.1

Source: Onibokun et al. 1986.

than three-quarters rely on electricity while thirteen percent use charcoal. For heating, forty-seven percent of the respondents use firewood, sixteen percent use electricity, twenty-nine percent use kerosene, and eight percent use gas. About sixty-seven percent of the respondents consume gasoline directly or indirectly. This high percentage is not surprising in the light of improved transportation found in most Nigerian cities. In fact, the granting of vehicle loans and the payment of travel allowances to workers on Grade Level 7 and above in Nigeria has accelerated the pace of acquiring and using motor cycles, private cars, and public vehicles.

The emergence of this pattern of energy consumption is influenced by the price of energy, supply reliability, convenience of use, and cost of energy appliances. Information on the extent to which these factors have aided the above pattern is presented in Table 4.19. Apparently, most of the respondents use kerosene for its low prices, supply reliability, and inexpensive appliances. Whereas, electricity is cheap, neat, and non-polluting, respondents feel that its supply is not reliable; also, the appliance is expensive. Gas is neat and non-polluting but is fraught with danger of explosion; the appliance is highly expensive and beyond the reach of the core area, which harbors the greatest number of low income people. Although firewood is highly polluting and not neat, the appliance is very cheap.

In sum, the detailed analysis confirms that whereas kerosene has displaced firewood in the cities, firewood is still consumed by low income groups who cannot afford the luxury of expensive energy appliances. This category of people constitutes more than thirty percent of the total urban population. Put differently, kerosene, electricity, and firewood constitute the major fuel sources for cooking in the urban areas in Nigeria. Other fuel sources include gas (restricted to the very small affluent class) and coal and charcoal (for the very low income urban dwellers). This suggests a categorization of energy consumers into high, average, and low income groups following the classification of urban dwellers into core, intermediate, and newer suburbs areas.

This study reveals a noticeable demand / supply energy imbalance in the cities, especially for fuelwood and electricity. Demand far exceeds supply, as a result of which a regular supply of energy cannot be guaranteed. The pattern of energy consumption in the cities suggests a significant transition from traditional energy sources to kerosene and electricity in the area of lighting and to kerosene in particular in the area of normal domestic cooking. However, there are elements of heavy reliance on energy combination and substitution efforts in the Nigerian cities for a variety of domestic and social activities. These efforts are usually reinforced by the variety of energy forms available, their relative prices, and the respective investments involved in converting to them.

Table 4.19
Reason for Using Energy for Cooking
by Type of Energy

		Electricity			Gas			Firewood		
		Ibadan	Kaduna	Enugu	Ibadan	Kaduna	Enugu	Ibadan	Kaduna	Enugu
1	Inexpensiveness	26.5	24.3	27.1	5.5	3.7	4.3	30.4	45.8	36.2
2	Neatness	20.1	18.5	21.5	20.1	15.8	17.8	5.4	10.8	6.3
3	Supply Reliability	2.4	4.1	1.8	10.4	16.5	12.1	41.5	39.8	36.2
4	No Substitute	45.5	48.2	44.5	0.5	1.3	1.4	3.4	6.8	2.8
5	Convenience	56.4	52.8	50.9	16.8	14.5	20.2	5.6	9.4	8.5
6	Danger-free	32.6	30.8	29.4	1.8	1.0	2.1	20.5	18.6	21.4
7	Non-pollutant	58.3	60.3	58.9	9.6	6.8	8.4	1.4	2.0	1.5
8	Inexpensive appliance	30.4	15.8	24.6	4.8	6.4	5.8	68.4	59.9	64.6

Table 4.19 continued

		Coal			Kerosene				Charcoal	
		Ibadan	Kaduna	Enugu	Ibadan	Kaduna	Enugu	Ibadan	Kaduna	Enugu
1	Inexpensiveness	13.4	–	15.6	45.6	48.5	40.9	10.4	15.8	12.6
2	Neatness	–	–	–	20.8	29.4	18.4	–	–	–
3	Supply Reliability	–	–	–	34.2	30.6	33.8	1.1	4.2	3.9
4	No Substitute	–	–	–	–	–	–	–	–	–
5	Convenience	10.2	2.8	9.8	19.5	15.6	20.1	3.6	3.8	2.4
6	Danger-free	–	–	–	2.8	5.6	10.5	11.6	15.1	13.3
7	Non-pollutant	–	–	–	10.4	11.8	9.8	–	3.6	3.4
8	Inexpensive appliance				30.3	26.5	32.1	15.1	17.8	16.9

Source: Onibokun et al. 1986.

Note: Columns add to more than 100% when individuals gave more than one reason for using a fuel.

Price as a dominant influencing factor is variously perceived by the Nigerian respondents. However, one restrictive factor in utilizing cleaner, non-pollutant, and long-range cheaper energy source (gas) is the investment involved in converting from one energy form to the other. Besides, consumers' behavior reveals that changes in energy prices would not significantly alter the pattern of energy consumption unless there are changes in the social class of the consumer. Generally, expenditure on energy consumption accounts for a small fraction of the household budget.

Any acceleration of the pace of energy development has implications for the quality of the environment especially with regard to the increased use of firewood. For example, bridging the urban fuelwood gap will aggravate the pace at which forest resources are currently exploited. This may consequently lead to deforestation as well as to wind and water erosion. Deforestation is already a function of household energy consumption.

Apart from deforestation, there are some social costs in terms of journeys made daily (eight to twenty kilometers) to gather firewood. The time allocated to this activity or to other adaptive energy-saving strategies represents an opportunity cost to society. Carrying heavy firewood loads over long distances, especially by low income urban dwellers causes spinal damage and problems in child-bearing.

Urban Management

Management structure and functions in Nigerian cities are in a state of flux. The history of local government and urban management in Nigeria has been characterized by a muddled approach where different ideas have been designed, adopted, and prematurely abandoned. This has led to disenchantment with local and urban institutions. At present, local and urban governments are given several responsibilities but without an appropriate financial base to perform them.

The Revenue Sharing Formula weighs heavily against the local and urban institutions – the state governments interfered in the disbursement and spending of the local government's statutory and locally-generated funds. Moreover, the locally-generated funds are quite minimal, hence the heavy dependence of the local / urban governments on externally generated funds. The ability and the capacity of the local / urban government to provide the essential services and amenities are thereby greatly hampered.

When the Military first seized power in January 1966, one of the most critical political problems which confronted the new administration was how to reorganize government at the local and urban level in order to provide a clearly defined scope of authority, responsibility, and functions, while at the same time maintaining an effective presence of state and federal authorities in the localities in order to be able to determine and control the pace and quality of development generated at the local level. At that time, in the Northern Region, unlike in the rest of the country, the system of local authorities was very strong indeed and the traditional rulers were in name and deed the "government" in their localities. What was therefore needed was to give strength to the governmental institutions at the local level in the south and to democratize the institutions in the north. Local government reforms in Nigeria went through difficult trials and errors. The period from 1966 to 1976 can be regarded as one of confusion. In 1976 a new structure of local government was introduced by an edict.

With the passage of the Local Government Edict of 1976, a single-tier system of local government replaced whatever was in existence in each of the states before the introduction of the reform. Two lists of functions were drawn up for local and urban councils. The first list allocated to the local government authorities included: sanitary inspection, refuse and night-soil disposal, control of revenue, slaughter houses, and public conveniences. The second list, which was to be passed to local authorities as they acquired the capacity to discharge the functions, included rural and semi-urban water supply. In neither of these two lists is electricity and urban water supply mentioned.

From 1976 and to the passage of the Revenue Allocation Act of 1981, the Federal Government made "annual grants" to local and urban governments, the amount of which varied from year to year. In 1976/77, 1977/78, 1978/79, 1979/80, and 1989, the following sums were made available respectively to local government: ₦100 million, ₦250 million, ₦150 million, ₦300 million, and ₦278 million. State governments were also required to do the same. These sums of money were distributed on the basis of twenty-five percent equally and seventy-five proportioned to population. In addition, all outstanding debts owed to the state governments by these 301 urban and local governments were written off. With the passage of the Revenue Allocation Act of 1981, local governments were allocated ten percent of the Federation Account. Table 4.20, however, shows the distribution of the Federal Government grants from 1976/77 to 1980. Local governments never received their statutory allocation regularly until the return of the military on 31 December 1983.

When the 301 urban and local governments were created and local elections held in 1976, the legal responsibility to transfer funds to the local government rested with the state governments. The Federal Government, however, set certain criteria which the state governments were expected to meet, and any deviation from the set guidelines required special approval of the Federal Government. In short, the creativity and management of urban and local governments was made the responsibility of the local level, the state government, and the Federal Government. The edicts which in 1976

Table 4.20
Grants Distributed to States for Local Governments
Between 1976 / 1977 and 1980
(million naira)

State	1976 / 77	1977 / 78	1978 / 79	1978 / 80	1980
Anambra	6.127	15.404	9.242	15.137	25.37
Bauchi	4.591	11.578	6.337	16.891	23.15
Bendel	4.645	11.579	6.947	14.657	20.64
Benue	4.585	11.456	6.870	18.444	18.99
Borno	5.293	13.383	8.030	15.289	17.40
Cross River	6.196	15.002	9.001	16.992	16.11
Gongola	4.885	12.063	7.238	16.589	16.67
Imo	6.241	15.660	9.396	16.356	14.87
Kaduna	6.636	17.092	10.255	16.650	13.87
Kano	9.094	22.740	13.644	21.864	13.40
Kwara	3.625	9.063	5.438	12.322	12.86
Lagos	3.161	8.152	4.891	13.382	12.75
Niger	2.924	1.313	4.381	13.342	13.73
Ogun	3.405	8.513	5.108	11.873	11.24
Ondo	4.990	2.485	7.451	14.136	10.09
Oyo	8.333	20.531	12.500	19.700	10.07
Plateau	4.046	10.117	6.070	14.080	9.45
Rivers	3.483	9.083	5.450	13.320	9.05
Sokoto	7.430	8.577	11.146	18.856	8.12
Total	100	250	150	300	276

Source: Data collected from the Federal Ministry of Finance, Lagos, by Onibokun et al. 1986.

established these 301 local and urban governments were not substantially changed in most states after the return to civilian rule in 1979. In particular, the requirements for altering the boundaries were not changed, despite the proliferation of urban and local governments, and many urban areas were split into several jurisdictions. This proliferation would have continued unabated if the military had not returned to power in December 1983. With this second intervention of the military, all state governments reverted to the position before September 1979.

The question of finance was probably more explosive than that of boundary adjustment. The Constitution requires the allocation of statutory allocation from the Federation account to be paid to urban and local governments through state governments. In many cases, the transfer of the allocation to local and urban governments was a mere paper transaction. Worse still, in some cases, neither the State nor Federal money was made available to local governments, not because federal statutory allocation was not sent but because the state spent it for its own purposes.

Local and urban governments in Nigeria rely heavily on externally generated revenue (i.e. revenue allocation from the federal and state governments). Apart from a few urban governments in Anambra, Kaduna, and Lagos states, externally generated revenue is as high as eighty percent and in some cases up to ninety percent. This is not healthy for urban and local government development. The size of the Federation account is very unpredictable, because it depends heavily on the international politics of oil. Therefore, unless the more stable internal sources of revenue are seriously exploited, the services which urban and local governments are expected to deliver cannot be delivered effectively. Yet state governments have appropriated some important sources of internally generated revenue, and unless these are restored, the local governments have little hope of discharging their responsibilities.

In each of the cities studied, the urban management structure is similar. Using Kaduna as an example, the main policy-making organ is the Council made up of elected and nominated members. The Council constitutes itself into a number of committees to which powers are delegated. Three or four of the members are elected to hold executive offices in order to exercise overall control over the various departments of government. These are supervisory councillors. Of the twenty-four members of Kaduna Council fifteen had no formal education whatsoever, while five had primary seven, two had middle four, and one had a pharmacy certificate. Even though the formal education of members was much different in the other two cities, not much difference can be seen in terms of the effectiveness of urban management.

In Ibadan, Enugu, and Kaduna, local government has always shared with the state and Federal Governments the responsibility for administering the area under its jurisdiction and more especially in the provision of services. In each of these cities, particularly in the last few years, urban governments are being made irrelevant in the provision of electricity, water, and waste disposal. More specifically, in all the three urban centers, the responsibility for the provision of electricity is that of the Federal Government. In Enugu, both water supply and waste disposal have been completely taken over by the state. Ibadan and Kaduna are not much different. In Ibadan, the waste disposal responsibility, has shifted so frequently between the state and the municipal government that it is difficult for the citizens to know who is responsible at any one time. The responsibility for water supply in Ibadan, Enugu, and Kaduna belongs to the state government. Kaduna local government has responsibility for waste disposal. However, as in the other two cities, most of the people interviewed agreed completely that the city council did not provide any services worth mentioning.

As S. A. Oladosu (1982) points out,

> The administration of social services in Kaduna [and the other two urban centers] is characterised by the absence of the public person or public authority with the duty of looking at the city as a whole, with a view to assessing its needs, weighing up the demands of its inhabitants, assessing the resources available with a view to relating these resources to needs and devising an order of priorities and an appropriate combination of social services.

The condition of human settlements in Nigeria, as evident from the three cities studied, is an indictment of the existing machinery. The rapid increase in population, the accelerated growth of urban areas, the complexity of urban problems, as well as the increasing involvement of several agencies in physical development and infrastructural provision and maintenance call for a more efficient coordination of strategies at both the federal, state, and local government levels. The machinery for managing urbanization needs to be revitalized and reorganized to meet the challenges.

Conclusion: Policy Recommendations

Any effort to improve the quality of urban life in Nigeria must necessarily start with an accurate head count. Until a reliable head count is available, provision of urban facilities will always be outdated before they are commissioned. Since census activities have been overtly politicized in Nigeria, this study suggests that cadastral surveys be made, interpreted, analyzed, and used as a surrogate for census counts. These types of surveys are capable of providing an equally reliable estimate of the total number of people in Nigeria, in addition to showing the various types of land uses by ownership.

The analysis in this chapter also shows the need to update, improve, and increase the levels of the various services provided to the urban inhabitants. However, an important policy decision that would improve the standard of services in the urban areas is the increasing decentralization of these services to the rural areas. Although the best educational, commercial, health, and transport services are concentrated in these urban areas, the continued pauperization and neglect of the rural areas make the urban areas islands of relative affluence in seas of misery. Thus, the people for these relatively neglected outlying areas will continue to migrate to the urban areas. It seems, therefore, that no adequate level of facilities can be provided for these urban areas until the population stabilizes and the rural areas assume some level of affluence or are provided with their own facilities and services. Thus, rural development is a prerequisite to urban management. This is where the use of intermediate or medium-sized cities as regional magnets or growth poles, serving as alternative nodes of development to the traditional large cities, will be useful. More importantly, Nigeria should adopt an urbanization policy aimed at controlling the birth rate and achieving balanced rural-urban development in order to minimize the rural-urban flow of population.

Because land management in urban areas of Nigeria is a shambles, there should be one land regulatory body in each of the urban areas. Moreover, the cities should use physical layouts and structure plans as tools for effective land control and administration. The various state governments should give the problems of urban areas more attention by giving them a greater financial share of their annual budgets to meet their increasing responsibilities. It is also essential for the different urban governments to explore other sources of revenue for the funding of the various responsibilities expected of them. As long as urban areas in Nigeria continue to grow, the efforts of policy makers should be directed to channelling the growth to a desirable end. Provision of essential facilities and amenities, preferably ahead of development, should be the goal of all urban governments.

The case studies emphasize the need to re-evaluate the relationship among the three levels of government in Nigeria in terms of the funding and management of essential facilities. There is also an urgent need to rationalize the institutional framework for the supply and management of the essential services. Unless positive steps are taken now, the quality of urban life in Nigeria will deteriorate faster and the future will be bleak, most especially for the urban poor.

Note

1. Within each state, three towns were relocated – the state capital, an intermediate size town, and a small town. Two hundred households were sampled in each town. The work was commissioned by the Federal Housing Authority, the Federal Mortgage Bank, and the Federal Ministry of Works and Housing. (See Onibokun 1985.)

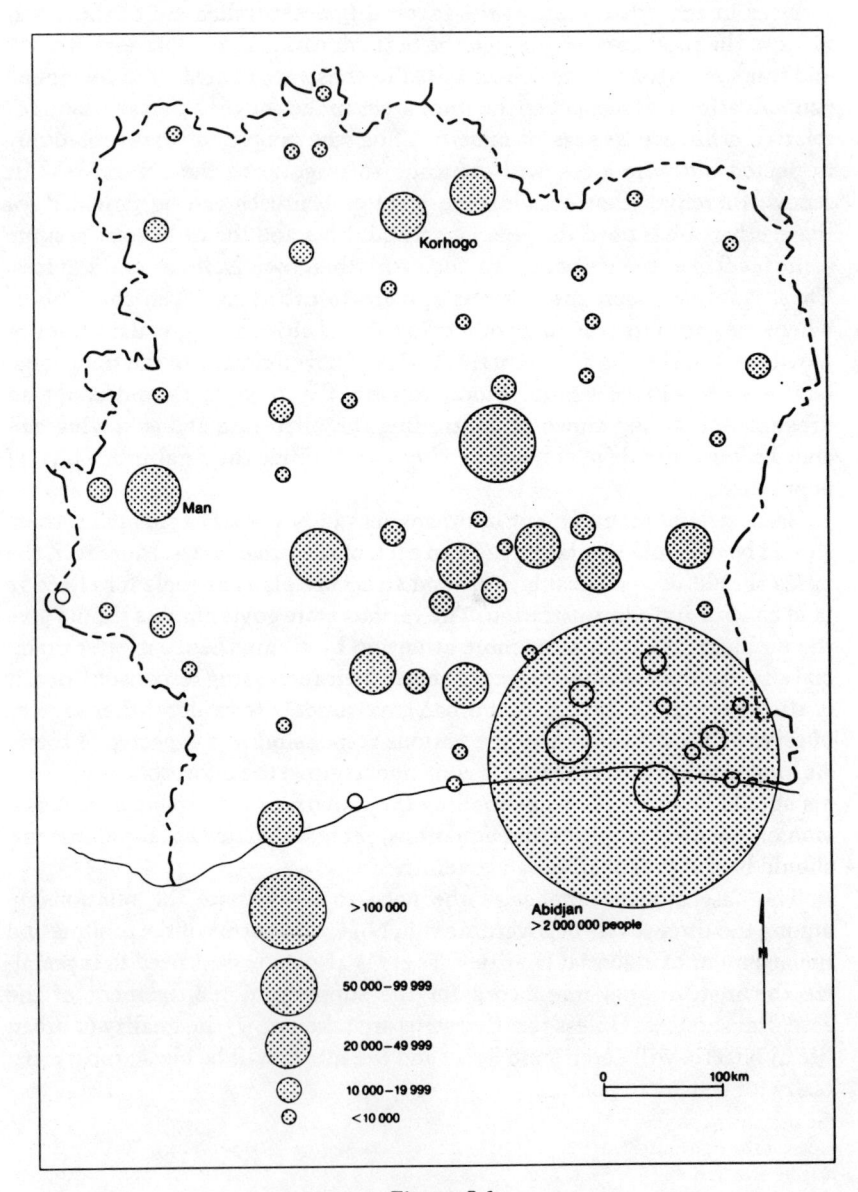

Figure 5.1
Côte d'Ivoire: Distribution of Urban Population

CHAPTER 5
Côte d'Ivoire: An Evaluation of Urban Management Reforms
Koffi Attahi

Introduction

The main aim of this study is to evaluate the first five years of operation of the reforms in the urban communes, which were undertaken in Côte d'Ivoire at the end of the 1970s. The first section analyzes the jurisdictions, management structures, as well as material, technical, and human resources of the Ivorian communes. The second section makes a similar analysis of the urban community, including the ten communes of the city of Abidjan. The third section presents a study of urban finances. The fourth section, after an examination of the exercise of authority of the decentralized communes, is an overall analysis of urban management reform.

Before beginning this study of urban management reform, it would be useful to locate this work within the perspective of the growing crisis in the provision of urban services and of the history of the development of local government bodies in Côte d'Ivoire. Since it achieved independence in 1960, Côte d'Ivoire has experienced an extremely rapid growth rate as a result of the combined effects of high levels of immigration and significant internal migration. Urban growth (10.5 percent per annum for Abidjan and 7.8 percent per annum for the towns in the interior) is clearly much higher than the rate of rural growth (2.3 percent per annum) and represents one of the most rapid rates of increase in this part of the continent. If present trends continue, by the year 2000 the urban population will have trebled in size. In 1984 there were 3.5 million urban inhabitants out of a total population of 8

I would like to thank Professors Stren and White, the administrators at IDRC in Ottawa and in Dakar, and the Ivorian Ministers of the Interior and of the Economy and Finance for having granted me their support. I would also like to thank the director of local municipalities, his colleague from the Treasury, and their collaborators; the mayors, town councillors, general secretaries, and persons responsible for the services of the communities visited; Mr. Gieger from the general secretariat for Administrative Reform and Mr. Kremien from the Treasury; Mr. N'Guessan, General Secretary of the City of Abidjan; the administrative staff of CRAU; and particularly the urban management team consisting of Loukou Brou, Koffi Enokou, Blaud Célestin, and Comoe Amoakon, all of whom are co-authors of this study. (Editors' note: this chapter was translated from the original French by Richard Stren, with assistance from Claire Letemendia.)

million. This urban population was roughly equally distributed between Abidjan – the economic capital of the country – and the towns of the interior. At this point, with fully forty-four percent of the country's population already urbanized, the problems related to such a massive urban expansion are becoming less and less manageable. Of these, the most central are employment, housing, infrastructural and superstructural facilities, and food and fuel provision.

Infrastructural and superstructural needs for the urban sector are massive. The country must provide housing, services, and social facilities for 250,000 to 300,000 new urban dwellers per year. In terms of housing alone, this implies a requirement for sixteen hundred hectares of land developed for construction and close to fifty thousand new dwellings per year. Just to cope with the problem of urban services, the state must make available significant financial resources. The case of the city of Abidjan is instructive. In order to guarantee the present level of facilities and services in Abidjan, the government must contribute nearly 100 billion CFA francs in investments yearly or close to forty percent of the Special Budget for Investment and Facilities (BSIE) of the nation. Confronted by this urban challenge, the government made some important political decisions during the 1970s. These decisions included the elaboration of a new urban policy, the reform of the urban administrative structure, and the transfer of the political capital of the country from Abidjan to Yamoussoukro.

Yet reform of urban management in Côte d'Ivoire had been initiated as early as the beginning of the colonial era. Grand-Bassam, on the eastern side of the lagoon, was in 1914 constituted as the first fully operating commune in the country. A year later, the city of Abidjan – slightly to the west – gained the hybrid status of "mixed commune." Not until 1952 could the third main town in the country, Bouaké, benefit from this status. These three communes were governed by regulations under the French municipal law of 1884, somewhat amended regarding the exercise of authority in order to be applicable to the colonies. To this initial framework was added the law of 18 November 1955, which allowed for only two categories of communes: one group involved the "full exercise" of powers in which the mayor was elected by a municipal council; and another group with "normal exercise" of powers was run by a mayor appointed by the state. The 1955 law gave the former "mixed" communes of Abidjan and Bouaké the status of "full exercise" communes and established the medium-sized towns of Daloa, Man, Gagnoa, Abengourou, Agboville, and Dimbokro as "normal exercise" communes. In line with the same decentralization initiative, the towns of Aboisso, Bondoukou, Adzopé, Dabou, Divo, Korhogo, Sassandra, and Ferké were given official status as "normal exercise" communes in 1959. Unfortunately, because of the absence of a decree enforcing application of the new regulations, this last group of communes was never able to function effectively.

In 1960, when the country was in the process of gaining national sovereignty, there were eight communes. But the new state did not judge it timely to encourage the movement towards municipalization launched earlier. Thus, in spite of the increase in problems resulting from a high level of urbanization, the state put a brake on the creation of new communes and refused to allow the release of funds necessary for the functioning of the smaller communes opened just before independence. Municipal elections were suspended. The management of "full exercise" communes was entrusted to designated mayors, and that of "normal exercise" communes fell to the charge of prefect-mayors representing the central government.

The failure to renew municipal councils and the absence of regular reforms of the municipal financial system resulted in the atrophying of municipal affairs in the country. Only in 1978 was a new law introduced to reorganize the communes. Under this legislation, twenty-seven towns in the interior and the ten main districts of Abidjan received the status of "full exercise" communes. A supra-municipal body was also instituted at the level of the Abidjan agglomeration itself – called the "City of Abidjan" – responsible for the co-ordination of regional development and the provision of certain services of regional interest to the population. Yet the new communes did not really begin to function effectively until the municipal elections of 1980. At that time, the new communes covered only 2,690,100 inhabitants or thirty percent of the total national population.

This chapter reports on a study of some of these newly-established communes. In addition to carrying out specialized studies of individual communes, our research team conducted interviews with officials from the Department of Local Government and from the treasuries of some of the communes. The sample selected, based on criteria of place, age, and size, included the communes of Man, Korhogo, Toumodi, Adjamé, Port-Bouët[1] and the City of Abidjan.

Functions, Structure, and Resources of the Municipalities
Functions
The wide jurisdictional range of the communes remains rather vague for the time being. Theoretically, all the jurisdiction exercised in the localities by the state and its decentralized administration should be gradually transferred to the communes. Several draft bills aiming to accomplish this are presently being studied by the General Secretariat of Administrative Reform. The new budgetary and accounting protocol of the communes takes this inevitable evolution into account; the communes now organize their activities into three categories: local government services, socio-cultural

and manpower services, and economic services. The so-called local government services essentially include highways and various road networks, town planning, the environment, hygiene, public sanitation, water supply, cemeteries, and funeral services. Socio-cultural and manpower services include national education, public health, welfare work, housing and accommodation, sports and leisure, and culture. As for the economic services, they include loans for agricultural and stock farming purposes, forestry, hunting and fishing, mineral resources, transport and communications, industry and trade, arts and crafts, and tourism. At present, the structures involved with these three service areas are essentially occupied by technical ministerial departments of the central government, together with the concessionary public service companies (such as the water and electricity companies).

Given the inadequate provision in the municipalities of qualified and experienced technicians and of material resources, as well as the low level of local budgets, the mayors are obliged to limit the range of their activities. There are few real functional conflicts; rather, communal action supplements the services of the state within the communal boundaries. Nevertheless, most of the mayors would like to have greater and more effective powers in the area of town planning and in the subdivision of land. For example, they feel that the state should permit them to assume the chairmanship of the land allocation committee presently in the hands of the prefects.

The effective exercise of municipal functions essentially involves three areas: public cleansing and urban planning; social services such as public health, education, and sports; and economic activities. As for urban planning and public cleansing services, the communes have exclusive power to collect and treat household refuse. They have sole responsibility for the establishment of plans (both master plans and operational plans, such as subdivisions) which are actually managed by the Ministry of Construction and Town Planning. They also provide fuel for the heavy construction machinery used for the maintenance of public roads. Interventions in the field of social activities, public health, and education are limited to planning and the construction of super-structural facilities (such as schools, dispensaries, and social centers) which are managed by the specialized technical ministries. Certain communes have some funds for helping the needy. Activities in the economic field involve the management of kiosks, markets, bus stations, abattoirs, swimming pools, and other facilities which generate funds for the communes. During the period immediately following the passage of the first legislation in 1978, communal involvement in these areas remained very modest, as they were not endowed with the means to essential the exercise of certain responsibilities. They carried out their functions according to the means available to them.

Political and Administrative Structures

In the analysis of municipal government structures, two levels must be distinguished: the political and the administrative. While the approach here is largely descriptive, I shall attempt, whenever possible, to go beyond pure description to see how municipal administration functions in reality. The Ivorian communes are regulated by Law No.80-1180 of 17 October 1980, which bears on municipal organization. According to the dispositions of this law, the government of a commune consists of two principal organs: the municipal council and the municipality.

The municipal council is in some respects the parliament of the city, the locus of debate on all political decisions relative to the conduct of the city's affairs. It is a body with a collegial character which expresses its autonomy through its own resolutions. The municipal council is composed of a mayor and a number of councillors, which is specified by law. This number varies with the size of the town. Municipal councillors are elected for a period of five years by direct, universal suffrage, through a list system with a single election. The municipal council meets for regular sessions three times a year under the chairmanship of the mayor, who may call special meetings whenever he feels this might be useful. All council meetings are open to the public.

The council regulates the affairs of the commune through its deliberations, ensures adequate living conditions for its population, intervenes in the planning of development activities in the city, and votes on and controls the implementation of the budget. The council comes under control of the central authorities, as it can be dissolved by a decree of the Council of Ministers; and some of its deliberations, notably those involving financial, economic, and fiscal matters, must be submitted for the approval of central government officials before they can be executed. Finally, municipal councils are helped by two standing committees: the committee for economic, financial, and public domain affairs; and the committee for social and cultural affairs.

The mayor and his assistants make up the executive body which constitutes what is commonly called the municipality in Côte d'Ivoire. They are elected by the municipal council at its first meeting. This election is by secret ballot; the winner by absolute majority is elected for a period of five years. The number of assistants to the mayor is proportional to the size of the commune.

The municipality is the intermediary between the municipal council and the services it provides. Among other things, it is responsible for the establishment of the agenda for council meetings, the coordination of development activities of the commune, the supervision of the collection of charges and various taxes, and the determination of the manner of implementation and of supervision of all communal works.

The mayor is the head of the municipal administration. Under the control of the central government and the councillors, the mayor prepares and sees to the carrying out of council deliberations. The mayor represents his commune before the courts and is responsible for the municipal police. Finally, he carries out the legal duties of a civil officer of the state.

In an attempt to avoid questionable recruitment, and to harmonize the structuring of municipal services, the Minister of the Interior, through a decree of March 1983, suggested the implementation of an organic structure which would apply to all communes. Highly simplified, this structure involved, in addition to the mayor's secretariat, four major departments under the control of a secretary-general. The typical organization chart of an Ivorian municipal administration would thus theoretically involve the following components: the mayor's secretariat, the staff of the secretary-general, the administrative department, the financial department, the technical department, and the archives. (The archives is a new section established by the central authorities to encourage communal officials to get used to collecting, distributing, and conserving official documents.) The proposed theoretical framework was respected by most of the communes visited in the course of this study, with the exception of Korhogo, which got slightly carried away in setting up a fifth department: socio-cultural affairs and manpower. The following sections explain the operation of the major municipal departments.

The mayor and his assistants are supported by a reasonably well-staffed secretariat. This office is generally directed by a chief officer (*chef de cabinet*). The responsibilities of this secretariat are wide and not very precise. They overlap in part with those of the secretary-general, a situation which constitutes a real and potential source of tension. The chief officer chosen by the mayor, often on the advice of the tutelary central authorities, handles "political" matters; looks after the implementation of instructions from central authorities, from the council, and from the municipality; registers and generally handles the confidential mail of the mayor; takes charge of protocol for public ceremonies and official receptions; and supervises the organization of council sessions. In most communes, the position of chief officer is filled by an administrative secretary trained at the National School of Administration. He is the privileged assistant, if not the personal nominee, of the mayor.

In two of the councils sampled, this post has not yet been filled. In the only interior commune at which the post was filled, the head of the archival service was the temporary chief officer. Moreover, in this same commune, under pressure from the mayor's assistants, the council refused the nomination of a central government officer to this post. The assistants to the mayor basically considered the responsibilities of this position to be theirs and not to be shared with a public servant. Such a notion of the exercise of this function on the part of the mayor's assistants can lead to an overlapping of responsibilities and create abnormal conflicts.

The general secretary is the intermediary between the municipality and its services. Under the authority of the mayor, the general secretary coordinates the activities of the municipal departments; maintains relationships with outside agencies; controls the implementation of instructions from the central government, the municipal council, and the municipality; sorts and examines the mail and prepares plans for correspondence; convokes the councillors, prepares for council meetings, maintains a secretariat for council sessions and for the meetings of the municipality; edits the minutes; and signs on behalf of the mayor for a certain category of correspondence. In fact, the general secretary supervises the municipal departments, holding regular meetings with departmental heads, coordinating budgetary estimates of the different departments, and directing the preparation and the implementation of both the initial budgets and the modified budgets. He presents to the municipality and council projects prepared by the departmental heads, as well as any decisions he thinks necessary to adopt in order to administer the commune effectively and economically.

In the absence of a legal counsellor, the general secretary gives an informed legal, administrative, and procedural point of view to the council and the municipality. This strategic position of general secretary has been filled in all the communes sampled by administrative cadres trained to the mid-superior level of the National School of Administration (equivalent to two years of higher education). In one of the communes sampled in the greater Abidjan area, this key post remains vacant after having had three occupants in less than four years. The functions of the position are discharged by the chief cabinet officer and the chief financial officer. Such a high level of turnover brings out real problems of collaboration.

The department of administration involves the following functions: the administration of personnel, civil law and the legalization of documents, the military bureau, the establishment and up-dating of electoral lists, youth and sports activities, and social and cultural activities. In the communes visited, only the sections relating to personnel administration and civil law were functioning. Personnel administration was working only partially, since the absence of a single statute for municipal administration has led to a situation whereby one part of the communal personnel is not under its jurisdiction.

Three categories of municipal employees may be identified: employees recruited and put at the disposition of the communes by the central government public service and paid out of the state budget, employees seconded by the communes, and employees recruited by and under the direct control of the communes. The first category is made up essentially of municipal officers. Their present perspective is not very appealing since they do not yet have a defined career path. While they await the statute covering municipal personnel, which would spell out rules and clarify choices, those within the local government system in charge of managing the communal personnel, along with the sub-section dealing with commune personnel in the Department of Local Government (Ministry of the Interior) are trying as best they can to provide municipal councillors, municipalities, and local department heads with the information necessary for rational and efficient management of their human resources. Unfortunately, because of a lack of qualified staff, the essence of their work concerns the management of new postings, the authorizations for absence from work, administrative leave, penalties, and nominations and promotions.

The drawing up and up-dating of electoral lists and the maintenance of the military bureau continue to occupy the time of the sub-prefecture of the central administration. As for sport and youth as well as for social and cultural activities, the municipal agencies which give support here are rudimentary, except at Korhogo where they are attached to a regular department. In the sectors where the presence of decentralized central government services is marked, the communes are involved in building social facilities and in subsidizing demonstrations. This important service is run by an administrative secretary.

The finance department is the most developed of communal departments. It is often run by an administrative secretary, assisted by officials who have specialized training in accounting. These officials look after sections which deal with the accounting of receipts, expenses, budgets, and accountable advances. This department faces a number of problems. Financial officials are only now starting to familiarize themselves with the new budgetary and financial procedures which have been in force in the communes since 1984. The application of these procedures has given rise to some hesitation on the part of communal authorities and agents of municipal services, who find them too complex and sophisticated. They have little experience in methods of estimating receipts because in all of the communes the level of collection based on budgetary provisions is low.

The archives exist in almost all the communes, but rarely function under the supervision of a full-time official. Quite often the chief of administrative services looks after this office on an interim basis. In spite of the importance which officials in the Department of Local Government accord to this service, it is still perceived by communal officials as of minor importance.

The technical services department is a strategic office since it constitutes the principal means of active intervention by the communes. In principle, the structure of this office includes the following sections: maintenance and hygiene; public and other road networks; town planning, housing, and research; and the garage. Because of a shortage of materials and qualified personnel, this department functions at a barely adequate level; its services have been reduced to the collection of household refuse, the cleaning of markets, and the maintenance of roads. The department is generally supervised by a public works technician. It has been called on to grow rapidly in most communes, since the analysis of purchases by the communes in 1983 and 1984 shows that most of their investments involved equipment for the technical services. The Ministry of Public Works, Transport, and Town Planning has begun seconding engineers and senior technicians to head up these local departments. It remains only to draw up a protocol of official collaboration between the technical municipal departments, on the one hand, and the services of the technical ministries (public works, town planning, and construction) and the concessionary companies which deal with urban public services, on the other hand.

Human, Material, and Technical Resources
At the beginning of 1985, two censuses carried out by the Ministry of the Public Service and the Department of Local Government gave the following results: central government civil service – 110,839 employees; municipal public service – 6,838 employees, of which 317 or 4.63 percent are seconded to the communes by the state. Of all municipal employees, 1,150 or 16.81 percent work for the City of Abidjan.

Next to the small number of seconded central government employees working at the local level, the largest contingent of communal personnel – 6,521 employees – was recruited directly and is under the control of the communes. The municipal public service is insignificant compared to the central government and is rather unevenly distributed amongst the communes since it is not proportional to the size of the population in each commune. In the communes visited, the ratio of the number of employees per 1,000 inhabitants varies from 4.90 for the small commune of Toumodi to 1.68 for the commune of Cocody. Surprisingly, and in spite of all efforts, the old and relatively rich communes of the Abidjan area – Adjamé, Cocody, and even the City of Abidjan – show the lowest ratios, 1.78, 1.68, and 0.50 respectively.

In general, communal employees are under-qualified. With the exception of those seconded to the communes by the state, almost all of the employees recruited by the mayors lack proper qualifications. In the communes visited, all the heads of department make this comment and complain of this situation, which very often forces them to carry through jobs themselves from conception to implementation. They attribute this to the lack of seriousness surrounding the reorganization of municipal personnel in the euphoric post-election atmosphere. Often mentioned were cases of sacking to "get even" with municipal employees who did not know enough to act neutrally during the elections; also mentioned was recruitment based on electoral criteria and nepotism rather than on objective competence.

Only the employees seconded to the communes – general secretaries and other department heads – have benefitted from a high level of training acquired in major professional schools such as the National School of Administration (ENA) and the National Upper School of Public Works (ENSTP). Yet they represent only 2.5 percent (Man) and 6 percent (Toumodi) of local personnel. After them comes the group with a secondary school diploma, office workers who often have, in addition, a professional diploma (accountancy, finance, secretarial service, or construction). Their importance in local departments varies from as little as 3.5 percent (Korhogo) to 12 percent (Toumodi). They are essentially office managers, supervising the work of ordinary office workers. Then comes the support staff with a full primary school education: simple office workers, typists, and ordinary clerks. They make up close to one-quarter of the staff and carry out their work under the direction of the departmental heads. The rest of the municipal personnel is composed of staff with no education whatsoever: illiterates. These people are laborers, guards, drivers, and janitors. They represent from 61 to 68 percent of the total number of municipal staff.

The division of communal personnel according to function gives some idea of the importance of the different departmental services. It varies considerably and demonstrates the primacy of the technical services. These departments employ almost 67 percent of the total staff while the financial and administrative departments share what remains, at 17.5 percent and 15.5 percent respectively.

The technical municipal services, moreover, are deficient in staff with obvious conceptual ability, such as engineers, architects, and town planners. By contrast, the administrative and financial services are run by seconded administrators or financial officers and accountants, as well as by administrative or financial officers. Under these conditions, it is difficult for the technical departments to take charge of projects. In many cases, these technical departments are poorly equipped to supervise the small planning projects for which they are trustees.

The communal staff is still waiting for a new statute. Such a statute should, in principle, regulate recruitment and the conditions of promotion of staff and define their rights and duties. If such a statute is to attract and retain highly qualified and experienced people, it must make certain provisions, including (1) a guarantee of the movement of staff from one commune to another; (2) a guarantee of parity with central government public servants and a "bridge" permitting movement between the central public service and the municipal public service; and (3) protection for local government staff against unfair removal (which can result from difficulties in working with certain mayors and councillors). The third condition might be obtained through the imposition of a minimal length of time for any posting and a maximum number of displacements of department heads to which the mayor would have a right during the course of a single term. Finally, at the present time, given the limitations on local government budgets, local authorities would experience real difficulties if the Minister for the public service carried out his idea of taking over control of seconded civil servants by controlling communal budgets.

The level of needs insofar as the material and technical resources of local governments is concerned is enormous. Many municipalities do not even have offices in which to house their departments after elections. This is why the most important elements in the investment plans of many local authorities involves the planning and equipment of offices. The level of equipment within the offices of the communes visited is satisfactory. Municipal technical services, however, are very under-equipped in terms of material resources. The three interior communes visited – Man, Toumodi, and Korhogo – have one maintenance vehicle for 7,436, 2,731, and 6,756 inhabitants respectively. The small commune of Toumodi seems to be the best equipped, although it has no grader and both Man and Korhogo have one. Man has also a steamshovel and a compactor vehicle.

With respect to technical means and other management tools, only the twenty communes involved in the study sample on urbanization in Côte d'Ivoire have any urban statistics at all, and these are already out of date. A significant effort was made to produce town planning documents (master plans and program plans), but unfortunately their implementation leaves a lot to be desired at the local level. Most of the program plans, for example, have not been used beyond the drawing up of triennial plans required by the central authority.

The local authorities lack the proper maps to plan at different scales, to undertake aerial photographs, and to bring the land registers up to date. As for management instruments, the local authorities have a whole arsenal of legal texts, decrees, and other such documents. They have all been obliged to operate under a totally new budgetary system; they must also present a three-year investment plan every year. These two instruments permit the rationalization of their activities and the execution of comparative analyses of their management. The communes are starting to become familiar with these new requirements.

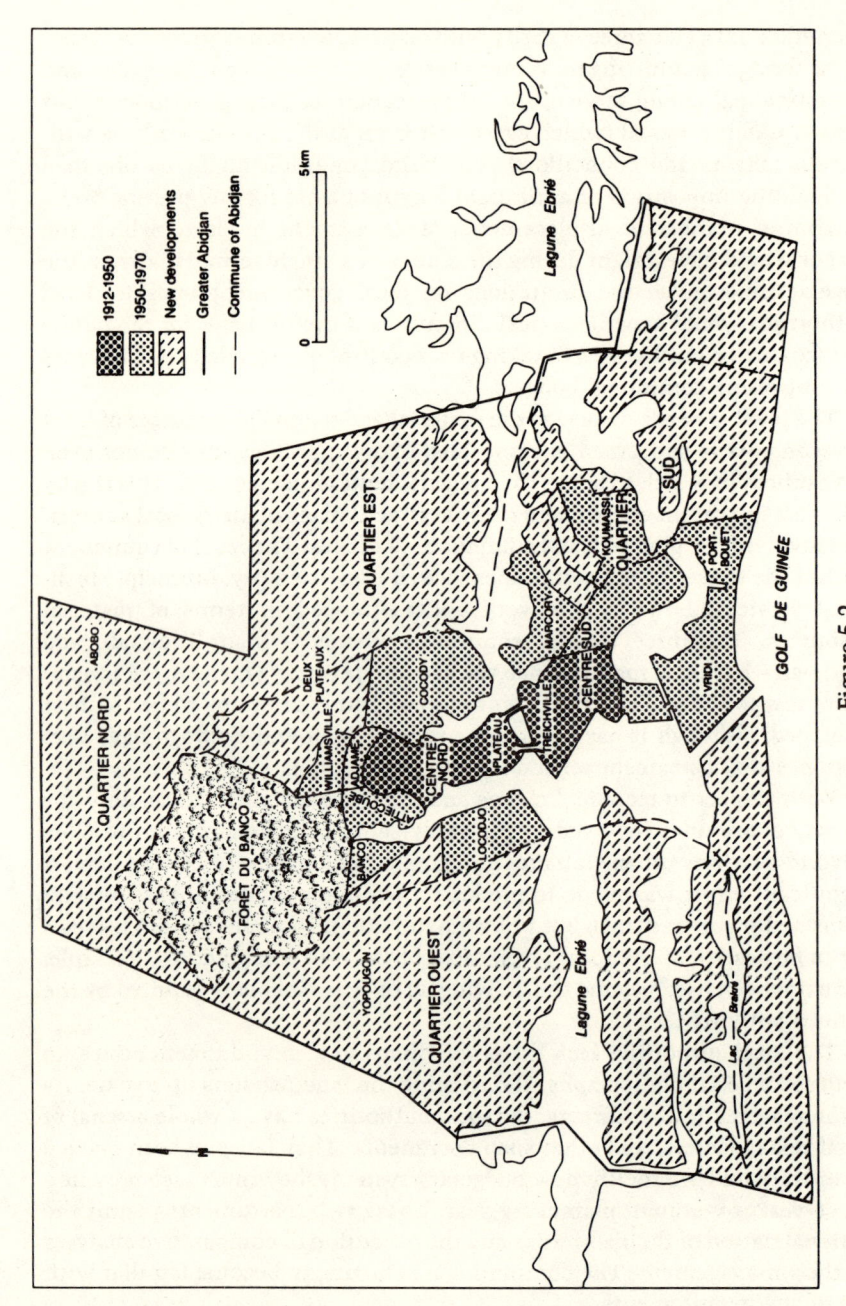

Figure 5.2
The Growth of Abidjan

Functions, Structures, and Resources of the City of Abidjan

The City of Abidjan is a territorial community with legal authority and financial autonomy. Composed of the ten communes of the greater Abidjan area, it is in fact a supra-municipal authority, created to deal with problems which go beyond individual municipal administrations without threatening the autonomy of these local authorities.

Functions and Powers

The City of Abidjan has defined responsibilities for the provision of urban services, forming an intermediary governmental unit between the communes and the central government. Nevertheless, its powers in relation to the communes remain rather vague. The law has not established a precise hierarchical order between the two levels of local government. There is, rather, a simple sharing of functions between the communes and the City of Abidjan without a real sharing of power. In fact, the communes of the greater Abidjan area have not lost their authority but have simply given up providing those services which the law considers of general importance to the whole urban area. Moreover, in the final analysis, the sharing of power is very limited, since the City of Abidjan is a federal-type body, controlled by the individual communes through their representatives on the City Council. The power of the City is therefore that which the municipalities are prepared to recognize. Although the state has conferred certain powers on the City, the exercise of these powers must be submitted in the last resort to the control of the municipalities. The City Council which adopts these regulations passes the budget and establishes the urban service departments.

The present unfortunate economic climate has not permitted the state to adhere to its original program of transferring powers. At present, the central administration continues to discharge certain functions, either as a result of the biases of the central technical departments or as a result of the bias of the urban public utility companies. The movement to transfer powers will gain momentum, however, and on this basis the City of Abidjan is developing and restructuring its departments. The powers already conferred on the City correspond roughly to those exercised by bodies known elsewhere as "urban communities" or "urban districts." They are strictly technical powers.

The present structure of the division of powers and the exercise of these powers among the state, the city, and the public utility companies does not present a coherent approach to urban problems. The technical departments of the City are confronted with a real problem of coordination emerging from all the policies and actions taken separately within the City's boundaries. Conscious of the danger which this lack of coordination represents in the longer term, the City of Abidjan has shown a desire to control and coordinate the activities of several large public utility companies. But it was quickly made known to the City that the exercise of certain functions, such as the provision of water and electricity as well as the construction of sewers, was not within the power of local authorities. The City must be satisfied with a simple right to take note of the activities of these companies, since it sits on their boards of directors.

Political and Administrative Structures
The political structures of the City of Abidjan are made up of its two decision-making organs, the council and the municipality. The Council of the City of Abidjan is the principal decision-making organ of the city. It is composed of the mayor of the City of Abidjan, the mayors of the ten communes of the greater Abidjan area, and of the fifty councillors elected by the ten municipal councils of the city, with five councillors for each council.

This system of representation has the advantage of putting every commune of the city on an equal footing in the Council, without consideration of demographic or financial weight. In introducing this theoretical equality amongst all of the communes, the system of representation has contributed to reducing potential tensions between the rich centrally-located communes and the poorer peripheral communes over the division of the tax revenues for the whole area.

The Council of the City of Abidjan deliberates over public matters involving its functions. The principal areas over which the City Council has exclusive or predominant responsibility are: (1) investments and development activities of the City; (2) loans; (3) the road system, traffic, and parking; (4) urban planning; (5) urban street lighting; (6) the regulation and development of public and private transport over the whole city area; (7) regulation of the public lands and properties; (8) planning, management and supervision of cemeteries; (9) the organization of first aid and firefighting services; and (10) the naming of streets, squares, and urban buildings. The municipal councils comprising the city are informed of the decisions and regulations decided upon by the City Council and must be consulted on any City project.

The Municipality of the City of Abidjan discharges the executive power of the city; it is composed of the mayor of the City and his assistants. The mayor of Abidjan is elected by the mayors of the communes of the city and the councillors elected by the different city councils. The mayor presides over the Municipality. Only the mayors of the Abidjan communes can be candidates for the mayorship of Abidjan. After having been elected, the new mayor loses his post in the commune and is replaced by a newly elected mayor. The present terms of the law do not provide for a hierarchical order between the assistants and the mayor. They all have the same status. The Municipality of the City of Abidjan meets at least once per month. Its functions are to carry out the decisions of the City Council, with the exception of police regulations; to prepare for Council meetings; to prepare and execute the City's budget; and to manage the revenues and the property of the City.

The mayor of the City of Abidjan represents the state, and as such he is responsible for the publication and the implementation of the laws, regulations, and decisions of the government; the implementation of public security measures; and the carrying out of economic development, social, and cultural policies defined by the government. In addition, in his role of representative of the City of Abidjan, the mayor chairs the meetings of the Council and of the Municipality, publishes the deliberations of the City Council, implements police regulations in the City, signs and executes Municipal decisions, directs the municipal administration and organizes the City budget, and supervises the accounts of the City in conformity with legal requirements.

The first organization chart of the City was established and adopted in 1981 in order to take back the functions which the state was supposed to transfer to the City in conformity with the spirit of the municipal reform. But with the economic crisis, the state felt it had to delay the transfer of certain functions. Thus, an incongruity developed between the structure of the departments of the City and the actual discharge of its functions. From that time onward, it was necessary to reorganize the services of the City as a response to the concern of the central authorities to bring the expenses of the City's services more into line with its means. The new organization chart restricted itself to the maintenance of traditional functions and to the establishment of those technical structures indispensable to the carrying out of the City's mandate.

The mayor is in charge of the municipal administration. He has the right to supervise and control all the staff working for the City. In spite of this heavy responsibility, he is not obliged by law to exercise his functions on a full-time basis. The mayor is assisted by an office which consists of his own secretariat, a mail office, and a number of technical counsellors. Six sections contribute to the functioning of his office: the office of external relations, the office of ceremonies and holidays, the press office, the office of the municipal bulletin, the security service of city hall, and the management office for city hall.

Under the mayor's authority is the general secretary who coordinates all the services of the city. His role involves seeing to the implementation of the mayor's instructions as well as those of the city council and the government; assuring that legal procedures and regulations are duly followed; attempting to improve the delivery of urban services; maintaining a secretariat for city council sessions and for municipal meetings in addition to preparing the minutes of these meetings; and, in general, planning, organizing, directing, controlling, and supervising the activities of the municipal administration. As this list suggests, the general secretary is the leading official of the urban administration. He maintains the link between the council, the municipality, and the officials and employees of the City. He supervises and takes responsibility for all the departments, officials, and employees of the City. He supervises the execution of the budget and attends to the rigorous observation of legal requirements, regulations, and decisions of the council and the government. This post is held by a public administrator selected from the ranks of the prefectoral administration. Five main departments are directly under the general secretary, namely: the Department of Management, Organization, and Methods; the Department of Tourism and Promotion; the Department of Youth and Sport; the Department of Culture and Education; and the Documentation Service. To assist him in his work, the general secretary of the City is seconded in his work by five functional offices and one general department of planning, called to coordinate the activities of the three technical departments.

The Department of General Administration involves three sections: a personnel unit which deals with questions of management of communal personnel; an ordinance section which handles specific aspects of personnel management involving retirements, work-related accidents, and union relations (this section is also in charge of litigation and archives); and a medical section which gives medical services to communal personnel and their families. The Finance Department has three sections: the expenditures section which takes on, specifies, and pays the expenses of the City in addition to preparing draft budgets; the receipts section which organizes the collection of the City's revenues, proposes other sources of revenue, and suggests means of improving the level of tax recovery; and the accountancy section, involved with the procurement, management, and distribution of nonspecialized materials as well as looking after the execution of contracts for public markets.

The Planning and Technical Coordination Headquarters is concerned with the planning of investments, with relations with agencies and technical enterprises associated with the City (such as the urban planning agency of Abidjan and SECI – the Infrastructure Company of Côte d'Ivoire), with the management of contractual services, and with the coordination of municipal technical services. Two sections are directly attached to this office. The first is the concessionary section, which oversees the activities of the urban services contracted out by the City or the state to private companies (the refuse removal company, the bus company, the water company, the electricity company). The second is the research section, which carries out technical studies, develops urban and architectural policies, and discharges the City's functions in the areas of construction permits, planning certificates, and the like. It also prepares estimates and tender documents. In addition, the Works Department has four sections: roads, building, equipment, and garage; the Food Hygiene Department manages the city slaughterhouses, controls sanitary standards for food supplies, and deals with stray animals; and the Environment Department manages park areas, cemeteries, and sports facilities in the city.

Human, Material, and Technical Resources of the City of Abidjan
The revised budget of the City of Abidjan which appeared in May 1985 showed 1,090 staff in the service of the City, representing a ratio of 0.56 municipal staff per 1,000 inhabitants. This rather low ratio may be explained by three factors. First, one of the functions which absorbs a lot of permanent labor, the removal of household refuse, is sub-contracted out to the SITAF (Industrial Company for African Transport), which itself employs around one thousand people. Second, the City of Abidjan is, in fact, no more than a structure of technical services. Finally, over the whole City area, three levels of government (supra-municipal, municipal, and central government) share urban functions.

Classifying the City's staff according to function provides a revealing picture the nature of the City administration: a structure of coordination and purely technical services. In fact, although the refuse removal services have been separated from the technical services, the latter employs 75.5 percent of the City's staff. Then come the administrative and financial services with, respectively, 14.77 and 9.63 percent of the total. The low profile of these two functions may be explained by the fact that funds arising from the fees accruing to the Civil Registry Office and the collection of various taxes are the prerogative of the ten communes. Thus, the administrative and financial agencies serve mostly as supports to the technical role of the City government.

The level of technical qualification of staff working for the City of Abidjan is higher than that of staff in the communes. Senior and middle-level staff with university degrees represent 4.86 percent of the total; then come technical staff with a secondary school diploma at 11.13 percent; and finally, a group with four years of secondary training at 13.3 percent. Support staff with primary school diplomas make up 21 percent, and illiterate workers (without diplomas) such as drivers, laborers, and equipment operators represent almost half the staff (49.31 percent). It is important to note that, unlike the situation in the communes, officials seconded to the City of Abidjan by the central government receive all their income and benefits from the City. The main exception to this rule is French overseas aid workers who benefit only from a housing allowance.

At present, the technical departments of the City are still building up in manpower, since City officials understand that the City will not be in a position effectively to carry out its mandate unless it can have at its disposal qualified technicians and managers who are respected by their counterparts in government agencies and, in particular, by their counterparts in the public utility companies. For example, the City does not have the resources or the means to audit efficiently the costs and fees paid to the company which collects refuse (SITAF), so that its costs have started to escalate. Thus, the payments to SITAF, which already took almost half of the City's resources (forty-nine percent) in 1981, represented as much as fifty-eight percent of the City's budget in 1983. The central government then instructed the Department of Major Projects (attached to the President's Office) to inspect SITAF on behalf of the City. But certain City officials realize that this Department has a tendency to take over the agencies which it inspects, while presenting itself as an intermediary between the City and "its" concessionary company. On the other hand, the fee for garbage removal is incorporated in the electricity bill. According to an agreement, the Electric Energy Company of the Ivory Coast (EECI), the sole utility for the production and distribution of electricity in the country, was supposed to turn these payments over to the City. Yet, knowing full well that the City could take only symbolic action against it, the EECI demonstrated bad faith in the execution of this undertaking. The City was forced, as a reprisal, to suspend payment on its own electricity bill for street lighting in order to pressure the EECI to live up to its agreement.

The City is well provided with material resources. Its fleet of vehicles consists of thirty-four light vehicles and sixty-four heavy vehicles as well as twenty-one construction vehicles, including six levelers, six loaders, six compactors, two bulldozers, and one excavator. This equipment is used for construction work, repairs, and the upkeep of properties and roads in the city. In principle, the maintenance of national roadways and communal roads is the responsibility of the state and of the communes. But given the limited means of the communes, the City helps out the communes.

The City also has two technical agencies attached to it: the Town Planning Agency of Abidjan (AUA) and SECI. AUA basically replaces the former Urban Planning Workshop for the Abidjan Area (AURA), which used to function within the National Office for Technical Studies of Development (BNETD), and then within the Central Office for Technical Studies (BCET) until they were dissolved in 1977 and 1980 respectively. According to its director,

> ... it is a lightly administered unit for reflection and synthesis. If it is to play an essential role in assembling, organizing and diffusing information about the

development of Abidjan, it is obviously not designed to deal with all of the problems which arise, nor to perform all research necessary (Belliot 1984, 4).

The agency has inherited a quantity of documentation emerging from the relatively venerable urban planning tradition in Abidjan. At the end of 1984, the agency possessed a staff of fourteen people, of which most of the six officials (including an engineer-urban planner, an urban architect, an urban planner, and a landscaper) were provided through French overseas aid. It has just been placed under the authority of the Department of Major Projects. Its research team regularly publishes an information bulletin. SECI for its part is in charge of developing urban lands and providing them with services and facilities. This agency has just been put under the control of the City and is now going to take the place of SETU (the Company for Urban Land and Infrastructure) in order to achieve more effectively the objectives of urban infrastructural policy.

Municipal Finance
The Structure of Municipal Financial Resources

Municipal financial resources in Côte d'Ivoire derive from five sources: tax receipts, receipts from fees and services, revenues from public property and investments, grants and other forms of aid, and miscellaneous sources. An examination of these sources sets the stage for a more detailed analysis of the determination of tax levels, their recovery, and the organization of municipal budgets. As in many other African countries, questions of taxation and financial resources are absolutely central to the effective operation of municipal administration. Côte d'Ivoire has already gone a long way in integrating the collection of its local resources with the administrative processes of decentralization.

Before the municipal reforms, the state had the responsibility to set taxes and to recover a large part of the tax resources of the municipalities. Since then, however, various responsibilities have been specified. Thus, by distinguishing according to the different levels of government involved with the determining and recovery of duties and taxes, two types of municipal revenues can be identified: revenues set and recovered by the state (Department of Taxation and the Treasury); and revenues established and collected by the communes.

Local taxes determined and collected by central government agencies have traditionally been divided into two categories. First, land taxes include seven taxes and fees, the total of which is the net revenue from properties. They can be further divided into two groups: tax on built land and tax on unbuilt land. The taxes on developed land include: the land-based share of developed properties (ten percent of net revenue), a surtax on insufficiently developed properties, refunds on the tax on property in mortmain, the tax on the net revenue of built property (five percent of net revenue), and a road and health tax (0.5 percent of net revenue). The tax on unbuilt land is made up of the land-based share of tax on unbuilt property and of the road and health tax. The second category of local taxes consists of business taxes and licenses. They include the products of business taxes (*la patente*), additional taxes and licence fees collected in the communes and systematically paid to the communes since 1982. The tax on betting for the City of Abidjan falls under this category.

Taxes set and collected by the local authorities consist of the following: a fixed fee for small traders and artisans, a tax on premises rented on a furnished basis, a tax imposed on communally-based revenues, and a tax on revenues imposed by the communes or by the City of Abidjan. The tax on revenues is made up of individual taxes on transport, advertising, sporting events, shows and night clubs, and the like.

Revenues from fees and services are an independent source of funds for the communes. They are mainly composed of remunerative taxes or income collected by the communes on the basis of services performed for the sole use of individuals or groups. The communes have the right to set the level of these fees and to organize the method of collection. They consist of revenue from general services, from local government services, from social and cultural services, and from economic services.

Income from public property consists of revenue from the leasing of land and buildings, from agricultural and industrial concessions, from other commune property, and from temporary use of public property. Income from the portfolio comes from communal investments in private or mixed enterprises, term and equity investments, and sales.

Subsidies and grants are being reduced at the present to grants for service paid by the state and to grants and other contributions by the state and other central government bodies for the purposes of the investment budget.

Miscellaneous receipts do not fit into the categories prescribed by the accounting system, such as money left over from previous operations, accidental revenue, and the like.

Organizing the Setting and Collection of Fees and Taxes

Since 1983 the Land Registry Department has been given the job of keeping the plot information up to date for the purpose of evaluating the land tax as well as the business tax, licenses, and other government taxes. Two filing systems – one having to do with the occupant of the land and the other with the owner of the land – contain files bearing on pertinent questions, such as changes of address and in family status, description of the properties, dates of the beginning and the end of exemptions, declarations of local estimates, and leaseholds. Once these records are carefully filled out, they are returned to the Land Registry Department which proceeds then to evaluate the properties and to establish rolls and notices. This stage takes account of temporary exemptions from tax, which are accorded to those undertaking new construction over a period of from five to twenty-five years.

Following the dispositions of Article 175 of the general tax code of Côte d'Ivoire, all land rent in taxes which is less than 21,000 CFA francs is automatically cancelled. The rolls and notices are then transmitted to the Treasury, which passes them to the municipal finance officers who also act as receivers. The latter send the tax notices by post to those taxpayers with an exact address. Notices which are not accompanied by a postal address are often remitted by hand by agents who track down the recipients. The taxpayers, once they have received their notices, must come to pay their taxes personally at the cashier's office. The cashier deposits the taxes in the account of the communes in question. Every two weeks, the cashier (*percepteur*) must fill out a form recapitulating all the taxes deposited, copies of which he sends to the commune in question and to the Treasury (section dealing with local government). The rate of recovery for both the business tax and the land tax is not particularly high. The land tax was paid at the rate of 32.17 percent in 1983, while business taxes and licenses were paid at the rate of 60.50 percent, for an overall rate of repayment of 46.57 percent.

The economic crisis of 1984 severely affected the recovery of business taxes and licenses and of the land tax, which were repaid at a rate of 51.12 percent and 20.91 percent respectively, for an overall rate of 35.99 percent. A number of factors combined to explain the weakness in recovering these two taxes. First, the target tax collection rate of sixty percent set by national tax headquarters, maintained by the Treasury for communal budgetary provisions, seems too high and unrealistic given the socio-cultural environment and the present economic climate. Second, the land tax is too high for the category of citizens who are asked to pay it. When the 15.5 percent constituted by local land taxes is added to the twenty-two percent of state taxes (service tax of ten percent, National Investment Fund tax of ten percent, and national contribution of two percent), the land tax represents, in total, 37.5 percent of the rental value of properties. This leads to some reluctance to pay. A third factor is that the conditions for repayment are not the best. One out of three Treasury offices which we visited in the course of our field work did not even have qualified staff to look after repayment. The two other offices can count on the services of only a single officer to locate errant taxpayers for a whole zone covering several cities. These officers are not even given vehicles or fuel for their work. They are thus obliged to wait for the taxpayers to come in and pay what they owe. Finally, there is no commission paid on the basis of returns for these officials. The municipal tax collectors are not held responsible for the level of tax recovery.

In addition, a number of smaller details were brought out in our investigations. For example, rolls and notices arrive late at the Treasury, with a rather high proportion of documents (ten to fifteen percent) without any postal address attached; these must be delivered by hand by the official collector. Again, at least one-tenth of the stamped envelopes come back to the Treasury marked "unknown at this address" – no doubt largely a result of the lack of honesty of certain landowners. And it is not easy to find the legal basis for pursuing errant taxpayers. The municipal collectors with whom we spoke noted that no Ivorian statute specifies the procedures for tracking down taxpayers; the collectors must look to French texts for this. Moreover, the quality of information is poor. Often the information contained in taxpayers' files is not up to date and does not reflect the real situation on the ground. As an example, the taxpayers whom we visited pointed out that, since the abolition of administrative leases by the state in 1983, they have lost more than half their revenue on built property; but the tax headquarters has not even realized this loss, since they continue to send out the same tax notices. Yet landlords are victims of poor information, since they have the right to a reduction in tax if they can produce documents showing a loss in income. They even mentioned the case of a businessman in Danané whose shops were closed following an official procedure in 1981, but who continued to receive notices for the business tax in 1985.

Beyond these rather technical points, the municipal collectors also claimed that there is no real political initiative to improve the level of tax recovery. They pointed out that it is, above all, the high state officials and important political personalities in the towns, exactly those people who should set an example of virtuous civic behavior, who refuse to pay their taxes. Tax collectors are powerless against these people because of their political contacts. Foreigners, on the other hand, are exemplary taxpayers, they said, perhaps because of their precarious status in the country.

Finally, the potential level of tax recovery for the land tax is negatively affected by two factors. First, there is the absence of land registers or the failure to bring existing registers up to date regularly. For example, the establishment of a simple register in the commune of Toumodi permitted that particular small local authority to increase the level of receipts sevenfold. Although the communal authorities in Toumodi questioned the results of this operation, the land tax base has definitely expanded in spite of some mistakes. Second, the excessive length of time given for tax exemptions to rental dwellings built by public development companies affects the level of returns. This is particularly the case in those Abidjan communes with the characteristics of "new towns" – such as Yopougon and Port-Bouët – where there has been very substantial development.

The organization of tax recovery by municipal departments varies according to whether taxes are set on the basis of a tax roll or whether they are based on evidence of receipts in the hands of the taxpayer. The major tax received through the tax rolls is the basic fixed tax for small merchants and artisans, which is imposed in all communes at rates determined by standards prescribed in the Finance Law. All the communes visited have a register of small businessmen and artisans who are not yet subject to the more elaborate business tax (*la patente*). They must pay monthly or even daily sums, either to the financial managers of the communes or to mobile collectors. The financial managers say that the level of recovery of these taxes is improving.

Taxes received on the basis of evidence of receipts are the most numerous. They are set by the communes, but the rate of taxation depends on specifications on permissible ceilings in the Finance Law. Generally, the communes keep ten percent of receipts on film shows, concerts, and sports events. Levels of service taxes vary with the services in question; civil registration fees run from 200 CFA francs for legalizations to 4,000 CFA francs for marriages. Parking rights and the occupation of space in bus stations along with taxi fees vary with the towns and with the number of seats available in the vehicles in question (from 200 CFA francs to 1,000 CFA francs per day). Places in the markets vary on average from 100 CFA francs to 150 CFA francs per day, depending on whether the subject occupies a covered or uncovered spot.

In all the communes visited the procedure of collecting tax is the same: the municipal receiver advances tickets to the revenue manager. The latter is personally responsible to the former. The manager gives up his tickets to the collectors, who are responsible for distributing them to the taxpayers in return for payments. Every day that the office is open the collectors must come in to deposit the money they have collected during the afternoon. The manager, in turn, deposits the moneys collected with the municipal receiver every two days. The receipts manager is responsible for all the taxes collected by the commune. For this, he receives a bonus (30,000 CFA francs in Man, for example). In Man, the collectors earn 40,000 CFA francs per month and can earn an additional commission of two percent every three months on the receipts they bring in.

The collectors often complain of their conditions of work. For example, those who are assigned to collect the fixed fee from small businessmen and artisans point out that the lack of transport (by which they mean bicycles or motorcycles) adversely affects their productivity. Others who work at the markets are constantly exposed to bad manners, insults, and threats of all kinds. They also speak of attacks by traders and especially by female hawkers. They lack suitable working equipment (such as uniforms, boots, bags, and even umbrellas). And they have difficulty scraping through narrow market lanes where there is no room to pass.

For their part, the managers point to fraud and irregularities in the work of the collectors. The most common fraudulent practice involves selling tickets of a value less than what should be paid, and pocketing a bribe in return. Some collectors simply fail to place tickets at the stalls of their friends, and are rewarded either in money or in kind. To limit irregular practices, the managers have instituted controls over tickets issued to third persons. Also, they frequently rotate the collectors. In Korhogo, for example, the main market was divided by the tax manager into twenty-three sectors, and the twenty-three collectors operated in different sectors every day, so that they did not return to the sector from which they started until twenty-three days later. The organization of work in this manner to prevent the development of friendship or under-the-table business interests between the collectors and taxpayers, as well as the control of tickets, has definitely contributed to reducing the level of fraud in the system. However, in one of the communes studied, the collectors themselves noted the practice of subletting stalls in the market.

In general, then, the development of municipal revenues has begun to take off. The transfers of resources which the transfers of functions are going to require will consolidate the communal revenue base. The state itself set the tone in 1982 through opting to reverse completely the direction of revenue derived from land tax and business taxes away from itself to the communes. But in spite of everything, much is left to do; in 1983 communal revenues were 9,700 million CFA francs or only 2.22 percent of the 435,250 million CFA francs collected by the state as total tax revenue.

Financial Analysis of the Budgets and Accounts of the Communes
An analysis of the structural evolution of the overall levels of the budgets of the communes and the City of Abidjan first shows a decline in the weight of the City of Abidjan, benefitting the other communes, especially the ten communes of Abidjan. Thus, in 1981 the City of Abidjan's budget effectively represented sixty-three percent of the total amount of communal budgets in the whole country. Since then, however, the City of Abidjan has experienced a progressive decline; in 1984 its budget represented only 30.15 percent of the total. At the end of the period, the City of Abidjan amassed only 41.86 percent of total budgetary resources. During the same period (1981-1984), the budgetary weight of the twenty-seven communes in the interior moved from 20.14 to 28.51 percent of the total. The growth rate is more marked amongst the ten communes of Abidjan, the budgetary weight

of which doubled from 16.85 percent in 1981 to 32.15 percent in 1984. The main reason for this increase lies in the new apportionment of the tax base between the ten communes and the City of Abidjan. In 1981 many of the new communes could not manage effectively, as a result of which the City of Abidjan took on their responsibilities. Yet since 1982 the new rules governing the slicing up of the fiscal pie have been applied, obliging the communes to designate 60 percent of their receipts to paying the costs of urban services. This amount was later judged to be excessive and revised; at the moment, it represents only 40 percent. Another reason for the rapid growth of the communes' budgets in relation to that of the City of Abidjan is that over the 1981-1984 period many of the communes introduced new taxes and improved the recovery rate of the others under their jurisdiction. These factors explain why the budget of the City of Abidjan experienced an average (negative) growth rate of −16.78 percent from 1981 to 1984, while the ten Abidjan communes and the twenty-seven communes of the interior had an average (positive) growth rate of 41.90 percent and 20.27 percent respectively. It might be concluded that the budgetary decline of the City of Abidjan can be attributed to a new emphasis on the individual identities of the Abidjan communes and those of the interior.

Analysis of the budgetary behavior of the communes and the City of Abidjan has been drawn from data collected by a study of the Department of Local Government entitled, "Budgets of the Communes: Overall Structures," gathered in 1984 and published in March, 1985. Tendencies in budgetary behavior are stressed because the statistics used do not come from administrative accounts but rather from budgets. It may, however, be that the tendencies revealed in this particular study are close to actual behavior, in that twenty-six of the thirty-eight budgets examined were modified budgets or documents which had undergone readjustments dictated by the actual circumstances of implementing the initial budgets.

The structure of budgetary resources is as follows: thirty-eight percent fiscal receipts, twenty-six percent cash payments and other service taxes, twenty-four percent state grants and grants-in-aid, and twelve percent patrimony revenues and miscellaneous receipts. Yet a closer analysis of the statistics shows that this distribution varies with the three categories of communes selected for the study. For example, while the twenty-seven communes in the interior counted on securing only twenty-seven percent of their resources from fiscal receipts, the ten communes of Abidjan estimated that they could extract from this source sixty-five percent of their receipts; meanwhile, the City of Abidjan expected to get only fourteen percent of its revenues from this source.

Cash payments and service taxes formed thirty-nine percent of the receipts of the communes in the interior, eleven percent for the ten communes of Abidjan, and thirty-one percent for the City of Abidjan. This particular behavior of the interior communes may be explained by the fact that this category of revenues represents their only autonomous source of revenue, and they are determined to develop it. Market fees and taxes on small businessmen and artisans constitute the bulk of this revenue.

The distribution of state grants and grants-in-aid varies a great deal. The largest beneficiary is the City of Abidjan, which gathers from this source fifty-two percent of its resources; next are the communes from the interior with twenty-two percent of their resources, while the ten communes of Abidjan derive only five percent of their resources from here. Although no precise rules govern the distribution of this aid yet, the small communes, the fiscal resources of which are not yet sufficiently developed, appear to benefit most frequently. For the same reason, this form of aid often represents more than half of the resources (fifty-four percent at Odiénné and fifty-six percent at Sassandra) of the communes in the interior, the greater beneficiaries. This being the case, the distribution of this aid implicitly attempts to compensate for the inequalities between communes, and simultaneously to correct economic disparities resulting from poor fiscal distribution over the country as a whole. Yet it may be argued that this practice does not function as well as the practice of grants-in-aid, which are the only means by which the state can give direction to the actions of the municipalities. This policy helps the central government attain certain specific objectives, through deciding at the same time to recompense attempts to install facilities and to generate autonomous resources in the municipalities. In the case of the City of Abidjan, which benefits only slightly from autonomous resources, this aid, which represents more than half of its resources, combines with the obligatory contributions of the communes of which it is composed.

Expenses can be divided into two categories: investment expenses and recurring expenses. The communes are encouraged by law to devote at least twenty percent of their expenses to investment. For the total budget of 1984, twenty-two percent of resources were put into investment expenses, while seventy-eight percent were devoted to recurrent expenses.

For all the communes, recurrent expenses were effected as follows: thirty-six percent for miscellaneous expenses, thirty-two percent for community expenses, twenty-five percent for expenses on general services, four percent for social and cultural services and manpower, three percent for economic services. Here again, a comparative analysis of the three categories demonstrates important behavioral differences in terms of budget distribution. The three categories of communes devote only a small portion to social and cultural services and manpower and to economic services. The ten communes of Abidjan apportion to these two areas five and three percent respectively, the City of Abidjan four and two percent, and the communes in the interior five and four percent of budgetary allowances for recurrent expenditures. These types of behavior may be explained by the fact that these areas are largely under state jurisdiction. In fact, as has already been emphasized, municipal services are paid for by the large technical ministries with the greatest means. While the ten communes of Abidjan and the City of Abidjan devote twenty percent of their resources to the functioning of general services, the communes of the interior give fifty-six percent of their resources to these services. This disparity may be explained by the youth of the institutions and structures of the interior communes: extra resources were required at the outset to consolidate these bodies. After this initial period of muddling through, the proportion of resources devoted to general services by the communes of the interior tended to diminish.

The proportion of recurrent budgetary expenditure devoted to community services in the ten communes of Abidjan (twelve percent), to the City of Abidjan (sixty-one percent), and to the communes of the interior (thirty percent) reflects accurately the existing picture as far as the functions are actually carried out. In the communes of the interior, these resources have mainly been used for the upkeep of roads, the removal of household waste, and leasehold programs. In the City of Abidjan, seventy-eight percent of the resources have been devoted to costs incurred by SITAF for the collection and transport of household waste in the Abidjan area, the rest being given over mostly to charges incurred by public lighting as well as maintenance of roads and parks. The twelve percent spent on this category by the ten communes of Abidjan allow them to discharge their legal functions in their respective areas. Miscellaneous expenses represent almost sixty percent of the recurrent budget of the communes of Abidjan, thirteen percent of the City's, and twenty-five percent of the communes' in the interior. The significant gap between the communes of Abidjan and the communes in the interior relates to the fact that the Abidjan communes have to transfer forty percent of their fiscal resources to the City of Abidjan as a contribution to its rates and that they are bound to reserve at least twenty percent of their resources as an investment budget. The twenty-five percent from the towns in the interior and the thirteen percent from the City of Abidjan mentioned above are their basic contributions to the investment fund. Thus, the City of Abidjan's investment effort is not as strong as that of the communes.

The structure of investment expenses in the communes and the City of Abidjan is as follows: thirty-three percent for investment in community services, thirty percent for superstructural facilities, twenty percent for general services, and ten percent for economic services. The behavior of the different categories varies according to need. The ten communes of Abidjan devote on average twenty-two percent of their investment resources to general services while the City of Abidjan and the communes in the interior contribute 25.9 percent and sixteen percent respectively. These resources have been put to building new premises and to renovating existing structures given over by the state for the use of the communes. For its part, the City of Abidjan has begun the building of offices for the municipal garage and the extension of the receiver's office.

The three categories of communes have all devoted more than one-third of investment funds to community services, with the following breakdown: twenty-eight percent for the ten communes of Abidjan, 40.4 percent for the City of Abidjan, and thirty-five percent for the communes of the interior. Road construction has absorbed the greater part spent, with urban planning (subdivisional) programs in second place in the towns of the interior. The disparity between the ten communes of Abidjan and the interior communes emerges from the relative difference in facility levels between the two categories.

The ten communes of Abidjan have attempted to exercise their functions with respect to superstructural (building) facilities by investing thirty-six percent of available resources in this area; the City of Abidjan has totally relinquished responsibility in this area, leaving intervention to the communes and the state by devoting to it only 0.3 percent. The communes in the interior have followed the same practice as the Abidjan communes, with a contribution of thirty-four percent. This fairly high proportion of the investment budget observed in the communes confirms the state policy of disengagement regarding the provision of superstructural facilities in the towns. These three categories of communes have all laid aside an average of ten percent for economic facilities. These investments have been used in the construction of small markets and slaughterhouses as well as the maintenance of bus stations.

The Exercise of Authority and the Evaluation of Communal Management

Although by law the municipalities are guaranteed a certain degree of autonomy, the state has judged it necessary both to give them assistance and to control their activities, partly because of their youth but above all because they deal with public property. The Ministry of the Interior has tutelary authority over the communes. It exercises this authority in collaboration with various technical ministries, such as the Ministry of Economics and Finance.

The Ministry of the Interior exercises its authority through the Department of Local Government. The role of this Department is not limited to simple controls on the management of the communes; it involves itself with communal administrations in order to provide a framework for them, along with technical and financial assistance. This office is rather poorly staffed in relation to the task it must perform. It includes an office of budgets, one for municipal personnel, one for administrative regulation, and a technical unit. Its regulatory activities are aimed at keeping the exercise of municipal functions within legal bounds. It has acquitted itself well in this area for, as has already been emphasized, the communes have at their disposal a highly elaborate arsenal of legal documents produced in record time. The risk here is that given the number and diversity of legal documents, certain officials may claim no knowledge of their existence or of the complicated manner of their application. The Department's controlling function over local communities consists of ensuring that legal and regulatory guidelines organizing municipal life are respected. These guidelines include respect for regular statutory meetings, the establishment of written reports on proceedings, and due regard for the duties of officials and municipal personnel. The Department's responsibility for technical assistance operates through advice to and consultations with municipal administration during the drawing up of budgets, mayor's accounts, and triennial investment programs. Intervention also occurs at the time of the drawing up of market title-deeds, and in the case of management problems involving municipal personnel. Inspection missions are common practice.

At the heart of the Department of Local Government is a technical unit. This unit must ensure that development programs and communal management schemes are consistent with general urban planning policies; and that operational urban planning projects respect the orientation and regulations of master planning documents. As far as questions about regulation are concerned, the Department of Local Government often has recourse to the guidance of the experts in the General Secretariat for administrative reform. Finally, the Department of Local Government is responsible for the training and development of commune personnel. A coherent policy in this area has not yet been achieved, yet it appears that the Department has opted for on-the-spot training, reinforced by seminars and short courses.

The authority of the Ministry of Economics and Finance is actually exercised through the sub-section of the Department of Local Government of the Treasury. This sub-section has worked out the new budgetary and accounting plan for the communes; as a result, this body follows up its application. It assists the communes in many ways. For example, the Treasury accountants in charge of funds in the communes are also municipal receivers, and as such, mayors' advisors and financial officers for the communes. Again, the sub-section of the Ministry dealing with local governments collects and assesses the financial data from the communes and produces regular summary accounts through which it may direct the financial management of the communes. And Treasury inspectors regularly perform unexpected audits of the financial affairs of the communes; if they discover anomalies, they report to the accounts chamber of the Supreme Court, which studies cases submitted to it and rules on the imposition of sanctions. Finally, Treasury plays a role in training personnel for communal financial services; and it sets out and controls the application of guidelines which organize the financial management of the communes.

The evaluation of the communal experience may be divided into three sections: the functioning of the existing political and administrative structures, an evaluation of financial management, and an evaluation of the extent to which the two main objectives guiding municipal reform have been attained.

On the whole, political structures have worked reasonably well. However, there have been many cases of lack of respect for the periodicity of council sessions and municipal meetings. And some standing committees have not functioned on a regular basis. The non-resident status of some mayors in their communes (i.e. mayors who do not permanently live in their communes) has slowed down certain important decision-making processes. A high rate of absenteeism at municipal council meetings has been recorded. In the communes under study, an analysis of the proceedings of meetings reveals that from 1981 to 1984 an average rate of absenteeism of twenty-five percent was recorded for council meetings. This high level of absenteeism may be explained by a number of factors. First, in some communes, the non-election of the individual at the head of the party list has resulted in the formation of factions, which has in turn imparted an unhealthy atmosphere to the councils. Second, the fact that councillors work on a voluntary basis creates a lack of motivation amongst some of them. Third, sometimes more than one-third of municipal councillors do not actually live in the commune they represent. Many of these councillors (and mayors) are high-status bureaucrats or businessmen living in Abidjan or other large towns. When they have to travel to council meetings, costs are incurred for which no adequate provision has been previously made in the municipal budget. Fourth, some private sector employers refuse to give councillors permission to attend meetings, although the law requires them to do so. Fifth, some councillors do not think their presence at council meetings is useful, especially when, in their opinion, the mayor does not respect the collegial nature of the council. Finally, some mayors simply refuse to delegate power to their staff. In one of the towns visited, a number of elected municipal councillors were posted far away from the commune, by the Minister with authority over the commune, apparently for purely political reasons. These interventions directed at council members had a discernible effect on the ratio of resident and non-resident councillors, and in turn influenced the rate of absenteeism to the exceptional level of 32.55 percent.

This incident indicates that municipal councillors, unlike members of Parliament, are not protected in the exercise of their duties; they remain extremely vulnerable and may be exposed to political reprisals. It should be noted here that the poor level of education attained by some councillors does not allow them to understand municipal problems or to follow and participate actively in council debates. This handicaps the democratic functioning of such bodies. For this reason, it would be desirable to see the translation of debates into the first language of the town in question and the adoption of this regional language as the second working language of the council.

As for the functioning of administrative structures, an important problem is that the definition of tasks is not very specific regarding the respective duties of the cabinet head and the general secretary. This ambiguity gives rise to some conflict. The general secretary, often wrongly suspected of having the ear of the all-powerful administration, is frequently excluded from access to certain documents.

Another problem is the absence of regulations concerning the status of municipal personnel, which leaves them with little security. This situation together with the low level of salaries paid to public officials will not encourage high-level technical staff to integrate themselves into municipal structures. Also, and partly as a result, the existing level of municipal personnel remains low. To deal with this problem, the National School of Administration should establish within itself a permanent section responsible for the training and development of municipal staff.

The framing of the political and administrative structures of the communes have so far been effectively put in place by the Department of Local Government in the Ministry of the Interior. After the establishment of management structures and tools, the problems that the communes may encounter concern the rational management of resources. But the Department of Local Government in its present form and with the means at its disposal cannot effectively deal with both the existing communes and the hundreds of new communes which will be created. It must be better provided with both human and material resources. In order to deal with the numerous problems and conflicts which arise from the functioning of such structures and in order to optimize the use of resources at the level of the communes, the Department should have at its disposal inspectors who are not only acquainted with management science but also capable of diagnosing the problems of commune management and making suitable recommendations.

Finally, within the confines of its existing duties, the technical unit should coordinate the programming and the execution of urban studies and investment plans in the communes, as well as the ordering of requests for matching grant funds. In order to do so, the Department should take over the Urban Investment and Management Fund (FIAU) initiated by the Ministry of Economics and Planning and should restructure its technical unit in the form of the Regional Fund for Rural Management (FRAR).

The evaluation of financial management in Côte d'Ivoire must distinguish between two categories: management mistakes and management misconduct. Management mistakes occur when the mayors, who are the main budgetary managers (*ordonnateurs*), fail to respect the rules governing receipts and expenses of the communes. The central authorities have registered four types of management mistakes encountered over the course of this first legislative period: exceeding credits which have been voted, resulting in budgetary deficits; incurring of expenses not entered in the budget or authorized by the central authorities; loans of money from commune funds; and the lack of regard for spending procedures relating to both council deliberations and public tenders. In the latter case, the law specifies that all purchases over 5 million CFA francs must be put out to tender. These regulations have not been followed in spite of Ministry circulars sent out to attract the attention of the mayors to the procedures involved in the tendering process for public purchases in 1982 and 1984. In 1984, nineteen public purchases were recorded of amounts over 5 million CFA francs, of which seventeen were made informally, only one after minimal consultation with the Ministry and one through an official tender document. The mayors, for their part, believe that the 5 million CFA franc threshold is too low and the procedure too lengthy. For this reason, they often present officials of the Department of Local Government with a *fait accompli*, expecting them to proceed to regularize the transaction after the fact.

Management misconduct occurs when the mayor or the agent of the commune, in defiance of the principle separating the duties of the budgetary officer and the accountant, involves himself in the manipulation of public funds. Five examples of this type of behavior have been observed in the Ivorian communes: the opening of accounts managed by the mayors themselves; the redirection of funds collected by municipal services without this being recorded by the official municipal receiver (a Treasury official); the use of funds for strictly personal purposes; the issuing of two sets of bills; and the collection of funds by unqualified agents, thus escaping the control of the registrar of receipts and the municipal receiver. As a consequence of these various corrupt practices, the accounts office, which was taken over by the Treasury, sent two mayors out of office. It was also supposed to pass regulations in the case of six others, but no follow-up has yet occurred.

Conclusion:
Achieving the Objectives of Urban Management Reform

Although all of the reports indicate that the Ivorian municipal experience remains essentially positive, it is important to ask whether the two main objectives of urban reform have been achieved, namely democratic participation in decision-making and the evaluation of needs, and the provision of rationalized urban services.

The democratic participation of the citizens or their representatives (the councillors) in evaluating local needs and making decisions for the communes has been achieved with great political difficulty. The problems involved in assuring the effective functioning of municipal councils have already been highlighted. Meanwhile, municipal councillors in their present context do not represent within council the various geographical areas which make up the whole town. Under such conditions, they cannot really be responsible to the people. Rather, they are responsible to the mayor, who had them elected as part of his list, so that they tend to follow his lead rather closely. The municipal councillor, as a result, is not the indispensable intermediary between the base and the political and administrative structures that he is meant to be. This seriously hampers the functioning of municipal democracy. Moreover, the present electoral method, in tending to produce strong mayors, simultaneously weakens the municipal councillors in the decision-making process. Some councillors consulted in fact recognized that the atmosphere in which they worked was uncomfortable; they realized that, in the final analysis, real power lay with the mayor who controlled the original electoral list (and thus was elected by the people), and not with the councillors.

The weakness of councillors at the commune level, along with the attitude and behavior of some mayors, may have created a sense of frustration amongst those councillors committed to democratic goals. To ensure the democratic operation of local political structures, a balloting method should be introduced whereby councillors would be elected at the level of wards or neighborhoods. This election would then be followed by the indirect election of the mayor, either by a simple count of councillors supportive of a specific candidate or by a vote of the elected councillors at the first council meeting. Furthermore, in order to improve the functioning of representational and participatory structures, mayors should not hesitate to make use of modern information sources and of consultative committees, which could be staffed by councillors and external experts.

Thus, the advent of municipal democracy has contributed to a change in the attitudes and behavior of local people in relation to their town. Urban areas no longer represent a temporary form of existence to which one must resign oneself until retirement age. Citizens are now concerned with their own living arrangements, management, and the quality of life provided in their urban environment. Neighborhood leaders have organized themselves into pressure groups working on the central and municipal administrations to obtain required community facilities or to prevent the installation of some economic facilities which might lower the quality of their environment if located in another area.

At present, the division of functions between levels of government in addition to the lack of human, material, and financial resources have acted as a brake on the achievement of the second objective, the provision of improved and rationalized public services. Confronted with enormous tasks, mayors have often been forced to make difficult choices. In general, the most urgent demands are those which are satisfied. Unfortunately, the failure to observe regulations regarding public purchases and the lack of technical personnel capable of carrying out new schemes lead to the conclusion that the economic criterion is not always respected. Yet some mayors have demonstrated a great degree of imagination in managing to install facilities at a relatively low cost. While the municipal reform process is still in its early stages, on balance it has shown sufficient success that government's cautious support can be strengthened.

Note

1. Adjamé and Port-Bouët are two of the ten districts comprising the City of Abidjan.

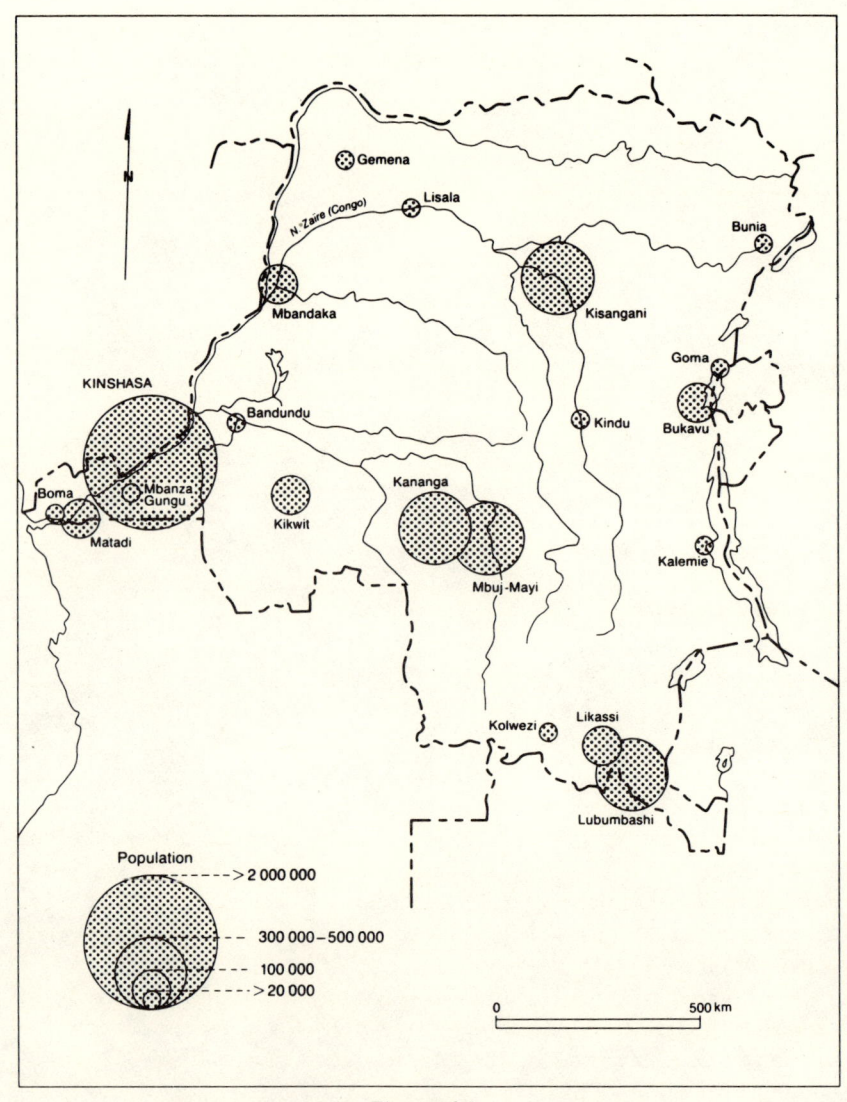

Figure 6.1
Zaïre: Distribution of the Urban Population, 1984

CHAPTER 6
Kinshasa: Problems of Land Management, Infrastructure, and Food Supply
Kankondé Mbuyi

Introduction

In 1970 Zaire's urban population of 4,500,000 represented close to twenty percent of its total population; by the year 2000 half the population of Zaire, probably 45 to 50 million inhabitants, will live in an urban environment. Kinshasa, the capital, will have reached a population of over 3 million in 1987 and perhaps between 6 and 7 million by the year 2000. The growth rate of towns, in spite of a noticeable economic recession, exceeds six percent per annum, while the areas peripheral to the town are growing at nearly twelve percent a year (see Table 6.1).

For many years, the economic situation has been characterized by a general stagnation of activity and employment in the modern sector. Market activity occupies more and more people, providing secondary employment jobs for women and the only means of survival for certain households. This rate of urban growth means each year that over 200,000 additional people must be fed and housed, thus requiring tens of thousands of new buildings, while public and private construction hardly provides a few hundred dwellings per year. Because of this situation, "self-help" construction has become widespread, turning the outskirts of Kinshasa into an immense building-yard slowly expanding in line with the feeble capacity of the poorest sectors to save and invest in construction. The problems encountered in acquiring a site and building on it continue to increase, as is witnessed by the unprecedented number of unfinished dwellings which have been in the process of construction over many years.

The impotence of public resources confronted by the magnitude of this expansion translates into an increasing slowdown in the development of infrastructure and amenities. Yet individual and community initiatives are coming to the aid of public efforts. The evolution and appearance of the urban center owe much to the initiative and dynamism of its citizens. In this fragile context, traditional approaches to urban management have had little impact. New mechanisms demanding greater responsibility on the

---

This chapter has been translated from the original French by Claire Letemendia and Rodney White.

Table 6.1
The Population of Zaire by Province

	Urban Population in Thousands					Total Population in Thousands					Urbanization Rate (%)	
	1975 N	1980 N	R	1985 N		1975 N	1980 N	R	1985 N		1975	1980
Kinshasa	1,679	2,410	7.5	3,302		1,679	2,410	7.5	3,302		100	100
Bas Zaire	493	676	6.5	900		1,574	1,768	2.3	2,007		31.3	38.2
Bandundu	471	660	7.0	896		3,068	3,486	2.5	3,995		15.3	19.1
Equateur	416	597	7.5	845		2,619	2,945	2.4	3,331		15.9	20.3
Haut Zaire	611	832	6.3	1,103		3,475	3,871	2.2	4,333		17.6	21.5
Kivu	500	718	7.5	1,036		3,812	4,495	3.3	5,330		13.1	16.0
Shaba	1,363	1,824	6.0	2,384		3,698	3,563	3.8	4,291		46.0	51.2
Kasai Or.	462	633	6.5	868		1,516	1,725	2.6	1,978		30.5	36.7
Kasai Occ.	439	657	6.5	900		1,872	2,111	4.4	2,410		25.6	31.1
Total Zaire	6,477	9,010	6.82	12,237		22,582	26,377	3.1	30,977		28.7	34.2

Source: Département du Plan, *Perspectives démographiques régionales*.

Centers are considered urban if their population exceeded 5,000 in 1975.
N = Number of inhabitants in thousands.
R = Annual average rate of growth between the two dates.

part of groups at a lower level, along with the emergence of better adapted networks of economic exchange and greater administrative decentralization, provide the foundations for a new attitude to urban centers and for a new conception of spatial growth and of the provision of goods and services.

Successful cases of spontaneous development are, however, rare. Usually they emerge from outside initiatives (for example, non-governmental organizations), in which the population has confidence to the extent of trusting it with funds and volunteer labor. There are many examples of this: bridges, the clearing of roads, etc. For the analysis of urban services the simple distinction between public initiative and private activity is inadequate. It is more fruitful to identify those essential needs which require collective action and to consider as an urban service any action or system which addresses such needs as security of tenure, family dwellings, food supply, drinking water, basic health care, environmental hygiene, security of persons and goods, and daily transportation. Some of these services, such as drinking water, transportation, and physical security, are managed by the State or large corporations. Others, such as food marketing and housing, lie within the sphere of private enterprise. In all cases, the community has some say in the organization, management, or control of such basic services and influences the way in which they function.

In the largest cities, the major problems are the lack of resources in relation to need in the domain of public finance, the lack of clarity in defining the responsibilities of various administrative levels, and the tenuous social organization of recent migrant populations cut off from their social roots. The lack of resources is evidently the primary cause of the insufficiency of utilities and the neglect of urban services. Although some financial flows emerge from the urbanization process itself (duties and taxes) or out of general services (food, health, schooling, transportation, drinking water, and energy), these resources are poorly managed.

It is understood that both decentralization of urban management and improved cost recovery are desirable. However, attempts in these directions have so far been ineffectual. The decentralized authorities lack the funds to fulfill their mandate and the flow of information up and down the hierarchy remains very weak. Within those generally difficult situations the case of Kinshasa, the capital city, is the most acute.

Only seven percent of household heads were born in Kinshasa; the rest come from the interior, sixty percent directly from the countryside. Yet from 1971 to 1975, Kinshasa has expanded more from natural growth than from migration. However, recent field evidence suggests that the mortality rate has begun to rise in the last few years.[1] It is important to view this rise in mortality in the context of worsening economic, nutritional and sanitary conditions, which prove particularly detrimental to certain sectors of the

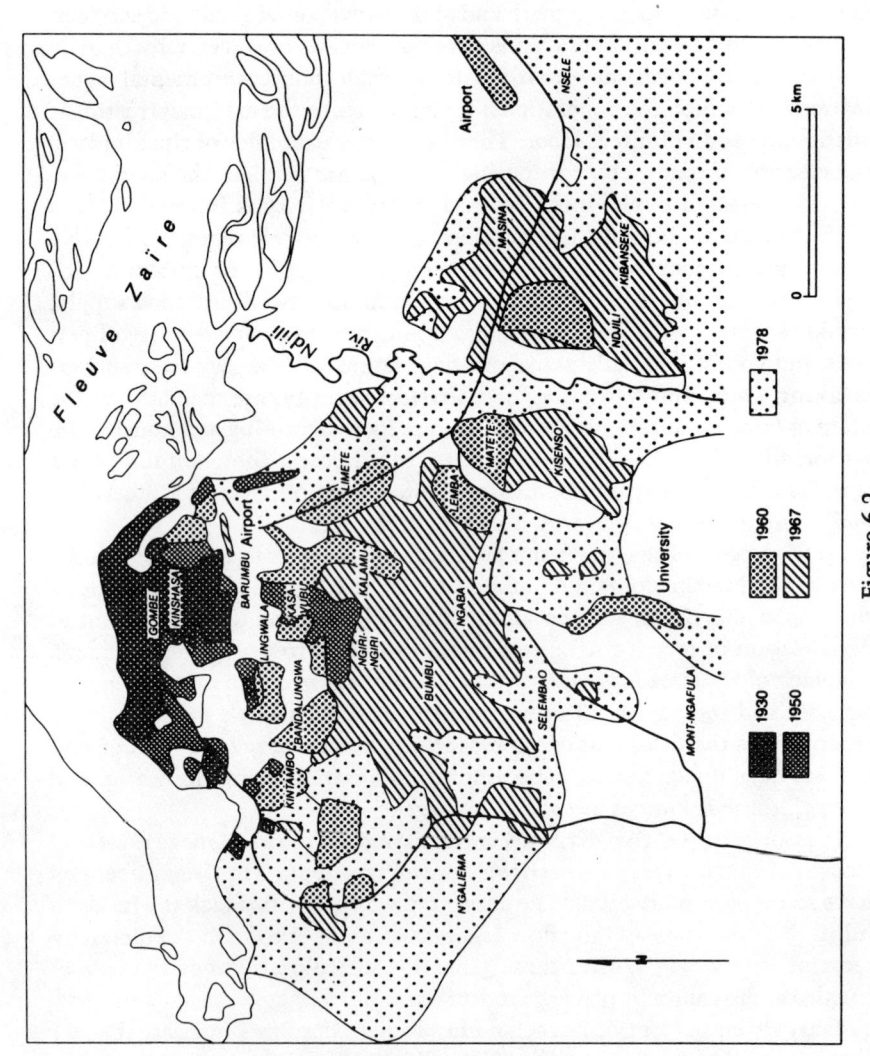

Figure 6.2
Kinshasa: Stages of Growth

population. Two important comments should be made with regard to migration. The number of women migrating appears to be increasing. (Since 1971, in absolute terms, their number has been greater than that of men.) Furthermore, the group of migrants coming from areas at some distance from Kinshasa is becoming more and more significant.

The site of Kinshasa is a constraint on its development. In terms of gradient, the city falls into two parts. First, there are eighteen thousand hectares of low-lying plains situated at an altitude of 250 to 350 meters. This huge plain is intersected by a series of rivers running generally from south to north, thus hampering the spread of urbanization. These rivers often overflow during the rainy season and for many days cause flooding in a number of badly drained areas. This situation is aggravated by erosion upstream which intensifies the run-off. Second, there are six thousand hectares of hilly area of slopes from eight to twenty percent in the southern part of the city. These areas are prone to erosion where dwellings are usually built without any precautions.

Slope	Surface Hectares	%
0-4%	14,740	60
4-8%	3,910	16
8-12%	1,710	7
12 and over	4,230	17
Total	24,590	100

Source: BEAU – SCET BCEOM

The allocation of space by land use is as follows:

Land Use	Surface Hectares	%
Living area (including public highways and local amenities)	10,450	70
Industries – businesses	1,510	10
Major public facilities and buildings	2,150	14
Ndolo aerodrome, military lands, reserved lands	880	6
Total	14,990	100

Source: BEAU – SCET BCEOM

Kinshasa occupies a loop in the river, an alluvial plain bordered by sandy hills on which any human settlement remains precarious because of the erosive tendency of the land. Since the 1960s expansion has filled the plain, and now the city is beginning to spread up the hills and flow out to the west, past River Ndjili, which for some time acted as the natural boundary of the agglomeration. The city, founded as a port, has developed along the river. It follows one major axis linking, parallel to the river, the administrative center, the business and commercial sector, and the two industrial zones. In addition to this privileged area (including the original residential zones), the city has spread out following a uniform grid, which constituted the pattern for urbanization laid down by the authorities until fairly recently. Kinshasa has retained the specialized character of its original neighborhoods and has flowed out to occupy, in successive stages, the whole of the site.

The city was formed around the industrial zones of Kintambo and Limete, the administrative center and the business center, in Gombé. A large boulevard links up these two main poles of the modern city. The old wealthy residential zones are the less densely settled parts of Gombé whereas new residential quarters have been established the surrounding hills, where climatic conditions are more favorable. The initial boundaries separating European areas from African ones have been maintained by the establishment of major public spaces (hospital, golf course, botanical gardens, military camps, etc). Beyond this "neutral zone," the old African neighborhoods of Kinshasa, Lingwala, and Barumbu have increased in density. The old Ndolo airport (situated on the outskirts of the city between the two wars), along with a military camp, today forms a second break, beyond which new estates – Kasa-Vubu and Ngiri-Ngiri – opened up in the 1950s. Planned residential areas designed to accommodate government employees have been created since 1960 by the National Housing Office. These districts constitute significant secondary centers (Lemba, Bandalungwa, Matete, and Ndjili). To the south of this group, grid-like plots were most recently opened up for planned urban development (Kalamu, Bamba, Makala, and Ngaba). The first unplanned settlements date from 1959, on the edge of Ndjili; these are rapidly spreading south and covering the flanks of the hills.

Housing zones may be stratified according to types of housing and defined social groupings: residential neighborhoods (Gombé, Ngaliema, Djelo Binza, and Joli Parc); planned neighborhoods (Lemba, Bandalungwa, Matete, and Ndjili); old estates (Kinshasa, Lingwala, Barumbu, and Kintambo); new estates (Kasa Vubu and Ngiri-Ngiri); southern extensions (Kalamu, Bumbu, Makala, and Ngaba); and recently extended peripheral areas (Masina, Kimbanseke, Kisenso, Selembao, and unofficial Ngaliema).

Land Management

The anarchic character of land ownership creates social inequalities and increases the cost of urban services. The land and construction laws were fundamentally altered by Law 73 / 021 of 20 July 1973 (modified by Law 80 / 008 of 10 July 1980). The essential principle holds that land is State property and that an individual may obtain a leasehold contract for a specific time period on the condition that he develops it. This principle of nationalization of land and its use derives from traditional African rural land allocation principles. The ownership of land law separates the right to benefit from the land and the ownership of private property consisting of the buildings erected thereupon. These buildings thus have a market value in the case of a termination of ownership. As far as the land is concerned, the holder of the concession must pay the State an annual rent, the amount of which is fixed at the time of the concession. In the event of a change of holder, the initial grantee would not be able to make any profit on the land; it is the State which will collect the annual rent from the new occupant.

The main principles of the law governing rental systems are:

Lease without option to buy (simple lease) – The length of the initial lease must not exceed fifteen years; however, it is renewable according to the wishes of the tenant for a new term at the price in effect at the time of the renewal. Upon expiry of the lease, the public authority may ask the tenant to take down anything he has erected.

Lease with option to buy – The length of the initial lease must not exceed three years. If construction is complete, conversion of the lease is consented to at the price determined at the time of the initial lease. If construction is not complete, two successive lease renewals of two years each may be given; conversion of the lease will be made at the price existing at the time of the sale, not at the price fixed at the time of the end of the initial lease.

The authorities responsible for private State land sales, concessions, and exchanges are the Commissioner of Land Titles for the city of Kinshasa (authorized to take over, hand out, or exchange private State lands under the conditions of the present ruling and inasmuch as their coverage does not exceed two hectares); the State Commissioner in charge of these lands has jurisdiction over agreement of terminations, concessions, and exchanges of State plots the extent of which exceeds two hectares. Where lands of this description exceed five hectares, the State Commissioner in charge of the lands will not exercise his jurisdiction on the matter without the authority of the Executive Council.

It has not been possible to put into practice the legal procedures established by the Land Law on a widespread scale within the urban agglomeration. In part, this is due to the complexity of the procedure and the cost resulting from the necessity of referring to intermediaries (whether officials or land surveyors) who charge a commission, thus discouraging new buyers from approaching them. In part, occupants holding titles predating the Land Law which have been invalidated do not feel the need to have their rights converted. Altogether, less than ten percent of plots are registered in the city of Kinshasa. This includes old plots which already had a land title dating from the colonial period. The rest of the agglomeration is still administered under the old system of the Lessor's Book and of the Plot Identification Card. The card acknowledges the right of the holder to occupy the plot and permits him to take various steps towards obtaining the Lessor's Book which was created during the colonial era. The Lessor's Book gives the inhabitants of the indigenous estates the right to occupy plots; the right was not only precarious but also easily revoked in certain conditions, notably the failure to develop the plot in one year from the date of the signing of the lease. The Lessor's Book has survived independence and continues today, and it is still considered by the population as a title of ownership in spite of being replaced by the 1973 law.

The official procedure described above is not the one most frequently used. In 1984, for twelve thousand new plots, there were only about eleven hundred new leasehold contracts. The legal proceedings being too lengthy and hard to understand, the parties concerned in most cases arrange matters in one of three ways. First, an arrangement may be made with the land surveyor in charge of putting the project into action, who assigns the plot and pushes the file as fast as possible through the Commissioner of Land Titles. This procedure is expensive as it includes the cost of the land, the charges for the file, survey costs, and the fee for establishing the contract; the total varies from 1,000 Z to 2,000 Z according to the proposed use of the land (1979 estimate). Second, the parties may approach the local government authorities who grant the land and sell a Plot Identification Card. Then, they arrange with someone who works in the Urban Planning Department to obtain a Lessor's Book. Third, one may buy the land from traditional chiefs who, in their turn, provide a receipt. With this receipt, the buyer approaches the Local Authorities to purchase a Plot Identification Card which will lead to the purchase of a Lessor's Book.

The traditional method of land acquisition is naturally more common in the extension areas because most of the people who acquire land in these areas have relatively modest incomes. A further reason is the very significant presence of customary chiefs who still exercise their rights within the rural lands. The well-known transfer of responsibility which, during the colonial era, transferred land from the traditional to the urban area governed by land law no longer exists. There is thus room for manoeuvre between traditional and urban land regulations. The continuing role of the customary chief interacts with the powers of the local administration which, although it has no jurisdiction over land affairs, distributes the lands.

As can be understood from this brief description confusion reigns at the root of the legal system of land grants. This problem has really become entrenched since traditional practices are ingrained in people's minds and they have become profitable to a considerable number of intermediaries.

Although, according to the books, the law removes any notion of land value, a land market still exists in reality. The effects of such an unbalanced system include a flourishing of anarchic construction, insecurity of land tenure, and scarcity of public resources.

On the plain, plot allocation follows a right-angled grid pattern; thus, for years, there has been a "spontaneous," yet orderly, extension. However, where land conditions are less propitious, as in the case of steep slopes or unstable soils, the division of plots becomes more problematic. Spontaneous construction is spreading up the sides of the hills, causing deforestation and erosion. Subsequently, these squatter areas become difficult to develop since costs would be out of proportion for the population thereby served. This consequence of uncontrolled distribution of land remains the most serious since it happens on the greatest scale.

A second consequence of the confusion in land management and the persistence of traditional legal channels is insecurity. What are the risks involved in not legalizing one's situation? What does or does not constitute a legal situation? Can one be expelled? The greater part of the households studied in Kinshasa have either a Lessor's Book, a Plot Identification Card, or both. Since they have a paper, whatever its validity, they consider themselves rightful owners. The administration has been so overwhelmed by the phenomenon of "spontaneous" settlement and rendered so incapable of the slightest action to deal with this situation that security of tenure may be considered a *fait accompli* by most of the inhabitants in the peripheral neighborhoods. Yet this security is more apparent than real, as others may come forward with other "rights" to the land, the latter having been distributed by other people through other channels. Other property conflicts which cannot be settled because of the lack of proper identification include trespassing on lots, construction contested by a third party, double or triple grants of the same piece of land, and contested inheritance (incompatibility between traditional and modern rights).

Two main types of land speculation contribute to increases in the cost of land. One minor speculation practised by a significant proportion of the population consists of the purchase of a number of plots by the same family, which multiplies its chances or retaining at least one, while all the time holding building capital for potential resale. In Kinshasa especially, a plot always represents an investment, however fragile its physical character or the legality of its appropriation. Another land and building speculation of a freer kind, designed to maximize accumulation, is of the "capitalist" type and can affect lands which have not been legally appropriated. The law of the strongest prevails in these conditions; the "anarchy" of Kinshasa's land systems benefits heavy capitalist speculation, even in the poorest of quarters, when it comes to the management and control of land.

In denying the existence of a land market and in permitting the development of highly lucrative private transactions, the State is depriving itself of resources which are sorely missed when it comes to providing services. In certain residential subdivisions, leasehold rights to a plot cost no more than 10,000 Z, whereas those already holding rights could resell them immediately without any development of the property at over 150,000 Z. Yet the construction of approved buildings on these lands would have led to an official resale value of only 60,000 Z. The State loses on two fronts: failure to capture the value of the transactions, and cost recovery of services. This situation occurs at a lesser rate in the peripheral zones, where plots may be obtained at from 20,000 Z to 30,000 Z while the official fees amount to no more than 2,000 Z.

Urban Services

Roads

The road network in Kinshasa is poorly developed. The general south-north direction of the rivers has imposed a pattern of main roads running in the same direction; the east-west routes are inadequate. Existing roads are inadequate in terms of surfacing. The zone of Gombé and its eastern extension, the zone of Limete, the planned estates of Volo, Bandalungwa, Matete, and Kalamu are served by surfaced roads; the rest of the agglomeration is generally accessible only by poorly maintained roads. Access to Kinshasa may be classed in either as "good and permanent accessibility" in the Northern zone (Gombé), where a number of asphalted roads form a closely knit network, or as "very difficult or variable accessibility" where the districts are often surrounded by routes which have been surfaced (Bumbu, Makala, and Ngaba in the South; Masina and Kimbanseke in the East). This category includes a population of about 500,000 people who have no access to public transport without a long walk, and therefore little possibility of travel over the whole urban area.

The road network was constructed about thirty years ago. At the moment, it contains nearly five hundred kilometers of asphalted roads. However, the lack of major transverse or peripheral roads, forces traffic to flow through the downtown in order to go from one suburb to another. As a result, the most underfinanced routes remain those built after 1960. They are basically inaccessible to public transport. The latter thus covers only fifty percent of the city, most urban travel being done on foot.

Water Supply

Water is provided in Kinshasa by three waterworks. In the West, the Lukunga plant treats water from Lukunga and the River Zaire and feeds the reservoirs of Ozone (7,500 m^3), Météo (300 m^3), and Djelo-Binza (150 m^3). The present capacity is 46,000 m^3 per day. The Ngaliema plant (60,000 m^3

per day) serves the South and East of the city. Other reservoirs are at Makala (12,000 m³) and Ngombele (2,500 m³). The capacity of the latter was planned to be increased to 220,000 m³ per day.

Water supply remains very uneven. As might be expected, the part of the city urbanized before 1960 is best served. Several levels of water service may be distinguished, based on the number of connections and the density of the network. These are high income areas which are one hundred percent connected; areas with eighty to ninety percent connections, which have a distribution system, but the number of connections is limited by the cost of being hooked up (Ngiri-Ngiri, Kintambo, and Kalamu); and areas with twenty to thirty percent connections where the network is limited to the main roads. The sale of water, therefore, flourishes in areas far from the network. In these areas of the city, people use well-water (on the plains or on the banks of rivers in hilly areas) or river water. In hilly areas, where the water table is deeper, a few people have been able to dig wells operated by hand pumps, and the water is sold to the people at 500 Z per month. Others have built large concrete cisterns, which provide water for several days. These unreliable methods serve half the urban population. Well-water from shallow wells in the badly serviced zones, which have no water supply, is not to be trusted, since it is often obtained from overcrowded sites without storm or waste-water disposal systems. Water is frequently contaminated by faeces. Moreover, access to the wells usually requires a fee.

Notable efforts have been made to improve water supply in underprivileged areas. The current program covers the main needs of the southern extension areas: Bumbu, Makala, Ngaba, and Masina. Water is brought to fifty percent of the plots. The cost of the connection, without the cost of the meter, is charged to the occupant, but payments are in installments.

Stormwater Drainage
The area is drained by several rivers. The Gomé and Bitshaku rivers, running East-West, drain the Kinshasa depression. The Bitshaku (formerly the Belgica) has been made into canals and covered over most of its area. Its downstream section passes through the industrial zone of Ndolo and cuts important traffic axes (roads for heavy vehicles and railways) by major engineering structures which limit its capacity. Some of the South-North rivers are covered over in their downstream sections (Funa, Basoko, Yolo, and Bumbu). The Funa, for example, has had its bed altered over the confluent of the Cabu branch, and the junction functions well. On the other hand, some structures are in very poor shape; some flows are often interrupted by water conduits crossing the openings the wrong way, holding up solid waste and creating serious blockages. A progressive correction of the problem, along with maintenance of existing openings, is required for most of the canals.

The rivers are generally on enough of a slope to sustain proper flow; but much erosion leads to much sediment in suspension. The downstream bed of the rivers, therefore, fills up progressively, accelerated by the discharge of solid and household waste (near marketplaces and unplanned dumps). Cleaning-out has already been undertaken by the Department of Public Works for a number of years, but upkeep is not possible for the whole network.

The stormwater drainage system affects the state of the roads and poses a great problem. Blockages of water resulting in the flooding of roads during each rainy season is due to the presence of sand in the networks, the growth of vegetation, drain covers which have collapsed and obstruct water flows, insufficient slope, and the shallowness of the water table in some areas.

A number of problems thus emerge. In the business sector, the original network is being changed into a single system by illegal connections of waste water joining the stormwater drains, causing impoundment of water, bad odors, and the proliferation of mosquitoes. In some planned estates, there is a fairly good covered network, but because of poor maintenance, it is mostly out of order. The old estates (Barumbu, Kinshasa, and Limgwala) have a covered earthen network to carry stormwater but the network fills up with sand, the earth ditches deteriorate, and, as the water table is too high, there is little absorption. The new estates (Kasa-Vubu and Ngiri-Ngiri) have a well-developed primary and secondary network, although the tertiary network is highly inadequate. In the hilly areas, with the exception of the upper income residential areas, there are serious erosion problems. In the extension zones of Kimbanseke and Masina, where there is no drainage system, the problem is less serious because of the sandy quality of the soil and the small slopes, which allow for better absorption. In general, the problems of drainage systems result mainly from a lack of coordinated and sustained maintenance.

Household Waste
Individual measures vary according to the level of urbanization. In upper income residential quarters (Gombé, Binza, Limété, etc), each building is equipped with a septic tank.[2] The efficacy of these tanks is doubtful, since they are generally not maintained. The business sector was originally served by septic tanks. With increased construction and the densification of the central quarters, the installation of septic tanks has become more difficult, and illegal connections emptying directly into the river started to appear. Because of this, the underground network of Gombé works like a unitary system. Through lack of maintenance and the entry of surface garbage as a result of the lack of grills over openings, the network functions very badly. It is common to see streets full of stagnant water and flooded buildings during the rainy season. This network must be cleaned out, even though it will be a difficult operation and will require specialized equipment.

In the densely-populated older neighborhoods, the number of tanks is much lower, and many plots supposedly equipped with septic tanks in fact have tanks which require emptying. The condition of these tanks is not reliable; the last emptying in the example surveyed here was two years ago, for which the charge is anyway quite high (around 150 Z). The tanks are not very water-tight and, given their high density, produce serious groundwater pollution through household effluent. Pollution is bad whether the water table is high or low.

A considerable number of people throw used water into the ditch surrounding their plot, if there is one. Others throw water directly onto the plot, into a disused well, or a septic tank. However, most people using the last two methods also throw part of their used water into the ditches. Most people drink water from polluted wells, incurring serious risk of waterborne diseases. Industrial waste must not be forgotten in a discussion of waste water. Most plants emitting polluted waste are concentrated in the industrial sectors, although some are located in the center of the city. In the absence of proper regulation, the government cannot control the disposal of industrial waste. The latter is thrown directly into the drains; those drains then pass through inhabited areas and are a significant source of pollution. One must also be concerned about the disposal of water used by hospitals; generally there is no treatment.

Collection of household waste and cleaning are not carried out in a coherent way. Only a few residential quarters (Gombé, Limété, and Binza) and the central market are on a regular, although inadequate, pick-up route. In the rest of the city, household waste is put out on the road, on illegal dumps, in stormwater drains, or buried in plots. In the peripheral neighborhoods, the lack of viable roads handicaps or prevents the collection of household waste. The presence of a minimal covered road upon which collection points would be positioned appears to be a primary condition for the development of coordinated action in this sphere.

The removal of waste is the responsibility of a number of privately contracted businesses. The "Crossroad" Company is responsible for this service at present, working under contract and with limited means. Dumps are emptied by staff who fill up container lorries. Elsewhere, teams of public service workers perform periodic clean-ups of the downtown roads.

Electricity

The electricity used in Kinshasa is produced in Lower Zaire by the Inkisi and Inga groups, whose energy output exceeds their needs. Energy is distributed by SNEL (the National Electricity Company) and sent to Kinshasa by two lines: Inga 220V is received by substations in Lingwala and Limiga; Zongo-Sanga 132V is received by substations in Makala and Gombé. Apart from these main substations, numerous links have been established for the rest of the city. The Middle and Low Tension networks are completely underground. Three levels of service can be identified. First are the residential quarters and the zones of Lemba, Matete, Volo, and Bandalungwa, which have a well-structured network. Second are Kintambo, Kasa-Vubu, Ndjili, and the old estates, where some plots are connected. Third are the southern peripheral extensions which have no electricity at all.

Housing
An estimate made for Kinshasa gives an annual housing demand of about 34,000 new dwellings for a population growth of about 190,000 people (6.6 percent a year). This demand is certainly not satisfied under existing conditions, given the high cost of construction which has exceeded any increase in income. The results of such a dramatic housing shortage in the urban areas are sufficiently well known that it is not necessary to list them all here. However, it should be noted that the housing shortage has created a high degree of land speculation and a sharp increase in rents. Speculation and the charging of excessive rents have serious consequences for the housing of low income groups. From 1974 to 1981 the average rental increase in Kinshasa may be estimated from available data at fifteen percent for estate housing and over 360 percent for high quality housing.

The poor are the most affected by these rental increases. Confronted by land speculation which discourages them from purchasing property and makes rents prohibitive, they are left with only two solutions: they can move into urban neighborhoods which are already turning into slums, as a result of increasing population density, or into squatter areas which are usually located on sites unsuitable for modern construction (dry valley basins, steeply sloping hills, etc.) or upon which building is not officially permitted.

Since 1932 an "Advancement Fund" has extended financial loans for the construction of "Native Quarters" or the purchasing of houses. These loans were theoretically long term (fifteen to twenty years) at fairly low interest rates (below five percent per year). Financing was jointly assured by one's employer and the colonial authorities, part of the cost remaining to be paid by the future owner. This fund allowed for various construction projects to be completed which were really quite considerable for their time. It is difficult to estimate the importance of these efforts. One official report quotes a figure of 57,000 houses financed by the Fund[3] from 1952 to 1960. Meanwhile, a Royal Fund established in 1955 gave money to 23,000 families to subsidize the purchase of housing.[4]

A new direction was taken with the creation in 1945 of the Ministry of Native Estates, later to become the Ministry of African Estates (OCA). This body was designed to build, acquire, manage, and maintain houses for people of moderate income. The formula of prebuilt construction on a tenant purchase basis thus replaced the individual housing loan system, making it possible for a series of dwellings to be constructed on land developed for that purpose. The official report quoted earlier indicates that, for the portion not covered by personal contributions, tenant purchase lasted fifteen years at a rate of three percent a year, something which is difficult to imagine today. The same report quotes the OCA as being responsible for 32,000 houses completed in this way. The planned estates thus correspond to totally prebuilt units delivered by the OCA through tenant purchase. On these estates the largest households (on average containing 9.5 people) were found in 1975; moreover, these estates contained the highest proportion of employed people and of owner-occupants (57.3 percent as against an average of 45.5 percent) with very little temporary construction.

In 1965 a new public body was formed called the National Ministry of Housing (ONL) with the initial aim of building houses as much as putting out mortgage loans for the purpose. The ONL also took over the duties of the OCA and the Advancement Fund; in particular, it ensured the management of the old housing estates, which were gradually being permanently ceded to their new owners. In 1968 all lending activities were taken out of its hands. Around this time, the ONL actually began to build. The ONL had survived on the income from rents and State subsidies until 1976. Because of a lack of long-term financing, the Ministry was able to build only seven hundred houses from 1970 to 1974, of which half were in Kinshasa and the other half in Lubumbashi. The ONL continues to manage these estates and maintains itself through construction operations outside the housing sector.

In 1971 a new initiative was taken in the establishment of the National Housing Bank (CNECI), designed to collect savings and distribute medium and long term loans to people for building, acquiring, or renovating modest housing. Because the regulations under which it was created provided it with this possibility, CNECI has actually devoted itself to prebuilt construction operations through tenant purchase just as the ONL did. CNECI completed nearly 850 houses from 1971 to 1975 in the North and South Salongo estates of Kinshasa. Completion has not, however, always followed initial planning. The financial situation of the CNECI has deteriorated because of the pressures of massive inflation; a new attempt was made in 1978 to oblige some companies (those in which the State has some interest) to donate to the CNECI three percent of the total amount paid in employee's salaries in the form of a ten-year loan to be repaid at three percent a year. Only a few companies followed through, but this allowed the CNECI to complete the Salongo project.

The churches have established some interesting projects in the field of low-cost housing. Unfortunately, they are still very limited andexperimental. One example is the Christian Church of Zaire (ECZ) which has undertaken a project called "Housing for Humanity." This pilot project, built with community participation, includes the construction of 150 houses and accompanying facilities in the Mount Ngafula district. At present, about twenty houses are finished and occupied. The Church receives contributions from international organizations, thanks to which it can produce materials for the use of the people. The project has encountered problems in execution because of the lack of permanent financial resources and increased costs of materials in the marketplace. Furthermore, rapid cost recovery is not assured by the way in which loans are repaid.

Parastatal companies involve themselves in many ways to improve the living conditions of their employees by constructing or renting houses, by sub-contracting to other companies to construct, and by providing materials loans to employees. The term "self-help" housing is somewhat misleading in that it gives the impression of the future owner laboring himself to construct his own home. In fact, a number of methods are involved. Although there are occasions when the head of the household actually picks up tools himself, it is much more common for him to hire workers, although family members may help from time to time. Usually the future owner not only coordinates the project by assembling the necessary requirements (land, money, and plans) but also supervises the actual task of building, ordering materials, ensuring their arrival, and coordinating their use.

Recourse to self-help housing in Zaire, as in a number of developing countries, is hardly cause for surprise; it allows for considerably lower expenditure since most of the fees for construction are avoided. From this perspective, self-help housing mobilizes workers who would previously have been unemployed; this process is therefore highly beneficial, although benefits may not be translated immediately into financial flows. Moreover, since credit is difficult (if not impossible) to obtain, this is the only method which allows for the adjustment of household savings and investment.

Public Transport
The limited capacity of public transport groups leaves open a great market for private transport which meets half the urban transport needs. In Kinshasa, private transport is organized through private companies or through the informal sector. In 1976 over forty percent of public transport vehicles were devoted to special, school-time, worker or officials' needs. No evaluation of these vehicles has been made. Three types of vehicles are used by the informal sector. These are the *fula-fulas*, which are heavyweight and should normally carry sixty passengers but often carry one hundred; the *Kimahimalis*, which carry up to thirty passengers; the taxi-bus, *Kombi* or little trucks, which carry fifteen to twenty; and shared taxis, which are normal

cars making stops en route to pick up to six passengers. It is difficult to evaluate this mode of transport because of the way it is run (some vehicles are used for other purposes as well) and the importance of stoppages resulting from breakdowns, lack of spare parts, or age of the vehicles. A 1983 survey gives the following totals:

Vehicles	Available	In Service
Fula-fulas	450	150
Taxi-bus	900	350

Education

This commentary focuses mainly on primary and secondary schools. Kindergartens and higher education have not been included. Two forms of this schooling are provided: the state schools and the religious schools (Catholic, Protestant, Kimbanguist, and Moslem).

The primary school population for the city is estimated at 307,318 pupils (Houyoux Inquiry 1975), with almost as many girls as boys. The level of school attendance at the primary level is over ninety percent. The contribution of the religious groups is very important. It seems that, at least quantitatively, primary school facilities respond to demand. In 1960 the city had a significant infrastructure, thanks to which it was possible to deal with the increased school population by introducing the double stream system in schools. In the southern and peripheral extension zones, such a system would really have been inadequate without the creation of new schools in these areas by the missions. In spite of all these efforts, the situation is often uncertain. There are on average sixty pupils per class, frequently in a makeshift classroom without tables or benches.

The Secondary School population has been estimated at 76,469 pupils (*Atlas of Kinshasa* 1975) in which there are twice as many boys as girls. Since 1960 the lack of schooling has begun to be felt; supply no longer fulfills demand, especially in the new neighborhoods of the southern and peripheral extension zones. Lack of schools in these areas forces children to travel long distances to find education, largely in older areas such as Gombé, Kasa-Vubu, Ngiri-ngiri, and Ndjili.

Health

The main medical facilities are situated in the Gombé zone, far from the most densely populated areas. The South and East of the city have only university clinics or the Ndjili health center. Along with the large medical facilities (*Atlas of Kinshasa* 1975), there are about one hundred dispensaries and health centers. Half of these are State-managed, the others being dependent on the missions or private funding. In the latter case, health care standards

Table 6.2
Distribution of Facilities by Zone

Zone	Markets	Social Total	Football Fields	Basketball Courts	Cinemas	Centers	Libraries
Gombé	4	20	8	–	4	–	4
Kalami	4	19	3	1	5	5	1
Ndjili	6	18	6	–	4	2	–
Ngaliema	11	16	1	–	3	1	–
Kimbanseke	9	15	3	–	3	–	–
Kintambo	4	12	3	–	3	1	1
Kinsenso	7	11	2	–	2	2	–
Barumbu	3	10	2	–	3	2	–
Makala	7	10	–	–	2	1	–
Matete	2	10	3	–	4	1	–
Kinshasa	1	10	2	–	6	1	–
Limete	4	7	2	–	1	–	–
Lemba	3	8	1	1	2	1	–
Kasa-Vubu	2	7	–	–	4	1	–
Ngiri-Ngiri	1	7	1	–	4	1	–
Lingwala	3	6	1	–	1	1	–
Masina	5	6	–	–	1	–	–
Bandalungwa	2	5	1	–	1	1	–
Bumbu	2	5	1	–	1	1	–
Selembao	3	5	–	2	–	–	–
Ngaba	1	3	–	–	1	1	–
Nsele	–	1	–	–	–	–	–
Mont Ngafula	–	1	–	–	–	–	–
Total	87	212	41	4	54	21	5

are very mediocre, yet for over one-third of the population, they provide the only access to medicine.

Other Facilities
These include sports, recreational, and cultural facilities. There is a sad lack of sports facilities, and those existing are concentrated in the North of the city. Swimming pools and tennis courts are used only by a minority of foreigners. Apart from football fields, Kinshasa is basically without sports facilities. Aside from cinemas and markets, other facilities are very sparsely distributed over the whole of the city. (See Table 6.2.)

Food and Housing:
Two Essential Services for the Urban Population
An analysis of consumption budgets reveals the importance of food expenses, which this study calculated at fifty-seven percent of the household budget in 1986. Even so, nutritional levels are unsatisfactory. This underlines the fact that provisions of basic foodstuffs in this city of 3 million inhabitants and the distribution of food produce are a major factor for urban management.

In order to estimate the quantity of provisions arriving by road, the Bureau d'Etudes d'Aménagements Urbains (BEAU) conducted a study with the Department of Agriculture from April 1984 to March 1985. During this period, in the last or second last week of each month, control posts were set up along the roads running from Bas-Zaire and from Bandundu. The vehicles transporting foodstuffs were stopped and their cargoes inventoried. A study of the same type had been done in 1974 / 5; it is thus possible to judge the way in which the situation has evolved. Table 6.3 summarizes the main products (a total of 251,000 tons in 1984). In a ten year interval, the local products brought in along the roads have remained fairly constant while during the same period the population of the capital has almost doubled. It thus appears that the rural hinterland of the capital has not responded to the increasing demands of the city. This situation reflects a stagnation in rural production or its very minimal growth. Any increase is absorbed by the expansion of the rural population.

One important element to note is the significant diminution (thirteen percent) in the delivery of manioc. Manioc forms the basis of the diet of Kinshasa's population, which is obviously extremely sensitive to its availability in the marketplace. Imports of oil products, palm oil, palm nut and palm cabbages, peanuts, sesame, etc. have remained stable in 1974 and 1984 while fruit and vegetable imports have stayed at the same level. Meanwhile, the quantities recorded here are certainly an under-estimation, since

Table 6.3
Fresh Produce by Road (tons per annum)

	Road to Bas – Zaire				Road to Bandundu				Total			
	1974		1984		1974		1983		1974		1984	
	T	%	T	%	T	%	T	%	T	%	T	%
Manioc	73,400	51	41,000	33	70,900	50	84,400	67	144,300	101	125,400	100
Oil Products	18,000	63	14,800	49	10,600	37	15,300	51	28,600	100	30,100	100
Vegetables	13,800	99	12,200	84	200	2	2,400	16	14,000	101	14,600	100
Fruits	13,400	96	17,900	100	600	4	80	1	14,000	100	17,980	101
Fish	19,400	99	400	89	200	1	50	11	19,500	100	450	100
Animals	1,890	35	850	50	3,500	65	850	50	5,390	100	1,700	100
Cereals	–	–	5,200	38	–	–	8,500	62	–	–	13,700	100
Tubers	–	–	1,900	54	–	–	1,600	46	–	–	3,500	100
Wood	1,400	93	12,200	84	100	7	2,300	16	1,500	100	14,300	100
Charcoal	10,400	78	22,000	74	3,000	22	7,800	26	13,400	100	29,800	100
Total	151,690	63	128,250	51	89,100	31	123,280	49	240,790	100	251,530	100

Source: BEAU, 1985.

production in the market gardening belt of Kinshasa has definitely increased during this period.

Imports by road only take up one part of Kinshasa's consumption. The total amount consumed is provided in Table 6.4. Cereal consumption has almost trebled during the ten years, an increase almost twice as rapid as that of the population. Whereas in 1974 manioc constituted twenty-eight percent of consumption and cereals twelve percent, in 1984 cereals formed thirty-two percent and manioc nineteen percent. Thus, cereals are supplanting manioc and, given their greater caloric values, this is an improvement in the structure of consumption. However, eighty percent of all cereals are imported. At the same time, national maize production is increasing very rapidly. At Shaba, (in the south-east) domestic production now satisfies two-thirds of urban consumption. Is such a change possible in Kinshasa? Oil products and sugar depend on domestic agro-industry; but the latter has not expanded its productive capacity to match the growth in population. Per capita consumption has declined markedly. This is a negative aspect of the balance-sheet which could, however, be easily met by national production. The increase in meat consumption only compensates for the reduction of fish consumption. In 1974 fish imports from the area were in the tens of thousands of tonnes. Now the level is very low, and financial difficulties have done a great deal to restrict the import of salt fish. Malt imports have also fallen. Although brewing remains an active industry, a reduction in the population's disposable income has brought with it a marked drop in consumption.

Much of the fresh produce is imported, a great part being destined for consumption by foreign residents. Some reduction in imports is accounted for by the reduction of foreign residents and by a lowering of purchasing power. Fruits and vegetables (along with sources of energy) are certainly underestimated mainly because of the lack of information regarding imports along the Ndjili valley routes which serve the market-gardens and forest zones of Kasangulu.

Two main conclusions can be drawn from the consumption estimates. First, there is a very marked reduction of food supply provoked by an income reduction of forty percent. This corresponds fairly well to the comment made by many inhabitants of Kinshasa that they now only take one main meal per day. Second, the structure of consumption has changed, cereals becoming the main source of consumption, and meat substituting for fish. The increase in cereal consumption has been made possible by external imports of food aid, but internal reasons also account for the change. Immigration in Kinshasa is now much more influenced by populations originating in Kasai (south-central Zaire), for whom maize constitutes the staple food. Their very significant presence in Kinshasa has changed consumption

Table 6.4
Estimate of Consumption in Tons,
Kinshasa, 1984

Food	1974 (BEAU) tons	%	1984 tons	%
Cereals	86,035	12.2	235,613	31.8
Manioc	198,355	28.2	141,441	19.1
Oil Products	103,018	14.6	101,545	13.7
Tubers	–	–	3,500	0.5
Vegetables and fruit	49,749	1.1	38,623	5.2
Sugar	52,259	7.4	55,714	7.5
Meat	9,618	1.5	40,000	5.4
Salt	6,718	1.0	7,738	1.1
Malt	31,224	4.4	19,756	2.7
Fish	31,582	4.5	8,203	1.2
Animals	6,620	0.9	1,700	0.3
Fresh Produce	127,536	18.2	84,826	11.5
Total 1	702,695	100.0	738,659	100.0
Fuelwood	13,648		17,403	
Charcoal	29,800		31,100	
Total 2	47,203		44,748	
Total 3	785,862		747,443	

habits. In nutritional terms, this is certainly progress. In terms of external dependence for Kinshasa, it is a negative move. Yet the development of domestic maize production, along with rice, could decrease the relative dependence on imports. This should be one of the goals of national agricultural policy.

In terms of the distribution of food produce, Kinshasa markets of different levels may be identified, without counting the floating markets which grow up around the presence of certain activities (restaurants, fairs, and livestock markets). Most important are "first order markets" which form central poles for greater Kinshasa. These are the Grand Marché, Gambela, and Simba Zikita, situated in the heart of the old neighborhoods (Kinshasa and Kasa-Vubu) and serving the whole of the agglomeration. Grand Marché and Simba Zikita offer manufactured goods in over thirty percent of their stalls. Grand Marché specializes in beauty products, Simba Zikita in ironmongering.

All markets across the city share a series of traits. Some are permanently built (Grand Marché, Gambeal, and part of Ndjili). Others, recently renovated, are made of solid metal structures, the foundations of which have been redesigned to improve their functioning. But most are temporary. The overall impression is of an enormous hive of activity under rapidly constructed and often unsanitary conditions. One walks through long lines of stalls linked and winding, encumbered by posts or by leaky roofs. The paths fill up with muddy refuse as soon as it rains. In other markets, or even in the first and second order of markets on the edges, one even finds goods laid right out on the ground. Yet in spite of their initially confusing and colorful atmosphere, the markets offer, upon closer inspection, a strong internal organization. Buyers and sellers know their business and are well acquainted with the division of the stalls even if the order changes. Each market from the largest to the smallest divides up into specialized areas: manioc, fresh vegetables, fruit, flour and grains, fish, meat, small groceries, etc.

The major markets are directed by an official (administrator) chosen by the zone (by the city in the case of important markets) and an assistant. A committee functions among the public administration agents, the elected member of the business women's organization (AFECOZA), and the member of the JMPR (the Popular Revolutionary Youth Movement) responsible for political activities and propaganda (MOPAP). Every day, the officials (elected businessmen) are designated for each cell (a variable number of sellers usually representing one product) and are responsible for the collection of the daily tax of 6 Z. Vacant stalls are also noted, and waiting sellers are put in contact with owners. Although this might all appear disorganized to the outsider, the market actually functions on an effective system of relationships. The cleaning of the market is done twice weekly by the sellers. *Salongo* (common work) takes place between 7:00 *am* and 9:00 *a.m.*, and rubbish is cleared out of the market towards a depot. Using the weekly taxes (6 Z per person per week), the officials rent a lorry or carts (20 Z per cart per journey) which removes the rubbish to an uncontrolled public dump, or an informal pick-up is made by the town representative.

The daily taxes go to the Local Authority. The officials are convinced that a higher daily tax could be levied (10 Z to 20 Z) if conditions were improved (care of the stalls, concrete flooring, water outlets, etc.). Sanitary conditions in the market are inadequate. Toilets are unusable because of lack of maintenance. The officials are sure that regulations regarding use would be accepted if funds were raised effectively for upkeep as in the case of the improvement of the toilets. Waste disposal remains a major concern: given the lack of a public collection, the officials propose a reorganization of the markets to sign a contract with a well-equipped cleaning company.

The female business representatives complain about food sale conditions. Although inadequate, food provision remains the carefully guarded prerogative of transporters who are not willing to expand their business as the existing conditions are sufficiently profitable. Some women have already invested in the purchase of lorries to improve delivery and are convinced that stronger competition would permit product costs to fall, increase sales, and improve their incomes.

The problems of stocking and gaining access to the market are also important. Especially for small enterprises, transport and merchandising on the way to the market (taxi or cart) represent an extra cost. Those small business people hope to be able to stock their merchandise in stores on the market site (an issue left up to private initiative) on the payment of reasonable tariffs.

The extraordinary dynamism and the volume of daily exchange which they represent underline the importance of the markets in the struggle to improve the urban system. The balance between taxes and services rendered to the business people and, indirectly, to the consumers are at the root of a development of such activities. The environment remains a concern as a guarantee of minimal sanitary conditions. Although existing economic conditions may restrict new projects in terms of infrastructure, efficient management and the improvement of the food provision system offer some hope for future improvement.

Conclusion

In the final analysis, three general problems in the management of rapid growth can be identified: a lack of management and control of urban planning; a lack of necessary resources for the new decentralised authorities; and a lack of data on the cost of urban services. With regards to the first problem, Kinshasa has about 350,000 plots, if one looks at the average level of occupation as just under ten people per plot. Meanwhile, less than one quarter of the plots are officially registered. The latter are concentrated in the downtown area and the old neighborhoods. The peripheral extension zones almost completely escape regulation and are often left to complete anarchy. Among some of the irregular situations and some of their serious consequences are: construction on steep slopes, provoking erosion and involving prohibitive development costs; the building of houses in areas subject to flooding, in which, apart from the unsanitary conditions, it is often the State which has to take responsibility for disaster victims in the case of floods; building on agricultural land; damaging peri-urban agriculture essential for feeding the urban population; and the lack of respect for payments for utilities.

This is not an exhaustive list, and these cases do not result from the contrary nature of individuals, but from the absence of a system of land acquisition and development which can respond to the housing needs of the expanding population common to large African cities. What can one do if land is inaccessible but settle oneself wherever one can? Even though it is illegal, at the risk of allowing practice to supercede codified rules, such spontaneous housing really is becoming, if not legal then at least, permitted. Would it not be better to channel urban growth rather than vainly attempt to constrain it? The most faulty urban legislation is that which fails to point out the best way to use land and fails to make the best use of collective finances. Would it not be better to resolve the gap between legal process and common practice in land distribution? Obviously, the State must reinforce legal procedure, but only with the means to make it generally applicable. Should not land regularization practices in the old districts and simplified procedures for the registration of urban land ownership in the new districts be developed? Has notice been taken of the significant land speculation market which profits certain privileged parties to the detriment of public finances? The establishment of a land fiscal policy which captures the funds needed to manage and equip urban land must now become a priority.

With regard to the second problem, local authorities are really responsible for urban services using local duties directly linked to the services provided for the local population. Meanwhile, urban Zaire is experiencing a time of administrative change, in which authority is in the process of being transferred from the central government to the localities. Decentralized bodies have been created, but even if their authority is well-defined, they have very few means with which to exercise it. The staff serving them depends almost completely on the central authorities for the fixing of its size, its selection, and the payment of basic salaries.

Studies of urban planning and the maintenance of urban roads still depend completely upon central bodies (BEAU and the National Department of Roads and Waste Disposal respectively) for their execution. Finally, in practice, because of a lack of their own financial resources which could be spent here, all investments depend on the State, which plans, finances, and ensures their execution. In the face of such a complexity of structures, as much organizational as financial, it is difficult to identify the specific tasks which fall to the decentralized bodies. Their role seems ill-defined, apparently limited mainly to planning.

Finally, the financial structure of the urban services analyzed does not easily give an immediate impression of the cost of each one. Even in the case of roads and drainage (the costs of which are identified in the State budget), the distribution of expenses at the level of each body does not appear, perhaps because many expenses remain centralized at the level of the Executive Council and not the Department responsible. In the case of household waste disposal, the Department of Roads contributes. The city budget only takes care of fuel expenses and night workers' pay. Obviously, this lack of understanding of the costs and the practices underlying them hampers the search for a better way to organize urban services. This does not mean to say that one could not arrive at an evaluation of the cost of each service, but it does mean that such a task would require methodical and scrupulous investigation of the various factors involved.

The principle of "cost recovery" should be at the base of any new system. This is no real innovation, since the only sectors in which major projects have been possible are water and electricity, which use fees charged for their services. As far as the other services are concerned (road sweeping, garbage collection, etc.), only on-site recovery of the costs will permit the State to launch projects which meet the needs of the people.

At present, there appears to be no process of coordination within the urban system. Public lighting can be installed along a road without prior warning being given to the Department of Roads. Urban land may be distributed to persons without regard for its suitability. No action is taken to bring services or economic activities to the peripheral neighborhoods which have sprung up. Responses to needs of all kinds work on a piecemeal basis. Because of a lack of suitable dumps, piles of rubbish block the roads.

It is fair to say that the management of the urban system of Kinshasa has been overtaken by events. The financial resources and the organizational structures are simply inadequate to deal with the problems. The State remains officially responsible for a host of services which it cannot provide. To meet their needs, households and communities have adopted various strategies. As the official land allocation system is unworkable, it is circumvented. To feed the city, a network of markets functions, albeit at a very low level of basic hygiene. Food could be provided more cheaply if competition in the transportation sector were more open; better services could be financed by the stall-holders if they had more autonomy in management. However, beyond the truisms of the need for "better-management," "full-cost recovery," and so on, solutions must be found within the everyday realities of Kinshasa.

Notes

1. Editors' note: In a personal communication, Mr. Mbuyi explained that the evidence is drawn from monitoring the number of burials. Presumably, the inference is drawn with respect to some estimate of the size of population served by a particular cemetery.

2. This is usually obligatory for all new construction and is included in the procedure for obtaining a building permit; but almost all construction in the low-income neighborhoods escapes this procedure.

3. Report of 14 February 1981, *Social Affairs*.

4. Loic Ricard Report (ILO expert) 1981.

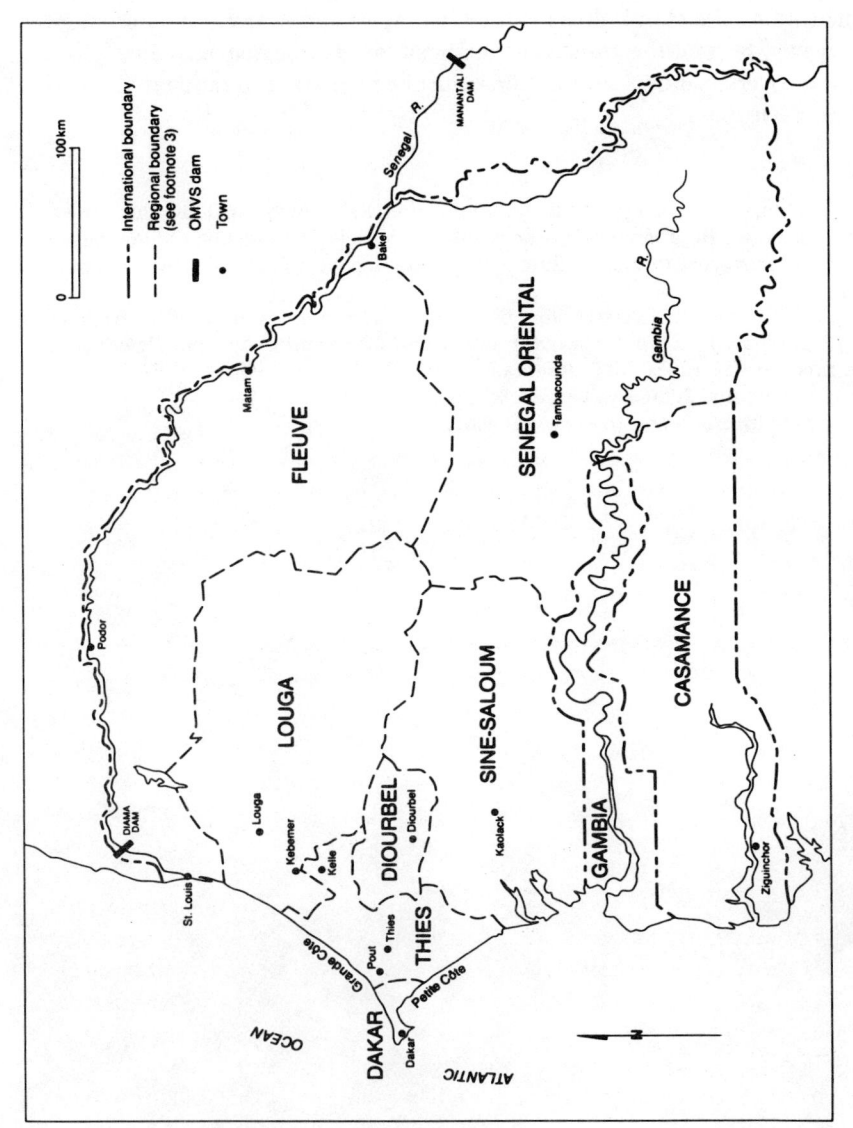

Figure 7.1
Senegal: Regions and Principal Towns

CHAPTER 7
Appropriate Standards for Infrastructure in Dakar

Thiécouta Ngom

Introduction

The rapid growth of the Dakar agglomeration has given rise to many problems of urban management. Despite countless surveys on various aspects of the urban system there is a lack of basic information essential for proper urban planning. Furthermore, despite detailed master plans and lengthy policy statements, there is a lack of specificity on the standards to be attained. This chapter reports on a series of surveys which the Centre de Recherche pour l'Habitat, l'Urbanisme et l'Architecture (CRHUA) – a department of the *Ministère d'Urbanisme* – carried out in 1985-86 to attempt to meet some of these needs. In the course of the surveys, CRHUA provided an accurate delineation of the official *quartiers* (neighborhoods) of Dakar and a complete inventory of public infrastructure. On the basis of these surveys, the average level of service available to the *quartiers* was calculated and the relative level of service was noted in hopes of defining appropriate and attainable service levels. The study focuses on health, education, and waste management.

Urbanization and the Provision of Services in Senegal

Most of the towns of Senegal were founded in the colonial era either as bases for military expansion (Saint-Louis, Gorée, Kaolack, and Bakel) or as administrative centers. Yet economic activity provided the main stimulus for their growth and development. The towns served as intermediaries for the collection of agricultural goods (peanuts and gum arabic) and for the distribution of manufactured goods. These factors, while giving the towns a particular economic function, created also a double disequilibrium. First, the towns display a distinctive morphology, in which a "European neighborhood" (known variously as the *escale* or *Plateau*) monopolized economic and administrative activities in contrast to generally unplanned "native neighborhoods." Second, the most important Senegalese towns are located within

---

Other members of the team which produced this report are Boubacar Fall, Oumar Wane, Mamadou Lamine Bob, and Abdoulaye Cisse.

This chapter was translated from the original French by Rodney White and Claire Letemendia.

250 kilometers of the coast, in the region which specialized in the export of agricultural products.

The hierarchy developed in two stages, each following a different principle. In 1960, at the time of Independence, the development of the towns was primarily influenced by their position in the hierarchy. As a result of their economic or administrative role, urban centers such as Dakar, Rufisque-Bargny, Ziguinchor, Diourbel, Louga, Saint-Louis, Kaolack, and Thiès experienced a rapid expansion in total population. Since the 1970s any settlement of at least ten thousand inhabitants (a threshold chosen by the Department of Statistics) or of five thousand and over (according to the urban code: Chapter 2, Article 7) may be defined as a town. In addition to this numerical criteria is a political / administrative one which ensures the promotion to urban status of ten regional capitals, thirty headquarters of *Départements*, and a number of district headquarters.

Senegalese towns may thus be identified either by their function or by their size; this definition results in a multi-level hierarchy in which Dakar acts as a metropolis because of its administrative, economic, cultural, and demographic importance. The regional capitals play a limited role, acting only as intermediaries linking Dakar with the rest of the country, while smaller centers are considered towns only by their size or by their administrative role, as their economic base is essentially rural in character.

The urban population, estimated in 1984 at 2.5 million or forty percent of the total population, is projected to reach nearly 5.2 million by the year 2000. Almost forty percent of this growth may be attributed to migration; the rest is due to high birth rates projected at 3.2 percent. Most important is the Dakar Region (Dakar and Rufisque); with a population estimated at 1,087,000 by the 1976 census and an average growth rate of 5.6 percent per annum, it will account for fifty-six percent of the urban population of Senegal by the year 2000. Inevitably, this rapid rate of urban growth will have a profound impact on the provision of public services in Senegal.

Housing: The housing problem has still not been solved, despite several policies designed to support the housing sector. First, the state builds housing estates using two agencies – Société Immobilière du Cap-Vert / Cap-Vert Building Society (SICAP) and Office des Habitations à Loyer Modéré / Low Cost Housing Board (OHLM) – and has invested 32.5 billion CFA francs in 19,400 housing units. Yet demand still far exceeds supply. Second, in 1973 the government initiated a "sites and services" scheme designed to provide anyone of a specifically defined income group with a plot upon which he may build according to his own preference. Today, about eleven thousand plots have been distributed in Dakar, yet there is a waiting list of 39,000 or four times the size of the program. The program operates also in Thiès (sixteen hundred plots on seventy-five hectares) and Kaolack (fourteen hundred plots). Third, the establishment of the Banque de l' Habitat du Sénégal / Housing Bank of Senegal (BHS) in 1979 revived interest in low-cost housing; the Bank has financed nearly ten thousand housing units in five years.

In spite of all these initiatives, a housing crisis remains in Dakar partly because of the high cost of building materials. From April 1980 to March 1981 only 1,025 building permits were issued for the whole of Dakar. The housing crisis is exacerbated by the lack of building space in the large towns, where access to land ownership has become a major worry. Because of this situation, land speculation is common, especially in Dakar where speculators will not hesitate to sell land illegally, even though it was supposedly nationalized in 1964.

Waste Management: Most Senegalese towns have no provision for the removal of household and public waste. Garbage is removed spasmodically. Only Dakar, Saint-Louis, Kaolack, Thiès, and Louga have sewage systems. Generally, the inner urban population has access to these facilities, while the most densely populated peripheral areas are left to their own devices, thus creating a serious health problem.

Water Supply: Urban water supply is provided from surface water in Saint-Louis, Dagana, Podor, Matam, Bakel, Kédougou, and Dakar (twenty percent) by the SociétéNationale d'Exploitation des Eaux du Sénégal / National Board for Water Supply of Senegal (SONEES). In Dakar, some households rely on private water connections (36,620 in 1980 / 81) and others on public standpipes (88,726 in 1980 / 81), while a further 5,484 households must buy their water from carriers. With the increase in population and the effects of the drought (which has reduced the level of both Lac de Guiers and the water table), water supply is still problematic (Ba et al. 1983). Today, the estimated shortage is 23,000 cubic meters per day. The situation is worse for the other towns than for Dakar because of a lack of distribution networks and the small amount of water available.

Energy Supply: Energy is provided from primary sources such as fuelwood and charcoal as well as by electricity produced by a network of interconnected power stations which cover the major towns in the regions of Dakar, Thiès, Diourbel, Kaolack, Fatick, Louga, and Saint-Louis. Other urban centers are supplied by isolated generators which function intermittently. The most important energy source for household purposes (i.e. cooking) is provided by fuelwood and charcoal in rural and urban areas respectively.

Health: Despite all efforts to develop and improve them, health and sanitation facilities remain inadequate and very unevenly distributed. In 1982 the ratio was 1 bed per 1,310 inhabitants in hospitals, 1 per 1,900 inhabitants in regional health centers, and 1 per 1,820 inhabitants in maternity centers. A strong concentration of these facilities may be observed in the west of the country, and in particular around Dakar and its suburbs.

Education: The level of schooling in Senegal was still quite low in 1979; only thirty-two percent of children from six to ten years of age were attending school. This level has been improving by about six percent per annum. In 1982 the 1,795 elementary schools, totalling 8,577 classes, received 452,679 pupils, eleven percent of whom were in private schools. This increase, however, has been surpassed by a high demand for educational facilities, especially in the Dakar Region.

Transport and Communications: There is an extensive network of motorable roads (3,612 kilometers of asphalted roads in 1982 and 11,150 kilometers of roads surfaced by laterite or earth) in addition to the railway network (1,032 kilometers of single-track and 70 kilometers of double track between Dakar and Thiès). The latter is important for freight only (especially phosphates); transport for passengers and for other goods is provided by the road network, which provides rapid and regular links between the towns. In Dakar, urban transport is the responsibility of the Société des Transports en Commun / Public Transport Board (SOTRAC), which operates twenty regular bus routes. To this service are added the 760 privately operated minibuses and 2,500 taxis. In other urban areas, public transport is provided by taxis, minibuses, and horse-drawn carts. Inter-urban transport is supplied by taxis seating seven persons and minibuses seating fifteen to twenty-five. There is also a regular connection by sea and river between Dakar and Ziguinchor as well as between Saint-Louis and various towns in the Senegal River Valley. These operations deal mostly with freight. Air Senegal also provides linkages to Dakar, Saint-Louis, Ziguinchor, Tambacounda, and Kédougou.

Meanwhile, throughout the 1970s and 1980s the Senegalese economy has been characterized by a low growth rate (below the growth rate of the population) because of climatic fluctuations and a serious deterioration in the terms of trade. The average annual increase in the GNP was only 1.6 percent. The Dakar Region accounts for eighty-seven percent of salaried jobs and fifteen percent of the GNP; in other regions salaried workers represent only ten percent of the employed.

From this analysis of urbanization and the provision of public services in Senegal, the importance of Dakar is evident as it has resulted in a concentration of political and economic activities and the extreme primacy of Dakar in relation to the rest of the country. Some steps are being taken to reduce this imbalance. These steps include an institutional framework which favors the autonomous development of local communities, a legal framework which stimulates industrial decentralization, and an investment code which favors businesses which locate outside Dakar. However, at a time of very slow economic growth any reduction in the imbalance will be slight.

Research Methodology

The survey was limited to the First and Second *Départements* of the Region of Dakar, known as the *Départements* of Dakar and of Pikine. (See Figure 4.) These two *Départements* include all the continuous built-up area as well as the coastal strip which connects Dakar to the old ports of Rufisque and Bargny. With the cooperation of the administrative and local authorities, access was granted (via the *préfets* of the First and Second *Départements*) to the official list of neighborhoods and the names of their respective Heads (*Chefs du Quartiers*). The First *Département* is subdivided into four districts (*arrondissements*) while the Second *Département* separates into eight sectors (*secteurs*). A series of maps were obtained from the Ministry of Urban Planning and the Land Survey Department at scales of 1:1,000; 1:2,000; 1:5,000; and 1:10,000.

After certain basic information had been gathered, a list of facilities was produced. This was divided into fifteen categories represented by letters from A to P, with numbers in each category providing a more detailed breakdown (as in the following example).

B Health Facilities

B 1 Clinic

B 2 Health Center

The survey of facilities, management, and users required five different questionnaires, including a general questionnaire referring to all of the various facilities, a guide designed to direct the interviewers towards a consistent working method, a questionnaire on medical facilities, a questionnaire on educational facilities, and a questionnaire on waste management and water provision.

In order to assure uniform preparation of the list, a coding manual was prepared. The sampling framework for more detailed work was based on eight steps:

Step 1: Calculation of the average level of service provision at the scale of the *Département* level (for all facilities except those serving a national or regional need, such as hospital, high school, university, etc.)

$$\frac{\text{population of given } Département}{\text{number of actual facilities}} = \text{number of persons per facility}$$

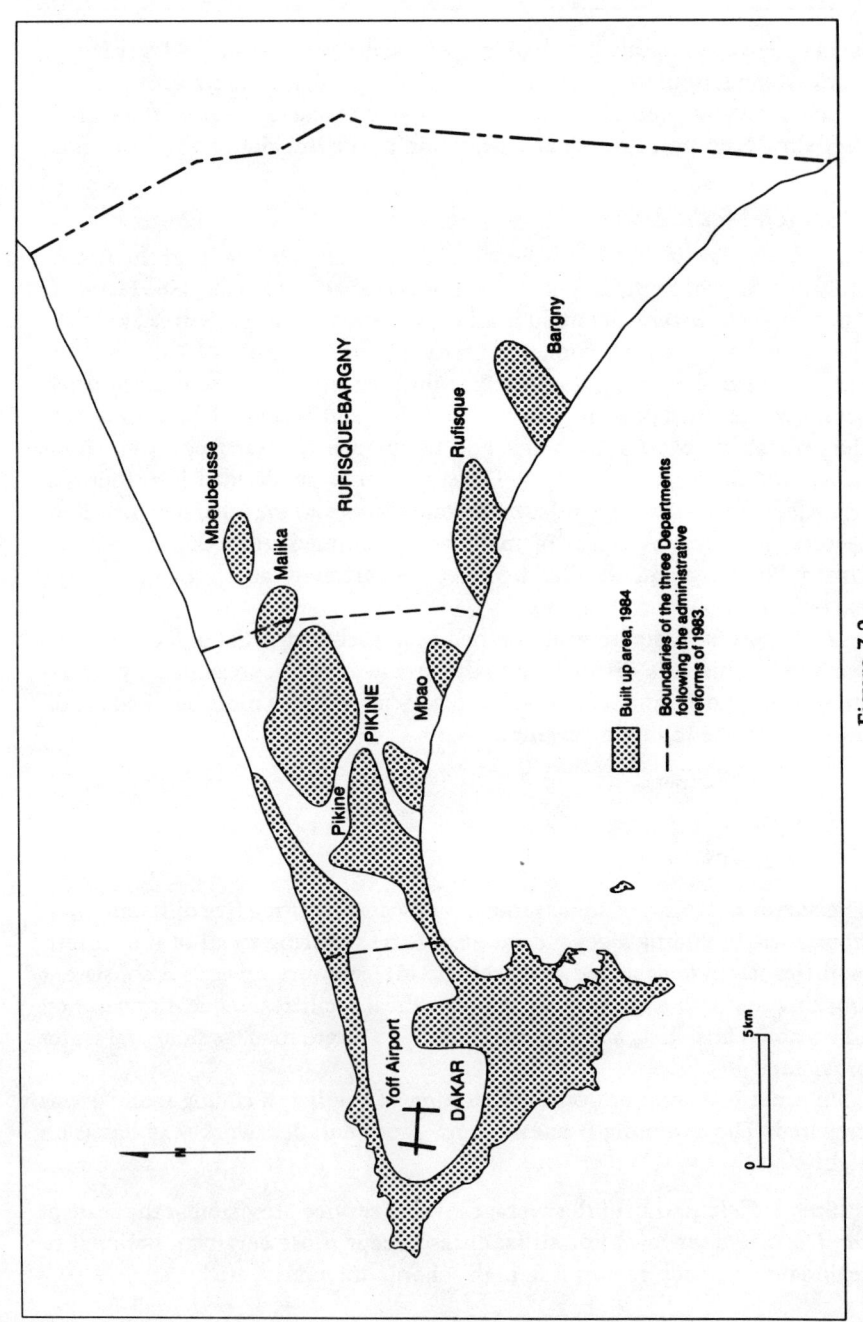

Figure 7.2
The Region of Dakar, 1984

Step 2: Evaluation of an expected ratio of facilities per neighborhood and per district on the basis of the ratio at the departmental level

$$\frac{\text{population of a given neighborhood}}{\text{divided by departmental ratio}} = \text{theoretical number of facilities}$$

Step 3: Application of above method to all facilities per neighborhood and per district (expected service level)

Step 4: Enumeration of the number of existing facilities per neighborhood and per district (actual service level)

Step 5: Evaluation of positive or negative variations by percentage determined in the following manner

$$\frac{(\text{actual facilities} \times 100)}{\text{expected facilities}} =$$

Step 6: Classification of the neighborhoods by level of service for each type of facility so that the following four categories may be identified

— no service at all (without facilities)
— poorly serviced (from 0-75 percent of the *Département* norm)
— normal service level (76-150 percent of the *Département* norm)
— overequipped (above 150 percent of the *Département* norm)

Step 7: Development of a table integrating the results from the four categories

Step 8: Selection of a sample of neighborhoods and types of facilities for study purposes to include the most representative cases and the most extreme.

The interviewers had to make local Heads of the various neighborhoods (*Chefs des Quartiers*) aware of the purpose of the work at hand, not only to secure their collaboration but also to identify the neighborhoods themselves and to mark down their boundaries on maps. In some cases, in neighborhoods where roads were neither named nor numbered, this task could only be accomplished by having the Head accompany the research team to point out boundaries and mark them down on maps. The researchers were required to make an inventory of existing facilities and eventually to mark out plot boundaries on the maps. The team members were able to obtain the list of existing facilities and their location from technical departments or bureaus responsible for the installation or maintenance of facilities. These data were then compared with field results. Maps were drawn up showing both neighborhood boundaries and the type and precise locations of facilities, after having first plotted on a single map of 1 / 5000 information made available through the smaller maps. Finally, estimates of the 1985 population were made on the basis of the 1976 census. (The research methodology

Table 7.1
Districts and Neighborhoods of the *Département* of Dakar

		Neighborhoods as Surveyed		
Districts	Official Neighborhoods	Number	Number of Plots	Estimated Population
I	21	21	8,465	76,185
II	27	23	4,349	91,329
III	60	77	22,592	271,104
IV	59	54	12,277	159,601
Total	167	177	47,683	598,219

Table 7.2
Sectors and Neighborhoods of the *Département* of Pikine

			Neighborhoods Surveyed		
Sectors		Official Neighborhoods	Number	Number of Plots	Estimated Population
I	"Derrière la Voie Ferrée"	10	14	2,192	18,417
II	Diamaguène	70	111	16,947	90,214
III	HLM Guédiawaye	31	22	4,083	19,285
IV	Médina Gounasse	36	15	5,706	27,474
V	Nimzatt et Angle Mousse Guédiawaye	15	10	1,392	6,314
VI	Pikine	72	55	10,585	110,491
VII	Premier Guédiawaye	21	13	3,923	29,931
	Total	255	240	44,828	302,126
	Golf-Sud	12	–	–	–

and results are described in detail in CRHUA's Final Report, *Les équipements urbains à Dakar*, July 1986).

Research Results

Demographic and Administrative Background

Table 7.1 shows the results of the field survey of the neighborhoods in the First *Département* (Dakar), with the number of occupied plots and the population estimated by district according to the adjusted 1976 census. The survey identified 177 districts in the whole of the *Département*, as opposed to the 167 noted on the official list. This variation is due to the discovery that some neighborhoods have only fictitious political subdivisions, while other neighborhoods do exist even though they are not on the official lists.

Of the eight sectors which constitute the *Département* of Pikine (the Second), seven were surveyed. (See Table 7.2.) The eighth, Golf-Sud, includes a large part of the sites and services scheme (Parts I to VI) and another zone which is not mapped. The observed variations between the number of neighborhoods on the official lists and those surveyed in the field result from the same factors indicated in the Dakar *Département*. In Pikine, another important point is that *Département* authorities do not have available to them all of the lists of neighborhoods and neighborhood heads. Aside from this, certain neighborhoods were mistakenly listed where they did not belong.

In the Pikine *Département*, there are two different types of neighborhood heads. In one type, the heads are appointed by an administrative directive from the Ministry of the Interior; they are called "decision-makers." In the other, the heads, called "witnesses," are appointed through testimonials from political representatives. The first type is found mainly in the old neighborhoods (the Pikine sector) and the second mostly in the other sectors, which are populated largely by people who have been dispossessed of their land from the First *Département* of Dakar. The "witness" may find himself in a variety of situations. First, he may be entirely responsible for a neighborhood. Second, he may live in the same neighborhood as the "decision-maker," in which case he serves as second-in-command. Third, a number of "witnesses" may be in the same neighborhood with a "decision-maker," but in this case their role is not clearly defined. There are also a small number of heads of neighborhoods who fit into neither of the categories defined above. These heads apparently work as volunteers, hoping only to be of some use to the people of the neighborhood they represent.

Neighborhoods of the Pikine *Département* also have some of the irregularities (extensions, arbitrary divisions, and interpenetrations) found in the neighborhoods of the First *Département*. Moreover, the occupation of new plots takes place in an uncontrolled fashion, especially in the Diamaguène-Yeumbeul sector where there is still available land. This explains the

Table 7.3
Population Distribution
in the Dakar and Pikine *Départements*

	Dakar	Pikine
Plots		
Total	47,683	44,828
Number of neighbourhoods	177	240
Average per neighborhood	269	187
Population		
Total	598,219	302,126
Total plots	47,683	44,828
Average per plot	12	7
Average per neighborhood	3,380	1,259

Table 7.4
Pupils Per Class, *Département* of Dakar

District	Elementary School	Junior High School	Secondary School
1	47	44	41
2	53	47	48
3	61	47	42
4	64	40	25

presence of small neighborhoods which were created in a manner which does not qualify them for any public services.

As shown in Table 7.3, the average number of plots per neighborhood in the First *Département* is 269, as opposed to 187 in the Second *Département*. The average number per plot in the First *Département* is 12; in the Second it is 7. The average population per neighborhood in the First *Département* is 3,380 inhabitants while in the Second it is 1,259. Moreover, the Pikine *Département* sectors are disproportionate in terms of both surface area and population; the most populated (the Pikine sector with 110,491 inhabitants) surpasses the least populated sector (Nimzatt and Angle Mousse Guédiawaye with 6,314 inhabitants) by 17.5 times. In the *Département* of Dakar, the most populous district (the Third, with 271,104 inhabitants) is only 3.5 times higher than the least populated district (the First, with 76,185 inhabitants).

The disparity in size of the neighborhoods in the two *Départements* leads to the conclusion that the setting of boundaries to the neighborhoods is not based on criteria well-defined by the administrative authorities. The extent in area of each neighborhood is strictly linked to the influence of the neighborhood Head upon the inhabitants. The manner in which other public services break down their operating area (e.g. SONEES and the police force) is not the same as the administrative one, nor are they consistent with one another.

The Distribution of Services

This section identifies the level of facilities for each district in relation to their respective populations, including spatial distribution and the level of service per type of facility.

Health

Health facilities are organized in a hierarchy from the hospital to the clinic, although some retain a specialized purpose. A clinic, known as the "maternity clinic," functions at a village level, treating first aid needs, emergencies, and child birth. A health care center and an urban maternity clinic are found at the headquarters of the rural community as well as in the towns. A medical center, located at the *Département* headquarters, is organized like a hospital, usually providing up to one hundred beds, and includes a maternity clinic, modern medical facilities, emergency services, and a laboratory. A hospital is a regional institution in which all illnesses other than those particular ones assigned to the care of specialized facilities are treated. Some hospitals, such as Dantec, Fann, Albert Royer, Principal, and Thiaroye – all in the Region of Dakar – also serve a national population. A center for maternal and infant health (PMI) specializes in the care of mothers and their children.

Disparities among the various Districts of the Dakar *Département* reflect both the age of each district and the activities engaged in by its inhabitants. Out of the 208 medical facilities in the *Département*, the First District has 108 or 52 percent; the Third is next with 54 or 26 percent; the Fourth follows with 29 (14 percent); while the Second has a total of only 18 (8 percent). For private pharmacies, the socio-economic level of the population in the various districts influences the distribution of such units. As a result, the First District has only 2,822 inhabitants per unit as compared to 22,832 persons for the Second; 15,947 for the Third; 22,800 for the Fourth.

The *Département* of Pikine is the least well served as it developed more recently and much of it is unplanned. Unlike the *Département* of Dakar, Pikine has only three major health facilities: the Dominique health center installed in the sector of Pikine and the Baudouin Center located in First Guédiawaye (both recently established); and the health center of Pikine Guinaw-Rail. These facilities offer additional services due to the distance from the large hospital facilities concentrated in central Dakar. The Dominique center of Pikine (a dispensary transformed into a health center) serves the following sectors: Pikine, First Guédiawaye, and DVF (*Derrière la voie ferrée*) – the settlement area known as old Pikine.

In cooperation with Belgium, Senegal has just completed two very important health centers for its people, consisting of health clinics structured in the same way as a health center. In fact, they are "small relay hospitals" which provide the kinds of treatment available in large health centers. These two centers, located in First Guédiawaye and DVF, supplement the Dominique center of Pikine, which is always completely flooded with patients. Completed a few years ago, the First Guédiawaye center functions as a Maternal and Infant Health Care unit (PMI), providing facilities for maternity needs and a health clinic with thirty beds. The DVF clinic, designed in the same way both in terms of form and function as that of First Guédiawaye, is a little smaller in size. They owe their establishment to the new State policy called "Health for Everyone."

The Ministry of Health is responsible for major investments to improve health care under the Four Year Economic Development Plan. Other organizations, such as the Commune, private social groups, or individuals are developing projects in cooperation with the Ministry. Private Services include doctors' offices, clinics, and pharmacies. Their practice and their presence are regulated, and they cannot exist without State authorization. However, their location generally depends on the availability of potential clients. This means that although a concern for planning may be expressed, requisite criteria evidently include a certain flexibility in terms of the precise location of the facilities. In some instances, as in the case of pharmacies, a service population is fixed by law (fifteen thousand persons for the

Dakar area, and thirty thousand for the other areas) and a market radius (from one thousand to two thousand meters according to the zones). The population and radius criteria are subject to revision every five years.

All construction of health facilities in the Dakar *Département* during the period 1979-85 was private, with the exception of one health center in the Fourth District. The private sector provided one clinic and five doctors' offices in the First District, one doctor's office in the Second District, three clinics, two pharmacies, and eight doctors' offices in the Third District, and one health center, four pharmacies, and four doctors' offices in the Fourth District. In Pikine *Département*, most of the facilities established in that period were public, with the exception of one birth clinic (eighteen beds), three doctors' offices, and four pharmacies.

Education
The educational system, which accounts for over thirty percent of the national budget, is composed of several levels: Pre-school education, elementary school, general junior high school and technical school, secondary school and technical school, professional education and higher education. Pre-school education covers children from two to six years of age and is mostly privately run, although public pre-school educational facilities are expanding noticeably (twenty-three percent from 1981 to 1984). Children enter elementary school at the age of seven and remain for six years. The goal is to achieve a one hundred percent attendance rate; however, of the population of school-age children from six to eleven years old, only thirty-five percent were in school in 1980. The distinction between the general junior high school (ninety-one percent of the total in 1980) and technical school will soon be eliminated, making way for a single program designed especially to strengthen education in the sciences and to generalize the teaching of technical skills.

Secondary school and technical school are divided into first, second, and final classes. Admission rose from 1,293 pupils in 1960 to 16,855 in 1980, with an average increase of 14.5 percent per annum. From 20,897 pupils in 1981/2, the stream grew to include 24,049 pupils in 1983/4, an average yearly increase of 7.3 percent. This number is higher than that given by the Sixth Four Year Plan (6.9 percent). The general Secondary Stream takes in 80 percent of those leaving Junior High School. Meanwhile, the Technical School at this level has been neglected for a long time and grew only 13.9 percent from 1978 to 1982.

The Ministry of National Education controls various kinds of professional institutions with different training programs and involving different types of people. Conventional-style establishments recruit pupils from the third class of the secondary level. The nine professional institutions took in only 1,196 pupils in 1983 / 4, as opposed to 1,236 in 1982 / 3. This small decrease is due especially to recruitment restrictions imposed by the admissions office and by low salaries. Higher education includes the University of Dakar, which has four faculties and six schools and institutes. From Independence to the present day, the university population has multiplied tenfold from 1,012 students in 1960 / 1 to 10,467 in 1983 / 4.

Although the *Département* of Dakar is well-served compared to the rest of the country, it is far from satisfying the requirements of the population. There is also a disparity among districts in terms of the distribution of schools related to the age of the neighborhoods and the standard of living of the inhabitants. Elementary Schooling includes a total of 1,618 classes and 93,637 pupils (56 per class) in the *Département* of Dakar. Distribution of people per class in relation to district is shown in Table 7.4. The different levels of service between the various districts reflects the problems experienced by the people in assuring their children a good education.

In general, professional institutes located in the First *Département* serve students on a national basis from all regions in the country. Twenty-eight institutions concerned with national education were surveyed; 281 classes and workshops with 8,627 enrolled pupils were studied giving an average of 31 pupils per class. Social centers are the responsibility of the Ministry of Social Development and cover a wide range of activities of interest to both young and older women, including retirees. There are 9 social centers, with 29 classrooms and 1,913 enrolled in classes.

In general, the *Département* of Pikine is less well equipped than the *Département* of Dakar. The latter benefitted from a time of relative prosperity and confidence in the 1960s, and it has continued to benefit from investment in new infrastructure especially in the private sector. The oldest part of the *Département* of Pikine (*Pikine Ancien*) was built to the standards of the 1950s and 1960s. The post-1970 growth is largely unplanned with very little infrastructure. The older standards of health and educational facilities was planned for the Sites and Services project but most were cancelled because of a shortage of funds. The whole of Pikine has only one technical high school, no secondary schools, and only three social centers.

Water Supply
This section of the report focuses on the problems of water supply by standpipe (used by those who do not have access to a private connection), the spatial distribution of these facilities in the First *Département*, and investment policy regarding standpipes. Water supply in the Dakar area has always presented problems partly because of low productivity and excess demands placed on pipelines and partly because of the deficit between maximum available production (165,500 cubic meters / day in 1985) and the average

needs of the Dakar area (180,200 cubic meters / day). Water supply in the urban areas of Senegal is provided by both private connections and by public standpipes. Private connections exist mainly in high or middle income areas where water pipelines have been installed; public standpipes are used in areas without adequate distribution networks and for lower income groups in the underprovisioned zones.

According to the CRHUA survey, in the 117 neighborhoods of the First *Département*, forty-eight percent of the population use private water connections, while fifty-two percent rely on public standpipes and water carriers. Distribution of private connections varies from sixty-eight percent of the population in the First District to seventeen percent in the Fourth.

In the *Département* of Pikine, stress has been laid upon the introduction of standpipes, given the poor supply of sources of drinking water. Thus, 434 public standpipes were surveyed. Their distribution amongst the sectors in terms of their respective populations provides the following ratios: Pikine 1,513 persons per standpipe; First Guédiawaye 831; Nimzatt and Angle Mousse Guédiawaye 574; HLM Guédiawaye 536; and Diamaguène-Yeumbeul 434 persons, giving an average of 696 persons per standpipe.

Waste Management
The treatment of solid and liquid waste is a major problem in Dakar. Generally, according to the Hygiene Department, the elimination of used water, household waste, and human waste is effective for only one quarter of the houses of Dakar. As a result, nearly one-sixth of the total solid human waste produced daily in Dakar (a mass estimated in 1976 at sixty tonnes) is dumped outside proper toilet facilities; this causes a great amount of filth in highly populated neighborhoods. The lack of solid and liquid waste elimination facilities in these areas gives rise to ill-health and discomfort for the inhabitants.

The collection and elimination of liquid waste in the *Département* of Dakar is the responsibility of public authorities. Sewage networks, open drains, and public toilets are used for this purpose. Sewage networks in the First *Département* form interdependent sub-systems, one known as the "downtown," another as the "Hann Fann" network, and another as the "Médina / Gueule Tapée" network. Open drains, designed to draw off storm water are Canal IV, Canal IVa, Canal VI, Canal VIa, and the Gueule Tapée canal. All of these drain water from the downtown area and part of the industrial zone. Public gratings, in some cases constructed in a makeshift fashion, are found mainly in such neighborhoods as Grand-Dakar, Médina Colobane, and Rebeuss. In these neighborhoods, the people generally get rid of used water by throwing it either on the ground, into the canals, into the openings of storm water drains, or into unplanned public drains. Public toilets are estimated at 117 (not counting school lavatories) and are distributed thus: twenty-one in the First District, twenty-eight in the Second, thirty-two in the Third, and thirty-six in the Fourth.

Reasons for the poor situation must be sought at both the level of public agencies (State and local) and at that of the community. Public agencies are in part responsible for establishing and managing waste disposal infrastructures and for taking measures to safeguard public health. Responsibility at the citizens' level should include participation in the waste disposal schemes put into practice by the State and by local communities.

Street sweeping and the collection of household waste is not performed uniformly over the whole of the Dakar area, and significant disparities exist amongst the three *Départements* and among neighborhoods of the same district or sector. Garbage collection is the responsibility of the Industrial Agency for Urban Waste Disposal of Senegal (SIAS), an agency supported by mixed financing to which the Dakar Urban Community has assigned the duty of waste collection since 15 April 1985 on a five year contract. The agency functions within the *Départements* of the region of Dakar, which all present different needs because of the extent of urbanization within each and the condition of the roads within their respective neighborhoods. SIAS collects from 950 to 1000 tonnes of waste per day over the three *Départements*, yet the rate of collection remains high only in those neighborhoods which possess good roads. The vehicles used for pick-ups are adapted to the type of sector they serve, and thus vary in capacity from three cubic meters to sixteen cubic meters. As in the case of human waste disposal, management of garbage disposal always operates at a deficit (connected to overdue payments not yet made by the Urban Community and the State), resulting in poor service for the people. Waste disposal networks are also insufficient, covering not even half the urban area.

Street sweeping and garbage collection is divided into separate sectors of administrative responsibility. No data were obtained on the fifteen hundred employees of SIAS as it exists now, but the former garbage disposal agency Société Africaine de Distribution et Promotion (SOADIP) (Waste Management Agency for the Dakar Commune) used, for one hundred inhabitants, 2.4 trips for the First District, 1.4 in the Second and the Third, and 0.5 in the Fourth.

Garbage collected in 1979 per person per day in a sample of neighborhoods was in the following quantities:

Downtown	1.14 kg
Médina	0.64 kg
Grand-Dakar	0.51 kg
Sicap-OHLM	0.65 kg

Ngor-Yoff 0.24 kg
Moyenne Dakar 0.49 kg

Collection levels are higher in neighborhoods which have good roads to provide access to pick-up lorries. In these neighborhoods, collection is on a daily, household, and individual basis. In those neighborhoods without good road access for lorries, the situation on 1 August 1985 (the date upon which SIAS began its activities) was characterized by the presence of forty-three illegal dumps in the *Département* – seven in the First District, four in the Second, seventeen in the Third, and fifteen in the Fourth. Each of these dumps will be provided with a common container of six cubic meters, according to the technical director of SIAS, in order to improve conditions.

Until very recently, the *Département* of Pikine had only a small number of drainage networks for liquid and human waste disposal, mainly in the OHLM estates (government low cost housing). Water collected in these networks is treated in a small purification plant. In view of the low rate of service, public toilets provide the main communal means of waste disposal in the department. Consequently, the survey examined sixty-eight public lavatories with 1,037 cubicles (not counting school toilets). These toilets were extremely badly distributed amongst the sectors. There are no public toilets in DVF. For the 389 potential users of Médina Gounasse to satisfy their daily needs, there are only twelve working cubicles.

As in the First *Département*, the collection and elimination of household waste in the *Département* of Pikine are the responsibility of SIAS. SIAS has divided the *Département* into six pick-up zones which are different from the administrative sectors. Fifty-four containers in service up to 1 January are used a public dumping areas. The spatial distribution of these six-cubic-meters-capacity containers in relation to the resident population is as follows:

DVF	18,417 persons
Pikine	9,207
Médina Gounasse	9,158
Premier Guédiawaye	7,483
Diamaguène-Yeumbeul	3,733
Nimzatt Angle Mousse	3,157
HLM Guédiawaye	1,928

A January 1986 study on household waste gives an average of 0.20 kilograms of waste per person per day, confirming an earlier study in 1978 of BCEOM which estimated an average of 0.24 kilograms per person per day in Pikine.

The construction, upkeep, and renovation of essential waste water disposal services are a State responsibility under the Fourth Social and

Economic Development Plan. Local Authorities have control over urban health policy dealing with such issues as the collection and treatment of household waste as well as the building and maintenance of communal sanitation facilities (amongst which are public toilets, public drains, and sewers). Less than two percent of the community budget is spent on investment in and the operating of waste disposal services.

Garbage disposal falls under the general budget of the Local Authorities, which has been drastically unbalanced by heavy staffing expenses amounting to fifty-three percent in 1984. This disequilibrium has an impact on waste and garbage disposal services. In terms of garbage disposal, the largest investment made by The Dakar Urban Community (approximately 200 million CFA) was the construction of a compost plant for household waste on the Rufisque Road at the site of a former controlled dump. This plant has actually only been in operation for three years because of premature breakdown of equipment, lack of a market for the compost, etc. Given that garbage disposal is linked directly to the state of the roads, policy in the former area should be preceded by a significant effort on the part of the community to improve roadways so that neighborhoods insufficiently served may be opened up to garbage collection lorries. In these neighborhoods, especially Pikine, carts are employed to pick up household waste and deposit it at points on the route of the SIAS lorries.

Until 1978 public conveniences were under the management of Community Technical Services; then the Dakar Urban Community signed a management contract for these facilities with the "Senegal Business Agency," and from this date on, practically no new toilets were built, as may be gathered from the 1984/5 community budget. The construction of public toilets is subject to a geographical disequilibrium because of the gap between proposed and actual provision of new services. To this is added the existing scarcity of public lavatories in areas without proper waste disposal. Taking as a starting point the standard set by the community (one public toilet to serve one thousand users), more than three-quarters of all potential users have not been accounted for by the Dakar Community in its building project for public lavatories. This situation poses serious hygiene problems for low income neighborhoods which will be so very poorly served under such circumstances.

In terms of investment expenditure, the most recent figures surveyed are in connection with the 1984 / 5 budget; public toilets fall here under the heading of "Health-Hygiene." According to policy decided on 31 March 1985, the Urban Community of Dakar allocated 3 million CFA francs to the planning and construction of the whole of the sub-sector "Health-Hygiene," an allocation which seems ridiculous when one considers that the construction of a single public toilet facility exceeds this amount. Over the same period, the Urban Community of Dakar allocated 112.7 million CFA francs to "Health-Hygiene"; but none of this has yet been spent. This situation suggests that the program to build new toilet facilities for the public is no longer being pursued by local authorities. It might further be supposed that the population itself is taking control over the public facilities; studies on the population *per se* will more accurately confirm this hypothesis.

Municipal Management

This section surveys the working characteristics (definition of a commune, categories of communes, the way in which a commune is established) which govern all of communes in Senegal and which explain the special nature of the new Commune of Dakar. A commune is a group of people from the same place united by a solidarity derived from living together, eager to pursue their own interests, and able to find the means for such action within the national community as a whole and within the spirit of national interest. It is a decentralized group vested with legal responsibility and financial autonomy. There are two types of commune in Senegal. The first type is a Common Law Commune. There are twenty-eight of these, including the three new communes of Dakar (Dakar, Pikine, and Rufisque-Bargny) with the exception of regional headquarter communes. In these communes, municipal government is constituted by a municipal council and a municipal office, composed of the Mayor and his assistants. The Mayor represents legal authority within the commune and consequently has extensive powers. The second type is a Commune by Special Statute. These are the nine regional headquarter communes, with the exception of Dakar. In these communes, the municipal government is composed of a municipal council, the municipal administrator, and his assistant. Here, the role of Mayor has evolved into that of Commune Administrator, a high-ranking official appointed by decree. He is assisted in his duties by a similarly appointed official. The Commune Administrator exercises his powers through the control of the Municipal Council.

A commune is established by decree. Only adequately developed localities with sufficient resources to meet necessary expenditures and balance their own budgets may achieve commune status. By law, a commune must have a population of at least one thousand people. The establishment decree fixes the name, headquarters, and boundaries of the new commune.

The Dakar area is unique because of its degree of urbanization and its small size (550 square kilometers) for a total population of 1,161,677 inhabitants in 1980.[1] Furthermore, the task of reforming its administrative system is particularly difficult. The last reform (Law No. 83-48 of 18 / 2 / 83 on the reorganization of the Cap-Vert area) created three *Départements* – Dakar, Pikine, and Rufisque-Bargny – each of which (in accordance with the general form of Senegalese administrative structures) is administered by a *Préfet*, without the office of a *Sous-Préfet*. The name "Cap-Vert Region" has been replaced by that of "Dakar Region," with a Governor and a Regional Council at its head.

The Decree 83.1129 of 29 / 10 / 83 further created three new communes in the Dakar region: the commune of Dakar (which corresponds territorially to the *Département* of Dakar), the commune of Pikine (which corresponds territorially to the *Département* of Pikine), and the commune of Rufisque-Bargny (which includes the village of Sindou, with Rufisque as the main center). The Urban Community of Dakar (CUD) was created to coordinate the three communes under the direction of a President and a committee composed of delegates representing all of the communes. The Dakar Region has two rural communes: Sébikotane and Sangalcam, which are not part of the Urban Community of Dakar. The CUD is responsible for the management of public services of an intercommunal nature as well as those which are of such importance that none of the three communes can handle them singly.

Two levels of political bodies govern the functioning and management of the communes. The first is the Municipal Council, composed of some councillors who represent the people and some who represent social and economic interest groups. The councillors representing the people are elected for a term of five years by universal suffrage, and their number is fixed on a *pro rata* basis according to the number of inhabitants in each commune. This number varies from thirteen to fifty-nine councillors. Councillors representing social and economic interest groups are designated on the basis of their capacity to be most representative within the conditions fixed by decree. Their number is also fixed on a *pro rata* basis according to the number of resident inhabitants in each commune. This number varies from two to ten.

The Municipal Council, composed of the Mayor, his assistants, and the municipal councillors, meets four times per year. It has authority over all commune matters, except for those for which the Mayor is personally responsible. It issues statements on all business submitted to it on both a legal and an administrative level. It may also issue directives on all matters of local interest.

The Mayor is elected by secret ballot by a majority of votes from the Council. He may have no more than twelve assistants, whatever the size of the commune. He performs a dual role. He is the Commune Administrator, and as such must prepare and put into effect the decisions of the Municipal Council, a task for which he is solely and wholly responsible. His activities are supervised by the Municipal Council. He is also the State representative, since he is responsible for the execution of general security measures and all of the special functions designated to him by law (representative of the civil government and possessor of legal signing power). He is also responsible for the municipal police.

The Committee of the CUD is composed of ten delegates elected by secret ballot. The existing distribution of delegates amongst the communes is as follows: three for Dakar, three for Pikine, and two for Rufisque-Bargny. The purpose of the CUD is the management of one or many services of interest to the commune as a whole, and as such it is responsible for road construction and maintenance, street sweeping and general cleaning, the removal and elimination of household waste, the management of the municipal hospital of Abass Ndao, the management of the municipal slaughterhouse of Dakar, the management of the Moslem cemeteries of Soumbédioune and Yoff as well as the Catholic cemeteries of Bel-Air and Hann Mariste, the management of the training center for municipal staff, and the liquidation of debts of the former commune of Dakar. Up to the present, this distribution of duties has still not been put into practice completely.

The President is elected from the delegates representing the three communes and sitting on the Committee. His duties are those which have been given to the Mayor by existing laws and regulations. As such, he carries out the decisions of the Committee.

Generally speaking, either a service is contracted out to the private sector (to which bills are paid very irregularly by the communes) or it is the responsibility of the commune services. In some instances, it is the State (the central government) which oversees the functioning of an urban service. Several different levels of jurisdiction thus emerge as shown in Table 7.5. The personnel from the CUD and the three communes listed in the 1985 / 6 budget are tabulated in Table 7.6. In spite of the considerable number of staff employed in technical services, service falls far short of the expectations of the people. Absenteeism, inefficiency, lack of supervision, and lack of facilities emerge as the main causes of this situation.

While it has not been possible to give an account of all the material resources at the disposal of the various communes of Dakar, vehicles per urban service listed in Table 7.7 provide some idea of how these resources are used. Vehicles play a key role in ensuring the effectiveness of urban services for the population. The first point of interest is that of the eighty-four vehicles for the commune of Dakar and the CUD, only thirty-four are in service. The most striking deficiencies are in ambulances, sanitation, and Abass Ndao Hospital; in all of these, only one vehicle is operating for a population of nearly 600,000. Were it not for State intervention, service for the people would be non-existent.

During the first year of the application of the new municipal reform in

Table 7.5
Responsibility For Services

	Services	Executing Agent[1]	Supervising Agent
1	Land-use control		Ministry of Urban Planning and Housing
2	Transport	(a) SOTRAC (P) (b) informal sector (P)	Ministry of Services
3	Electricity	SENELEC (P)	Ministry of Industrial Development
4	Telephone	Postal and Telecommunications Bureau (S)	Ministry of Communications
5	Water supply	SONEES (P)	Ministry of Water Resources
6	Drainage and sewage	Soc. Sénégalaise des Travaux Urbaines (P)	
7	Road construction and maintenance	Roads and Bridges Dept. (S)	Ministry of Services
8	Street lighting and traffic lights	SENELEC (P)	Ministry of Industrial Development
9	Public spaces	The communes	
10	Market maintenance	CUD	
11	Street cleaning	SIAS (P)	CUD
12	Solid waste	SIAS (P)	CUD
13	Public and school toilets; ditches	Soc. Sénégalaise Entreprise des édicules scolaires (P)	CUD
14	Burials; cemeteries	CUD (some); the communes (others)	
15	Municipal slaughterhouses	SIAS	CUD
16	Municipal hospital (Abass Ndao)	CUD	

[1] (P) = private; (S) = State. "Private" may include a significant percentage of public ownership.

Table 7.6
Personnel with the CUD and the Three Communes

Personnel	Total	Technical Services
CUD	1,340	876
Dakar	1,351	72
Pikine	545	52
Rufisque-Bargny	266	19
Total	3,502[1]	1,019[2]

Source: Department of Local Government: Staff and staffing costs for the communes, on October 1, 1985.

[1]Excluding delegates from the neighborhoods.
[2]Excluding administrative personnel who cannot definitely be accounted for.

Note: The above figures differ amongst the sources consulted.

Table 7.7
Vehicles Owned by the
Dakar, Pikine, and Rufisque-Bargny Communes

Function	Dakar		Pikine		Rufisque-Bargny	
Central Services	48	(27)	11	(11)	11	(9)
Undertakers	4	(3)	1	(1)	1	(1)
Ambulances	10	(1)	1	(0)	2	(1)
Sanitation	11	(1)	–		–	
Police	3	(1)	–		–	
Abass Ndao Hospital	8	(1)	–		–	
Total	84	(34)	13	(12)	14	(11)

Source: Technical Assistance Project for the Rehabilitation of Urban Management, Part 4: Municipal Policy, Urban Services, August 1985 (Ministry of Planning and Cooperation, World Bank).

The number of vehicles actually functioning at the time of the survey is shown in brackets.

Dakar, expected resources for the Commune of Dakar alone reached 4,667.5 million CFA francs (1 FF = 50 F CFA) or 67.69 percent of the total projected receipts from the three communes (see Table 7.8). The importance of fiscal receipts (57.83 percent) should be noted, followed by that of municipal taxes (24.33 percent), rents (15.22 percent), and other receipts (1.61 percent). Together these budgetary resources represent 7,802 CFA francs per person for the Commune of Dakar, the most populous of the three communes (598,219 inhabitants). Yet there is a deficit in receipts, mainly in fiscal and municipal tax receipts, with a recovery rate of only about fifty percent.

Provisional working expenses for the Dakar commune account for 68.57 percent of the total for the three communes. Investment expenses account for 14.7 percent, personnel for 27.3 percent, and working expenses for 58 percent, thus adding up to a total charge of 7,229 CFA francs per person for the Dakar commune, not including the part reserved for the CUD.

Between 1984 / 5 and 1985 / 6 there was a significant decline in the budget of about 48 percent over the total of expenses, especially in the case of regular expenses other than personnel. Moreover, the total budget of the three communes and the CUD shows a decline of 1.16 percent in 1985 / 6, with a total deficit of 6,299.3 million CFA francs owing mainly to unplanned expenses.

Conclusions

In spite of the effort that has been made to distribute power amongst the State, the CUD, and the communes, a great deal of confusion remains

Table 7.8
Receipts of the Communes
(1985-1986 Budget in CFA millions)

Item	Dakar	Pikine	Rufisque-Bargny	Total	Structure (% of Total)
Fiscal receipts	2,743.3	965.4	278.9	3,987.5	57.84
Municipal taxes	1,128.3	364.1	185.2	1,677.6	24.33
Rents	728.2	248.5	141.7	1,118.4	16.22
Other receipts	67.8	23.2	20.0	110.9	1.61
Total	4,667.5	1,601.1	625.8	6,894.4	100.00

Source: Same as for Table 7.7.

because of a lack of clear identification of the existing division of power and responsibilities amongst the various structures. The responsibility of local groups is frequently diluted in the hands of the State, which still has final authority in most matters. The absence of real public services, apart from the technical services which were transferred from the former communes of Dakar to the CUD, creates a serious gap between the structures which have theoretically been put in place and the manner in which they really operate.

Almost all urban services are contracted out by local authorities with very little follow-up on delivery. The role of local authorities in the provision of services under their jurisdiction remains highly theoretical. The accumulation of debts owed to the enterprises responsible for delivering services threatens the functioning of the whole urban system. For example, by July 1985 the maintenance of public toilets, traffic lights, and public lighting were no longer to be relied upon. Demand further and further exceeded the financial means of the communes and the CUD, a condition exacerbated by bad management.

This study of urban services in Dakar has not fulfilled all of its initial objectives, but the team has still managed to shed some light on certain aspects which have been previously neglected. New information has been provided on the actual boundaries of the neighborhoods and districts, an exhaustive list of actual services in place has been drawn up, and finally, an account has been given of investment policy for urban services and of the municipal management under the new administrative reform of the Community of Dakar.

The methodology applied has allowed for greater organization of fieldwork for the surveying of neighborhood boundaries and the facilities in these areas and for the transcription of these results onto maps. From the boundaries of the neighborhoods may be revealed the real socio-administrative situation and the weakness in spatial organization of the Dakar urban area. The listing of existing facilities has made it possible to demonstrate the way in which each service studied is distributed (health, education, water supply, and waste disposal) over the urban area; but above all, it highlights the significant gaps between service levels in the different neighborhoods. The investment policy regarding the services studied does not follow a particularly rational planning strategy; on the contrary, it is subject to a kind of anarchy dominated by those with investment capability (politicians and donor agencies). The study of municipal management in Dakar makes it clear that in spite of efforts to rationalize the system there are still a great many problems with the provision of services for the population.

This study is extremely timely, since it has already attracted the attention of the local and administrative authorities (CUD, Ministry of the

Interior, and National Census Office) as well as of other researchers. As first recommended in this report, it is hoped that the present study will lead to further research, especially in establishing standards for the provision of services and the basic elements for a coherent and efficient policy for urban services. It is also to be hoped that other services (than those which were the object of this study) might be investigated in the field. This kind of study could also be extended through a sampling system to the rest of the urban and semi-urban areas of Senegal, especially the middle-sized towns and regional capitals, which could in turn lead to the establishment of national standards for urban services for different levels of the urban hierarchy. This would provide the urban planning process with working tools to improve the choice of facilities, their size, and their location.

Notes

1. Study of the Dakar Urban Master Plan; Synthesis of urban data; Household studies – SONED Afrique – BCEOM, January, 1982.

CHAPTER 8
Local Government and the Management of Urban Services in Tanzania
Saitiel Kulaba

Introduction
This chapter will outline and analyze some of the problems of urban growth and the management of urban services in Tanzania, as exemplified by six urban centers: Dar es Salaam, Mbeya, Tanga, Morogoro, Moshi, and Tabora (see Figure 8.1). According to the August 1978 National Population Census, these six urban centers accounted for 46.4 percent of the country's total urban population. The efficiency and productivity of these towns have a major impact on the economy of the country and on the well-being of the majority of the population.

Past studies on urban growth in Tanzania have several shortcomings. For example, growth (including migration) has been studied mainly at the aggregate demographic level. Little work has been done on intra-urban differences or on the relation between growth and the access to and management of urban services (Project Planning Associates 1968; Hutton 1972; Hayuma 1984; Kulaba 1979; Mascarenhas 1966). Past studies on local government and finance in Tanzania covering the post-independence period of the early 1960s reflect many of the problems of a newly-independent country in a state of transition to nationhood (Dryden 1968; Warrell-Bowring 1963; Lee 1965; Penner 1970). But with few exceptions (Stren 1975; Kulaba 1981), there has been little research on the urban impact of Tanzania's development philosophy of Socialism and Self-reliance, as this philosophy was articulated in the late 1960s and onwards. As a result of the major emphasis on rural development by the Arusha Declaration of 1967, a number of important constitutional, legal, and administrative changes have taken place in the country; these changes have profoundly affected the status, operations, functions, and organization of local government in Tanzania. This study aims to fill part of the gap in our knowledge of recent urban growth and its implications for the finance, delivery, and management of urban services. The challenge facing urban local governments in Tanzania is to solve these pressing urban problems within an environment of limited resources and institutional constraints.

The study towns have a number of common characteristics: a growth rate of six to eighteen percent per annum; a narrow tax base and an inelastic

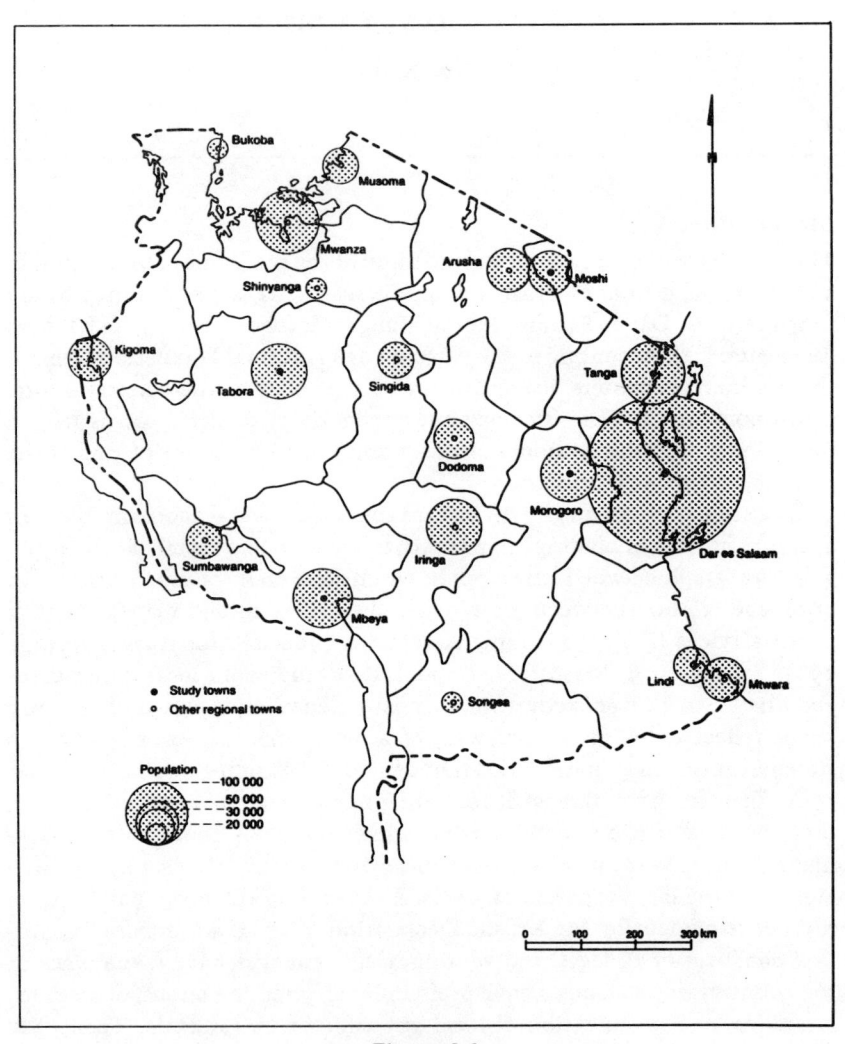

Figure 8.1
Tanzania: Study Towns and Cities

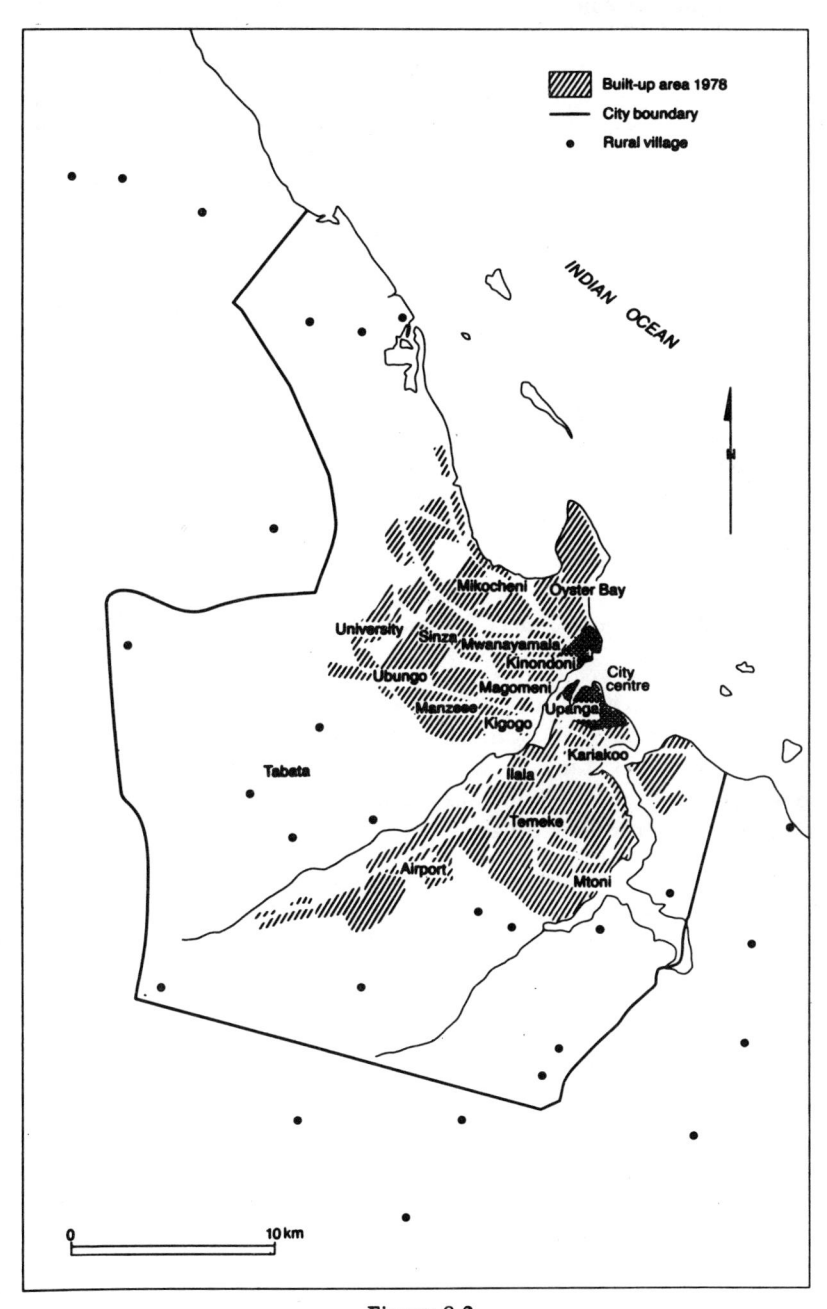

Figure 8.2
Dar es Salaam: Areal Extent

tax structure, hence insufficient revenue to finance the provision of more and better services; inadequate maintenance of infrastructure, which continues to deteriorate every year; and a lack of co-ordination among the various organizations involved in urban management and development. Other characteristics of the individual study towns are discussed in the following paragraphs.

Dar es Salaam: This is a major metropolitan area. With a population of 757,346 (1978 census) and an estimated 1.6 million in 1986 over an area of 1,100 square kilometers, the city is the largest and most densely populated urban area in Tanzania. Notwithstanding the 1973 decision of the ruling Party – CCM (Chama cha Mapinduzi) – and the government to shift the capital of Tanzania from Dar es Salaam to Dodoma in the center of the country, Dar es Salaam remains the largest seaport and the industrial, commercial, and communications center of Tanzania. Although of a low standard when compared to developed countries, Dar es Salaam's network of infrastructure and utilities is by far the best in the country. All the major transportation routes by air, sea, rail, and road which connect various parts of the country as well as those which connect Tanzania with the rest of the world originate in Dar es Salaam.

Tanga: This town had a population of 103,409 within its township boundaries in 1978. By 1986 the estimated population was 197,000, over an area of 360 km^2. A seaport, Tanga is one of the oldest towns along the East African coast, with a number of industries and tertiary activities. In recent years, it has been economically stagnant.

Mbeya: This municipality had a population in 1978 of 76,606 within its township boundaries or 78,111 when the population of its suburbs which form part of Mbeya Urban District was included. The town had an estimated population of about 153,000 in 1986, covering an area of 174 km^2. Mbeya is located in a region with a healthy climate, fertile soils, and a high mineral and agricultural potential. The development potential of the town is, however, blocked by inadequate power resources, infrastructure, and utilities.

Tabora: This municipality, with an area of 120 km^2, had a population of about 67,392 in 1978 as an urban district. Tabora had an estimated population of about 106,000 in 1986. It is located in a region of low agricultural and industrial development potential and a rather dry climate. Tabora is one of the oldest towns in the interior of East Africa; its initial expansion dates back to the early trading caravans of the thirteenth century. Tabora town is a service center with a number of tertiary activities (especially education establishments) and very few industries. The town has a narrow tax base and declining economy.

Morogoro: This municipality, covering an area of 63.3 km², had a population of 61,890 in 1978 within its township boundaries and 74,114 as an urban district when the population of its suburbs was included. By 1986 it had an estimated population of about 120,000. It is located in a vast region of high agricultural potential with especially fertile soils and an excellent climate. A fast growing town, Morogoro has attracted a number of industries because of its proximity to Dar es Salaam (being 176 kilometers from the harbour of Dar es Salaam) and has become the second largest industrial center in the country after Dar es Salaam. Its recent physical expansion, like that of Mbeya Municipality, poses difficult development options for planners, decision makers, and urban administrators. Although planners hope that Morogoro's growth will ease the congestion of Dar es Salaam, the town has yet to get better roads and adequate power and water supplies.

Moshi: This municipality, with an area of 56.5 km², had a population of 52,223 in 1978 as an urban district. It had an estimated population of about 131,000 in 1986. Moshi is a commercial town where land values and population density are high. It is located in an area of scarce and very fertile agricultural land on the slopes of Mount Kilimanjaro.

Over the whole country, an estimated urban population increase of about 350,000 people per annum and the accompanying physical extension of the towns is a continual strain on the limited services available. In terms of land requirements, this substantial population increase requires from 770 to 850 hectares for residential plots alone per year, assuming an average density of four hundred persons per hectare. When other land uses such as roads, open spaces, primary schools, and urban dispensaries are also included, the total annual land requirement rises to as much as 1,150 hectares. Such an expansion means building the equivalent of two serviced municipalities a year, each the size of Mbeya Municipality. Since experience has shown that it is cheaper to plan ahead of new development – especially to install infrastructure, utilities, and community facilities – the need to expand the planning capacity of urban councils and a consequent demand for more trained manpower, finance, and equipment is therefore obvious.

Urban local governments also face the challenge of creating productive employment opportunities which can pay for urban services. As John Friedmann (1973, 154) has argued, "Urbanization is no longer regarded as an unfortunate by-product of planned industrialization whose consequences governments should learn how to constrain, but as a set of powerful development forces in its own right."

A particularly difficult task facing urban councils is the construction and maintenance of surface drainage channels which are more important in Tanzania than in temperate climates because of the problems of tropical rainfall and attendant seasonal flooding. Storm water drainage tends to be overlooked in the design and construction of urban roads. A weak development control system has also led to the erection of buildings on natural drainage systems, to man-made surface drainage channels, and to a considerable amount of dumping of refuse in such areas. Such construction practices often exacerbate seasonal flooding as was the case in the Mtoni area in Dar es Salaam in May 1986, where flooding resulting from heavy rains destroyed more than two hundred houses. Strengthening of development control using available resources is a major challenge facing urban councils.

In general, most of the pressing needs of urban development involve construction and finance. There is need for a complete reconstruction of most urban roads which are in a bad state of disrepair as a result of neglected maintenance, for the provision of new schools and dispensaries, and for the construction of new housing. A recent policy announcement in Parliament in 1986 states that urban and rural district councils must henceforth raise locally most of the finance they need for both their recurrent and development budgets. The central government has also announced a substantial reduction of grants as of January 1987. This raises the question of how and from which sources urban councils will raise adequate revenue. Possible further deterioration in the standard of municipal services – especially refuse and garbage collection, sewage disposal, mosquito control, environmental sanitation, roads, and water supply – appears inevitable unless immediate action is taken. The high rate of rural-urban migration is making these issues and the design and implementation of pragmatic policy measures to meet them a matter of urgent attention. The following sections discuss what some of these measures could be.

Urban Growth and Urbanization Problems

Tanzania, with an estimated population of 22.3 million people in 1986 (an annual rate of increase of 3.5 percent), has an urban growth rate of 9.2 to 12 percent per annum (Kulaba 1981). The most recent National Population Census of August 1978 estimated Tanzania's total population at about 17,516,610 of which 13.78 percent lived in urban areas. While in mainland Tanzania 13.25 percent lived in urban areas, on the islands of Zanzibar and Pemba, urban residents comprised 32.55 percent of the total population. The two islands are therefore more urbanized than the mainland. The significant growth of the urban population in Tanzania is the direct result of the three major factors: rural-to-urban migration; the natural population increase of the urban population; and a change in geographical boundaries of urban areas.

A large net rural-to-urban migration accounts for the bulk of the urban growth in Tanzania. For example, the percentage share of net migration in urban growth from 1970 to 1975 was found to be sixty-four percent while the share of urban growth resulting from natural population increase was thirty-six percent over the same period (Newland 1980, 10; Renaud 1981, 165-66). Results from our survey study of Dar es Salaam show that eighty-one percent of the respondents were not born in the city; similar results were obtained for the other main towns included in this survey.

Recent droughts and floods in some rural districts have added to the flow of urban migration. Moreover, the proliferation of lucrative petty trade, especially in major urban centers since the beginning of the 1980s, has attracted a large number of rural youths as well as retained those already in urban areas. As Table 8.1 shows, the urban population on Tanzania Mainland increased 18.5 times in a period of three decades while its share of the country's total population increased fivefold over the same 1948-78 period.

Over the 1967-78 period, the urban population on Tanzania Mainland more than trebled in size and its annual growth rate rose (from 6.0 percent over the 1957-67 period) to 11.1 percent. The annual growth rate of the country's total population also rose from 3.0 percent over the 1948-57 period to 3.3 percent over the 1967-78 period, and the trend is likely to continue. If the 1967-78 urban growth rates continue, the combined total population of the nineteen main towns (which accounted for about 76.6 percent of the country's urban population in 1978) will have more than doubled in just over seven years – from 1,664,088 in 1978 to 3,329,176 by March 1986 (Kulaba 1981, 84). Dar es Salaam City Region accounted for 38.5 percent of the country's urban population in 1978 and is expected to have a population of over 3.6 million at the end of the century. Population projections suggest that the total urban population of Tanzania will increase more than fivefold, and one in every three people will live in urban areas by the year 2000.

Such a redistribution of the national population will call for drastic changes in current policies. Urban development must be given more importance and resources than at present, and rural development and agriculture must be made more productive. A related problem has to do with the unplanned or "squatter" settlements as they are sometimes called. The present growth rate of twenty-two to twenty-five percent per annum in the unplanned areas of major urban centers means that their population is doubling every four to five years, thus straining further urban infrastructure and facilities. The large proportion of the squatter population to the total urban population in Tanzania calls for changes in attitudes and policies toward the development of these low-income settlements because squatter settlements are no longer marginal settlements as they were in the 1950s and early 1960s. Both the central government and urban local governments face the challenge of harnessing the human and financial resources available in these settlements so that these become a national asset and not an economic and financial liability.

The six study towns will account for about 55.2 percent of the total urban

Table 8.1

Population Growth Trends in Tanzanian Study Towns, 1948-2000

	Population				Annual Growth Rate (%)			Population Projections	
	1948	1957	1967	1978	1948-57	1957-67	1967-78	1990[1]	2000[2]
Dar es Salaam	69,277	128,742	272,821	757,346	7.1	7.8	9.7	1,918,400	3,641,000
Tanga	20,619	38,053	61,058	103,409	4.8	4.0	4.9	239,000	453,600
Mbeya	3,179	6,932	12,479	76,606	9.1	6.0	17.9	233,600	424,400
Tabora	12,768	15,361	21,012	67,392	2.1	3.2	11.2	173,000	332,100
Morogoro	8,173	14,502	25,262	61,890	6.6	5.7	8.5	153,000	290,044
Moshi	8,048	13,726	26,864	52,223	6.1	7.0	6.2	123,700	234,800
Total	122,014	217,316	419,496	1,118,866				2,830,700	5,376,300
As % of Tanzania's Total Urban Population:									
	64%	59.7%	69.2%	49.6%				54%	55.2%
Tanzania Mainland Total Urban Population:									
	183,862	364,072	685,547	2,257,921	6.5	6.0	11.1	5,193,000	9,745,700
Tanzania Mainland Total Population:									
	7,480,400	8,785,500	11,958,654	17,048,329	3.0	3.1	3.3	24,354,000	32,729,800

Source: Bureau of Statistics, *Recorded Population Change 1948-1967, Tanzania Population Census, Vol. II*, Government Printer, Dar es Salaam; Kulaba, 1981, Table 5.2, p. 84.

[1] Assuming a 7% urban growth rate.
[2] Assuming a 6% urban growth rate.

population of Tanzania by the year 2000. Hence, the share of the urban population of the six study towns in the country's total urban population is expected to rise over the 1978-2000 period. Therefore, any policy measure aimed at strengthening urban management and the improvement of living conditions in the six urban centers is likely to benefit more than fifty percent of the urban population of Tanzania.

The present high rate of population growth is likely to continue for several reasons. For example, life expectancy has increased from an average of about forty years or less at the time of independence in 1961 to fifty-five years or more now. Similarly, since fifty-one percent of the population is in the reproductive age group of fifteen to forty-five years, a high fertility rate will contribute to a large natural population increase in the next decade even if each couple were to decide to have only two children in their lifetime. Further success of government efforts to control the six killer diseases – measles, whooping-cough, polio, diptheria, tuberculosis, and neo-natal tetanus – will contribute to a substantial reduction in infant mortality. Therefore, whatever population control or family planning measure is undertaken, it will have a small impact in reducing the natural population increase in the foreseeable future. This has important implications for urban growth. With an average birth rate of ninety to one hundred births per day, Dar es Salaam is the city with the third highest birth rate in the world (Kulaba 1985b).

High birth rates and the in-migration of a young population mostly in the fifteen to thirty-five age group (according to the survey results) imply a broad based population pyramid. A broad-based population pyramid, in turn, creates an inflated demand for education and health facilities, especially primary schools and mother and child clinics whose provision and management are essentially the responsibility of local councils (both rural and urban) in Tanzania.

Expansion of township boundaries is another major source of urban growth in Tanzania, increasing significantly the area and number of people which urban local authorities have to deal with using the limited resources and vehicles at their disposal. If left unchecked, these urban population growth trends could force a dramatic rearrangement of national priorities and a consequent distortion of investments in the economy. Investments geared to arrest the deteriorating situation in the urban fabric could take away scarce resources from high priority areas such as rural water supply, primary schools, dispensaries and clinics, and agriculture.

At this point it is necessary to say something about the methods of research used for this study. The main data for the study was collected through records and documents in the form of government enactments, annual plans, reports, circulars, directives, and statistics; and through field interviews with officials at all levels of government. Similarly, documents on the history of local government, and financial records in the case of urban councils, were explored. At the same time, however, it was necessary to get an idea of the magnitude of urban problems as seen through the eyes of ordinary people, and measured against statistics which were not drawn from official sources. Accordingly, in 1986-87 the research team administered seventeen hundred questionnaires on housing and the socio-economic characteristics of the respondents as well as seven hundred questionnaires on the perception of general urban management problems to a random sample of heads of household (and the houses they lived in) in the six study towns.[1] The largest single subgroup was the 660 questionnaires administered in Dar es Salaam. These houses consisted of a total population of 9,828 or 2,606 households. This gives an occupancy rate of 14.9 persons per house, about 4.0 households per house, and 2.4 persons per habitable room. The average household size is 3.8 persons.

An analysis of the socio-economic data furnished by the 660 respondents interviewed in Dar es Salaam shows that thirty-two percent are in paid permanent employment, two percent are in temporary employment, twenty-seven percent are in self-employment, thirty-three percent do family work, while six percent do farm work or keep dairy cattle. None of the respondents claimed he (or she) was unemployed. Even the nine retired officers interviewed were found to be engaged in some income-earning activities such as farming or trade. The distribution of income was rather uneven. Eighteen percent of the households were in what would normally be considered a low-income bracket (earning up to Shs.2,000 per month), twenty-nine percent were in the middle income group (earning from Shs.2001-4,000 per month), thirteen percent were in the upper middle-income group (earning from Shs.4,001-5,000 per month), while a substantial proportion (forty percent) were in the upper income group, earning from Shs.5,001 per month and more.

One possible explanation of such an income distribution may be the fact that a large number of the households interviewed (seventy-two percent) earn supplementary incomes from a number of activities such as farming, dairy cattle, poultry keeping, piggeries, business or petty trade, repair work, or work in garages; still others get a substantial part of their food requirements from their farms. Another possible explanation is the fact that 49.4 percent of the households reported more than one member of the household employed (thirty percent of these additional workers in the formal sector, seventy percent in the informal sector). Since the early 1980s the earning of supplementary income from other economic activities – especially petty trade – has become common amongst urban residents who earn a regular salary or wage. The figures on income distribution should be interpreted with care because many of the respondents, especially those living in spontaneous settlements, clearly earned substantial incomes from such petty trading activities as the selling of home-made foodstuffs, fruits, soft drinks, and the like. This became obvious when their reported expenditures were matched with their reported incomes. The general tendency was to understate income "from other sources" when it involved petty trade because traders are wary of government tax collectors and tend to dissimulate income from poultry keeping, cattle, and pig raising since township by-laws do not allow the keeping of farm animals and poultry in urban areas. As a result, reported expenditures were higher than reported income. Many respondents felt freer to state their expenditures on various items – notably food, clothing, education, transport, fuel for cooking purposes, and indoor lighting – than they did to state their incomes.

Data on housing tenure from the Dar es Salaam survey indicates that about fifty-six percent of the respondents own the houses they live in, thirty-nine percent are tenants, and five percent stay in relatives' or parents' houses free of charge. The majority (82.6 percent) of the total 2,606 households who live in the 660 houses covered by the housing survey are tenants. Sixty-three percent of these tenants rent one room per household, twenty-one percent rent two rooms, and thirteen percent rent three rooms. Only four percent rent four rooms or more. This pattern of renting one or two rooms by eighty-three percent of the tenant households reflects the low rent-paying capacity of the majority of urban residents both in Dar es Salaam and in the other main towns of the survey.

The survey also identified a number of houseowners for whom some interesting socio-economic data may be presented. Of the 371 houseowners that could be interviewed in Dar es Salaam, only seventeen percent are in the low-income group, twenty-seven percent are in the middle income group, while the largest proportion (fifty-six percent) are in the upper middle-income to high-income groups (i.e.those earning more than Shs.4,000 per month). As for the financing of house construction, seven percent of the houseowners relied solely on a housing loan from the Tanzanian Housing Bank (THB), the major source of housing finance in Tanzania. Another two percent used their own savings supplemented with a THB loan, while the largest percentage (sixty-nine percent) relied exclusively on their own or their family's savings to finance the construction of their housing. A small number (ten percent) used profit and income from their business to finance construction. One implication of these statistics is that the role of the THB in financing housing construction and improvement is very small. The majority of houseowners rely on their own savings. Indeed, only two percent of houseowners obtained loans from their employers. The role of employers in financing the housing of their employees in Tanzania is insignificant in the total volume of housing finance.

Local Government and Urban Management Before and During the Decentralization Program

Local Government and Development

Since the beginning of the 1960s, the concept of "development from below" has had considerable appeal. Both within and outside government circles, observers and practitioners have recognized the importance of local institutions and public participation in decision-making and development. The rationale behind this interest is that the support and understanding of the populace at the grassroots level are critical to the success of planning and development strategies designed by national governments. Thus, according to one authority on local government, "if this institution is given some degree of autonomy it can be a useful instrument for implementing the planning strategies designed by the center and for communicating the information on which strategies are based from the bottom to the top" (Penner 1970, 61). Lady Ursula Hicks (1961, 6-7) has argued that local government

> ... is an attempt to give the people their own socialism, not to rely upon a central government socialism, which must seem to be (and would no doubt for some time have to be) imposed from outside.... Economic activity by local government may well be the best way in which "the people" can play a part in the organization of their own economic development.

Other writers have expressed similar views (Alderfer 1964; Cheema and Rondinelli 1983; Dryden 1967, 1968; Picard 1979). But of most importance for Tanzania was President Julius Nyerere's strong support for the notion of local government with considerable autonomy, as embodied in his statement that

> ... there must also be an efficient and democratic system of local government, so that our people make their own decisions on the things that affect them directly, and so that they are able to recognize their own control over community decisions and their own responsibility for carrying it out. Yet this local control has to be organized in such a manner that the nation is united and working together for the common needs and for the maximum development of our whole society (1967, 11).

Further in the same document he argued: "The development of Tanzania cannot be effected from Dar es Salaam; local initiative, local co-ordination of plans and local democratic control over decisions are also necessary" (1967, 34).

Local governments are also seen as instruments for the mobilization of resources needed to meet the recurrent costs of operating and maintaining capital projects. This interest stems from three major sources:

... (a) the push to decentralize government decision making, (b) the desire to improve the relative quality of life in secondary cities and rural areas both for its own sake and to slow the rate of migration to the largest cities, and (c) the recognition that local governments might be in a better position than the central government to capture local taxable capacity outside major cities and to determine appropriate local service priorities (Bahl, Miner and Schroeder 1984, 215).

Being closer to the people than central government, local governments are better placed to mobilize local resources needed for local and national projects. Thus, interest in local government dovetails with discussions of the necessity for more decentralization in the operation of government. According to Shabbir Cheema and Dennis Rondinelli, the desire to decentralize central government authority with respect to the planning, implementation, and management of development projects arose from three converging historical factors:

... first from disillusion with the results of central planning and control of development activities during the 1950s and 1960s; second, from the implicit requirements for new ways of managing development programs and projects that were embodied in growth-with-equity strategies that emerged during the 1970s; and third, from the growing realization that as societies become more complex and government activities begin to expand, it becomes increasingly difficult to plan and administer all development activities effectively and efficiently from the center (1983, 10).

Financial autonomy or having a major independent source of finance under the control of local governments is considered central to the true meaning of local government (Hicks 1961; Hepworth 1971; Penner 1970; Alderfer 1964; Mawhood, 1983). Local governments are thus instruments for building and strengthening democracy in a country and a means of building leadership qualities at the local level. Efficient local government is a means to rapid economic development. Many African countries have experimented with decentralization policies and programs (involving local government) with various degrees of success (Conyers 1981; Mawhood 1983; Reilly 1983; Rondinelli 1983). Many of the reasons cited for the failure of decentralization programs have to do with lack of resources and trained manpower, a situation which is exacerbated by rapid staff turnover, inefficiency and corruption, and real or perceived threats of disintegration of national policy (Picard 1979). But central governments should also take part of the blame especially where (1) central government has been reluctant to give enough financial resources to local authorities for the duties they have to discharge; (2) central government did not provide the required trained and qualified manpower for local governments; (3) decentralization was conceived and implemented without a clear understanding of its implications and without taking into account the socio-political climate and economy of a country; (4) the capacity of local government to assume larger roles in development planning and management was not understood or was overestimated.

Sometimes decentralization has been designed on the basis of orthodox models of local government and attempts have been made to implement it in its ideal form. But without clearly defined goals and objectives and without taking into account the socio-political environment of the country, decentralization has little chance of success. Indeed, in Africa, when the boundaries of districts coincide with tribal boundaries, the process of transferring powers to local governments may mean that "greater local powers will lead to political disintegration" (Hicks 1961). The transferred services could also deteriorate below tolerable levels because of lack of adequate resources and good management. In countries where the opposition party controls some local authorities (i.e.the majority of the councillors belong to the opposition party), there is a temptation to impose greater centralization and strong supervision by central government (Mutizwa-Mangiza 1986).

Furthermore, the English model of local government, notwithstanding its merits, is only appropriate for countries where both the central and local authorities have a common purpose and interest, where the people think as one nation, and where decentralization receives mass support at the grassroots level as an opportunity for participation in decision-making. What ought to be recognized is that local governments are part of one government and that the areas under their jurisdiction are part and parcel of one nation. There is not, and cannot be, absolute autonomy for local government.

From the foregoing discussion, a number of observations on local government can be made. First, since it is closer to the people, local government has the ability to come face to face with the people's problems. Second, local government provides an opportunity to people and their institutions to develop leadership qualities and skills. Third, local government is a potentially effective means of resource mobilization for the implementation of development projects and the provision and management of basic services. Fourth, local government is a means of establishing and promoting community participation in decision-making, planning, and development, and of strengthening democracy in a country. Finally, because of its location and the participation of elected councillors, if it is given the necessary support and requisite resources, local government has a greater potential to respond effectively to the aspirations and needs of people than does central government. Local government is not a technical problem to be solved merely by the provision of more resources or by enacting laws or constitutions specifying its functions and relations with central government. It is part of society. As such, it has to be viewed in terms of its contribution to the attainment of societal goals and objectives. It is on this understanding that the evolution and performance of urban local governments in Tanzania over the past two decades will now be examined.

A Historical Perspective on Local Government in Tanzania

Before decentralization in 1972, local government in Tanzania was a replica of the British local government system. Each local government authority was characterized by (1) a council composed of unpaid part-time elected councillors; (2) co-option through a committee system of a few individuals on the basis of their experience, training, or background in local government; (3) a semi-autonomous status and clearly defined areas of jurisdiction; (4) multipurpose activity; and (5) powers to make by-laws and raise revenue within its own jurisdiction. Management of local council affairs took place through a specialized system of committees, with the full council as the dominant power. The employed staff (i.e. the salaried and wage employees) were (and still are) answerable to the local council and not to central government.

The functions which local authorities performed (and to a large extent still perform) have included the provision and management of primary schools and urban dispensaries and clinics, refuse disposal, drainage and sewerage or sanitation, roads, water supply, fire-fighting services, mosquito control services, and the control of buildings and trade within their areas of jurisdiction. A direct tax base was provided by the site rate and house tax. The second important source of finance was central government grants given to urban councils. Other important sources included various fees and charges including fifty percent of motor vehicle licence fees.

In 1946 the Municipalities Ordinance No.26 empowered the Governor to establish municipalities and provided for the appointment of councils and regulation of their activities. These bodies, though not popularly elected, were to have legislative and executive powers. The Local Government Ordinance No.35 of 1953 enabled the Governor to establish town councils, county councils, and district councils. The constitution of a city or a municipality was made by an order under the Tanganyika Ordinance (Cap.105). The basic law used was the Local Government Ordinance (Cap.333), but the detailed application to any particular council was enshrined in the council's legal instrument made by the Minister responsible for local government with the approval of Parliament; this instrument contained the number of members of the council, their method of election or appointment and their assigned powers and duties. Locally elected, unpaid, part-time councillors have always been an important feature of local government in Tanzania. Besides elected councillors, there has been a tendency to nominate a few councillors on the basis of their experience, ability, and participation in civic affairs.

The first local authority to be established under the 1945 Municipalities Ordinance (Cap.105) was the Dar es Salaam Municipality (now the City of Dar es Salaam) set up in 1949. It was followed in 1954 by the Tanga Town Council (now Tanga Municipal Council). At the time of independence in December 1961, there were two categories of local authorities in Tanzania: (1) eleven urban councils and six rural district councils established under the 1953 Local Government Ordinance; and (2) thirty other rural district councils brought to different levels of constitutional development under the old Native Authority Ordinance (Dryden 1967). The new independent government took over these local authorities which had, according to Stanley Dryden's authoritative account, three major problems:

> ... the body of elected councillors who now have responsibility for the progress of their home areas were, for the most part, ill-equipped to shoulder such responsibility. In general, they were poorly educated, they had little knowledge of the purpose and practice of local government and they were uncertain of their role as councillors within the system itself.
>
> ... the quality of local authority employees was variable ... and, in general, poor at the time of Independence.
>
> ... the lack of adequate finance to improve and expand the services which were already in existence. The most important of these were administrative, educational and medical (1967, 100-01).[2]

In 1963 three more urban local authorities were established to make a total of fifteen urban councils. The set-up of the urban councils was not changed until early 1974, when urban local governments were abolished and a new system of organizing government machinery was consolidated. Then, in 1978 the fifteen urban councils were reinstated; in 1980 three more urban councils were created, and in 1981 a fourth new urban council was created to reach the present total of nineteen urban councils throughout the country.

In order to harmonize and improve terms of service and the manpower position of local government authorities, a Local Government Service Commission (LGSC) was established by Parliament in July 1962 under section 128 of the Local Government Ordinance of 1962. Service in all local authorities was deemed unified with effect from January 1963. The LGSC was given powers to transfer senior local government officials (e.g. executive officers and treasurers) without the employing authority's consent as one way of protecting them against improper local pressures and the manoeuvering of elected councillors.

The establishment of a one-party state in 1965 and the incorporation of the supremacy of the Party into the Constitution brought another major change to the organizational structure of local governments in the country. Local governments were integrated into the national party apparatus by the nomination and inclusion of a few party officials in local government councils, as provided for under the new legislation. For instance, the District Party Chairman became the ex-officio chairman of the rural district or urban council in his district. A few other party officials were also nominated for each local authority. In addition, all candidates aspiring for council seats had to be screened by the District Party Conference and two candidates for each vacant seat presented for public choice. The objectives for integrating party and administrative hierarchies in the country were: (1) to facilitate political cohesion and unity; and (2) to influence the perception of development goals at the local level by transmitting information on the new policy of Socialism and Self-reliance down the party hierarchy. In other words, the structure and composition of local government authorities had to conform to the new political philosophy and objectives. Notwithstanding this integration, urban councils remained under the guidance and general supervision of a central government ministry responsible for local government up to the decentralization period in 1972.

A third major change was the abolition of the head or personal poll tax payable by all able-bodied adult males, announced in Parliament in June 1969 by the Minister for Finance in his Budget Speech for 1969 / 70. Its abolition was in response to a public outcry that the tax collectors used harsh and inhuman collection practices which had resulted in a number of deaths in Mwanza Region in 1969. In many peoples' minds, the tax was still associated with past colonial practices. But its abolition deprived local government authorities of their major source of revenue.

The Decentralization Program and its Aftermath for Sanitary Services and Housing

In 1972 rural local authorities were abolished and placed within a newly instituted, decentralized government structure. When urban councils were officially abolished effective January 1974, the sources of revenue from which they obtained their finances were also taken over by the central government. New senior staff – many of whom had no experience in urban administration – were brought to urban areas. Most of the Regional Development Directors and District Development Directors appointed to be the top civil servants in the regions and districts were agricultural and veterinary officers with training in agriculture and livestock. Officers with the experience in urban management and the management of urban services were transferred to other government departments or parastatals. The new staff working for urban areas – integrated into the rural administrative system as parts of districts and regions – had a rural development bias. This bias led to a rapid deterioration in the standard of urban services and infrastructure.

The decentralization program was recommended by McKinsey and Company Inc., a large management consultant company with offices in the UK and the US. Before its introduction in the urban areas, the program had been in force for about one year in the rural areas. The introduction of the system in the urban areas was intended to bring about uniformity and balanced development. It was envisaged that under the program, urban administration would be easier, and there would a faster pace of development and provision of services in the whole country. This was based on the assumption that urban areas were more developed than rural areas and hence the former had to be stalled in order to allow the latter to catch up. Indeed, the overall development strategy of the decentralization period was heavily biased in favor of rural development. For instance over the entire 1974-78 decentralization period, Dar es Salaam City and Mbeya Municipality received a total of Shs.16,037,000 and Shs.8,369,000 respectively for all their development projects, including annual maintenance of infrastructure and services. This amount was like a drop in the ocean compared to their needs, to say nothing of the fact that Dar es Salaam had over ten times the population of Mbeya yet received less than twice the amount received by the smaller municipality. The amounts were also smaller than the sums given to any rural district.

Essentially, the government deconcentrated its powers by transferring some amount of its administrative and financial authority from the center in Dar es Salaam to regional and district governments. Through deconcentration, the government shifted the workload of the center to regional and district authorities as extensions of central government. The regions and districts were given powers to plan and implement programs within guidelines set by the government. Regions were also given financial powers to control and spend their money once their budgets were passed by Parliament, without reference to a central government ministry. Hence, Regional Development Directors as the top civil servants in the regions were made accounting officers for their regions. When the local authorities were abolished, the local officials were absorbed into the national civil service. The ten ministries, whose activities were decentralized, were instructed to post high-level personnel to the regions and districts to act as technical advisers to the leadership at regional and district levels in order to improve planning and project implementation.

Basically, under the new program, it was anticipated that development could be achieved through the exercise of greater "initiative by the local committees." When the program was announced, the press talked about a "reality of democracy" and "trust in the people." The purpose of the Tanzanian decentralization program was first and foremost political. The rationale for it was to increase development by stimulating grass roots participation in decision making and planning. Now more than sixteen years after decentralization was undertaken, it is evident that one of the shortcomings of decentralization is that it failed to achieve that purpose of effective decision-making at the grassroot level and stifled self-help activities by the masses.

Two related explanations are commonly given for the failure of decentralization. First, it is asserted that there was usurpation of power by the government bureaucracy at the regional and district levels which, at times, were not accountable to the people but to the central government. The local areas did not control either the personnel or the funds allocated. Second, while one original goal of decentralization was economic development through greater managerial efficiency, some have argued that this goal was not achieved because people were alienated from the system. Evidence for this point is the fact that people's participation in self-help development projects came almost to a standstill.

As regards the development and management of urban areas under the decentralization program, after only four years of the abolition of urban councils, there was a public outcry over the deterioration in urban conditions. In particular, people were concerned with basic services like water and power supply, sewage disposal, refuse and garbage collection, roads, fire protection, and malaria control. In October 1976 the Prime Minister formed a committee headed by a Minister of State in his office to study and make recommendations to him as to how these services should be efficiently managed. The committee included some Members of Parliament and some high level technocrats. Among the many recommendations of this committee were:

(1) The prevailing overemphasis on rural development at the expense of urban areas should be done away with. Instead, development of both rural and urban areas should be seen as complimentary.

(2) Urban centers should be graded and those with higher growth rates should be allocated adequate numbers of competent personnel.

(3) Urban laws and by-laws should be enforced as they had been before the decentralization exercise.

(4) Adequate funds should be allocated to urban councils for basic services. It was observed that approved budgets for urban services were not in conformity with the amount requested.

Table 8.2
Target and Actual Cesspit Emptying for Three Weeks,
June – July 1985, in Dar es Salaam
(number of trips)

Week	Ilala Zone		Kinondoni Zone		Temeke Zone	
	Target	Actual	Target	Actual	Target	Actual
20.06.85 to 28.06.85	100	42	150	68	120	22
29.06.85 to 5.07.85	100	24	150	67	120	32
6.07.85 to 12.07.85	100	17	150	48	120	12

Source: City Council Records, Dar es Salaam, August 1985.

Table 8.3
Main Sources of Revenue of Tanzanian Urban Councils
from Local Taxes, 1985 / 86

Type of Taxes	Amount in Shillings	Percentage
Development levy	246,690,000	55.23
Rates on dwellings	73,244,400	16.40
Trading on licences	60,915	0.01
Market dues and fees	29,923,900	6.70
Others	96,713,900	21.65
Total	446,633,115	99.99

Source: Tanzania, 1985.

(5) Urban recreation areas should be maintained. This recommendation was made after discovering that under decentralization, financial resources allocated to maintain such services were totally inadequate and were decreasing each successive year.

Under decentralization, the Treasury funded the entire budget of the urban councils. Preference in resource allocation was in favor of rural areas, with attempts being made to integrate urban and rural services. This process led to a serious deterioration in urban services. In particular, machinery and maintenance equipment were in very short supply. While importation of new machines and vehicles was limited by the scarcity of foreign exchange, the quality of the few available machines was affected by the lack of spare parts. For these reasons, the City Council of Dar es Salaam had only ten trucks for refuse collection in 1982; thirty-five trucks were not working because of a lack of spare parts. A year later, the position was still the same.

Another service which was and continues to be heavily affected by the scarcity of resources is sewage disposal. During the 1970s the situation deteriorated seriously. It had not improved by August 1985 when the whole city had only two cesspit emptiers, only one of which was actually in working order. When the two cesspit emptiers are working, they normally operate in Kinondoni zone (one vehicle) and Ilala zone (one vehicle). The third major area of Dar es Salaam, Temeke, is not provided with the service except on specific occasions. This service is highly inadequate, as Table 8.2 shows. Not only is the capacity for cesspit emptying abysmally low for the whole of Dar es Salaam (where a high proportion of permanent dwellings are connected to septic tanks) but also the capacity of the system is far below target. During the third week surveyed, for example, only seventeen percent of the target was met in Ilala zone, thirty-two percent was met in Kinondoni zone, and ten percent was met in Temeke zone. As the fieldwork for this study was being completed in August 1986, the situation had marginally improved; both cesspit emptiers were working, and a third was expected to be operational again in the near future.

The only mitigating factor is that several organizations have their own cesspit emptiers. These are public institutions and include the prisons, the National Housing Corporation, the Tanzania People's Defence Forces, the police, and the Tanzania Electricity Supply Company (TANESCO). There is even one private citizen with his own cesspit emptier. All those cesspit emptiers provide services on a hire basis. The average charge is, however, very high – from Shs.400 to Shs.600 per trip – compared to Shs.60 per trip charged by the Dar es Salaam City Council.

But even with this additional availability of cesspit emptiers, the service is still very poor. The result is that people live with flooded water closets and latrines for many years. Sanitary conditions are particularly poor in Dar es Salaam's squatter settlements with high densities like Manzese, Mwananyamala, and Tandika-Mtoni where many residents have pit latrines which are almost filled up. The Dar es Salaam City Council does not provide cesspit emptying services to most of these areas because of the lack of such vehicles and because many houses in these unplanned areas are inaccessible. The results of the questionnaire survey were revealing on sanitary questions. Many people in the survey, especially in Dar es Salaam, suggested that Council employees doing the work of cesspit emptying are not well supervised. This situation gives more reign to dishonest practices such as demands for financial inducements from the residents. Thus, instead of the City Council getting revenue, individual staff may profit.

Data on sanitary facilities in individual houses indicates the extent of the problem. In Dar es Salaam, 88.9 percent of the 660 houses visited had only simple pit latrines dug into the ground. Another 5.6 percent had somewhat more elaborate "ventilated improved latrines," while only 4.5 percent had toilets connected to either septic tanks or the sewerage system. In general, many people (or families) are obliged to share a single toilet or latrine with others – 60.7 percent of the Dar es Salaam households surveyed had to share sanitary facilities in this way. This overburdens the latrines, which becomes a serious health problem during the rainy season when the water table rises. Twenty-one percent of the surveyed households reported overflowing latrines during the rainy season. This problem is acute in the low-lying areas and valleys commonly occupied by squatters. Overflowing of pit latrines tends to contaminate shallow sources of water supply in low-income settlements, where field surveys have shown that sixty-four percent of the houses do not have a piped water supply inside their houses or on their plots.

As for services obtained, only 6.2 percent of the households surveyed reported that their houses get cesspit emptying services. Another 11.2 percent stated that the sewerage emptying service is costly and not reliable, while 69.4 percent reported that they do not get any emptying services from the Dar es Salaam City Council.[3]

A final important area of services is housing and the allocation of serviced urban land. For a decade after independence, the Tanzanian government implemented a policy of slum and squatter clearance through the National Housing Corporation. As a means of modernizing the built environment in several major urban centers, this policy met with limited success. Then in 1972, Tanzania adopted a sites and services and squatter upgrading approach to the improvement of housing conditions in urban areas. In arriving at this decision, the government took into account four major considerations: (1) the provision of conventional, finished public housing was becoming too costly for both the state and individuals to afford;

(2) the "target groups" (i.e. low-income families) were not gaining access to the supposedly "low-cost" finished public housing provided under the slum clearance program; (3) Tanzanians have for a long time been providing for their own housing needs in any case, and this pattern will continue; and (4) Tanzania's development philosophy emphasizes development originating from the people themselves; the government's role should thus be geared to facilitating housing construction on the basis of self-reliance.

To support this innovative approach, the government established the Tanzania Housing Bank (THB) in January 1973. One of the major functions of the THB is to promote housing development by making technical and financial assistance available for sites and services and squatter upgrading schemes, housing cooperatives, Ujamaa villages, and other owner-occupied housing schemes. Once the THB was in operation, the government approached the World Bank for support; a project agreement was signed with the International Development Association (IDA) in 1974 for a large sites and services and squatter upgrading project.

Carried out through the Ministry of Lands, Housing, and Urban Development, the basic sites and services approach under Phase One of this project involved the provision of 8,932 surveyed plots with basic services in planned residential layouts in Dar es Salaam, Mwanza, and Mbeya. These plots were to be allocated to low-income families. This approach was expected to accommodate and even contain the proliferation of squatter settlements in a planned urban context. The project also involved squatter upgrading, which consisted of providing community facilities such as primary schools, health and nutrition centers, urban dispensaries, and permanent markets for designated squatter neighborhoods. The approach also incorporated the provision of secure tenure and basic infrastructure and utilities – such as water and electricity, storm water drainage, roads, and street lighting on major roads. About 8,800 squatter houses in Dar es Salaam and Mbeya were expected to benefit under Phase One of this program. While thirty community facilities were originally to be provided, in the end only twenty-five were built as a result of cost overruns.

In spite of the small decrease in community facilities actually built, the project has been a success in most respects. In the process of implementation, the cost per serviced plot increased fifteen percent from Shs.3,020 to Shs.3,480. This cost increase led to the trimming back of the number of sites and services plots from 19,600 planned plots to 8,964 actual serviced plots or forty-three percent of the original target. On the other hand, upgrading costs proved to be fifteen percent lower than expected, so that 14,600 instead of only 8,800 houses were able to benefit from upgrading, an increase of sixty-six percent over the original estimate.

While it was originally estimated that a total of 194,000 people would benefit under Phase One of the World Bank scheme, the actual number that benefitted by 1980 turned out to be about 231,000 people, for an increase of 19.2 percent. According to current estimates (1986), there are some 17,800 houses in the upgraded areas. This increase is due to the densification process which has taken place in the upgraded areas. Phase Two of the scheme, which provided for more serviced and upgraded plots in Dar es Salaam as well as in Iringa, Morogoro, Tabora, and Tanga, has also benefitted more people than was originally envisaged.

There are two main criticisms of the scheme. One is that many of the occupants of the sites and services area – judging by the value of the finished houses – clearly earn more than would have been possible were they all in the original "low income" target group. A second criticism is that infrastructure (especially roads and surface drains) has been poorly maintained by the local authorities, with the result that the quality of services has deteriorated. In the end, the problems of infrastructure maintenance in Tanzania's towns described above will affect even these internationally-financed, large-scale urban schemes.

In spite of the relative success of the World Bank project in providing upgrading benefits to houseowners already living in squatter areas, the level of provision of newly serviced plots has not been very high on a annual basis. Indeed, the inability of the planning system to provide an adequate number of planned and surveyed plots (i.e. with no services) is a major cause of Tanzania's housing problems. For example, Dar es Salaam Region needs about ten thousand housing units (or surveyed plots) annually just to meet the needs of its annual population increase. But the Dar es Salaam City Council has been able to provide on the average about 2,000 to 2,150 surveyed plots a year, for a total of 23,865 plots over the 1978-87 period. Hence, the Dar es Salaam City Council has been able to meet only about 26.5 percent of the demand for planned and surveyed plots over the same 1978-87 period. Mbeya had about four thousand applications for surveyed residential plots on its waiting list in 1984. But it has been able to survey a total of only 3,924 plots over the seven-year period from 1978 to 1984. As a result, in 1985 as much as 70.4 percent of the estimated housing stock of 13,500 dwelling units the Municipality was located in unplanned and unsurveyed areas. In Tanga in the 1978 / 79 financial year, there were two thousand new applications for plots, but only 330 plots were surveyed and allocated to individuals. In all, from the 1978 / 79 to 1982 / 83 financial years, there were eighteen thousand applications for plots, but only 1,282 plots were surveyed and allocated by Tanga Municipality; this amounts to only five percent of the demand. Given the present shortage of land surveying equipment and of land surveyors and support sources, together with a lack of adequate funds to pay compensation to the owners of property and crops in the areas to be surveyed and rapid population growth, the waiting lists of applications for surveyed plots in the main urban areas of the country are likely to get longer with each successive year.

As these waiting lists grow, people are obliged to build in unplanned areas. The abolition of urban local authorities under the 1972 decentralization policy further exacerbated the growth of squatter settlements because it left urban areas without the authority to enforce development control conditions or to effectively regulate and guide urban building activity. Indeed, the 1972-78 decentralization period, with its rural development bias, was characterized by widespread flouting of urban by-laws and building regulations. What took place in urban areas was the invasion of whatever vacant land people wanted to develop.

Three other factors led to the mushrooming of squatter settlements and shanty housing in urban areas during the decentralization period. First, the land reforms of the early 1960s, which placed all land in Tanzania under public ownership, encouraged urban residents – especially those who wanted to construct their own housing but could not get a plot from the government's land office – to build on whatever vacant land they could find. Second, rural inhabitants who migrated to towns went there with the traditional norms of rural communities. Rural inhabitants own land under a customary land tenure system and build their houses without having to submit a building plan to any government body. As a result of this rural background, many migrants constructed their housing without seeking and obtaining a building permit and without getting a title deed or leasehold from the Lands Department of the government for the pieces of land on which they built their houses. In addition, they started to grow vegetables and a whole range of crops like maize, bananas, sweet potatoes, cassava, and rice in the vicinity of the huts and houses they constructed in order to supplement their meager incomes. Finally, the absence of a proper planning authority to supervise the implementation of master plans made the task of controlling urban land uses difficult. Particularly important from the town planning point of view was a lack of commitment on the part of the Regional Development Councils (1) to adhere to correct and effective implementation of master plans and (2) to enforce development control conditions.

These attitudes, and the stigma of lawlessness implanted into people's minds by the abolition of urban councils, have proved difficult to erase even ten years after the reinstatement of the councils. The Party's policy of encouraging urban residents to undertake gardening and other forms of cultivation on their plots in order to produce food after the 1974 nation-wide drought and food shortage has led to all forms of agricultural practices in the towns. Many of these practices constitute a direct breach of basic urban health and safety regulations. For instance, practices like the keeping of poultry, pigs, and dairy cattle as well as the growing of permanent crops and fruits are a health risk to both owners and neighbors in a crowded urban setting. The common practice of CCM Party and higher administrative officials of abrogating stop notices and demolition or eviction notices issued by urban authorities to people who break urban by-laws and building regulations has further strengthened the feeling of lawlessness. This tendency for many people to appeal to the Party, even where the culprit deliberately invades vacant public land zoned for other uses, or breaks building regulations, has exacerbated Tanzania's urban housing problems. This is but another legacy of the decentralization period which will not quickly recede.

However, the decentralization policy and program can be credited for doing four things. First, it created job opportunities in the regions and districts for senior, middle level, and junior civil servants who were found redundant in Dar es Salaam. Second, it brought central government (but without increasing democracy or people's participation in decision-making and planning at the grassroots) closer to the people. Third, decentralization placed all civil servants of the ministries whose functions were decentralized under one system of leadership and under one employer in each region. (The Regional Development Director was in charge, with the Regional Commissioner as the political head of the region.) This made it possible for the civil servants in each region to work as a team. Finally, the transfer of qualified and experienced officers from Dar es Salaam to the regions and districts to take up positions created under the decentralization program increased the ability of the regions and districts to plan and implement development programs and to make decisions on how to spend their budgets approved by Parliament without reference to any central government technical ministry in Dar es Salaam. On the other hand, these advantages have now become a disadvantage, since it has proved administratively and politically difficult to reduce the large central government bureaucracy created during the decentralization period even after the reinstatement of urban councils and rural district councils, which has made the positions of Regional Development Directors and District Administrative Officers redundant. Indeed, one may argue that Tanzania is now over-governed when the supremacy of the CCM Party is also taken into account.

Management of Urban Authorities and Services: The Present Situation

Background

In Tanzania, the power and authority of the state is divided constitutionally among the CCM Party, the central government, and local authorities. Part VIII section 145 of the 1984 revised Constitution of the United Republic of Tanzania stipulates that local government authorities shall be established at all levels in accordance with the respective law as passed by Parliament. Section 146 of the Constitution states the primary objectives of local government as being devolution of power to the people. The Constitution requires all authorities to involve people in development activities, to provide local government service in their respective areas, to maintain law and order, and to strengthen democracy. It is thus clear from the new Constitution that Tanzania would like its towns and cities to be important units of democratic local self-government.

The Local Government (Urban Authorities) Act of 1982 has become the major legal framework for the present organization of urban local authorities. According to this Act, every local authority is governed by a council. The council, in turn, is composed of councillors elected from each ward within the town, municipality, or city; members of Parliament representing the constituency within which the town is situated; five or six other members nominated by the Minister responsible for local government; and the National Member of Parliament elected from the region in which the council is situated, if he is resident in the area. Unlike the situation before 1974, the Chairman of an Urban Council or the Mayor of a City or Municipality now has to be an elected councillor. Since 1982 the Local Government Service Commission has been reconstituted to perform the same functions which it performed prior to the abolition of local governments. Finally, the Local Government Loans Board was established in 1985, as provided for under the Local Government Finances Act No.9 of 1982, "for the provision of development works and services," to extend loans to local authorities.

A typical urban council governs through six standing committees with the full council – which is required to meet once every three months – as the dominant power. These committees are: Administration and Finance, Health and Social Welfare, Education and Culture, Works and Communication, Town / Urban Planning, and Trade and Economic Planning. Corresponding to these committees are six functional departments which are responsible for the management and implementation of decisions of the respective committees. The Human Resources Deployment Act (1983), aimed at making every able-bodied person engage in productive employment, has added a seventh committee, the Human Resources Deployment Committee, to the councils.

At an operational level, the work of the councils is carried out under the direction of a Chief Executive or Director, appointed by the President of the United Republic of Tanzania. He is personally accountable for the funds of the urban council. The Heads of Departments constitute the Management Team of each urban authority, under the chairmanship of the City / Municipal / Town Director. They advise and assist the Director in the implementation of the council's resolutions.

For administrative purposes each urban area, with the exception of Dar es Salaam, is an Urban District and an electoral constituency with an elected Member of Parliament and a District Commissioner who is assisted by a District Administrative Officer (the head of the civil servants in the district). The District Commissioner is the political head of the district and is responsible mainly for the administration, planning, and development of the villages and suburban hinterland of the respective urban area; the town council is responsible for the urban area proper. The District Commissioner and his staff are responsible to the Prime Minister's Office while Town / Municipal / City Councils and Rural District Councils are responsible to the Ministry of Local Government and Co-operative Development and Marketing.

Dar es Salaam City Region represents a particular case. The region is divided into three districts (Kinondoni, Ilala, and Temeke) as it was during the decentralization period. Each district is headed by a District Commissioner, assisted by the District Administrative Officer. Each district also has an elected Member of Parliament. The whole of Dar es Salaam City Region, which includes Dar es Salaam urban proper, is headed by a Regional Commissioner assisted by the Regional Director of Administration, who is in turn head of all civil servants in the region. The Regional Commissioner, the three District Commissioners, and their staff are responsible mainly for the administration, planning and development of the rural hinterland of Dar es Salaam which is not fully urbanized. Dar es Salaam City Region has also one National Member of Parliament representing Dar es Salaam City proper. According to the 1982 Local Government (Urban Authorities) Act, the four Members of Parliament in Dar es Salaam are co-opted councillors of the Dar es Salaam City Council.

Under the present regulations, the central government has retained a number of controls and checks over local authorities. For example, all by-laws made by urban councils have to be endorsed by the Minister responsible for local government before they can come into operation. The central government decides on the qualifications of the administrators who run local governments. And proposals to raise new taxes or to change existing taxes have also to be approved by the Minister. But perhaps most importantly, since local authorities are heavily dependent on central government grants for their recurrent and development budgets, their budget proposals have to be approved both by the Ministry responsible for local government and by the Treasury. The actual composition of those budgets is determined by local authorities themselves taking into account overall national policies and budget guidelines issued by the Treasury each year for all government Ministries and Parastatals who depend on the Treasury for their money. A final central government control is an annual auditing by the government's Controller and Auditor General.

The Finance of Urban Services

According to the Act establishing urban councils and to the Local Government Finances Act No.9 of 1982, local councils are empowered to collect revenue. The most important sources of revenue for the 1985 / 86 fiscal year are shown in Table 8.3 in which it is obvious that, for all urban councils in Tanzania, the development levy is the major source of local revenue. Table 8.4 looks at the performance of this levy, which is paid by all able-bodied adults from the ages of 18 to 65 in urban and rural areas. Hence, revenue from this source is expected to rise as the population increases. All the six study towns exceeded their targets in tax collection from the development levy in 1984 / 85. However, tax collection over a more recent nine-month period (July 1985 to March 1986) shows a declining trend with only fifty-three percent of the target total development levy collected. The performance of urban councils in collecting the smaller taxes – especially the tax on small businesses and the urban hut tax – has been worse.

The councils are charged with the responsibility of almost all development activities within their areas of jurisdiction. The schedule in the Local Government (Urban Authorities) Act No.8 of 1982 is very exhaustive. The specific powers conferred on the local authorities by the Act deal with a very wide variety of functions involving the overall welfare of the locality in question. Health services, public health and sanitation, agriculture, roads, primary school education, sewerage, building control, fire-fighting, and refuse disposal are all responsibilities of the councils. Although there is a well-defined line of ministerial authority from the center, the government's policy is to ensure that the exercise of this central authority is kept to a minimum.

Financial resources are important for the provision of urban services. The central government needs to make sources of local government finance more elastic. At the moment, the central government takes taxes that are easy to collect (such as income taxes, usually deducted at source from wages and salaries; duties; and license fees), leaving the politically and administratively more difficult taxes to local government. Table 8.5 shows how the local urban authorities were financed over the 1978-87 period for their development projects. This amount reflects somewhat less than two percent of the national development budget – clearly a disproportionately low figure, considering the economic importance of urban areas and the fact that the 1978 census showed that 13.8 percent of the country's population lived in towns. The amount is also very inadequate in the face of the complex problems urban authorities are expected to solve. Thus, even in the present July 1987 to June 1988 fiscal year, urban councils have been allocated only Shs.263,941,000 (equal to 1.53 percent of the total development budget of Shs.17,255 million) in spite of the official statement of May 1987 that the

Table 8.4
Performance in Tax Collection of the Development Levy
in Selected Tanzanian Urban Authorities,
1984/85 – 1985/86

Urban Authority	Estimated Target Tax (Shs.)	1984/85 Actual Revenue Shs.	%	Estimated Tax Revenue (Shs.)	1985/86 Actual Revenue[1] Shs.	%
Dar es Salaam	80,000,000	104,425,642	130.5%	120,000,000	56,000,000	46.6%
Mbeya	10,000,000	10,336,100	103.4	10,000,000	6,476,560	64.7
Morogoro	7,400,000	9,270,020	125.3	7,400,000	5,454,455	73.7
Tanga	8,800,000	14,270,244	165.2	12,100,000	9,400,000	77.7
Moshi	2,800,000	4,607,000	164.5	7,000,000	6,003,700	85.7
Tabora	4,000,000	3,758,900	94.0	10,000,000	5,040,000	50.4
Total	1,130,000,000	146,667,906	129.8%	166,500,000	88,374,715	53.1%

Source: Tanzania, 1986.
[1] Nine-month period only.

central government would increase grants to urban authorities so that the latter could improve services. Until now (1987), urban local authorities have been one hundred percent dependent on central government grants for the financing of their development projects. Only in the last fiscal year (1986-87) have some towns been able to raise a proportion of the funds they require to finance their development projects. In the foreseeable future, urban authorities cannot expect to obtain grants from central government adequate to finance the provision of new urban services which will both match the needs of a rapidly growing urban population and provide for the necessary rehabilitation of existing urban infrastructure and services. The reasons for this financial stringency include a declining national income, the competition of many national projects for the same limited funds, and Tanzania's emphasis on rural development and recently on agricultural development in order to attain national self-sufficiency in food production.

Urban councils are also dependent on central government grants to finance the recurrent expenditures of maintaining vital municipal services and staff salaries. Thus, in 1983 / 84, total expenditure on salaries of nineteen urban councils in Tanzania was sixty-four percent of the total recurrent costs of these councils; in 1984 / 85 the figure was 64.5 percent. For Dar es Salaam, whose total recurrent expenditure in recent years has been about one-third of the total figure for all nineteen main towns in the country, the proportion spent on salaries was sixty-two percent in 1983 / 84 and 61.7 percent in 1984 / 85. Partly as a result of this expenditure pattern, the annual recurrent budget of urban councils has been far greater than their annual development budget each year over the 1972-87 period. This trend is likely to continue in the future.

One implication of these figures is that shortage of manpower is not the major cause of the present deterioration of urban services. The major problem would seem to be the underutilization of the existing pool of technical and managerial staff because of lack of proper tools and equipment.

Sanitary Services

The 1978 reinstatement of urban councils seems not to have contributed to an improvement in vital municipal services. Of special interest is the case of refuse collection (as shown by Table 8.6) and sewage disposal. For instance, while both the population and area of the main towns have been expanding over the past decade, the capacity of urban authorities to collect and dispose of an increasing amount of refuse has been declining. Virtually all urban authorities in Tanzania have a totally inadequate number of refuse collection vehicles, as compared to the daily amount of refuse produced in urban areas. The refuse collection capacity is low partly because most of the vehicles are either in poor mechanical condition or are not working at all. As

Table 8.5
Urban Local Government Authorities Development Budgets, 1978-1987
(in thousands of Tanzanian shillings)

	Urban Council	1978-79	1979-80	1980-81	1981-82	1982-83	1983-84
1	Arusha	6,745	7,905	9,690	6,600	4,520	4,730
2	Bukoba	4,842	1,842	4,419	3,481	3,635	3,885
3	Dar es Salaam	36,060	21,352	30,482	12,642	10,345	10,812
4	Dodoma	300	5,479	8,369	5,650	3,318	3,623
5	Iringa	2,594	4,636	4,837	3,882	5,379	3,375
6	Kigoma / Ujiji	3,655	3,309	5,608	5,105	3,938	3,841
7	Lindi	4,254	1,524	4,831	2,775	3,552	2,856
8	Mbeya	4,158	3,002	5,005	5,400	4,894	4,864
9	Morogoro	5,204	3,529	5,179	5,200	4,212	5,216
10	Moshi	4,022	3,233	5,980	3,445	3,203	4,280
11	Mtwara	3,542	3,165	4,928	3,308	2,497	3,197
12	Mwanza	5,852	5,546	8,110	6,135	4,428	4,422
13	Musoma	3,465	3,380	5,310	3,918	4,008	4,006
14	Shinyanga	–	–	1,670	4,145	2,976	2,976
15	Singida	–	–	1,471	4,170	2,820	3,700
16	Songea	–	–	2,156	4,283	5,220	3,920
17	Sumbawanga	–	–	–	–	3,437	4,500
18	Tabora	3,460	3,747	5,217	3,721	2,800	2,650
19	Tanga	6,283	7,530	9,530	6,640	4,770	4,770

Total Urban Areas:

		94,466	79,179	122,792	90,500	79,950	80,623

Total Tanzania Development Budget:

		5,823,600	7,186,800	9,342,000	6,622,400	4,816,000	15,630,000

Urban Areas as % of Tanzania Total:

		1.62	1.10	1.31	1.37	1.66	0.52

Source: Ministry of Local Government and Cooperative Development.

Table 8.5 continued

	Urban Council	1984-85	1985-86	1986-87	Total	Absolute Change[1]	% Change[1]
1	Arusha	5,220	5,087	4,500	54,997	−2,245	−33
2	Bukoba	3,375	3,844	3,500	32,823	−1,342	−28
3	Dar es Salaam	19,496	22,088	32,992	196,269	−3,068	−9
4	Dodoma	4,086	7,972	6,000	44,797	5,700	1,900
5	Iringa	3,404	4,000	3,500	35,607	906	35
6	Kigoma / Ujiji	3,583	4,065	3,500	36,604	−155	−4
7	Lindi	3,612	3,350	3,500	30,284	−784	−18
8	Mbeya	4,653	5,000	9,500	46,476	5,342	128
9	Morogoro	3,981	3,350	3,000	37,871	−2,204	−42
10	Moshi	3,385	3,260	15,400	46,208	11,378	283
11	Mtwara	2,350	3,000	3,000	28,987	−542	−15
12	Mwanza	4,486	3,550	3,000	45,529	−2,852	−49
13	Musoma	4,114	5,000	4,500	37,699	1,035	30
14	Shinyanga	2,910	3,000	4,000	21,677	2,330	140
15	Singida	3,761	3,400	3,000	22,322	1,523	104
16	Songea	2,795	3,526	6,828	28,728	4,672	217
17	Sumbawanga	3,536	3,320	11,500	26,293	8,063	235
18	Tabora	2,424	2,706	3,500	30,225	40	1
19	Tanga	5,670	5,124	4,500	54,817	−1,783	−28

Total Urban Areas:
| | | 86,841 | 94,642 | 129,220 | 858,213 | 34,734 | 37 |

Total Tanzania Development Budget:
| | | 6,560,000 | 6,828,000 | 15,859,000 | 78,667,800 | 10,035,400 | 172 |

Urban Areas as % of Tanzania Total:
| | | 1.32 | 1.39 | 0.31 | 1.09 | | |

[1] 1978-79 – 1986-87, or for period over which development budget allocated.
Calculations in last two columns take account of inflation over the period indicated.

Table 8.6
Refuse Production and Collection,
Tanzanian Urban Councils, 1986

Number of Refuse Collectors

	Required	Available	In Good Condition	In Bad Condition
Dar es Salaam	50	20	6	14
Arusha	17	5	2	3
Tanga	20	3	2	1
Mwanza	15	7	2	5
Dodoma	15	5	2	3
Mbeya	15	6	4	2
Iringa	8	6	3	3
Lindi	6	4	2	2
Mtwara	6	4	2	2
Musoma	5	3	2	1
Tabora	6	2	1	1
Sumbawanga	5	2	1	1
Singida	4	2	1	1
Moshi	15	5	3	2
Morogoro	9	3	2	1
Songea	5	3	2	1
Shinyanga	5	2	1	1
Bukoba	5	2	2	–
Kigoma	6	3	2	1
Total	217	87	42	45

Source: Tanzania, Ministry of Local Government and Cooperative Records, Dodoma, March 1986.

Table 8.6 continued

Daily Refuse Production and Collection

	Estimated Production (tons)	Estimated Collection (tons)	Amount Uncollected (tons)	Amount Collected as % of Production
Dar es Salaam	1,200	262	938	21.83
Arusha	170	30	140	17.65
Tanga	200	36	164	18.00
Mwanza	174	30	144	17.24
Dodoma	200	42	158	21.00
Mbeya	300	90	210	30.00
Iringa	81	24	57	29.63
Lindi	40	25	15	62.50
Mtwara	45	15	30	33.33
Musoma	80	15	65	18.75
Tabora	30	15	15	50.00
Sumbawanga	54	20	34	37.04
Singida	84	10	74	11.90
Moshi	120	33	87	27.50
Morogoro	75	15	60	20.00
Songea	45	25	20	55.56
Shinyanga	40	20	20	50.00
Bukoba	42	15	27	35.71
Kigoma	20	6	14	30.00
Total	3,000	728	2,282	24.27

Table 8.7
Number and Condition of Construction Equipment
in Tanzania Urban Areas as of 31st December 1985

Type of Construction Equipment	Number Available	Number in Poor Working Condition[1]	Number Not Working	Numbers Required
Graders	13	9	4	24
Tarboilers	5	3	2	20
Water bousers	6	6	–	26
Rollers	7	7	–	20
Tipper lorries	44	38	6	91
Concrete mixers	4	3	1	26

Source: Ministry of Local Government and Cooperative Development Records, Dodoma, March 1986.

[1] Includes those in such bad mechanical condition that once they break down they have to be written off because it would be too expensive to import spare parts and repair them.

Table 8.8
Estimated Cost[1] of Repairing and Reconstructing Roads
in Tanzanian Study Towns
(Shs. million)

	Murram or Gravel Roads	Tarred Roads	Total Cost
Dar es Salaam	986.0	1,200.0	2,118.0
Mbeya	288.8	78.0	366.8
Morogoro	260.0	60.0	320.0
Moshi	80.0	231.0	411.0
Tabora	460.0	96.0	556.0
Tanga	89.0	264.0	353.0
Total	2,163.8	1,929.0	4,092.8

[1] 1984 / 85 prices.

a result, as Table 8.6 demonstrates, urban authorities can only collect a small amount (twenty-four percent) of the estimated refuse produced every day. In the study towns, the situation is typical for the country: Tanga is able to collect only eighteen percent of the daily refuse produced, followed by Morogoro at twenty percent, Dar es Salaam at twenty-two percent, Moshi at twenty-eight percent, Mbeya at thirty percent, and Tabora at fifty percent.

An even more dismal picture exists for sewage and foul water disposal in urban areas. According to the calculations of the Ministry of Local Government and Cooperatives in March 1986, Tanzania's nineteen main towns required 164 cesspit emptiers to remove the amount of foul water being produced. Of this number, however, only forty-seven are available in Tanzania, and of these only twenty-four are in good working condition. The result is that only thirteen percent of the estimated urban production of sewage and foul water is regularly disposed of. For the study towns, Dar es Salaam disposes of a derisory 0.3 percent of its foul water; this is followed by Tanga at nineteen percent, Mbeya at twenty-one percent, Tabora at twenty-five percent, Moshi at twenty-nine percent, and Morogoro at thirty-three percent. Ironically, Morogoro, with a population of less than a tenth of its neighbor, Dar es Salaam, is able to collect almost ten times more foul water than the largest city in the country.

The present deterioration of urban services is a complex financial, technical, and managerial issue. Improvement of the quality of urban services to acceptable standards which meet the needs of a rapidly growing urban population requires a heavy injection of foreign exchange, imported capital and machinery, competent and experienced technicians and managers, and proper utilization of the scarce plant and machinery available.

Urban Roads and Transport
Today in Tanzania, most urban roads are in poor condition, with many pot holes and blocked storm water drainage channels. The main explanation for this state of affairs is a lack of resources, both in technical personnel and in heavy construction and maintenance equipment. As Table 8.7 shows, many of the available graders, tar boilers, tipper vehicles, and concrete mixers needed for the maintenance and construction of urban roads are defective; and those that are in working order fall far short of requirements. Aside from personnel and equipment, urban areas lack even basic inputs like tar to do even road patching work. The Ministry of Local Government and Cooperative Development estimates that, for proper maintenance of the tarred roads only in Tanzania's main towns, some twenty thousand tons of tar would be necessary. Only about two percent of this total was on hand in March of 1986. In any case, simple patching up work cannot significantly improve the road networks in the urban areas; a great deal of reconstruction is necessary.

Based on Ministry estimates, the cost of reconstructing urban roads in the study towns is shown in Table 8.8. Based on the estimates in Table 8.8, the total cost of necessary road reconstruction works in each town would be far greater than the amount of money for all development projects given to each urban council by the central government each year (as shown in Table 8.5).

Shortage of heavy construction equipment and lorries, rather than technically qualified personnel, is the major constraint urban councils face in their efforts to repair and reconstruct urban roads. The shortage of construction equipment and funds has in turn led to the present underutilization of the available manpower. For example, after the 1986 heavy rains, it would have cost Dar es Salaam City Council some Shs.2,500 million to reconstruct tarred roads while general repair of all murram / gravel roads would have cost about Shs.25 million – a total cost of Shs.2,525 million for all murram and tarred roads. However, Dar es Salaam City Council had an approved budget of Shs.10.4 million for the maintenance of both tarred roads and murram roads in the 1986 / 87 financial year. This works out to 0.41 percent of the amount of money required for the adequate maintenance of roads in the city.

Public transport provision is also grossly inadequate or altogether absent in the urban areas. With the exception of Dar es Salaam, the study towns do

Table 8.9
Number, Condition, and Carrying Capacity of UDA Buses, Dar es Salaam

Type of Bus	Number Working	Number Not Working	Total	Seating / Carrying Capacity	Carrying Capacity When Overloaded
Articulated, i.e., Ekarus buses	7	32	39	150	240-250
Leyland buses	73	24	97	90	140-150
Mercedes Benz buses	48	5	53	90	140-150
Mini buses	20	2	22	26	31-40
Total	148	63	211		

Source: *Dar es Salaam City Transport (Shirika la Usafiri Dar es Salaam Ltd) Records*, August 1986, Dar es Salaam.

not have public transport serving their residents. In each town, two to five private minibuses serve several areas only. Usafiri Dar es Salaam (UDA) (Dar es Salaam City Transport) is a parastatal organization with a mandate to provide public transport in Dar es Salaam. UDA operates normal 90-seat buses, 150-seat articulated passenger buses and 26-seat mini-buses. The mini-buses operate alongside regular UDA buses though not on all transport routes. The whole fleet consists of 147 ordinary buses, 39 articulated buses, and 25 mini-buses, for a total of 211 buses. As Table 8.9 shows, only seventy percent of the buses were working and on the road according to the latest survey during August 1986.

Many of the UDA buses are not in good mechanical condition because of a shortage of tires, tubes, and imported spare parts. Although the UDA fleet is expected to carry up to eighty percent of urban passengers in Dar es Salaam, UDA's performance has declined since 1983. In that year, a UDA survey showed that an average of 358,000 passengers were carried per day through the UDA transport system. Two years later, in 1985, the average had slipped to 218,000 passengers per day. This decline is due mainly to a reduced fleet of serviceable buses, though it is also partly a result of the legalization (since 1983) of private mini-buses which are licensed to operate on specific routes within the city. By 1986, some three hundred of these buses (called *dala dala* locally after the Kiswahili word for the silver Shs.5 coin used as a fare) were on the road, operating alongside UDA buses. While the *dala dala* buses have gone a long way to alleviate urban passenger transport problems, they do not offer a long-term solution to the transport problems of Dar es Salaam. Many of these private buses are mechanically defective and pose a risk to city commuters.

Water Supply
Water supply is another important urban service. Clean water has been one of the most difficult and expensive services to provide because of rapid population growth and the extensive physical development pattern of most Tanzanian towns. Most urban water supply schemes were built more than thirty years ago when these towns were relatively small. For example, the water supply system in Moshi was built in 1956 when the population of the town was only about thirteen thousand. Since then, the scheme has undergone expansion in 1980, but the present system meets less than fifty percent of the demand for water in Moshi. Similarly, the Tabora urban water supply system was built over 1977-81 at a cost of over Shs.8 million. The system was constructed to serve an estimated population of 67,800 people, with a capacity of 9,761 m^3 per day. But by 1986, the actual supply of 10,000 m^3 per day was considerably less than the actual demand of 18,900 m^3 per day.

Most urban water supply schemes in Tanzania face a number of financial and technical problems. The most important of these include low pumping capacity; a lack of standby capacity; old generators; treatment plants operating at fifty percent or less of their capacity; shortage of reservoirs; inadequate trunk mains; lack of nearby new sources of water; a frequent lack of imported chemicals for water treatment and purification; and insufficient funds for operation and maintenance, including the purchase of spare parts.

The water supply situation is serious in Dar es Salaam where the scheme is very old. Although the water scheme has undergone a number of rehabilitation exercises and expansion programs, the demand of 264,000 m^3 (or 264 million liters) a day considerably exceeds the supply of 182,000 m^3 – notwithstanding the fact that the installed capacity is 270,000 m^3 per day. Shortages of water have become common, with many areas of the city doing without water for several hours a day or even for days.

At the level of individual households, water connections are inadequate in Dar es Salaam. Out of the households surveyed, 47.1 percent do not have a piped water supply either inside or immediately outside their house; another 32 percent reported a shared piped water supply. Only 20.9 percent of all the households sampled had a private piped water supply. Of the households without a piped water supply, 67.2 percent buy this water from their neighbors, while 25.7 percent draw their water from public water kiosks or standpipes. Unlike the situation in many other African cities where many people purchase water from water sellers, only 7.1 percent reported buying water in this fashion. On the average, however, water consumption is very low in Dar es Salaam, with 39.8 percent of the households using up to 120 liters per day, 30.7 percent using from 120 to 200 liters per day, and 31.5 percent using over 200 liters per day. As the average household size from our survey is 3.62 persons, these figures mean that at least 70.5 percent of the population (and possibly more) of Dar es Salaam receives less than the accepted international standard of 90 liters of water per day. Indeed, the average water consumption is only 23.6 liters per person per day.

At an institutional level, water shortages affect many major industries and organizations in Dar es Salaam, notably the University of Dar es Salaam (where water for office buildings and student residences is rarely available), the Urafiki Textile Mills (the largest textile mill in the country with more than four thousand employees), Tanganyika Dyeing and Weaving Mills Limited (SUNGURATEX) with more than 2,100 workers, and the Dar es Salaam-based Kilimanjaro Textile Mills. For example, SUNGURATEX received only 500,000 gallons of water per day for a few weeks in October and November 1986, when the factory needed 1 million gallons (*Daily News* 8 November 1986). And in mid-March 1987, KILTEX sent its 638 workers on a two-month compulsory leave because of financial problems and a water shortage at the mill (*Daily News* 17 March 1987). The KILTEX move came at a time of widespread water shortages in Dar es Salaam as a result of the destruction of a section of the power line because of a bush fire north of the city. Then, in April 1987, most areas in Dar es Salaam experienced a water shortage for a whole week after a water pump burst at the lower Ruvu station. The lower Ruvu scheme supplies seventy percent of the city's water supply. These dry spells, which are often the result of a combination of water and power outages, cost the nation hundreds of millions of shillings in terms of lost production of goods and services.

Recently, the government was forced to take strong measures to improve tax collection and to raise taxes on beer, hard and soft drinks, and cigarettes in order to cover a Shs.3.35 billion deficit on the 1986 / 87 budget (*Daily News* 8 April 1987). Announcing these tax measures, the Minister for Finance, Economic Affairs and Planning, Cleopa Msuya said that a combination of a lack of spare parts, power problems, and water shortages had so affected industrial production as to produce a serious shortfall in government revenue. But arguably, raising tax rates on non-essential goods cannot solve the problem of frequent water shortages and power failures in urban areas, which in turn adversely affect production. Goods which are not produced include such essential commodities as clothing, fertilizers, farm hoes, ploughs, and pesticides, which are essential for rural development. The root cause of these conditions is under-investment in urban infrastructure and services. An over-emphasis on rural development as if rural and urban development were mutually exclusive is short-sighted in the extreme.

Conclusions and Recommendations

On the basis of the foregoing discussion, a number of conclusions and policy implications may now be brought out. First, it is clear that rapid urban growth in Tanzania will continue at least for the foreseeable future. Urbanization is an inevitable part of the development process. Pragmatic policy measures should therefore be devised and applied to guide urban development into planned and serviced areas. Provision of employment opportunities to the large pool of untrained migrants from the rural areas or their channelling into productive self-employment could turn the present rapid increase of the urban population into a windfall for national development. Stimulation of construction activities in the popular housing sector – where construction is labor-intensive – would provide a large number of employment opportunities to many artisans and to the unskilled labor force. It would also act as a training base for educated youth to learn and acquire various skills needed in modern industry and other sectors of the national economy. At the same time, it would simultaneously provide much-needed and better housing to urban residents.

Second, efficient urban councils are an important means to meaningful local democracy and rapid national development. But in order to be efficient, the urban economy needs adequate and regular water supply, electricity, well-designed and constructed road networks, an efficient urban transport system, and reliable refuse collection and sewage disposal services. Inadequate urban services limit the efficiency and growth potential of firms and industries, imposing large costs on both the firms and the national economy. Well staffed, adequately funded urban councils, which are efficiently managed and have adequate heavy construction and maintenance equipment, could turn Tanzania's urban areas into a real engine of national development and prosperity.

Finally, the present legal framework is adequate in providing power to people at the grassroots level and in providing for the accountability of the councillors to the electorate. Both acts of Parliament and various constitutional provisions provide adequate powers and authority to local authorities to raise revenue and render services to the people and areas under their jurisdiction. Nevertheless, in recent years central government grants accounted for sixty percent of the entire recurrent budget of urban councils, and for one hundred percent of their development budgets. In his June 1986 Budget Speech, the Minister for Finance and Planning proposed a reduction of central government grants to local authorities from the present level to less than thirty percent of their recurrent budgets, and to less than fifty percent of their development budgets. In practice, therefore, urban local authorities will have to devise and apply new fiscal measures to raise more revenue locally; otherwise, they will face a financial crisis with urban services deteriorating even further to very low levels indeed.

At the same time as they must be concerned with improving their sources of local revenue, urban local authorities must strengthen the enforcement of local by-laws. The main outcry from councillors at the moment is that enforcement is ineffective and at times totally lacking. The national authorities have wider powers but the police force is pre-occupied with central government duties and cannot spare adequate time for the enforcement of local by-laws. In order to ensure that urban by-laws are enforced, each urban authority should have its own police force in the form of metropolitan police. Urban councils should then be left free from outside political interference in ensuring that their by-laws are sustained. In general, if urban authorities are to effectively manage rapid urban growth and improve the delivery of urban services, the strengthening of their financial and institutional capacities ought to be given the highest priority.

Notes

1. A sample of wards, houses, and households in each case study town was randomly selected. Where there were many wards in a town, all wards were numbered

and a sample of five to seven wards drawn by lot. Since each ward is divided into three to five CCM Party Branches, a sample of two or three CCM Party Branch areas was also randomly selected. In these Branch areas, housing questionnaires were administered to four houses randomly chosen for every ten houses under a ten-cell leader. The only exception was the selection of Manzese Ward in Dar es Salaam. Manzese was specifically selected because it is the largest urban squatter settlement and residential neighborhood not only in Dar es Salaam but also in the whole of Tanzania. The survey on general urban management covered all Heads of departments and most of their assistants in the six urban councils, and from fifty to seventy percent of the councillors in the study towns, along with the municipal director and mayor (or chairman) in each town.

2. This problem has remained the chronic weakness of the local government system in Tanzania. For instance, by the time local governments were abolished in 1972, many of them were failing to pay salaries of their primary school teachers.

3. The recent grant of refuse collectors and cesspit emptiers by the Japanese Government to Tanzania for distribution and use by seven urban councils (Dar es Salaam, Arusha, Mwanza, Dodoma, Tanga, Mbeya, and Moshi) should help the efforts of these urban councils to keep their areas clean.

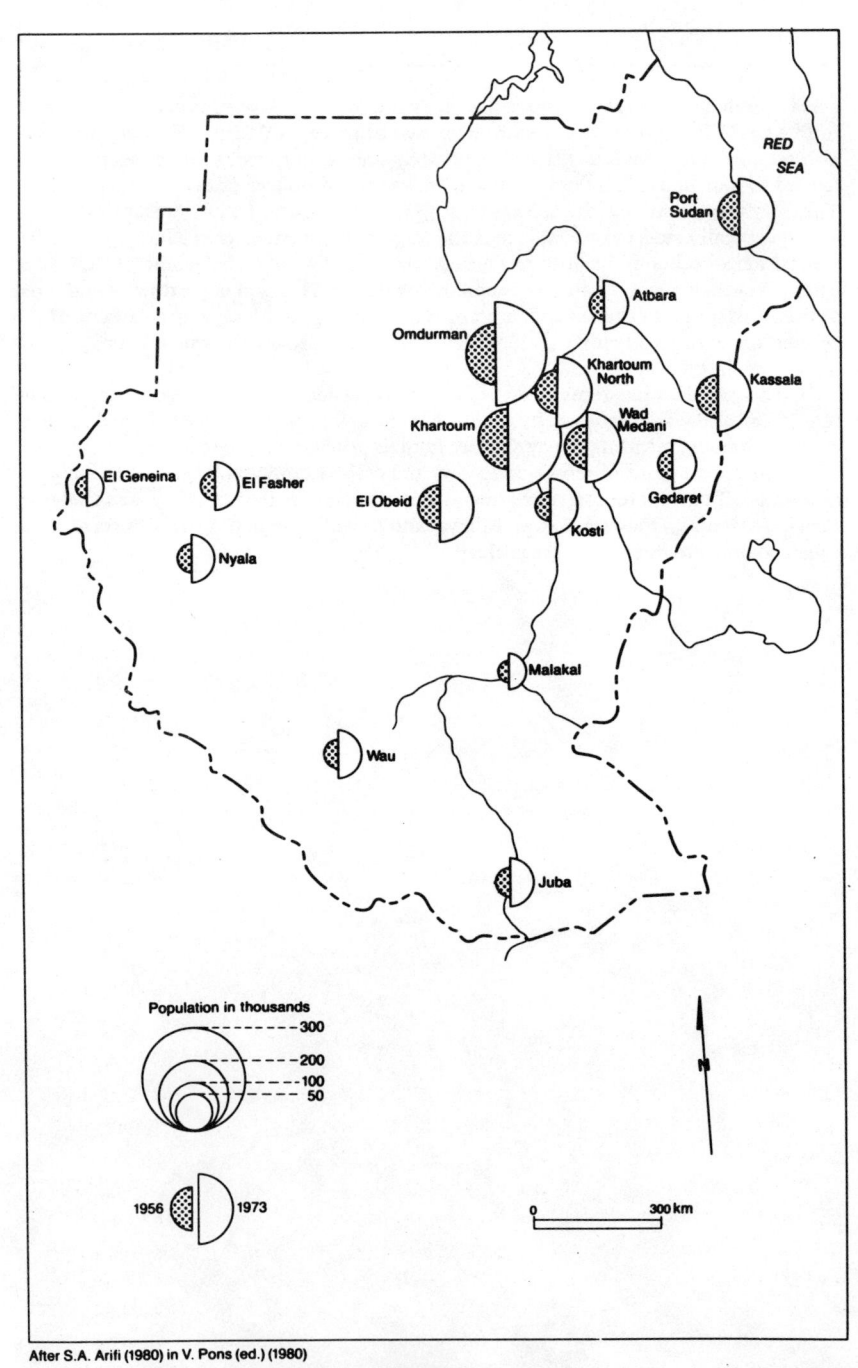

Figure 9.1
Sudan: Distribution of the Urban Population, 1956, 1973

CHAPTER 9
Management Problems of Greater Khartoum
Mohamed O. El Sammani, Mohamed El Hadi Abu Sin, M. Talha, B.M. El Hassan, and Ian Haywood

Introduction

The Sudan has a four thousand year history of human settlement along the Nile and its tributaries. Only recently has the balance between what is rural and urban presented a real management and economic problem. The complexity of this problem stems from the country's character – a blend of indigenous, Islamic, and Western culture, economy, and politics. Mismanagement and poor planning, exacerbated by the increase in oil prices and the global recession in the 1970s, have hindered attempts to attain balanced regional and urban development. Severe environmental stresses have also added to the country's economic problems. In order to appreciate better the Sudan's urban problems, the understanding of these parameters is essential.

Sudan covers an area of 2.5 million km^2, stretching over 20° latitude from north to south, and embracing a wide range of ecological zones – pure desert, semi-desert, savannah, and equatorial forests. A varied geography has generated equally diverse types of land use systems, such as nomadism, a peasant agricultural economy, modern irrigated agriculture, and mechanized rainfed agriculture.

The Nile river system constitutes the most important single physical feature for human settlement and development. The country has two axes of productive development and human concentration: a north-south axis represented by the Nile and an east-west axis represented by the central belt (lat.13-18°N). To the south, resources are of high potential, but not easy to tap because of political unrest and inaccessibility while to the north, resources (away from the Nile) are highly marginal and very expensive to develop.

The historical and political development of the Sudan is very difficult to review; yet the broad outline can be summarized in five major historical phases. The first phase was an early civilization on which was superimposed an Islamic culture, mostly in North Sudan. Elsewhere, indigenous cultures maintained their integrity up to the present. A second and much later phase involved exposure to the outside world after the Turkish invasion in 1821 and the British incursion in 1889. A third phase consisted of the short period of the Mahdist state, from 1884 to 1898. A fourth phase, the period of

Anglo-Egyptian condominium from 1899 to 1956, brought the country into close contact with the outside world, bringing at the same time new forms of economy, administration, and urban style. Finally, the fifth phase, the independence period, has been characterized by political instability, which in turn has adversely affected economic progress, leading to the present situation of economic recession, energy and food shortages, and overriding urban problems.

The most important aspects of population are natural growth rate, migration, and the processes of redistribution. The first national census of 1956 gave a population of 10.3 million; subsequent censuses in 1973 and 1983 showed populations of 14.9 million and 20 million, respectively. The average annual natural growth rate is estimated to be from 2.5 to 3.0 percent, for a doubling time of from seventeen to twenty-three years. The projected population for year 2000 could be as much as 34 million. One of the most alarming statistics subsumed in the overall growth rates is the rapid growth of the Sudan's urban population. From a low level of eight percent of the total population in 1956, the figure rose to sixteen percent in 1973 and thirty-two percent in 1983. Extrapolating at this rate, the expected urban population in 1993 could be sixty-two percent of the total population. The largest urban area in the country, Greater Khartoum, alone accounted for thirty-five percent of the total urban population in 1983. In that census year, Greater Khartoum had a population of 1.5 million while the second largest city, Port Sudan, had a population of only 200,000, giving an urban primacy ratio of approximately 7.5:1.

The country's economy is characterized by a sharp dualism between a small, highly localized modern sector in irrigated and mechanized rainfed agriculture and an urban-based industrial sector on the one hand; and a broad, diverse, traditional sector on the other hand. Most of the urban-based and agro-industries are concentrated in Greater Khartoum and along the middle Nile axis.

The economic setting and linkage between the modern and traditional sectors was favorable and self-adjusting up to the late 1960s. The rural areas were able to feed their populations and discharge some migrants into the urban areas. This economic setting has, however, been profoundly disturbed by two major factors. The first factor is the "spearhead development" strategy of picking areas of high potential in order to serve the interests of foreign investors in agro-industries, and irrigated cash crop schemes. The result has been not only increasing regional economic disparities but also the displacement of a large population into urban areas. In Greater Khartoum at least sixty percent of the population were first generation migrants after 1970.

The second major disruptive factor was the successive years of drought, pushing more marginal people into urban areas, particularly Greater

Khartoum. In 1984, for example, over 120,000 moved to Greater Khartoum as "environmental refugees" from Kordofan and Darfur (Leyla 1986; Sohair 1986). The economy is overburdened by the influx of refugees sharing meager resources with the existing population. Refugee estimates in 1985 were as high as 2 million (Refugee Commissioner's Office, Khartoum, 1986). Approximately one million of them are in the Eastern region, where there is one Ethiopian refugee for every three Sudanese. A large number of these refugees have gravitated toward Greater Khartoum, most illegally, looking for work and hoping eventually to migrate abroad.

A major response to the economic recession in the country has been out-migration of skilled workers and professionals into the Arab countries. Although this form of selective migration has injected significant levels of remittances into the economy, it has, on the other hand, deprived the country of productive elements who are the key to the support and execution of development projects. Further concerns about the economic consequences of remittances are that (1) most of such remittances are spent to provide for the basic needs of the family left at home; and (2) most of the surplus generated by remittances is handled by middlemen, land speculators, and currency merchants, and much of it is channeled into petty investment in urban land and into commercial transactions. Most of the money is trapped in these businesses and does not find its way into productive investment in either rural or urban areas.

The extent of emigration for work outside the country is substantial, as shown in the results of a survey of one thousand households which we carried out in Greater Khartoum in 1985. The survey, whose methodology is described in detail elsewhere (El Sammani et al 1986), was based on a random selection of household heads, stratified according to a list of quarter councils in six major kinds of residential areas: "first-class" areas; "second class" areas; "third class" areas; community-planned neighborhoods; squatter neighborhoods with few refugees; and squatter neighborhoods with a concentration of refugees. In the end, fourteen neighborhoods were surveyed. Table 9.1 shows that, while the process of emigration has been going on for some time, it has accelerated in recent years. Thus, households in the table are broken down according to the period during which members emigrated: 1970-1974, 1975-1979, and 1980-1985. The figures are further broken down between male and female household members, and according to the proportion of support the household estimated it received from the emigrants during these periods. The table shows that not only do the unplanned residential areas send a higher proportion of their male members overseas for work, but the proportion of the household income depending on remittances is much higher than in the more established (and richer) areas.

The interplay of the purely environmental conditions, nature, and

Table 9.1
Emigration of Khartoum Household Members and their Remittances to Household Budgets, 1985[1]

Sample Areas	Time of Emigration of Any Member of Household					
	1970-74		1976-79		1980-85	
	M	F	M	F	M	F
Est: 1st class, 3 towns	6.20	6.20	25.0	25.0	28.1	9.30
1st class, 3 towns, U.P.	13.30	13.30	20.0	13.30	26.60	13.30
2nd class, 3 towns, Est.	0.0	0.0	5.80	29.40	35.20	29.40
2nd class, 3 towns, U.P.	0.0	0.0	40.0	0.0	60.0	0.0
3rd class, 3 towns, Est.	10.40	2.60	34.30	3.40	43.40	5.60
Mahdiya, 3rd class, planned, Est.	8.30	8.30	37.50	8.30	29.10	8.30
Wadnubawi, old, unplanned, U.P.	15.30	0.0	30.70	0.0	53.80	0.0
Ushara south, new, planned, Est.	0.0	0.0	20.0	0.0	80.0	0.0
Thawra, new, planned, U.P.	0.0	0.0	33.30	0.0	55.50	11.10
Hag Yousif, popular, Est.	0.0	0.0	40.0	0.0	60.0	0.0
Umm El Ghora, popular, U.P.	7.10	0.0	21.40	0.0	71.40	0.0
Salama, squatter, Est.	0.0	0.0	50.0	0.0	50.0	0.0
Mayo, squatter, U.P.	0.0	0.0	6.25	0.0	93.75	0.0
Diem, refugees	0.0	0.0	6.20	6.20	75.0	12.50

Est. = established. U.P. = under process of development.

[1] Figures represent the percentage of households in each neighbourhood. The total used for these calculations was 1,000.

Table 9.1 continued

	Emigrant Contribution as Proportion Of Household Budget			
	¼	½	¾	All
Est: 1st class, 3 towns	63.64	18.18	9.09	9.09
1st class, 3 towns, U.P.	33.33	33.33	0.0	33.33
2nd class, 3 towns, Est.	75.0	0.0	25.0	0.0
2nd class, 3 towns, U.P.	50.0	0.0	0.0	50.0
3rd class, 3 towns, Est.	43.24	18.02	10.81	27.93
Mahdiya, 3rd class, planned, Est.	28.57	14.29	14.29	42.86
Wadnubawi, old, unplanned, U.P.	40.0	20.0	20.0	20.0
Ushara south, new, planned, Est.	25.0	0.0	0.0	75.0
Thawra, new, planned, U.P.	25.0	25.0	12.50	37.50
Hag Yousif, popular, Est.	33.33	0.0	0.0	66.67
Umm El Ghora, popular, U.P.	0.0	14.29	14.29	71.43
Salama, squatter, Est.	0.0	0.0	0.0	100.0
Mayo, squatter, U.P.	60.0	40.0	0.0	0.0
Diem, refugees	33.33	22.22	11.11	33.33

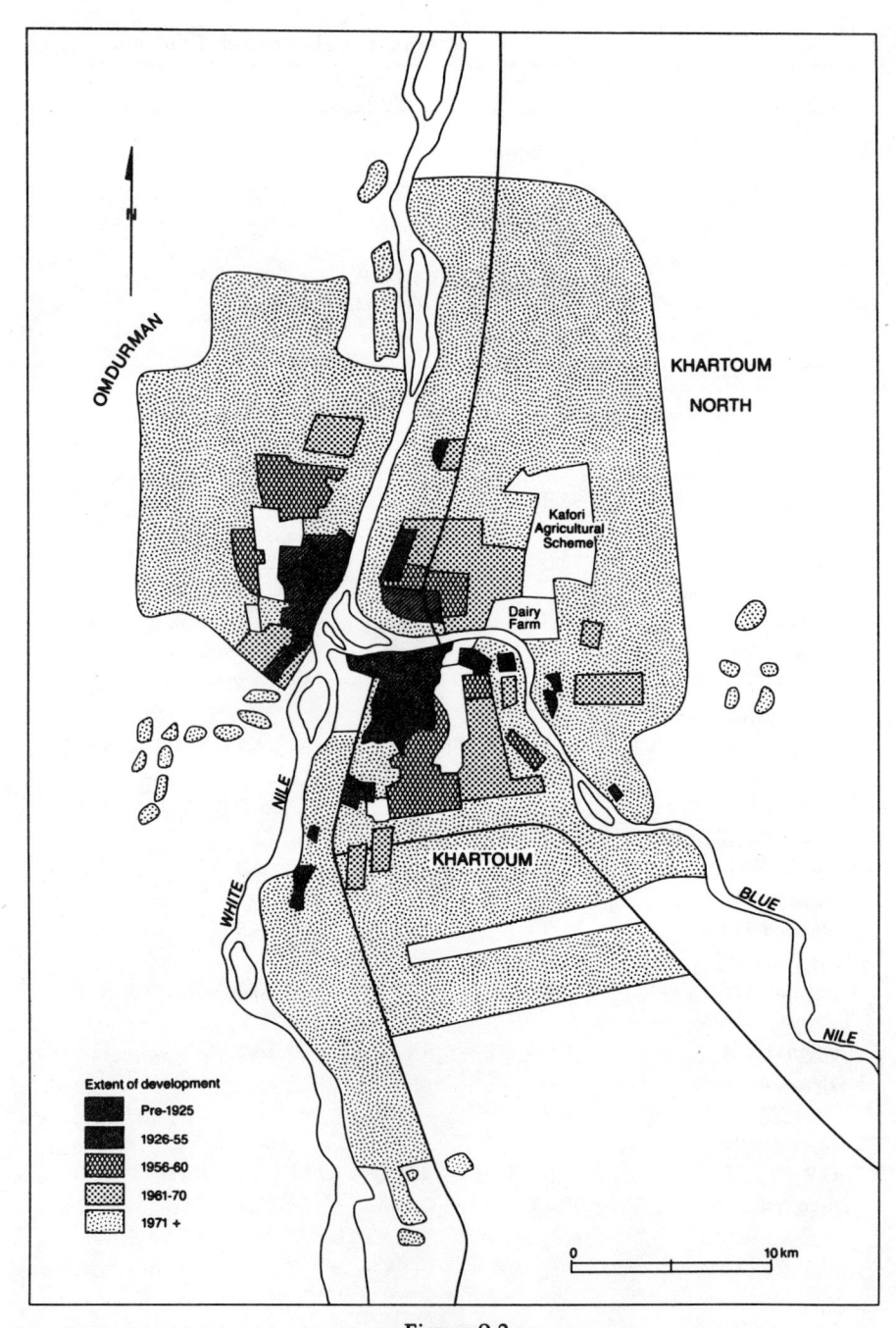

Figure 9.2
The Growth of Khartoum

pattern of development strategy (mostly capitalistic) and the resultant population dynamism has shaped the urban problems of Greater Khartoum. The inefficiency of the urban authority in handling such problems is the main cause of the "urban crisis." The purpose of this study is to examine the management of Greater Khartoum's urban area in order to assess the effectiveness of the administrative response to pressing urban problems. Realizing that the urban authority has limited capabilities because of the shortage of finance, skilled manpower, and basic supportive technology, this study is also meant to examine how this reflects on the availability of basic services in the urban milieu. As a substitute for publicly-provided services and amenities, people are opting for self-help solutions to their immediate problems. The overall objective of this study is to arrive at a series of relevant recommendations aiming at (1) the improvement of the administrative system and (2) the delivery of services in the most economic way.

The Demographic Factor

Sudan gained independence in 1956, by which time the Three Towns had grown together as a single entity although each retained its distinctive identity and primary functions. Omdurman had grown as a national, business, and residential center; Khartoum North had grown as a residential and industrial center; while Khartoum, as an administrative center and a center of Western culture, and was the site of most of the higher order services in the capital area.

In 1906 Greater Khartoum had a population of 78,087 which rose to 202,381 in 1931, showing a growth of 159 percent. Thereafter, the growth rate was moderated by a slight decline during World War II. The population then increased by 40 percent from 176,209 in 1942 to 245,736 in 1956; the growth rate was 219 percent growth from 1956 to 1973 and 72 percent from 1973 to 1983. In 1983 the population of Greater Khartoum stood at 1,343,651. Greater Khartoum's average annual population growth from 1956 to 1964 was approximately 6 percent compared with 6.9 percent from 1964 to 1973 and 7.3 percent from 1973 to 1983. An estimated 60 to 70 percent of such an increase is the result of net migration. The pressures of such rapid population growth have led to the emergence of shanty towns, accounting for over 60 percent of Greater Khartoum's population and an even higher proportion of its residential built-up area.

Within the Greater Khartoum urban complex, Omdurman (the site of the traditional heart of the urban area) had the lowest rate of growth in the period 1942-56, while Khartoum North had the highest growth rate. After 1956 the growth rate of Greater Khartoum was dominated by that of Khartoum North and Khartoum. The rapid increase in the growth rate of Greater Khartoum during the period 1956-73 coincided with the industrial boom of

Khartoum North. From 1973 to 1983 the growth rate continued to accelerate well above the national average and the average of the eight major towns.

Three main factors are responsible for the rapid growth of Greater Khartoum: (1) the administrative functions associated with its status as a national capital; (2) the high concentration of industry, business, educational, and health services; and (3) the excessive immigration attracted by actual and imagined job opportunities, reinforced by the environmental conditions in the rural areas. It was estimated that about sixty percent of Greater Khartoum's population growth from 1960 to 1975 resulted from migration from rural areas or lesser urban centers. The interplay of the above variables is well illustrated by the functional interrelationship of Greater Khartoum with the rest of the main centers in the country. As a result, Greater Khartoum represents the largest urban concentration in the country with 32.4 percent of the total urban population and an estimated population (in 1986) of 1.8 million.

In brief, the trend of demographic growth of Greater Khartoum can be seen to have five major characteristics. First, there was steady growth during the British colonial period, associated with development in urban-oriented industries and improvement in infrastructure and services. Second, there was a rapid increase in growth after independence, related to the continuation of the British policy of generating more services and economic development in Greater Khartoum. The rapid rate of growth during this period has been closely associated with the excessive migratory process. In this context, Greater Khartoum's urban primacy has not been challenged and it continues to dominate the country's urban and rural landscape. Third, the highest level of population increase is recorded among recent immigrants and low income groups now dominating the urban scene. Fourth, although the rate of growth in terms of population is increasing, the economic prosperity of Greater Khartoum is declining. The result is a rapid deterioration in urban life styles and a strong trend towards "ruralization" (Stren 1986). Fifth, as a result of the dramatic growth rate, there is a polarization in the standard of living, dividing the city into sharply contrasting segments in terms of living conditions and the quality of material life. This polarization is also evident in housing conditions and facilities, plot size, rent levels, additions to housing facilities, and the like. For instance, in the first class (established) area sampled in this survey, thirty-five percent of the houses had three or more toilets; in the unplanned areas, most houses had only one toilet (or latrine), and not one house sampled had more than two. As for plot size, ninety-eight percent of the first class (established) plots, ninety-three percent of the first class (developing) area plots, fifty-four percent of the second class (established) plots, and twenty-eight percent of the second class (in process of development) area plots were over six hundred square meters in size. By contrast, almost all of the plots in the unplanned areas are less than five hundred square meters in size, with many in the poorer squatter areas being less than two hundred square meters.

Thus, the place of Greater Khartoum in the national context and the demographic trends describing its growth are closely associated. The increasing national dominance and parallel rapid population growth are responsible for the fast degradation of the urban environment. It is reasonable to conclude that immigration, along with a low level of investment in urban services, is pushing Greater Khartoum into what may be called an "urban crisis," demanding a proper evaluation of the problems and the development of an appropriate planning system to secure clearly defined objectives.

City Planning

As the population growth rate of Greater Khartoum accelerated, the discrepancies increased between the need for a functional organization of the urban fabric and the actual planning and administration responses. The structure of the administration in which planning agents are to function is very complex.

Population growth rates have been accompanied by changes in the social and economic organization of the Three Towns which are reflected in the urban structure. The process of physical growth has consisted of the creation of mainly residential areas at the perimeter combined with changes of land use towards the center as low density housing areas have been redeveloped to provide for new commercial uses or for higher density forms of residential accommodation. In the center, this process has resulted in new multi-storey developments affecting both land values and patterns of land use. Urban blight takes place as land values rise faster than property values, until the value of a site exceeds the value of the building on it and redevelopment takes place. As a consequence, a fragmented pattern of land uses develops with new high density developments of new land uses appearing alongside low density established land uses. The lack of adequate provision of services or the development of a hierarchy of roads serving different functions leads to inefficient movement patterns and an erosion of environmental quality. The process of deterioration itself accelerates as the pattern of land use change affects land values and encourages further changes of land use, which themselves pose additional loads on an already inadequate urban infrastructure and poor service delivery systems.

The mechanisms for controlling development in the Three Towns consist of simple zoning and housing classification systems. These mechanisms are based on planning standards derived largely from the grid pattern of development and land use zoning system which were used in the original colonial development of Khartoum. However, in the immediate post-independence period, the government recognized that the application of such standards was inadequate. In an effort to develop a more systematic form of planning, the government commissioned Doxiadis Associates of Athens in 1959 to prepare a master plan for the Three Towns. The resultant proposals applied the familiar Doxiadis orthogonal grid to the Three Towns in order to provide a structure for both the rationalization of existing urban uses and future urban expansion to the north and south. The plan was a comprehensive study which included both a general development strategy and detailed proposals for the layout of neighborhoods and subcenters. However, the lack of an effective planning administration and mechanisms for the control and promotion of development meant that the proposals were never formally approved or implemented, although they did have some influence on the detailed layout of neighborhoods.

The high rates of population growth which the Three Towns were experiencing meant that the Doxiadis proposals were soon overtaken and outdated. In 1977 a second attempt to produce a master plan for the Three Towns was made, and the Mefit Consulting Group of Rome was chosen. Its brief was more wide-ranging, as they were to prepare a new master plan for the Three Towns in the context of a sub-regional transportation study. Comprehensive studies were again undertaken, resulting in a set of inter-related regional and local proposals, including detailed policies for improving and upgrading existing urban areas. Some initial efforts were made to implement the new plan, but the same lack of administrative procedures, coupled with political antipathy to planning, prevented the proposals from being formally approved. Although the plan has affected some decisions, such as the proposal to relocate the airport, it has largely been overtaken by events and fallen into abeyance.

Because of the lack of a formally approved plan, control of the growth of the Three Towns operates only on an *ad hoc* basis. New areas for housing are allocated and sub-divided using the same basic grid layout and classification system established during the colonial period, although efforts are presently being made to reduce planning standards to allow increased densities and lower service costs. Housing areas are provided with space for commercial building and social services including schools. However, the lack of government resources means that frequently basic infrastructure services and social services are not provided. As a result, in many areas of the conurbation, communities have developed self-help associations in order to provide such essential services. Money is collected through both voluntary donations and compulsory tolls on traffic. The funds are then used, in conjunction with the community's own skills and labor, to provide roads, infrastructure, and community services. Such community associations, which are often organized through the local mosque, also act as political pressure groups to ensure that main services, such as water and electricity, are provided to the housing areas, with the community arranging the internal distribution.

The distribution of sites is, however, unable to keep up with the demand caused both by natural increase and in-migration; the result is the growth of large squatter settlements of spontaneous dwellings around the perimeter of the Three Towns. The local authority has a rather ambivalent attitude with regard to these settlements. Where it feels the pressures are too great or the illegal settlements are seen to conflict with what are considered to be more legitimate needs, they are frequently demolished and the inhabitants instructed to return to their rural areas of origin. In other areas, particularly where the communities are able to organize themselves into political pressure groups, they follow the same pattern of organized self help not only to provide themselves with services but also, ultimately, to gain legal status and land ownership rights.

At the same time as growth is taking place at the periphery of the Three Towns, increasing commercial pressures at the center are resulting in largely uncontrolled changes of land use as low density residential development is demolished to provide sites for higher density blocks of flats or offices. This centrifugal displacement of uses is creating both a deterioration of environmental standards in the Three Towns as a whole as well as increased development pressures at the periphery.

The general impression of the conurbation is that of uncontrolled growth, resulting in vast areas of characterless urban sprawl surrounding a core area of rapidly changing buildings and land uses. This has resulted in poor accessibility to basic services, which in most spontaneously rising quarters does not exist at all.

The failure to control the growth of Greater Khartoum stems from the lack of an effective administrative system with proper development control and forward planning functions, backed with the appropriate planning legislation. The lack of proper development controls has led to changes of use, with the allocation of sites for new development occurring in an uncoordinated manner and resulting in considerable diseconomies, both in the use of land and in the functioning of the urban area. The lack of a proper forward planning function has meant that it has not been possible to predict the needs of the future growth of Khartoum to ensure that sites and their related services are provided in advance of demand.

The basic reasons for the failure to develop and maintain an effective planning administrative machine are the lack of resources necessary to ensure the provision of the appropriately skilled administrators and a failure to recognize the significance and implication of many development decisions. In many instances, decisions are essentially political; but failure to consult professional staff working in the administration leads not only to the alienation of those staff but also to decisions based on poor political reasons rather than good technical ones.

The Management of Greater Khartoum

Greater Khartoum's urban administration is an established local government system according to which the three adjacent municipalities of Khartoum, Omdurman, and Khartoum North assume direct responsibility for running the urban ecosystem of Greater Khartoum. Structurally, the urban management system of Khartoum comprises a three-tier system with neighborhood councils at the bottom, the town councils in the middle, and the city councils at the top. The city council is fully electoral, locally autonomous as a corporate body with a legislative capacity, and duly authorized to take decisions in accordance with its warrant of establishment specifying its functions and duties.

The entire structure of Greater Khartoum's urban system consists of a network of 367 neighborhood councils, thirty-one town councils plus another ten specialized councils for industrial areas, central areas, and specialized markets, in addition to the three city councils mentioned above. While the city council comprises a number of town councils ranging from a maximum of fourteen in the case of Khartoum city to a minimum of six town councils in the case of Khartoum North, town councils consist of several neighborhood councils, with an average of seven for each. The membership of the base and middle level councils is limited to twenty-four elected members.

The council at each level is formed into a number of specialized committees such as environmental health, education, finance, public works, commerce, agriculture, public transport, and public order. Some of these committees are statutory, with finance as the core committee, while others are optional, and the council may or may not decide to set them up. The average number of specialized committees, in the case of the city and town councils, is eight.

This hierarchical structure, which gives the Greater Khartoum urban management system its unique character, together with its specified duties and functions, has been based on three major principles. First, the neighborhood councils are meant to function to facilitate grass-roots involvement to deal with running neighborhood-oriented services by generating self-help and promoting self-reliance. A second function of town councils is to promote cooperation among neighborhood councils to deal with services that by their very nature are necessarily shared among them. Finally, it is the role of the city councils in each of the three towns to ensure that action concerning central issues is coordinated and integrated among town councils. This is particularly important with regard to the provision of higher order services and development projects that are beyond the capacity of individual town councils and at the same time fit into the activities of the national capital level authorities.

The urban structure of Greater Khartoum consists of a variety of residential class-types, including first, second, third, and fourth class planned areas, intermingled with over ninety squatter areas and extensive spontaneous settlements. Some of the planned residential areas are well established while others are still in the process of being established. The resultant heterogeneity of the town council areas, formed of different neighborhoods, has a direct bearing on services demand and provision as well as on the town council's general performance.

Both the economic viability of administrative units within an urban system, as well as the social cohesion among the constituent neighborhoods, are central to the way the councils perform their duties and functions. Communities that are of the same or similar economic and social standards are likely to have a similar perception of priorities and the quality of life to which they aspire. Moreover, they tend to be more cooperative as taxpayers, more likely to generate self-help schemes, and more likely to be consensual and rational in their decision-making process. They usually work out their agendas with similar resolutions that are practical in the sense that they ensure beforehand that they have the resources necessary to implement them. These characteristics are likely to obtain in town councils which cover residential areas containing similar class neighborhoods. This is obviously more the case in neighborhood councils than in higher-level councils, as these are base administrative units where more mutual understanding will prevail.

However, the very nature of neighborhood councils as administrative units means that there is a limitation on their jurisdiction and competence, dictated by the council's administrative capacity in terms of population size and revenue sources. Hence, the functions and responsibilities specified for them, by-laws and regulations, are those strictly confined to activities at the neighborhood level only. They, therefore, must depend on town and city councils to provide social and basic services, such as primary health care centers that, of necessity, have to be shared with other neighborhood and town councils. Through their representatives on town and city councils they seek services which often are beyond their capacity to utilize to the fullest.

There are many challenges for the future. The Greater Khartoum urban management system was initiated by the British in the late 1930s and still is, with its complicated system of different tiers and wide representation by the population, a pioneer system in Africa. However, the mounting problems and constraints that are currently posed seem to be too complex to be readily surmountable by the present machinery of urban administration. These problems, not unlike those of many of the other large capital cities treated in this volume, include an unwarranted and uncontrollable urban growth that frustrates the provision of social services and local development, particularly in view of the already strained resources. A second major problem area is the extent of the city's squatter settlements, now numbering well over ninety residential areas. This has been further aggravated by the recent unprecedented intensity of drought and desertification experienced by much of the country, culminating in whole villages moving from the countryside into the capital city area. A third problem involves the shortcomings of the city administration's fiscal performance. These shortcomings seem to be in-built weaknesses of the system – for example, the chronic deficit of the annual municipal budget, some of which can be attributed to the large element of salary (called "Chapter I") in the budget. Other problems of urban administration involve the low viability of administrative units and coordination of services, a low level of popular participation, and a general inefficiency and incompetence of urban management personnel in Greater Khartoum. These problems and constraints obviously represent a telling indictment of the Greater Khartoum urban management system; the elements of the crisis in Khartoum are not, however, uncommon in primate cities in the developing countries.

City Finance

Greater Khartoum city councils have eight main sources of revenue: (1) assigned taxes, which are originally central government taxes, according to the 1954 Act but have been assigned to local government councils to enable them to meet their public financial obligations – examples are the house tax, based on one-twelfth of a house's annual rental value, and the entertainment tax; (2) local rates, which are levied on houses as a certain percentage of their annual rental value; (3) licensing fees, such as trader's licenses, public health licenses, and building permit fees; (4) rents on the properties of councils, such as shops, sheds, and specialized markets built by councils for the dual purpose of providing special services and raising revenue; (5) grants-in-aid from the central government, which actually constitute over sixty percent of the annual total revenue secured by Greater Khartoum city councils; (6) revenue accruing to city councils from local development projects they have established, such as agricultural and animal production schemes; (7) fees on special services, particularly in the areas of environmental health and veterinary services; (8) loans from banks, which are not actually resorted to as yet since they do not seem feasible to deal with real problems of deficits and insolvency.

More important than fees and formal taxes for much urban development in the Sudan, however, is the element of self-help. Sudanese communities are basically oriented towards self-help and self-reliance as an integral part of their indigenous culture. As a result, neighborhood councils, at the base of the structural hierarchy of the urban administrative system, have been made to depend mainly upon their own revenue sources for the services and facilities they wish to support. Local communities seem to be predominantly inclined to contribute to education and health projects, but they have also financed water projects and local roads. The amount of funds generated by self-help campaigns for financing different projects of services and development in Greater Khartoum reached several million Sudanese pounds in 1985.

This strong culturally-based commitment among the Greater Khartoum urban communities to contribute financially to the provision of social and basic services and local development needs to be carefully revised and rationalized. The reason for this is that outside donors tend to contribute funds only for the construction of services and institutions without giving due consideration to running expenses, personnel provision, equipment, and coordination of the proposals with other budgets and appropriate local plans and priorities. Such shortcomings in the system of contributions by local communities account, through irrational planning, for some of the problems encountered in the urban management of Greater Khartoum. There is a need to consider a better utilization of community resources by coordinating community efforts with official plans and programs. The extent to which this is important can be seen in the following analysis of the operation and effectiveness of city-wide utilities and health services.

Conurbation Utilities

Due to the expansion of the city by the early 1920s, the water supply system had become inadequate. Consequently, as early as the 1920s, the authorities constructed a series of water treatment plants based on perennial Nile water, to cope with the increasing demand. As the water supply from these works proved to be insufficient, because of the continuous growth of the city, the authorities had to resort to ground water sources to augment the urban water supply. The return to ground water was dictated by economic as well as technical reasons. The installation of treatment plant facilities is financially beyond the budgetary limits allotted for such services. The ground water installation proved to be cheaper and more locally-controllable compared with the already overloaded urban water connection system. In community planned quarters (Abu Sin 1985), drilling of wells and the installation of house-to-house connections provide freedom of action without no reliance on the government-controlled main system.

The Khartoum Water Corporation (KWC) has recently achieved considerable success in increasing the supply of water to the Khartoum area. Since May 1982 supplies have increased from 110,000 m^3 per day to 260,000 m^3 per day. This was made possible by a program of rehabilitation of the existing water treatment plants, together with a program of intensive borehole drilling and connection work. The two activities have raised the output of the five water treatment plants to a capacity of 150,000 m^3 per day (compared to a design capacity of 90,000 m^3 per day) and have increased the supply of boreholes from 20,000 m^3 per day to 110,000 m^3 per day.

In spite of the increase in water produced for domestic purposes, some people, particularly in a few poor quarters, spend a substantial proportion of their income on buying water from vendors. Our 1985 survey shows, for example, that in the new squatter area of Mayo eighty percent of the households reported obtaining water from vendors; for other "popular settlements" such as Umm el Ghora and Hag Yousif, the figures are eleven percent in each case. Even for the newly-developing "planned" settlement of Thawrah, ninety-five percent of respondents purchased water from vendors. But on the positive side, the overwhelming majority of the respondents said that the water they received was healthy for drinking and that the cost of water was either "satisfactory" or "low." While almost all the respondents in first, second, and third class areas had a water tap in their house, a majority of respondents in all but two of the other areas sampled also reported taps in their houses. For the most part, such water supply services were obtained through community self-help activities.

The systems of disposal of sewage in use in Khartoum range from traditional pit latrines to conventional sewerage systems; the system in use is largely a function of the housing class type. Thus, older first and second class areas rely on sewerage systems, whereas newer first and second class areas use septic tanks. In third and fourth class areas most houses have traditional pit latrines and aqua-privies. Most squatter areas do not have any system, and open-air defecation is common. A few areas are also still dependent upon the bucket collection system (even though it has officially been abolished) while some areas have cesspools.

The Three Towns contain two sewerage systems at El Goz and El Haj Yousif. The first (commissioned in 1959) was designed to serve Khartoum town and the second (commissioned in 1971) mainly to serve the industrial area of Khartoum North. The two sewerage systems in use serve only fifteen percent of Khartoum, five percent of Khartoum North; and 0.5 percent of Omdurman. In total, they serve less than five percent of the population of the conurbation.

At present, the El Goz plant is overloaded since it was initially designed to handle 3.2 million gallons per day while it is currently treating 8 million gallons per day. Occasionally, and because of power cuts and overflow, the excess flow from the El Goz plant is diverted to the White Nile without any treatment, thus constituting a serious pollution hazard. In the case of the El Haj Yousif plant, planned second and third phases of construction were never implemented and the treatment plant is presently out of use because of corrosion problems and lack of maintenance. As a result, new sewage is by-passing the plant and being discharged on agricultural land nearby.

The deficiencies of the two sewage disposal plants can be summarized as follows: (1) lack of budget for running the system; (2) operation and maintenance problems (power cuts, lack of spare parts, and the like); (3) lack of qualified personnel, partly attributable to the emigration of skilled and professional staff mostly to the oil-rich Arab countries; and (4) the non-familiarity of industrial users of the system with the nature of its operation. To improve the sewage disposal situation in the Three Towns, these shortcomings need to be addressed. In the case of Khartoum North, the factory effluents should be brought under control so that the waste discharged will have an acceptable pollution load. The El Haj Yousif plant should then be brought back into operation and the construction of Phase II should be considered.

Other than the sewerage system just described, the septic tank seems to be the technology mostly used in the first and second class areas. The septic tank is even being used in some houses in the third class areas where it is gradually replacing the pit latrine. The aqua-privy is unsuccessful because of the low KAP since its effluents are released into ground water. The pit latrine stands as the most appropriate for third class housing but needs to be upgraded. Of the three types, the septic tank constitutes the most significant potential ground water pollution risk, if not now, then in the long run, as increasing use is made of ground water for the supply of drinking water.

The inefficiency of refuse collection is one of the most acute problems facing Khartoum at present. Theoretically, the organization of the service appears practical, with each of the four district councils of Khartoum being headed by a Senior Public Health Inspector responsible to the Director of Environmental Health in the office of the Director General of Preventive Medicine, reporting to the Health Inspector in each of the four districts, and assisted by Public Health Inspectors and sanitary overseers, assistant overseers and laborers. In 1986 2,290 workers (1,869 of whom were manual laborers) were involved in refuse collection in Greater Khartoum (El Sammani et al. 1986, 107).

Refuse is collected by the councils or contractors they employ, either on a house-to-house basis or from central collection points. Some refuse is burned at collection points, either by residents themselves or by sanitary overseers. The systems of collection in use range from carts and tractors with trailers to proper refuse collection vehicles either fitted with hoists for containers or compactors. In 1986 there were eighty vehicles (thirty of them tractors) in the refuse collection services of the Greater Khartoum area (El Sammani et al. 1986, 107).

Only first and second class residents pay for garbage collection. The poorer quarters do not pay; but neither is their refuse collected. In these areas, most people dispose of their garbage in open spaces. The survey asked respondents how their refuse was collected, whether they were satisfied by the present system, and, if they were not satisfied, what their reasons were for dissatisfaction. Except in the first and second class areas as well as in Ushara South (a new, planned neighborhood) and Diem (a refugee village), almost none of the respondents reported council collection of rubbish in front of the houses. In most of the spontaneous housing areas, people either dumped their garbage anywhere outside their house or took it to a collection place, where it was piled up. Almost everyone was dissatisfied with the refuse collection service (with the exception of the refugee village, where fifty-three percent reported that they were satisfied), the main reasons being given tending to be either the irregularity of the service (in the planned areas) or that the service did not at all cover the area where therespondent lived (in the spontaneous areas).

In general, there is a gross deficiency in the refuse collection system operating in the conurbation, resulting in a considerable hazard to public health. The deficiencies stem essentially from the lack of equipment and personnel which results from budgetary deficiencies, causing such depressingly familiar problems as a lack of spare parts, fuel and maintenance, and poor wages and salaries. However, the situation is somewhat ameliorated by the low rate of production of refuse – currently estimated at approximately 0.5 kilograms per person per day. The composition of the refuse, the large numbers of scavenging goats and other animals, the relatively low population densities, and the hot dry climate, all assist in reducing the problem.

As for energy supply, electricity service was first introduced into the Sudan in 1908 through the installation of a small thermal engine in Khartoum, producing a 1 MW supply. Since then, the production of electricity has been increased. Today, it is estimated at 444 MW. The city is supplied by hydropower, through the Blue Nile Grid from a dam on the Blue Nile, plus thermal power from the old Burri thermal station which was recently renovated. During the last two years the electricity supply has increased through the Power III project to reach 180 MW – comprising 80 MW from hydro power and 100 MW from thermal power. In spite of this increase, Greater Khartoum is still facing an acute electricity shortage. Hence, a new project (Power IV) is anticipated. This project is designed to generate 140 MW thermally.

The current policy adopted by the National Energy Administration (NEA) to overcome the existing shortage is through load shedding, increasing the supply from private generators, and holding back the extension of the supply to new consumers. Most electricity consumption from the main grid or from private generators is reported by first and second class areas. Most of the poorer areas have either limited access or no access at all to electricity, so they pay little or nothing for this facility. In any case, the family budget in poor areas is overstretched by the cost of transportation, education, medical treatment, social obligations, and the like.

Although the total installed generating capacity in the Blue Nile Grid is 444 MW, this has never been attained because of generation, transmission, and distribution problems. There are, however, considerable seasonal fluctuations in both supply and demand. In winter the demand drops to some 120 MW while in summer the additional cooling requirements increase demand, resulting in an overload of approximately twenty percent. At the same time, the demand is growing through population increase, agricultural and industrial expansion, and the rise in domestic consumption rates. But as a result of the low costs of electricity and unbilled consumption, the present supply is decreasing. This is due to the inefficient performance of all types of generating sources. Difficulties in improving the situation stem less from the lack of resources and more from management problems of poor record-keeping, the inefficient collection system of electricity charges, and the general opposition to increasing electricity prices, even for domestic uses.

Two main sources of domestic energy are used, mostly for cooking purposes. First, fuelwood and charcoal are used by the majority of the urban population. Second, gas is used by the rich minority. The infrequency of gas supply has made charcoal the most popular source of cooking fuel. It is estimated that Greater Khartoum is consuming over sixty percent of the commercially produced charcoal in the country. The price of a sack of charcoal (twenty-five to thirty kilograms) has increased from £S5 in 1970 to £S20 in 1985, and £S30 in periods of shortage. Empirical evidence suggests that it is cheaper to use gas when available. A fourteen kilogram cylinder (£S20) supports an average family for three to four weeks, while the same family needs three to four sacks of charcoal (total price £S60-80) for the same period. About fifteen years ago, people combined the use of wood, charcoal, and kerosene. At present, because of the unavailability of kerosene and the infrequent supply of gas, people are mostly dependent on charcoal. The reliance on charcoal and wood has serious problems for the biomass, with an inadequate replacement rate and resultant process of desertification. The off-take from the forests for fuel and furniture, in the urban areas, has proved to be irreplaceable by natural regeneration or regular planting of trees.

Health Services

Following the enactment of the 1983 National Capital Commission Act, health services in Khartoum were brought under the responsibility of the central government Commissioner for Health. Two general directors assist the Commissioner: one for curative services and the other for preventive services. The Director General for Curative Services is in charge of all general and specialized hospitals as well as teaching hospitals. Under the Directorate of Curative Medicine are the departments of radiology, laboratory services, dentistry, personnel, pharmacy, private practice, insurance, and paramedicals. The Director General for Preventive Medicine is responsible for three main departments: the Department of Health Programs, the Department of Training, and the Department of Planning and Information. The Director General is also in charge of the directors of health services in the four areas of the Khartoum Commission.

Medical services in the Sudan are still being divided into curative and preventive services as had been adopted by the colonial government's Medical Commission in 1924. Although the government in its National Health Plan for 1977 / 78-1983 / 84 adopted a primary health care approach for the delivery of health services, the old concept of curative and preventive services is still being followed.

The budget for health services is divided into three sections: Chapter I is for salaries; Chapter II is for services; and Chapter III is the development budget. For Chapter I, the commission had a budget of £S1,693,405 for 1983 / 84. For services, the commission requested a budget of £S20,091,273 but was allotted only £S8,611,573 for 1983 / 84. Chapter III expenditure is centralized with the National Ministry of Health. This limited budget has to provide health services for the estimated current 1.8 million population of Khartoum. The estimated expenditure on health per head in Khartoum Province is £S4.7 per year. This is only an approximate estimate, since typically the actual expenditure is less than what is originally approved because of liquidity problems.

Medical care is delivered through general and specialized hospitals and through health centers in the urban parts of Khartoum; for the rural fringe areas of the city, medical care is delivered through dispensaries, dressing stations, and primary health care units. Khartoum Province has fifteen general hospitals, ten specialized hospitals, forty-eight health centers, sixty-eight dispensaries, seventy-six dressing stations, and fifty-seven primary health care units.

The rural population of Khartoum is served by a system of dispensaries run by medical assistants and a nurse, by dressing stations run by nurses, and by primary health care units which are staffed by community health workers. In total, the rural and nomadic population of 458,648 is served by 201 health facilities. Many local health facilities in the rural fringe areas are in practice usually served by one health worker except for dispensaries which, especially in densely populated areas, are typically run by a medical assistant and a nurse. Assuming that all dispensaries in Khartoum are being served by two health workers, this would mean a total of 269 health workers to serve a population of 458,648 or 1 health worker for 1,705 people.

The hospitals in the conurbation as a whole are staffed by general practitioners and specialists. Their number in 1982 included 1,273 doctors, which represented fifty-eight percent of the doctors in the whole Sudan. These doctors served 3,595 beds distributed in all the specialized and general hospitals of Khartoum; hence, each doctor was responsible for 2.8 hospital beds.

Over the period 1981-83, there was a 7.5 percent decline in the number of doctors registered in the country. For these three years, the average number of doctors registered in the Medical Council was 438. This drop resulted from the brain-drain to the Gulf States, caused by several factors, the most important being the gradual degradation of medical services in the country.

Private medical practice has long been established in Sudan. More than five hundred private clinics of all different specialties, owned by consultants or general practitioners, are located in Khartoum. The only two requirements for opening a private clinic are completion of the one-year medical housemanship in the government hospitals after graduation from medical school and registration by the Medical Council. Similarly, approximately 154 private pharmacies in Khartoum provide a wide range of drugs. These pharmacies are run by graduate pharmacists who must be registered by the Medical Council.

The increasing number of doctors in private practice is a result of the current poor health services in Khartoum, as doctors leave the public system to practice on their own. Although the constitution states that medical care is to be freely provided for the population, the government is encouraging private practice to meet the increasing demand and to solve the problems caused by a very limited health budget.

An Overview of Khartoum's Problems

The highest rate of population growth in the development of Khartoum was during the period 1956-73 when the conurbation was estimated to have grown at around eight percent per annum. From 1973 to 1983 the growth rate was estimated to have fallen to approximately 6.5 percent per annum and, despite the recent influx of people resulting from drought and famine conditions, there is no reason to believe that the rate has not fallen even further. In spite of this downward trend in population growth, Khartoum's population is doubling in size every decade. The reasons for this high population growth rate are both high levels of natural growth and high rates of in-migration.

Efforts to control the physical growth of Khartoum have failed in the past and, at present, the conurbation is growing in an uncontrolled manner. The general planning problem is exacerbated by a number of cultural factors. Both Khartoum and urbanization are relatively new in Sudan, and it is doubtful if the process of urbanization taking place in Khartoum involves the fundamental changes of lifestyle or means of production involved in general definitions of urbanization. Therefore, a considerable mismatch is likely to exist between the demands of the citizens and the ability of the administrative mechanism to respond. This problem is further exacerbated by rampant inflation and incompetence in the administration leading to uncontrolled land speculation and corruption.

The administrative and financial system of the Khartoum conurbation has been in a continuous state of evolution and subjected to a number of structural changes dating back to colonial times. The last major change was in 1983 as a part of the national changes leading towards devolution and regionalization.

The current deficiencies of the administrative and financial system can be attributed to four main factors. First, the overall structure is too complex with too many bodies involved, particularly at the lower level. The result is an excessively complex chain of command and decision-making, frequently resulting in either conflict or inaction. Second, the legal and procedural instruments of government are outdated and, consequently, the administration is not able to respond quickly and effectively to particular problems as they arise. The third area of difficulty is the failure of the local government system clearly to define the separate functions and responsibilities of central and local government. More particularly, at the local level, the division of responsibilities between elected members and salaried officials needs to be clarified and their accountability to the public at large to be codified. The final factor is the inadequacy of financial provisions for ensuring effective urban management. On the income side, the tax base is both outdated and structurally inadequate to meet current demands. This deficiency is further exacerbated by incompetence and corruption in the collection of the revenue due to the local government. On the expenditure side, there is no clear system for developing budget priorities based on need or ensuring that the limited resources are used in the most cost-effective manner with the highest level of cost recovery.

The systems of water supply, sewage disposal, refuse disposal, and electricity supply are all inadequate both in the coverage of the urban area and the maintenance of the service. The service deficiencies which are clearly of the greatest concern are those related to sewage and refuse disposal. Without adequate collection and disposal systems, they pose a very serious threat to both public health and the environment.

The water supply system is working beyond its design capacity while the demand continues to rise. The coverage is poor, with the low income groups in squatter settlements suffering the cost of all through paying the most for water, often bought from vendors. Breakdowns and cuts in the supply system are common with more and more people resorting to the development of private sources and the installation of private storage systems. All these developments pose a serious risk of contamination to the supply.

The municipal sewerage system serves only about five percent of the Khartoum urban area. Even that system is susceptible to breakdowns when waste is discharged either directly into the river or onto open land. For the majority of residents in the planned areas, sewage disposal is by means of septic tanks or pit latrines, with the consequent risk of contamination of the ground water. For most people in the low income areas, there is no system of sewage disposal, and the need to defecate on waste ground is not only aesthetically offensive but also poses a further health risk through rural disposal of dried matter. The lack of an efficiently organized refuse collection and disposal system represents a similar degradation of the environment and potential health hazard. The situation would clearly be much worse if not for the scavenging functions performed by goats and the beneficial influence of a very hot climate on rapidly drying organic matter.

Because of the fluctuating characteristics of electricity supply and demand, the peak load can only be satisfied at certain times of the year. While this represents considerable inconvenience to the residents of Khartoum, it has a far greater significance on essential services and the productive sector where the inadequate power supply inevitably affects industrial production and the development of the country overall. The general problem with utility services is the lack of financial resources to provide both the necessary capital for the provision of the infrastructure and equipment and recurrent income to pay for running costs, maintenance, and adequate wages and salaries. The situation not only suffers from the effects of poor management and training but also reflects the lack of priority generally attached to the provision of urban utilities.

Although there has been a gradual build-up of medical services in Khartoum, resulting in all people having access to some form of medical service, the overall picture is of a declining service as population growth rates rise faster than investment in the service. As the budget allocations are cut, doctors migrate from the service, either into the private sector or abroad. The rapid expansion of the private health sector is evidence of both people's desire for proper health care and the ability of the upper income groups to pay for it. However, the running down of the state health service and the growth of the private sector means that a two-tier system of health care is developing with only the more affluent being able to have access to proper services.

The shortage of resources means not only a deterioration in the provision of existing services but also no possibility of the service developing new initiatives to help reduce the incidence of endemic diseases. In particular, although the government is now committed to the concept of primary health care, services are still based on the division of services into preventive and curative medicine.

Policy Recommendations

Significant changes in the population growth rate of Khartoum are only likely to occur over a long period of time as a result of economic and social changes. In the shorter term, population growth rates will be the key element in determining the demand for land, housing, employment, and related social and welfare facilities. Therefore, a much greater emphasis should be given to developing predictive population models which could serve as a basis for assessing the future demands likely to be put on the urban management system to provide appropriate facilities.

The considerable uncoordinated effort in the prediction of population trends is worth mentioning. The Family Planning National Committee is starting to work on the prediction of fertility trends. The Ministry of Education is attempting to project the number of pupils to be enrolled. The Department of Statistics is also attempting to project the population of Greater Khartoum through natural and net migration rates. Unfortunately, none of these efforts is coordinated with others to arrive at a predictive population model to help in estimating the needs and necessary action in planning and management.

Within this context, consideration also needs to be given to the problem of controlling population movement in the country and to reducing the migratory pressures on Khartoum. Such a policy would need to include a regional development strategy which would identify regional settlements and resources capable of development to increase regional economic and social opportunities. Such a regional strategy would also need to develop economic policies which could operate a series of incentives and disincentives to encourage industrial and commercial development in regional centers rather than in Khartoum.

Successful planning can be defined as maintaining balance in the urban ecosystem to ensure the preservation of environmental quality and the quality of life. For this objective to be achieved, it is necessary to develop a predictive system which will be able to anticipate pressures on the ecosystem and to release resources to ensure these pressures are absorbed successfully. This requires not only the development of a proper forward planning administrative system but also the development of the mechanisms, including necessary legal powers and sanctions to implement land use and development control policies.

However, for any planning system to operate successfully, there must be a clear conceptual framework. Therefore, a study of the hypothetical models of growth which could be adopted in Khartoum to enable a conceptual basis for action to be developed, responding to local needs and cultural perspectives, is urgently needed. At the same time, the limitations of predictive models in dynamic situations will need to be recognized and emphasis placed on a flexible process approach to planning capable of responding and reacting quickly to changing circumstances. Such a reactive system must have a wealth generating function built into it.

In view of the cultural conditions prevailing and the limited resources available in Khartoum, it has to be recognized that the only form of planning which will be able to succeed is one which positively and actively utilizes community resources. Such a system would reduce the administrative and financial demands on government and, at the same time, would ensure that local planning reflects the community's culture, aspirations, and needs.

The present structure of Greater Khartoum's city council has an adverse impact on the performance of the machinery of urban administration. An overall restructuring of the city council to create administrative units which are socially and economically more viable is an urgent issue. Decision-making in Greater Khartoum ought to be more responsive to the challenges of urban management. To secure this, local government needs to be guided by clearly defined policies, comprehensive plans, and well-designed programs worked out with the maximum possible involvement of all concerned. Such programs should include priorities which are more public-oriented, and they should address problems and constraints more objectively.

Decision implementation organs and instruments of Greater Khartoum ought to be revised, revitalized, renewed and restructured. In this connection, (1) council work procedure regulations should be updated; (2) a new specialized committee needs to be created to follow up the implementation of council resolutions (this should be formed of the heads of all the specialized committees of the town and city councils); (3) special council sessions should be periodically held for revising decision implementation; (4) selected qualified officials should be entrusted with the authority to implement decisions and in-service training courses should be specially designed and held for them; (5) the up-dating of local orders needs to be undertaken in all areas of public health, public works, markets, public order, and the like, in terms of coverage and types of penalties to be inflicted upon violators; (6) in order to minimize the volume of work to be taken to court with regard to violations of local orders, judicial powers should be delegated to certain administrative officials to make summary settlements and decide on penalties; (7) special courts should be set up solely to implement local by-laws and regulations, since these by-laws and regulations are instrumental in the efficient implementation of urban management decisions.

The Khartoum urban management crisis has a national dimension, and hence it should be addressed in a national context. The financial performance of the Greater Khartoum city councils is the core issue in view of the almost perpetual deficits which have been afflicting their budgets over the last twenty years. Measures to mitigate and perhaps finally eliminate these deficits should include (1) assigning more central and national capital level taxes to the Greater Khartoum city councils (this might include business profit tax or even a percentage of the national tax revenue raised in Greater Khartoum); (2) reassessing the house tax and local property rates (these have a great potential for revenue generation in view of the enormous residential, commercial, and industrial urban development that has been going on in Khartoum for quite a long time without being properly assessed and taxed); (3) restructuring the local tax collection system through reorganizing collection campaigns and employing more qualified personnel with appropriate authority (such an approach might result in more than doubling the current revenue of the Greater Khartoum city council); (4) allocating grants-in-aid according to more national criteria in order to make them more equitable and more instrumental in realizing their stated ends (though they represent about fifty-eight percent of the city councils' total annual revenue, the sum obtained is mainly allocated for Chapter I of the annual budget covering salaries and wages); (5) holding a special conference to discuss the whole issue of the role of finance in Greater Khartoum urban management.

Upgrading and extension of all the urban utility services is urgently needed, but the highest priority must be given to improving the sewage disposal system and the system of refuse collection and disposal. As an immediate step, a system of industrial waste disposal needs to be developed and appropriate charges levied. At the same time, the El Haj Yousif plant should be renovated and the El Goz plant expanded. Steps should be taken to develop an overall sewage policy for Khartoum together with detailed layout proposals. Such a scheme would need to identify priority areas where there are no sewage disposal facilities or where the existing disposal system poses a threat of ground water contamination. In areas where pit latrines continue to be used, consideration must be given to the introduction of an improved type with the local councils sponsoring their development.

An overall refuse collection and disposal system needs to be designed for the conurbation. This should include the development of house-to-house collection systems in the higher income areas with an obligatory charge reflecting the true cost of the service. In the low income areas, a more extensive network of collection points needs to be developed so that all houses are conveniently served. To ensure the operation of the system penalties should be enforced for the indiscriminate dumping of refuse.

A program for the development of the water supply system should also be prepared. Such a program would need to bring together the exploitation of both river water and ground water, along with the development of a distribution system. As a part of this program, new by-laws and regulations need to be developed concerning the standards to be applied when installing water supply systems in buildings. The water supply system should be seen as a self-financing activity, with charges reflecting the cost of supply. As a part of this program, greater emphasis should be given to conservation, with restrictions applied (through appropriate charges and penalties) to excessive private exploitation of water sources.

Similarly, a program should be prepared for the development of the electricity supply and distribution network. Priority in the supply of electricity should be given to essential services and industry. The development of this system should be based on full cost recovery, but consideration should also be given to the development of energy-saving programs. These should include the development of minimum building standards which, through reducing heat gain, could reduce the cooling load. If necessary a reduced level of provision should be also envisaged, with a program of regular cuts in supply built into the system. Alternative systems of energy also need to be considered further, including the possible application of solar energy.

For all public utilities, appropriate training schemes to upgrade skills at all levels of the system need to be developed. Particular attention needs to be given to the development of managerial skills and to systems of decentralization which give greater responsibility and autonomy to local managers.

The health services are failing in their vital role of contributing to the balance of the area's ecosystem. The obvious difficulty is the lack of resources. Clearly, it is not possible to envisage a health service in Khartoum operating on a cost recovery basis. However, recognition of the important and expanding role the private sector is playing would help to reduce the pressure on the state system. The development of the private sector should, therefore, be built into the balanced development of overall health service provision. A levy on the private sector would contribute a subsidy to the state system and consideration should be given to subcontracting the provision of some services to the private sector.

In the public sector the commitment to the development of primary health care facilities should be developed through a restructuring of the health service administration. More resources should be allocated by central government from tax revenue to the development of health services. If the tax system is raised and other utilities and services are put on a cost recovery basis, this should free resources for the development of health services. As a part of this process, greater emphasis will have to be placed on cost-effectiveness and the improvement of management systems aimed both at reducing the cost of services and at improving their delivery.

Conclusion

The trend of population growth and inadequate response to basic needs will continue so long as the deteriorating conditions of the economy continue. There is little chance of recovery in the rural economy in the near future unless drastic measures are taken in combating desertification, in consolidation of the food base, and in revision of the development strategy with respect to goals, execution, and funding management. The influx of rural population will, therefore, be likely to continue. This process is expected to increase because of strong "push" forces in rural areas and strong "pull" forces associated with the development of Greater Khartoum and an increasing urban bias. To cite a minor example, sugar prices in Greater Khartoum are controlled so that a pound of sugar costs only one-third of a Sudanese pound in Khartoum, as compared to two or more Sudanese pounds for the same quantity in the rural areas.

The population increase and generated needs for basic services are not matched by development in the provision of such services. As a result, there is further degradation in the quality of urban life. In attempting to cope with this crisis, the urban authority is hindered by severe financial, technical and manpower limitations. In the face is such massive inadequacies, two possible self-generated developments may take place. First, there may very well be a significant increase in community involvement in local service provision, as the development of the urban informal sector proceeds. Development in this direction will, however, limit the present urban authority in managing the urban ecosystem and will in effect hand over direct control of over forty percent of the built-up areas of Great Khartoum to the local community. A second possible development would be the intensification of self-sustaining regional development elsewhere in the country. This would have the effect of stabilizing the rural population. For this to happen, however, present development plans would need to be seriously revised, both to improve modern agriculture to provide necessary linkages with the traditional sector.

In fact, the problems of management of Greater Khartoum cannot be isolated from the current complicated problems of the country, which are administrative, political, and economic in origin. These problems need to be treated within an integrated development plan. For such a plan to take hold, the past policy of solving urban problems at the expense of development in the rural areas will have to be changed. The management of Greater Khartoum cannot continue to be burdened by the vast migratory influx which has resulted from failures in rural development; and urban development will have to be more responsive to rural needs.

CHAPTER 10
Urban Management in Nairobi: A Case Study of the Matatu Mode of Public Transport
Diana Lee-Smith

Introduction

Nairobi is in many ways an archetype of the African colonial city, having purely colonial origins which shaped its structure and management at the time of Kenya's transition to independence. Like other African cities, Nairobi was characterized after independence by a rapid increase in rural to urban migration, accompanied by the proliferation of small-scale trade and petty commodity production, including unserviced and unauthorized housing. Because formal institutional, legislative, and physical planning structures were not designed for and could not cope with this form of economic activity, it was labelled the "informal sector." To a large extent, the urban crisis in Africa can be measured by the failure to cope with this sector, while useful urban reforms have been those which are designed to accommodate or aid this sector.

A case study of *matatus* – the informal mode of public transport in Nairobi – can thus provide a useful example of the degree to which urban reforms may be necessary. Matatus are small motor vehicles, usually pickups or minibuses, which ply for hire along public bus routes. They were originally illegal, but became so popular after independence that President Jomo Kenyatta decreed in 1973 that they be permitted. It took another ten years for the legislation to catch up to this decree, although the planning process still has not done so.

Although the informal sector harbors the urban poor majority, it tends not to receive official attention and has been left to be self-supportive. The areas occupied by urban poor informal sector workers are the same areas officially not provided with the services which would normally be expected from a city government. This is not necessarily because of any misconceptions about the situation, but more likely because of concrete class interests associated with a specific pattern of accumulation.

There have been attempts since the 1970s to improve the conditions of the urban poor, mainly through international assistance from agencies such as World Bank and USAID. These agencies may correctly be perceived as agents of international capital. Nevertheless, their investment program is designed to promote capitalist petty commodity production through capital infrastructure and through increasing the productivity of the urban poor. This agenda coincides at some points with the interests of the urban poor, and thus some urban reforms that have been successful have been supported by international agencies. On the other hand, there are many constraints on effective implementation of policies aimed at the urban poor, and in many cases they fail to meet their target and end up benefitting higher income groups.

The various attempts at urban reform in Nairobi have included programs aimed at the urban poor such as sites and services housing, infrastructure improvement such as extension of the water supply, organizational redesign in City Council, and legislative reform such as the 1984 Matatu Act. Some of these, especially the last, will be described below. The specific case of the matatu mode of public transport illustrates the positive role of central government in enacting first a decree and then a legislative reform which regularizes an informal sector activity. It also illustrates the presence or absence of complementary supportive reforms at city level.

Research Methodology

This study of urban reform is a follow-up to an earlier piece of primary research carried out by Mazingira Institute in Nairobi. In October 1982 Mazingira Institute completed a study entitled *The Matatu Mode of Public Transport in Metropolitan Nairobi*. Because of the large amount of data available and the fact that a major piece of legislation formalizing matatus was enacted two years later, it was decided to carry out a further study in order more broadly to examine urban growth and reform.

The original study was based on a method developed by Mazingira Institute for research on policy-related subjects. The method identifies interest groups involved, who in turn identify the key issues or problems. This information was used to design surveys and case studies which describe the system to be examined as accurately and quantitatively as possible, and annotate the various issues. The issues were then presented, with the back-up data, to a workshop which involved all the interest groups. The first matatu workshop, involving government, the City Council, the Matatu Vehicle Owners Association (MVOA), the Automobile Association, Kenya Bureau of Standards, vehicle manufacturers, Kenya Bus Service (KBS), and the researchers, was held in early 1983. The second workshop was held at the end of the follow-up study, with the same interest groups and some additional agencies, including the Kenya Police, in July 1985. The intent of the method is to inform the various actors affected by the issues and to involve them in trying to achieve a consensus on useful courses of action to improve the situations which have been identified as problems.

The original matatu study (1979-82) consisted of several surveys carried out by Mazingira, both independently and in collaboration with Nairobi City Council. Thus, a users' survey was carried out on a sample of 352 heads of households in twenty-four locations in Nairobi, stratified by income group. Following a preliminary census of matatu ownership, an operators' survey was carried out on a random sample of vehicles using the twenty-nine terminals in Nairobi City centre. A total of thirty-eight owner-drivers, seventy-two employed drivers, and ninety-nine conductors were interviewed. Case studies were made of five matatu owners, three terminals, and one matatu association. Finally, an informal survey of car dealers, tire dealers, body conversion workshops, credit finance institutions, insurance companies, and the Registry of Motor Vehicles was carried out to gather contextual information, particularly on the economics of operating matatus.

The follow-up study on urban growth and reform – the basis for this chapter – relied on both primary and secondary data. Although the main source of secondary data was the 1982 matatu study by Mazingira Institute, other sources were also reviewed and utilized. In addition, a press cuttings file was kept which was particularly useful during the period of the passing and enforcement of the Traffic (Amendment) Act of 1984. Primary data were collected through structured interviews with relevant authorities and interest groups. These included City officials as well as finance and insurance firms and Matatu Association officials. This permitted the updating of the 1982 matatu study as well as acquiring data on other service areas.

At the final workshop for this study (9 July 1985), the following issues related to matatu operations were discussed: associations and terminals, credit finance, vehicle and passenger insurance, and commuter safety. All the interest groups directly involved in these issues attended the workshop. During the workshop, matatu operators complained of high insurance premiums which reduce their profit margins, while representatives of insurance firms criticized the bad claim records set by matatus and said that premiums cannot be reduced unless these records improve. It is worth noting that a Commission of Inquiry on insurance rates was set up in late 1986 and that the Mazingira matatu report was extensively used in evidence before this Commission. At the time of completing this chapter, the outcome of the Inquiry was still not known.

The Development, Planning, and Management of Nairobi

The City of Nairobi began less than a hundred years ago when a depot was established there during construction of the Uganda railway. It quickly became clear to the railway authorities that it was going to be impossible for them to cope unaided with the social consequences of the development they had initiated. And as the colonial government became involved, it also became clear that at least the expatriate communities must be associated with the necessary measures of social provision and social control. The Nairobi Township Committee, formed in 1900 with a mere six members, marked the birth of local government in the town. Thus, although it was originally laid out by railway engineers, Nairobi was born firmly within a political framework of imperial expansion.

Racial segregation was implicit in the earliest plans, which had separate zones for railway employees, European and Asian traders, as well as Asian and African laborers. Before the 1920s little consideration was given to providing services for Africans. Those not employed by the railways were seen as surplus to the needs of the town and a menace to health, law, and order. Thus, planning excluded a large part of the population. Nairobi was made a Municipal Council in 1919, but even at that time it did not in fact run many services. By 1935 it took over children's welfare services and clinics from the colonial government, and in 1943 it took over the African maternity hospital.

The 1940s saw the consolidation of settler power within the colonial government and the start of industrial expansion. A new master plan was prepared in 1948, with minimal services for Africans located near the new industrial area and European residences near the administrative center. The aim was to attract industrial investment. Subsequent years saw much economic expansion and further growth of settler power along with the growth of African opposition. African nationalism grew in the 1940s and 1950s, not least initially in the eastern part of Nairobi where zoning regulations permitted high density African housing. Meanwhile, Nairobi was steadily expanding, incorporating new peri-urban areas, though often against the will of the residents who had no wish to contribute to municipal funds. In 1950 Nairobi achieved the status of a city. The council was British controlled until 1962, one year before Kenya's full independence, when Charles Rubia became the first African mayor.

Transport had first become an issue in 1932, when the Municipal Council considered starting a bus service. However, the costs proved to be prohibitive, and public support was insufficient. Two years later, KBS started as a private concern, a subsidiary of United Transport Overseas (UTO) which operated in several countries. From that time, when it began with only two buses, KBS has held the official monopoly of transport in Nairobi, although this has become increasingly meaningless with subsequent legislation.

The situation inherited at independence in 1963 was that of a city designed for capitalist expansion, highly segregated by race and income, with extreme inequalities in the level of services provided in different areas. As with other African countries, independence meant the removal of colonial restrictions on freedom of movement and a rapid increase in rural-urban

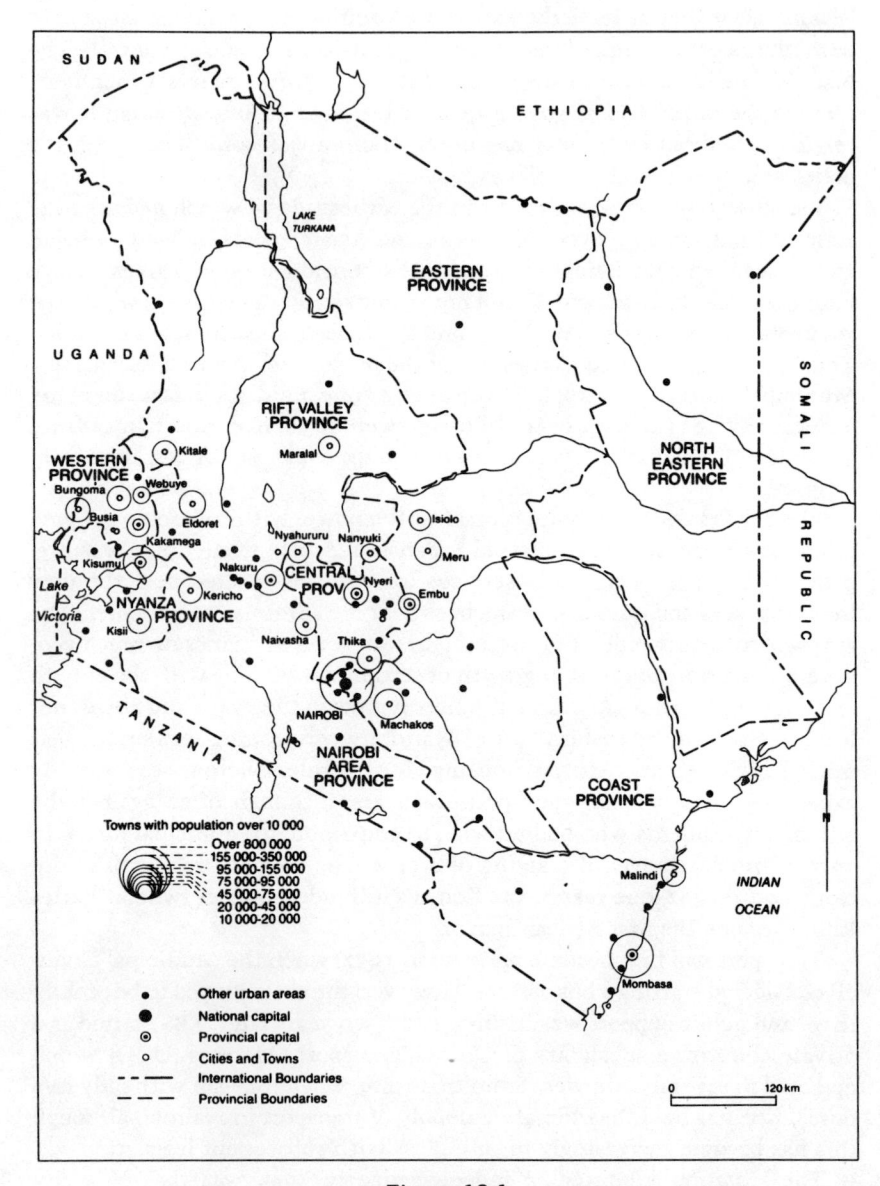

Figure 10.1
Kenya 1979: Towns with Population over 10,000

migration. Urban growth in Kenya has accelerated since independence, averaging 5.4 percent per annum in the first decade and 7.9 percent per annum in the second after independence.

One year before independence, a census showed Kenya had a population of 8.6 million, only nine percent of which was urban. The next census, in 1969, gave a national population of 10.9 million, ten percent of which was urban. The most recent census of 1979 gives a total population of 15.3 million, fifteen percent urban. The number of towns with a population of over two thousand almost trebled to ninety in the period from 1962 to 1979.

Urban growth was initially focused on the larger towns, although secondary towns experienced higher rates of growth during the latest inter-censal period. Figure 10.1 shows the distribution of population in urban areas in Kenya at the time of the 1979 census. The rapid growth of Nairobi after 1963 reflected the new government's employment policies which expanded African representation in government and industry, both of which were disproportionately located in Nairobi. While Nairobi grew in population it also grew in area. The area enclosed by the city boundary was extended at independence from 32 to 266 square miles. A large unserviced area was included within a jurisdiction already unevenly serviced.

The new government attempted to come to terms with its responsibilities to this rapidly expanding and underserviced population in several ways. Housing was a particular concern and was the subject of a special UN study in 1964 (Bloomberg and Abrams) and the Kenya Sessional Paper No. 5 (Kenya 1966). The National Housing Corporation (NHC) was established in 1967 for the specific purpose of building rental housing for the poor. The second Development Plan 1966-70 (Kenya 1966) expressed similar policy intentions. However, the housing built by the NHC was high cost and since it could not be afforded by the poor it was appropriated by higher income groups. The same applied to City Council rental housing (Stren 1978; Temple and Temple 1980).

The situation of rapid in-migration and unaffordable housing led to what was characterized as early as 1971 as the "self-help city" (Hake 1977). The Nairobi City Council (NCC) estimated that one-third of the city's population was living in unauthorized housing at that time, while the ILO estimated in 1972 that thirty thousand jobs in Nairobi were not officially counted and thus constituted an "informal sector" of the city's economy (ILO 1972). Andrew Hake stated that the self-help economy of Nairobi was creating more jobs, absorbing more people, and expanding faster than the so-called "modern" economy of the city, at the same time as it built many elements of an urban infrastructure and created a pattern of social organization to maintain itself.

During the 1970s Nairobi planners expressed the view that there was

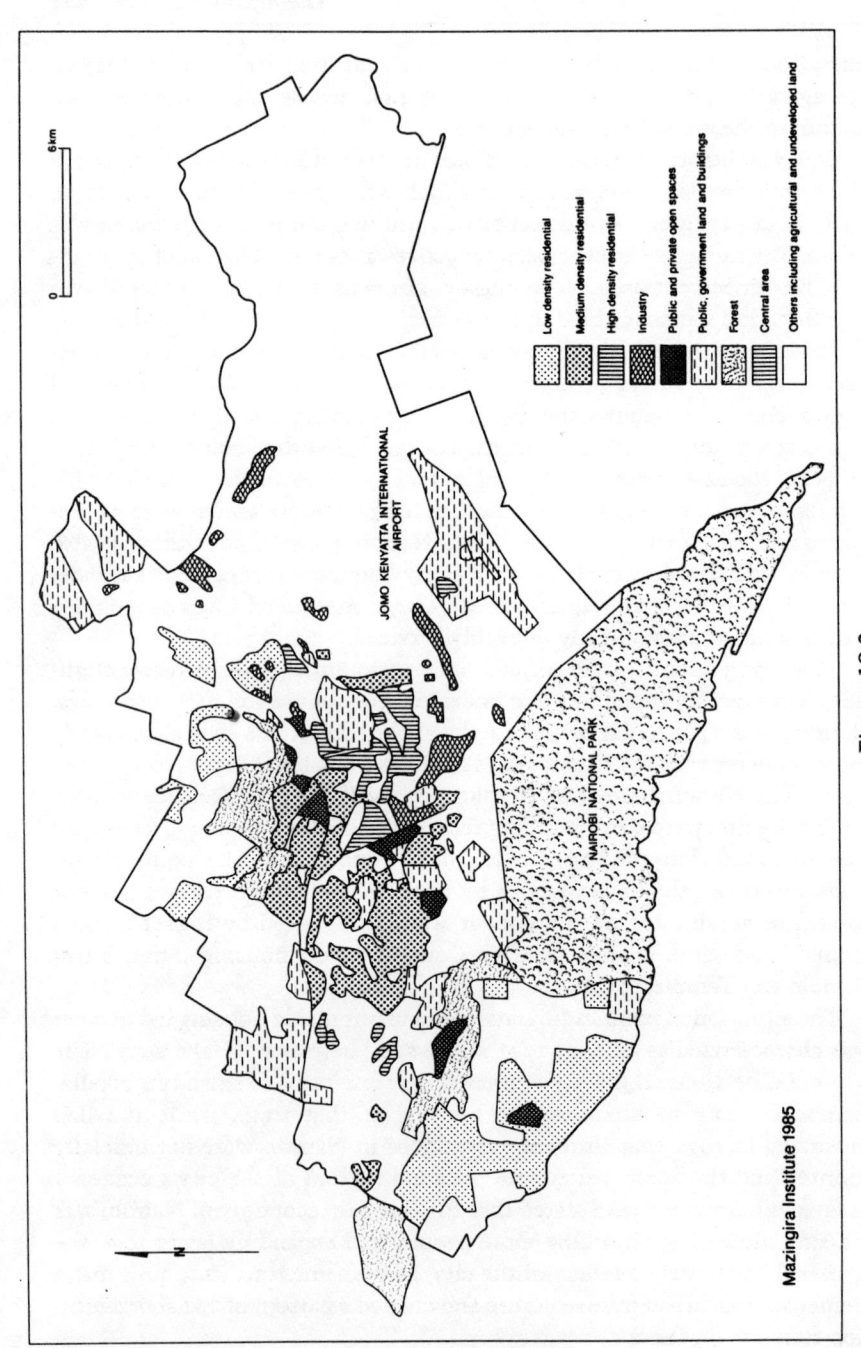

Figure 10.2
Nairobi: Land Use

virtually no coordinated planning of the city in the first decade of independence, only sectoral plans. But these sectoral plans by no means solved the sectoral problems. Migration continued because informal incomes were higher than anything that could be earned in rural areas. Housing plans failed to take account of the low income population's social-economic priorities – that is, to obtain minimal services at a cost they could afford while gaining access to the labor market. Thus, the unplanned city grew. By 1973 it was also clear that the city's water supply would soon be insufficient for demand while existing roads were already inadequate.

As a result of these sectoral pressures, the Nairobi Urban Study Group (NUSG) was formed in 1973 to develop the Metropolitan Growth Strategy and arrest the problem before it got out of hand (Nairobi Urban Study Group 1972). One of the main proposals of the plan produced by this group was to decentralize industry to an additional four locations apart from the existing industrial area. This plan, which was aimed at a better integration of work and housing areas and a corresponding alleviation of transport problems, has never really been implemented. The recommendation to set up a planning department within the City Council was not implemented until eight years later, in 1981, when the City Planning Department was established.

One fault of the Metropolitan Growth Strategy was its omission of any consideration of matatus in examining transportation in Nairobi. An example of the spontaneous generation of an informal transport network in a situation where formal public transport services are inadequate, matatus were originally completely illegal. For the decade before and the decade after independence, these converted pick-ups and minibuses operated against the law. They were therefore harassed by the police, although they survived and grew in numbers. In 1973 President Kenyatta legalized matatus by decree, exempting them from public transport licensing requirements. Although the NUSG might be excused for not planning for an illegal transport mode (since their report was concurrent with the decree), the new mode was not subsequently included by NCC in its physical planning in a systematic way. Matatus continued to compete for space with KBS buses, to use their stops, and to crowd into inadequate public spaces, often car parks, which served as their route terminals.

One of the general problems of implementation of the Metropolitan Growth Strategy has undoubtedly been the lack of power associated with the planning function within the overall decision making system and the reliance on "master planning" as an approach without effective mechanisms of plan implementation. However, it began to be realized in the 1970s that an emphasis on construction of urban infrastructure and other facilities to match projected growth was needed.

During the 1970s there was renewed effort to address the needs of the lowest income groups. Basic needs became the focus of government development plans (Kenya 1974) and programs aimed at poverty-alleviation were supported by international aid, chiefly the World Bank and USAID. NCC received large loans and credits mainly to expand its water supply and services and to build infrastructure for large-scale sites and services and core house projects. These must be considered successful to some extent, although not problem free. Within the overall context of deteriorating municipal finances, the extent to which they were mismanaged contributed to the financial and political crisis in city management in the early 1980s.

Water shortages became severe in the city towards the end of the 1970s and during the early 1980s. Even though a new supply was planned, there were repeated delays in implementation. Construction was delayed because of mismanagement, particularly in the awarding of contracts. Intervention by the World Bank – the major donor – after correct procedures were not followed on a tender award ultimately led to a two-year delay, which again entailed cost escalations resulting from inflation. The new water supply system finally came on line in early 1984. It made an additional 26 million gallons per day available, almost doubling the previous maximum of 29 million gallons a day, and was 20 million above 1984 demand.

Although NCC has not met the demand for low income housing in the city, very significant advances were made in the 1970s and early 1980s through a large scale sites and services program handled by a new Housing Development Department geared to low income users. Although this program only met a portion of the potential demand, it has been established that the lowest income groups were able to build and benefit from improved housing, although not without some intervening financial hardship and depending on adaptive support structures put in place through the Housing Development Department. No doubt the Housing Development Department could have expanded its activities to cope with a more substantial proportion of the city's needs were it not for political considerations which intervened.

Problems in the sites and services program arose because of cost increases, delays, and political interference. Internal studies showed that more low-income people benefitted in the first phase than in the second, where these problems became endemic. Many city officials (particularly those in the Department of Health) insisted on high standards which increased costs and caused delays. Delays in turn caused further cost increases because of inflation. There was political interference in the award of tenders and in the reallocation of housing plots, with the result that as many as one sixth of all plots may have gone to higher income people. Such interference became so severe in the early 1980s that it led, along with the deteriorating financial situation of the City Council, to the suspension of the Council, dismissal of its councillors and many officers, and the replacement of the council by an appointed City Commission in March 1983.

The financial problems of NCC, like those of all local authorities in Kenya, can be partly explained by the controlling role of central government, which was strongly reinforced at the time of independence, and the abolition in 1973 of Graduated Personal Tax (GPT), a major source of revenue for local authorities. Nairobi has built succeeding budgets on the central government grant in lieu of GPT, which was gradually phased out, and on unimproved site-value property taxes, which failed to be adjusted upwards for the decade 1971-81 to take increased property values into account. Even then, political resistance to such increases was strong. Water and housing revenues were adequate, but the overall lack of funds combined with mismanagement led to the city's financial crisis and subsequent collapse in the early 1980s.

Within this context of inadequate public sector resources and embryonic reforms which failed to find much political support, the drama of the urban transport sector has been played out in the years following independence. Unlike housing, water supply, refuse collection, and property taxes, which only attract public controversy from time to time when crisis threatens, the matatu industry has been the topic of almost continuous public debate for two reasons. First, there is the visible lawlessness of its operations and the accompanying daily discomfort and danger for many city residents. Second, the industry generates a substantial amount of private income for part of the urban population. This group appears to consist of a section of the middle class engaged in various other occupations (presumably including some decision-makers and people with political influence) and the upper echelons of self-employed people in the informal sector, namely those with more education, driving skills, and a small amount of capital. As a result of its political influence, this group has come into direct conflict with the interests of a multi-national company and is currently taking on the insurance industry.

Matatus as a Transport Service

The official bus service grew up with the relatively small colonial city. From the original two buses in 1934, it had expanded to 140 buses in 1968, carrying 105,000 passengers a day. Presently, KBS is seventy-five percent owned by a British-based multi-national company, United Transport Overseas Services, Limited, and twenty-five percent owned by Nairobi City Commission. It is the major means of public transport within the city, being used for twenty-seven percent of all journeys. However, it has by no means met the total demand for public transport; twenty-four percent of city residents walk because of the high cost of transport, and twenty-three percent use the matatu mode. The remainder of journeys are made by private cars (twenty-two percent) or other private vehicles such as bicycles or motor-bikes (four percent).[1]

Train travel does not figure at all. The option for a commuter train service using existing lines and stock was investigated by NUSG but was never pursued. This is unfortunate since existing rail lines already link various high density residential areas with the industrial area. The second most important mode, walking, has been neglected in transportation analysis and planning. The majority of people in the lowest income groups walk for economic reasons. Yet footpaths are poorly maintained, if not nonexistent, on many primary pedestrian routes. Resources are rather invested in catering for vehicular traffic.

Matatus – generally minibuses or converted pick-ups – operate along lucrative bus-routes by carrying passengers for hire. The name matatu is derived from the Kikuyu words *mangotole ihatu* meaning three ten cent pieces, the fare charged in the 1950s when they started operating. The Presidential decree of 1973 exempted matatus from Transport License Board requirements, categorizing them as Public Service Vehicles. (This is the category that applies to taxis and tourist buses as well as to public buses.) However, their situation remained only quasi-legal, since they continued being owned and operated as if they were private vehicles. They were therefore inadequately insured for carrying passengers and were also usually overloaded and poorly maintained. In the absence of any law specifically governing them, they tended to operate in an uncontrolled manner. Police harassment continued while the rate of breakdowns and accidents increased, attracting much public and media attention. Meanwhile, the anomaly of the KBS monopoly of public transport continued. (The monopoly was renewed in 1985.)

The first study of matatus was carried out for NCC in 1977 (Situma 1977). It identified the origins and destinations of matatus, their average daily number, the ridership, type and condition of vehicles, and the fare structure. It was recommended that matatus organize themselves in associations, and that a "public light bus company" be formed to supplement KBS. Other recommendations were made on insurance, licensing, vehicle inspection, taxation, and terminals. Although some of these recommendations were later taken up in the matatu legislation, the City Council itself did not make specific provision for matatus in its physical planning. For example, no provision was made to zone or allocate space for terminals where matatus could wait at their route terminus or to rationalize the space needed by them and buses at bus stops. However, the operators themselves did form associations in a more organized fashion, based on routes, and began to police themselves by setting up queuing systems and managing the terminals. They also lobbied NCC for terminals, which led the city to cede them some space previously zoned for other activities such as car parking. Thus, by 1979 several large terminals had been approved by the traffic police. "A terminal" means the space required by any vehicle service at the end of its route for turn-around, waiting, and staff refreshment. Buses usually use bus stations which are formally included in city planning. Matatus, however, have had to make do with reallocated parking meters or parts of city council car parks, which remain marked for their other uses and which they have to "defend."

In 1978 the Transportation Unit of NCC was set up as recommended by NUSG. A consultant's report on matatu operations proposed the possibility of a matatu assistance scheme to be funded by the World Bank as part of a larger urban transport loan (Barwell 1979). The aim was to provide funds to matatu owners and operators for the purchase of new and second-hand vehicles. The report also proposed the improvement of informal repair facilities and the construction of shelters for passengers. These proposals were never put into practice because the Kenya government could not find the funds for the local component of the project. Other proposals of the Transportation Unit were for bus / matatu lanes, improved pedestrian facilities, area traffic control systems, road improvements, and lay-bys for buses and matatus in specific areas. Again these were never put into practice because of the failure to implement the proposed World Bank funded transport project.

In 1980 a report was commissioned on a standard, diesel-fuelled matatu and a prototype vehicle was made by Leyland Motors (Coopers and Lybrand 1980). The proposed vehicle was to be assembled in Kenya, thus having employment benefits as well as producing cost savings through change in fuel type. However, it was later established by Automobile Association testing that the proposed prototype was not financially viable for operators.

Licensing, insurance, vehicle design, credit finance, routes, terminals, and the proposed change to diesel were the major issues identified by the 1982 research on the matatu industry carried out by Mazingira Institute, which forms the basis of this study. It is the only comprehensive study on matatus, being based on detailed survey data as well as financial and policy analysis. The Mazingira study found two thousand matatus operating in Nairobi in 1982, one half full-time and the other half part-time. The commonest type of vehicle was a converted pick-up, carrying fourteen seated and four standing passengers. On average, a matatu made an estimated four hundred passenger trips per day. Thirty-five percent of matatus were owner-driven, and it seems as if at least half the vehicles belonged to fleets of two or more vehicles in 1982. Although belonging to an informal sector industry and therefore generally paying no tax, matatu owners and operators generated Shs.1.6 million in fines in 1982 or Shs.1,600 per full-time matatu.

On the other hand, survey data indicated that the average matatu generated Shs.4,700 in bribes to policemen, or three times as much! Further details of these data are given in the various sections below.

The Traffic (Amendment) Act 1984, commonly referred to as the "Matatu Act," was a landmark in legislation since it formalized a previously informal activity. This informal activity had come to play an important part in the economy, providing a service industry to the low and middle level wage-earning urban population. The main provisions of the Act were the requirements for Public Service Vehicle licensing, police supervised annual vehicle inspection, passenger insurance coverage for a maximum of twenty-five passengers, minimum driver age of twenty-four years, and minimum period of holding a license of four years for drivers. A matatu was defined as "a public service vehicle having a seating accommodation for not more than 25 passengers excluding the driver, but does not include a motor car." A motor omnibus was defined as "a public service vehicle having seating accommodation for more than 25 passengers exclusive of the driver." Thus, the borderline between a public bus and a matatu is clearly defined legally as one of size.

Since the act became law in November 1984, enforcement of the licensing requirement has been strict.[2] Initially, less than half the matatus in Nairobi had the new licenses, and the lack of transport for commuters was almost as severe as it had been in previous years when "crack-downs" were made on matatus because of their illegality. Gradually, however, licensing proceeded, and numbers came back to normal. The number of registered "minibuses" in Kenya as a whole in fact increased by seventeen percent from 1984 to 1985, so presumably the number in Nairobi increased proportionately (Kenya 1985, 166). There was one noticeable difference, however, to observers in Nairobi: the numbers of smaller vehicles, especially pick-ups, decreased whereas the number of larger vehicles increased. Particularly obvious was the number of new large vehicles belonging to "lines" or fleets carrying commercial names.

The Act has addressed the issues of licensing, insurance, and vehicle inspection identified by the preceding matatu studies, but the issues of vehicle design, credit finance, routes, and terminals have not been addressed through any public planning or policy action. There is no public sector acknowledgement of matatu organizations such as route associations or of umbrella bodies such as the MVOA. Similarly, the physical planning response has so far been limited to allocation of terminals in response to lobbies. This is the type of "planning" which characterizes public sector dealings with the informal sector.[3] One may conclude that, despite formal legalization by government, the matatu industry still carries the stigma of extra-legality for the NCC physical planners.

The number of matatus operating primarily in Nairobi increased from four hundred in 1972 before the Presidential decree to fourteen hundred in 1976 and approximately two thousand in 1982. About half of these vehicles operate full-time, and the rest part-time in rush hours. Matatus operate along different routes in response to consumer demand. All routes converge on the city center. Seventy percent serve nearby residential areas, twenty-five percent the peri-urban fringe, and four percent the industrial area. The heaviest volume of traffic is to Eastlands, a densely populated and predominantly low-income area.

The number of matatus in Nairobi increased by over four hundred percent from 1973 to 1979, whereas the number of KBS buses increased by only fifteen percent. Also, the number of passengers per bus per day decreased from 1973 to 1977 but rose again thereafter, while the same was true of matatus. It is not possible to say to what extent this reduction was the result of the dramatic increase in the supply of matatus on the road, once they had been made quasi-legal by the President's decree. What is common knowledge is that both modes of transport are extremely overcrowded, especially at peak hours.

A matatu makes about four hundred passenger trips per day, and a bus at least twice as many. In 1973 matatus in Nairobi made 46,000 passenger trips per day whereas KBS made 242,000. In 1980 matatus in Nairobi made 201,000 passenger trips per day, whereas KBS made 273,000. Thus, the share of the market captured by matatus rose from sixteen to forty-two percent in the first seven years after the presidential decree, while the KBS share declined from eighty-four to fifty-eight percent. Nevertheless, both modes expanded in absolute terms, in the number of vehicles and passengers carried.

In 1982 three-quarters of Nairobi matatus were mini-buses or converted pick-ups carrying about fifteen passengers. About one-eighth were smaller vehicles such as saloon cars or station wagons plying long distances, while another eighth were larger vehicles such as the midi-buses carrying about twenty-two passengers. It appears that these figures will have shifted towards more larger vehicles after the 1984 legislation, although no reliable data are available.

The majority of matatu users are low income people, although the very poorest walk. Forty-five percent of journeys are to work, and thirty-two percent to school. Most people prefer buses for safety and comfort, but prefer matatus when carrying luggage. When asked, matatu users were not in favor of a standard design; city matatus need more space for passengers as well as a roof rack, while country matatus need more space for luggage. The users favored enforcement of restrictions on overloading, bus and matatu lanes in peak hours, separate terminals for bus and matatu, but the same routes to facilitate choice. They thought bad and undisciplined driving was the cause of accidents and that drivers should be over twenty-one, that they should be properly qualified, and that competition between drivers should be controlled. Ten percent of the riders surveyed had been in matatu accidents in the last three years. Although they preferred buses, most users did not want to discourage matatus, nor did most of them think any other form of transport should be started. Those that did (thirty-eight percent) favored a commuter train.

Thirty-five percent of matatus were owner-driven in 1982 while the majority were driven by employee drivers. The data on ownership of the employee driven vehicles are unfortunately not clear. When asked how many vehicles were owned by their employer, seventy-five percent of employee drivers and eighty percent of conductors would not answer. If it is assumed that those who said "only one" were telling the truth, then fifteen percent of matatus fall in this category. Of course, it is possible that some were lying, given the general concern about this question. In any event, it seems safe to assume that at least fifty percent of vehicles in Nairobi were owned by businessmen with fleets of two or more vehicles in 1982. The owners were described by their employees mainly as businessmen or employees in the private or public sector. As mentioned above, it seems likely that the proportion of vehicles belonging to fleets or lines has increased following the new legislation in 1984, although this is based merely on observation and not on any hard data.

Among the owner-drivers, most were sole owners not in partnership; half purchased them from savings; and one-third from official loans. Over half said it was their first vehicle, while the others appeared to have sold the first one to purchase a better one. Two-thirds of the vehicles were bought second-hand, and their useful life is about five years. Nevertheless, one-third of the Nairobi vehicles in 1982 were older than five years. Matatus make an average of ten return trips per day, each lasting about one hour, for a total of about two hundred kilometers per day. Four out of five matatu operators work seven days a week, about ten hours a day from the hours of 6 a.m. to 8 p.m. One in five works a six-day week. Thus, eighty percent of workers in the industry are working a seventy-hour week, ninety-eight hours including the afternoon slack periods.

Most drivers used regular petrol rather than premium, and very few used diesel because, although the fuel is cheaper, the vehicles which use it are more expensive, and there are shortages of both fuel and spare parts. Vehicles use one liter per five kilometers on average. Most drivers used new tires rather than retreads because of longer life (five months versus three months). Vehicles are generally repaired at informal *jua kali* (meaning "hot sun") garages. About half the operators had agreed on a mutual fare structure to avoid cut-throat competition and used the KBS fare structure. KBS in turn resorted to fare-cutting on the most popular routes. With an average fare of Shs.2 in 1982, the average income for a single matatu was thus Shs.800 per day.

As Table 10.1 shows, no matatu operators were illiterate. Fifty-three percent had primary education, and forty-seven percent had been to secondary school. Most owner drivers had completed at least four years of secondary education, were married, older, had more dependents and longer working experience than the employee drivers, who in turn had higher ratings on these variables than the conductors. Owner drivers tended to have long experience driving other commercial vehicles besides matatus than did employee drivers whereas conductors only had experience with matatus.

It is estimated that whereas a KBS bus generates 7.5 jobs, a matatu generates 2.5 jobs, including drivers, conductors, manambas (who direct passengers to vehicles at stops), garage operators, association officials, vehicle body-shop workers, and the like. Buses carry more passengers than matatus, but matatus create fifty percent more jobs per passenger carried (0.125:0.08). One thousand matatus are estimated to create 2,500 jobs, including 350 owner drivers, 650 employed drivers, 1,000 conductors, 150 manambas, 50 association officials, 300 informal garage operators, body workshop employers, etc. The costs of job creation are about the same for buses and matatus. Matatus mostly create employment for the poor. In 1982 a low income was

Table 10.1
Characteristics of Matatu Operators

	Owner-Drivers	Employee-Drivers	Conductors	All Operators
Primary education	42%	50%	61%	53%
Secondary education	58%	50%	39%	47%
Married	100%	67%	24%	53%
Number of dependents (mode)	8	3	0	–
Age (mode)	35	26	20	25
Years experience				
– mode	7	4	2	–
– mean	9	5	3	–

Source: Kapila, Manundu and Lamba, 1982.

Shs.1,700 per month and below. Employed drivers earned Shs.1,500, conductors Shs.900, and manambas Shs.660 per month. Owner-drivers were in the high income group, earning on average Shs.6,184 per month while informal sector mechanics earned a middle level income of Shs.2,500. Annual income generated in the matatu subsector in 1982 was an estimated K£5 million or about two percent of Nairobi's formal sector earnings and nine percent of the city's informal sector earnings.

An analysis was carried out on the profitability of the matatu business taking a typical vehicle, a Toyota "Hi-lux" pick-up carrying fourteen seated and four standing passengers. Costs involve vehicle purchase and conversion, registration, licence and insurance, loan payments, driver, conductor and manamba payments, fuel, tires, maintenance, bribes, fines, and other fees. Revenue is from passenger fares, carrying luggage, and hiring out the vehicle. It was found that the profitability of the matatu business depends on the length of the vehicle's operating life: the longer the life, the more profit. This partly explains why Nairobi matatus tend to be operated for long periods of time. Easier credit finance terms (such as a reduction in down payment from forty to thirty percent of total costs, a reduction in interest rate from fourteen to twelve percent and an extension in repayment period from eighteen to thirty-six months) would make entry into the matatu business easier for low income entrepreneurs who find the current terms difficult to meet. The twenty-seater matatu is most profitable, followed by the twenty-five-seater; the fourteen seater is least profitable. Matatus with roof-racks are more profitable than those without, and used vehicles are more profitable than new ones. Owner-driven vehicles are more profitable than employee-driven ones. The method of demanding that an employee driver pay a fixed sum daily and keep the surplus was found to be less profitable than collecting all earnings and paying operating costs.

Although "third party" insurance cover yields higher profits than "comprehensive" insurance, it carries higher risks of failure. And although diesel matatus are more profitable to operate, their higher purchase price makes them out of range of most owners. The Leyland diesel prototype, with fourteen seated and no standing passengers and no roof-rack, was confirmed to be unprofitable.

Prior to 1979 there were no matatu associations, each owner acting on an individual basis, This led to very disorganized operations both at terminals and along the routes, with every operator trying to lure passengers. In 1979 vehicle owners operating on various routes began to come together and set up associations to alleviate this problem. Frequent police prosecution for traffic obstruction was also a reason for forming associations to lobby City Council more effectively for parking space in the city center. By 1982 there were six associations, and by 1984 there were seventy-six. All associations are organized by routes. However, by 1984 only forty-one of the seventy-six associations had been allocated space for their terminals by NCC. Registration as associations (with the Registrar of Societies in the Attorney General's Office) was done after some operators ascertained it was the simplest form of organization to register, the requirements for cooperatives being too stringent. Membership fees of a typical route association were Shs.100 per owner in 1979 but rose to Shs.500 in 1982. The fees collected are used for association officials, offices, and the payment of rent for terminals to NCC. For twelve parking meter bays in the city center a typical association paid Shs.1,296 per month in 1982.

The case study association included in the Mazingira research had fifty-six members in 1982, fifty male and six female. Only nine percent were owner-drivers, the rest having other occupations running small businesses such as vegetable or tea kiosks or were wage-employed. Members were only allowed to operate a maximum of two vehicles on the route to prevent the domination by fleets, but owners were free to be members of several associations. Associations have a monopoly of service on their selected routes, through terminal management, but "poachers" do invade, particularly in the middle of the routes. Association officials supervise queuing at terminals and timed starts of vehicles in peak hours.

The MVOA was formed as an umbrella organization of all route associations in 1979. Although it acts as a lobby for the sector at national level, has introduced training, and published a journal in 1982-84, the MVOA is not formally recognized or responded to by government or NCC. In 1985 a breakaway association was also formed by some officials of MVOA. Called the Matatu Association of Kenya (MAK), it took the journal with it but has failed to achieve the same lobbying power and influence as the MVOA.

Urban Administration and Implications for Reform

While the public transport problems of Nairobi can be analyzed locally and sectorally, the dynamics of the overall policy questions addressed can only be properly understood in a wider context. Not only are urban problems merely a sub-set of the broad developmental issues faced by the whole country but also the implementation of transport (or any other sectoral) policies involves multi-purpose administrative structures at both the local and national level in Kenya. This section examines the organization of administrative and commercial structures locally and nationally in order better to understand the prospects for a reform agenda in the transport sector in Nairobi.

In the early 1980s, NCC had eight departments, each staffed by technical employees and guided by a committee of elected councillors. In addition, the Town Clerk's Department coordinated the others and constituted the legal arm of the Council. The Town Clerk was the chief officer as well as secretary to Council, while the Mayor was the chief elected official and chairman of Council, following the British model of local government. The following is a list of Departments and their sections:

City Treasurer – Purchasing, Technical, Audit, Establishment, Computer, Revenue, Accountancy;

Public Health – Cleansing, School Health, Health Inspectorate, Funerals, Epidemiology and Disease Control;

City Engineer – Architects, Estates and Development Control, Structural, Operations and Service, Highways, Parks;

City Education – School Staffing, School Supplies, School Advisors;

Social Services & Housing – Housing and Estates Administration, Markets and Trading, Family Welfare, Welfare and Recreation, Community Development, Bibliographical, Information and References;

Water & Sewerage – Commercial Water Planning, Design and Construction, Sewerage;

Housing Development – Administration, Community Development, Technical and Finance;

City Planning – Administration, Development Control, Forward Planning, Research and Land Survey.

Some departments overlap in function largely as a result of the addition of new departments as the city grew after independence. These additions were also attempts at reform through restructuring. Thus, the Water and Sewerage Department was separated from the City Engineer's Department which was already too big to cope with increased demand as well as planning and construction of new supplies. The Housing Development Department was added to implement the new self-build low income housing schemes rather than add this function to the Social Services and Housing Department which managed the rental housing built by City Engineers Department. The City Planning Department was finally separated from the City Engineer's Department in 1981, following the earlier recommendation of the NUSG.

The new Water and Sewerage Department was clearly aimed at increasing efficiency and budgetary control as well as expanding infrastructure, while the new Housing Development Department was aimed in addition at introducing an innovative administrative structure specifically to deal with low income people. Both were set up as a result of conditions the World Bank had written into loan agreements with the Council. Though both departments, particularly the Housing Development Department (HDD), have been criticized as duplicating functions and were opposed by the existing department heads, the reforms may be considered effective to the extent that, when all other funds were finished in the early 1980s, NCC was able to draw on the Water and Housing funds to replenish its General Fund. Those two departments were the only ones which were not incurring a loss and in fact had surplus funds. Although the tactic of using resources from these funds ultimately backfired (this was a major reason for the closing down of the NCC in March of 1983), this does not mitigate the general point that the two departments involved were running their own affairs efficiently.

The HDD was particularly resented by many NCC councillors and officials because, unlike all other standing committees of the council, there were several central government nominees on its guiding committee, the Housing Development Committee. The new departments were able to introduce better management methods and budgetary controls, to by-pass existing vested interests, and to pilot through a number of technical innovations. On the negative side, however, they were unable to address these issues within the Council as a whole, with the HDD in particular coming into conflict with the existing structure. Thus, the reforms, while partially successful, may also be seen as not radical enough.

The attempt to incorporate transportation planning as an integral function of NCC foundered through lack of funds as already described. The separation out of city planning under its own chief officer and the introduction of the forward planning function may be seen as a positive step, though results have yet to be seen. In the past, enforcement of zoning and other planning controls has been hindered by political interference. The corrupt allocation of public land to private individuals, particularly councillors, was one of the factors behind the suspension and dissolution of the City Council.

The dissolution of the elected council and its replacement by a City Commission in March 1983 may be seen as one attempt at reform, albeit a form of crisis management. Central government had previously intervened in the late 1970s by dissolving the elected Councils of Mombasa and Kisumu (the second and third largest towns in Kenya) and replacing them with commissions appointed through Ministry of Local Government. This was done for similar reasons of misallocation of resources and poor financial management, the elected councils being reinstated after a period of two or three years.

Earlier hints at similar measures being taken in the capital were warded off by Nairobi's powerful political lobby. This finally broke down in 1983 through a combination of financial crisis, internal loss of morale through mismanagement, and political divisions. The elected committee chairmen were replaced by appointed commissioners, who reviewed the decisions and recommendations of the various technical departments in their place. The complex system of reporting and review (which absorbs an inordinate amount of council staff time and resources) was not reformed. Thus, while political interference in decision-making was reduced, by early 1987 there still was no structural reform or streamlining of functions based on analysis of performance. It remains to be seen when and if government will reintroduce elected councillors based on the old wards or whether it will introduce a new system geared towards district development committees which have been introduced in the rural districts all over the country in step with the government's "district development focus."

The various political interests in Nairobi have yet to cohere in overt organizations or structures, although the Matatu Vehicle Owners Association and a Hawkers and Vendors Association are examples of emerging interest groups that can represent parts of the low income population in local political bargaining. Within NCC itself, councillors' representations of their constituents were often blurred or manipulated by ethnic, interpersonal, or other factional conflicts. Among the technical personnel, such extraneous factors have also often been influential, partly because of the influence which councillors had over employment within the Council.

Finally, while the policy conflicts over equitable provision of lower-standard services to the poor have often been seen as a confrontation imposed on local government by outside funding agencies, NGOs or even central government, this is a misperception. Such innovations and urban reforms have often been initiated as well as opposed *within* local government. Local authority personnel are not all faceless bureaucrats or tools of corrupt politicians but increasingly form part of an "invisible college" of urban reformers with personal links with enlightened NGOs, donor agency and central government personnel, and progressive local leadership. This group of people is handicapped by lack of public awareness as well as lack of support from many decision-makers. Public information on urban issues and urban reform is greatly lacking.

Nairobi's financial problems stem in part from the controlling role of central government which has restricted local sources of revenue. This control was established at the time of independence when the Ministry of Local Government gained the right to approve all council estimates as well as to over-rule other decisions. Then, in 1974 the central government abolished the main source of local authority revenue without providing alternative sources. This may be seen as part of a general move to control "urban bias" (Lipton 1977) and to curb the autonomy of such centers of wealth as Nairobi. On the other hand, it is doubtful how effective central government control has been in the case of Nairobi, where urban wealth has grown, as has urban poverty, while the formal structures have failed to capture enough of that wealth to sustain city services or to make them equitable. Apart from sporadic skirmishes with garbage collection (organized at one point by an army officer appointed by the President), the centrally controlled Commission established in 1983 has done no better than the abolished Council. At the time of independence, Nairobi was caught in the contradiction of expanding its spatial area more than eightfold and attempting to overcome colonial inequities, while maintaining not only the same budget but the same standards for services. This was compounded by the loss of GPT revenue ten years later.

Central government control was a source of conflict between central and city governments until 1983, often personified in political tension between the Minister and the Mayor. Charles Rubia, who asserted when he was Mayor that the Minister concerns himself with petty things rather than policy direction (Werlin 1974, 198), was caught on the other side of the conflict when he himself became Minister for Local Government later on. While local councillors complained of interference, central government complained of incompetence and the need for outside controls. Councillors' level of education and lack of substantive knowledge about city management were common causes of complaint. It was also said that councillors were more concerned with private accumulation of wealth than with the management of public services. However, it is doubtful whether higher education is in itself a guarantee of selfless public service. Democracy is based on the assumption of people governing themselves in their own interests. The record of Nairobi does not show that councillors, who come largely from the class of small producers and traders, have governed in the interests of that class, particularly of those petty commodity producers and traders classified as "informal."

In the absence of proper representation of low-income interests, it has been the *ad hoc* personal interventions of the Presidency that have been their main protection. President Kenyatta's decree protecting the matatus and President Moi's defence of the *jua kali* workshop owners in the early 1980s are the main examples. Historically important as these presidential actions may be, they cannot long substitute for a more societally integrated process of representation, planning, and legislation.

True urban reforms bring urban services to the bulk of the urban population on an equitable basis. The question remains whether public decisionmakers in central or local government who resist efforts to provide lower standard public services more equitably do so out of lack of a sophisticated understanding (for example, a belief that it is a capitalist trick supported by international agencies) or out of concrete class interests to protect their own potential access to property and services. The latter seems most likely, since few people astute enough to be elected to public office would fail to grasp the implications of policies involving cheap credit.

International agencies, unlike international capital operating through multi-national companies, have actively promoted the growth of small-scale capitalism in the private sector of African economies. The matatu mode of public transport is a good example of this; the World Bank was ready to assist small owner-drivers through credit, while the multi-national UTO was in direct competition with matatus. However, the scheme was never implemented. In the housing field, USAID and the World Bank support small scale contractors and owner / builders, while the increase in construction which their support entails also benefits larger-scale local and also international contractors, not to mention urban residents.

The development of small-scale production and service industries such as matatus is not usually favored by African governments because they are considered low-status (if the government is capitalist) or capitalist (if the government is socialist). Such responses beg the question of an appropriate strategy to develop urban production capacity in Africa today, as well as the question of equity in urban reform.[4]

The history of the matatu mode of urban transport in Nairobi clearly illustrates how one type of small scale entrepreneurism has been dealt with by central and local government in a capitalist system dominated by multi-national capital. From the colonial phase where multi-national control of the public transport sector was complete, central government (in the person of the President) moved to support small African entrepreneurs, though governmental structures were not geared to cope with them. It took a decade for legislation to catch up, although this must be considered reasonably fast when compared with technical and institutional change in some other countries. However, the planning process has not yet caught up. The response has been disjointed, particularly from local government where, in spite of some technical studies and *ad hoc* responses to the matatu lobby, no systematic plan or policy position has been developed. The major response has been from central government, in initiating and carrying through an innovative piece of legislation (albeit one which has benefitted the larger scale entrepreneur rather than the smaller). The exception to this was the initial proposal for the matatu assistance scheme, which came from City Council at the end of the 1970s. It was dropped after some discussions between KBS, NCC, central government, and the World Bank, despite the support of the latter, not least because of the lack of central government funds. After that the NCC transportation unit lost momentum and some members of this unit went over to work for KBS.

Historically, public transport in Kenya has been the province of the private sector, and interventions by the public sector have been dominated by central rather than local government. Policy issues affecting matatus raised at the July 1985 workshop are dealt with in the following section. Most of these issues fall outside the province of local government, except for the physical planning aspects which will be dealt with first.

Policy Options for the Matatu Subsector

Physical planning is the area of responsibility of Nairobi City Commission which most directly affects matatus. Up until 1979 no planning provision was made for matatu terminal parks, and the question of whether these, and the stops along the routes, should be the same as for buses, was not addressed by NCC. Terminals were allocated from 1979 on as a response to lobbying by the associations, rather than through a coherent plan based on assessment of demand. According to NCC's own assessment, in 1982 there were two thousand matatus in Nairobi, but at the same time only 797 were allocated terminal space. Furthermore, this space was taken from already under-provided private vehicle parking spaces. Problems of congestion were compounded by buses and matatus sharing terminals, whereas separate terminals are preferred by operators, KBS, and users alike. NCC has not been entirely negligent, for the issue of "permanent" matatu terminals has been debated. Proposals that these be outside the city center (in the same way that low-income housing and markets are zoned) have been understandably opposed by matatu operators because they implicitly favor the KBS, with its terminals within the city center.

Another proposal has been for central city terminals for urban matatus and outer city terminals for the long distance routes. Given the overcrowding of the city center, such an alternative seems more equitable. However, a proposal by the City Engineer's Department for several large matatu terminals in the city center was rejected subsequent to the new legislation, apparently based on NCC's persistent concern that KBS has a "legal" monopoly.

A properly planned separate terminal system for buses and matatus would benefit users, matatu operators, and the police by reducing prosecutions for illegal parking; but it represents an apparent threat to KBS because of competition. The perception of such a threat would, however, seem to be unrealistic in view of the present excessive demand for transport compared with supply by both modes, and in view of users' stated preference for buses as safer and more comfortable. NCC and KBS resistance to a properly planned development for both modes is not of particular benefit to anyone and perpetuates urban congestion, reduces legal revenue collection, increases harassment (together with potential illegal revenue collection), and overloads the police and courts.

The issue of stops along routes has never been addressed by central or local government in planning or legislation. It is up to the city to provide stop space for matatus as well as for buses and clearly to designate whether stops have separate lay-bys or how vehicles should behave if lay-bys are shared. This is an important and urgent task for the city's Department of Planning in consultation with traffic planners. Now that matatus have been legalized, planning for them should be removed from short-term and political considerations. This is a clear example of the need for improved professional methods in NCC.

The history of matatu owners organizing route associations and establishing an umbrella organization to lobby for their interests has already been outlined. This organizing enabled the industry to gain access to city space for terminals and initiated more controlled behavior at stops and terminals. Although owners rather than operators formed the associations, restrictions were put on large fleets dominating routes. The main umbrella organization (MVOA) was formed in 1979 and a breakaway organization (MAK) around the time of the new legislation. Neither the constituent nor the umbrella organizations have been officially recognized or dealt with by the central government or by NCC. MVOA has received much criticism from the breakaway association, the press, and the public on misuse of funds. It nevertheless remains a powerful lobbying force.

Associations are of advantage to NCC and the police in that they assist in terminal management and payment of terminal charges. They are of advantage to members in representing their interests, and a beginning has been made in organizing driver and management training courses and starting a magazine. However, other types of support systems for matatus, such as credit financing, business, and legal advisory services, are needed but have not yet been addressed. A major problem with the industry at the moment is that matatu owners may reinvest their profits in any field, so that such profits do not serve to improve the industry as a whole. This situation could be improved by the formation of matatu cooperatives, which would not only manage routes and terminals but also financing. Such a development should benefit the smaller operators more equitably as they would gain access to credit as well as to other support services which only those with larger capital can currently achieve. This is a reform which can only be achieved by organization of the owners themselves. In the current situation where the number of owner-drivers appears to be decreasing, the chances of such organization are reduced. However, if such a move were to be encouraged and facilitated in the public sector, either through NCC or the Ministry of Cooperative Development, it could undoubtedly assist in a more balanced and controllable growth in an industry which is currently somewhat out of hand.

The suggestion during the 1970s that NCC collaborate in a matatu assistance scheme with credit provided by the Industrial and Commercial Development Corporation was never implemented. Vehicle credit finance is not an area that directly concerns city administration, but rather needs to be implemented through private sector finance houses with government support and encouragement.

Nairobi's finance houses do not generally give credit for matatu purchase, and definitely not for second-hand vehicles. Operators who have loans often disguise the application, for example, as the purchase of a farm pick-up. Only thirty percent of owner-drivers obtained credit, although most would have liked to, according to the 1982 survey. Finance houses perceive matatu owners as bad risks and are uncertain that they can manage their operations properly. It is not known whether legalization has changed these views. The small operators are the ones least likely to get credit as they seldom have other forms of security or influential people who can act as guarantors or contacts with finance institutions. An increase in credit for matatu purchases would benefit the industry through growth. However, present loan terms are restrictive. Extending credit to the purchase of second-hand vehicles would make a big difference as the cost is less than one-third of a new vehicle and the rate of return is more than double. Down payments could also be reduced from forty to thirty percent to give better access to more borrowers in the industry.

Matatu cooperative savings and credit societies would be another important step forward for the matatu industry. Not only could they give loans to members but they could also guarantee members' loans with other finance houses, obtain funds from the Cooperative Bank, and get assistance from the Ministry of Cooperative Development in training members on accounts and management. In the absence of such reforms, the result of the 1984 "Matatu Act" seems to have been an increase in new vehicles owned by business people with more capital.

Before the 1984 legislation, matatus generally lacked insurance cover for both the passengers and the vehicle as a passenger carrier. Owners of vehicles bought on loan, however, had to take out comprehensive insurance, which is five times more costly. After the 1984 legislation, matatu insurance rates were more than doubled because of the coincidental dissolution of the Kenya Motor Insurance Pool which underwrote heavy-risk vehicles, including buses and matatus. Government stepped in to ask Kenya Reinsurance Corporation to establish reasonable rates and to try and revive the insurance pool which had been suffering heavy losses. When these moves proved ineffective, the government set up a Commission of Inquiry on insurance rates in 1986. Another problem with insurance is overloading, since matatus are either uninsured for the actual number of passengers carried or are expected to insure for an unsafe number. Improved police enforcement should be the solution to this problem.

Because of the high cost of insurance, matatus make much better profits when they carry less insurance and take bigger risks on losing their vehicles. Unfortunately, this means they also force their passengers to share this higher risk. This is not an issue which affects city administration but rather the private sector and government. It is a difficult issue to resolve, although more credit finance, better enforcement, and better maintained vehicles would help. Matatu associations or cooperatives could also help by negotiating better group insurance rates.

Public safety was the central issue which led to the "Matatu Act" or Traffic (Amendment) Bill of 1984. All matatus are now required to be registered as public service vehicles and to undergo an annual inspection. However, the quality of driving and the attitude of drivers and conductors have hardly changed; Nairobi matatus still overload and drive carelessly. The new legislation cannot by itself improve passenger safety, but three reforms, if undertaken by the industry itself and government, could result in a marked improvement: (1) better law enforcement by the police; (2) the application of labor laws to the matatus; and (3) the formal organization of matatu owners.

The police force is entrusted with enforcement of the law, and it is their responsibility to ensure that matatus do not overload, are mechanically fit, and are driven carefully. However, the 1982 Mazingira study shows that, before the "Matatu Act," when the simple provisions of the Highway Code could have been called upon, an average of six percent of a matatu's earnings went in bribes to traffic police. Thus, disregard for traffic regulations may be equally assumed among operators and enforcers. It is not clear that such attitudes have changed with the enactment of the new law.

Several provisions of the new law bear on safety: the age and experience of the driver, the annual vehicle inspection, and compulsory insurance cover. The 1982 data shows very few drivers under twenty-four or lacking experience, so that it is unlikely that this requirement alone would affect their driving. MVOA's schemes for driver training courses were interrupted by the enforcement of the Act and the disruptions within MVOA, so that these have not yet had any effect. It will be up to the Kenya Police to enforce the other provisions on vehicle condition and insurance, rather than continuing with harassment and encouraging evasion through corrupt practices.

Most matatu operators work ten hours a day, seven days a week. Since they work in two shifts, they may actually be on the job fourteen hours a day including the four-hour afternoon lull. These excessive working hours have not been raised as an issue by operators, probably because owner-drivers are motivated to earn more by working as long hours as possible, while employees are not organized or represented by any organization. Furthermore, most drivers and conductors are hired on a daily, casual basis. The fact that they can be hired and fired whenever the owner chooses encourages carelessness. They can also earn more in this way than if they were limited to a legal working week. Moreover, the method of fixed payments of many employees encourages reckless driving; because they can retain any profits above a given daily amount, they try to make up the amount due at all costs.

These conditions are unlikely to change until the industry is more formalized and owners are required to conform with labor legislation; so far, no organized group has asked for these arrangements. Meanwhile, the exhaustion of operators is likely to continue to contribute to unsafe driving. A further Traffic Amendment Act was in fact reviewed by parliament in 1986. Among other provisions, it proposed to make long hours of driving illegal. Such an amendment would certainly be difficult to enforce as it is difficult for police checks to establish how long someone has been driving. Enforcement of labor laws would probably be simpler.

Conclusion

As an example of an informal sector activity in transition to the formal sector, the matatu mode of transport in Nairobi offers a useful case study for urban reform. However, because of the nature of the transport sector and the responsibilities of the local authority, many issues of reform in the sector cannot be addressed at local government level, but must be taken up by central government through legislation, guidance, or incentives to the private sector.

The main role of the local authority is in physical planning, and here the conservatism of NCC is apparent in its unwillingness to deal openly and directly with the "informal sector" because of the colonial legacy of the illegality and poverty of this sector and because of the domination of international capital. The weakness of the planning function is also apparent, as well as the political inadequacy of low-income interest groups. Neither such interest groups nor the public nor the decision-makers are sufficiently aware of the rights of these low-income groups or their best options. In this respect, the case study of matatus has parallels in other sectors, such as housing, where colonially-originated norms also hold precedence over concerns for the welfare of the vast majority of the population in the provision of vital urban services.

Notes

This paper is based on two research projects carried out by Mazingira Institute: The Matatu Mode of Public Transport in Metropolitan Nairobi, 1980-82, and Urban Growth and Reform, 1984-5. The first project was carried out by a team of researchers at Mazingira and the findings are contained in the report cited here by Kapila, Manundu and Lamba. The second was carried out by Winnie Mitullah of Mazingira Institute, whose 1985 report is also cited here. The material contained in the present article relies extensively on these two earlier documents and substantive guidance provided by Davinder Lamba who directed the two research projects.

1. All figures given in this section originate from Kapila, Manundu, and Lamba (1982) unless otherwise indicated. The surveys were carried out in late 1981 and early 1982.

2. Mitullah (1985) is the source for information cited on the results of the Traffic (Amendment) Act, 1984.

3. Another such example would be the installing of water kiosks in slum areas on the insistence of politicians at the time of disease outbreaks. The official stance of NCC is that every individual house must have a connection, and such kiosks are therefore "extra-legal" though necessary, and thus accepted with the label "informal."

4. Since this was drafted, progressive reforms legalizing matatu-type vehicles have been made in Tanzania and Malawi.

Conclusion

The seven case studies analyzed in this book are representative of a wide variety of conditions among the states of Africa – western, central, and eastern; Anglophone and Francophone; humid and semi-arid. It should, therefore, be possible to draw some general conclusions from the seven countries that might have some relevance to sub-Saharan Africa as a whole. All the countries have a rapidly growing population which is rapidly urbanizing. Urban governments have been overwhelmed by the influx; services have deteriorated, and jobs have not kept pace with the growth of the urban labor force. Attempts to subsidize the urban food supply (domestic and imported) and urban services have floundered. Governments have turned to administrative decentralization, community self-help, privatization, and full-cost recovery in attempts to retrieve a modicum of control. None of these policies has yet reversed the general trend of deteriorating urban conditions, though it could be argued that conditions might be worse had they not been attempted. It is now widely appreciated that rural conditions are even worse than urban conditions, and this is the root of the urban management problem. Some African governments have tried to redress the problem of rural underdevelopment as well; but few can show much evidence of success.

The urban management crisis which is described in every chapter of this book is a complex syndrome. Among its major elements are the financial inability of local and national governments to provide critical urban services, the inadequacy of administrative and skilled technical personnel to operate urban services and to maintain infrastructure, and the ineffectiveness of local communities in the local administrative and political decision-making process. While some of these problems exist even in developed countries, their coexistence in Africa in the face of historically unprecedented urban growth and extreme poverty constitutes a real crisis. This study has put together elements of the urban management crisis in the hope of providing some practical commentary that may be of use to African urban

---

This concluding chapter was prepared by Rodney White from discussions with the contributors and notes on the three seminars at which the original working papers were presented.

governments. This conclusion attempts to disentangle the interwoven impacts of exogenous and endogenous factors and to relate them to the policy reforms that have been undertaken across the continent.

The exogenous conditions affecting post-independence development are widespread and diverse. Traditional climatic variability has produced more than average drought years since independence, and this has had a heavy impact on all seven countries, although regional heterogeneity masked this in Nigeria, Côte d'Ivoire, and Zaire. Aside from rainfall, the price of petroleum has disturbed the continent most. Even oil-rich Nigeria has been pushed through a boom-and-bust period which has hardly been conducive to orderly economic development. As the oil price softened in 1981, the American dollar appreciated strongly, keeping the balance-of-payments pressure on oil-importing countries. Throughout the late 1970s and early 1980s the world economy has experienced difficulties, ranging from recession to weak, often imperceptible, recoveries. The terms of trade for Africa's primary goods compared with industrial goods have been generally (sometimes strongly) unfavorable. Plagued by self-doubt, the leading industrial economies have drifted through monetarism, Thatcherism, Reaganism, and generally towards protectionism. The agricultural policy of the European Economic Community has become the Sorceror's Apprentice of world trade, mindlessly piling up unusable surpluses. The "Butter Mountain" reached 1.2 million tons in 1987, nearly ten times higher than it had been in 1982. To this, one could add more than 7 million tons of wheat and millions of tons of other foodstuffs (*The Economist* 11 July 1987, 52).

The growing cost of services (especially urban services), stagnant markets for exports, and the cost of servicing and repaying debts acquired in the optimistic 1960s have pushed nearly every African country to the brink of insolvency. Many have only one or two days of foreign exchange reserves in the treasury, and they survive by rescheduling their debts and – on a national scale – stalling their creditors, just not answering the telephone. Now, at a time of zero or even negative capital flows, the countries of Africa are advised by the International Monetary Fund to save their way out of the crisis by cutting public spending, devaluing their currencies, and cutting urban subsidies. But even if these seven (and other African countries) had been managed in an exemplary fashion, most (if not all) of them would still have been in difficulty because of a combination of an adverse global economy, rapid population growth, and the heightened expectations which accompanied independence. Added to the climatic, economic, and demographic problems has been the instability brought by political forces, particularly the Cold War between the superpowers, white South Africa's aggressive struggle for survival, the fall-out from the Arab-Israeli conflict, and many other persistent wars.

In these circumstances, it is easy to see why some of the reforms described in this book – administrative decentralization, improved policy coordination, and the revision of building and service standards – have been stillborn. With national economic concerns high on the political agenda and few additional resources to strengthen local administrative structures, effective implementation of those urban reforms which entail additional expenditures and more official appointments will have to wait their turn. By the same token, however, other reforms such as privatization (or contracting out) of services and the improvement of the tax collection system at the local level have a much better chance for support, as they promise to relieve the state of some of its burdens.

What then are the policy lessons that can be drawn from this experience, given that exogenous factors will continue to perturb the continent in the foreseeable future? Are there some lessons for improved urban management that can be applied even in circumstances of very limited public cash flow, high urban unemployment, and stagnant rural productivity? Is it simply a matter of watching while the rich minority takes care of its own interests and the situation of the poor majority deteriorates? The studies in this book suggest otherwise. This analysis of the rise and fall of urban public policy suggests that some remedial steps are available even in the present adverse situation.

Urban Management Should Be Adaptive

The classical Master Plan has not withstood the pressure of rural-urban migration. In Dakar, the Ecochard Master Plan guided urban growth for over ten years, and its lines can still be traced on the ground. But the population of the *Département* of Pikine is now greater than that of the *Département* of Dakar, yet as this study indicates, the level of services is much lower. In the Dakar surveys described in Chapter 7, the official neighborhoods – the smallest administrative units – were mapped out for the first time; a complete inventory of urban infrastructure was made. Until this had been done, the responsible agencies did not know if the companies to whom maintenance had been sub-contracted were doing their work or not. This represents a small beginning perhaps, but a vital one. Without information, there can be no management.

The old belief that secondary growth centers could reduce the rate of rural-to-urban migration should be abandoned. There are other reasons for promoting smaller centers, but a visible effect on the rate of growth of the largest cities is not one of them. Instead, urban management should adapt to the likelihood of continuing inflows from the countryside. Perhaps a major shift of policy in favor of the rural economy would reduce the flow, but again, this should not be the principal objective. What a pro-rural policy should produce is an increase in productivity to help feed the cities and to raise rural incomes. If this later reduces the flow of migrants, there are additional benefits.

The study of Kinshasa shows that domestic agricultural production has not kept pace with population growth. Far from it, the flows of agricultural goods into the city have scarcely increased over the last decade. True, some foreign residents have left, but even so, the diet of the remainder must be greatly impoverished, even allowing for the cultivation of more food within the city limits. Observations seem to indicate that infant mortality has started to rise again. If so, this would be the worst possible news, as it would further postpone the completion of the demographic transition. (Although the impact of mortality on fertility is disputed, it can hardly be imagined that a rise in mortality is likely to be conducive to a fall in fertility, under current conditions.)

The surveys in Kinshasa also indicate that market stall-holders could distribute more and cheaper food if a few circumstances were changed − if the additional fees which they were willing to pay should go to their market organization and not to the local authorities; if competition for transport were more open; and if they had safe places to store their goods on-site overnight. This seems not much to ask for and would involve minimal costs to the government. In a more prosperous market, the Ministry of Health would have a better chance to upgrade the sanitary situation.

If Kinshasa seems to be eating incredibly little food, then Ibadan is drinking incredibly little water. If the population and water supply figures are correctly reported, then the inhabitants are surviving on less than thirty liters per day, well below the minimum for maintaining an urban population in an acceptable state. Yet the city of Ibadan is surrounded by underutilized reservoirs of water. They are not released because half the pumps at the waterworks were never installed, and those that are installed are often idle because there is no foreign exchange to import the purifying chemicals. (The same blockage resulting from lack of foreign exchange has been reported for the main reservoir serving Dakar and for the water treatment facilities in Dar es Salaam.) In this case, the administrative structure has not adapted to the urgent need to provide Ibadan with more water. There is no urban authority which can influence the foreign exchange allocation priorities of the Central Bank of Nigeria. It was not necessary before the economic downturn, and there has been no adjustment in the years in which this situation has steadily worsened.

Many more examples could be produced. The fact is clear that urban management is often not sufficiently adaptive even in those cases where the change would cost very little money. Ironically, the communities and decision-makers which are aware of the problems do not have the authority to make the necessary changes.

Urban Management Should Be Integrated

Every large organization throughout history has struggled to find the best way to structure its activities so that the system functions reasonably well. For African governments – both central and urban – the favored organizational form is sectoral. The Department of Finance is staffed by economists, the Ministry of Public Works is run by engineers, and so on. Departments and Ministries compete for scarce resources; they cooperate only when forced to do so by a higher authority. Staff secondments do not always solve the problem, as reported in the Nigerian study.

The African urban management crisis has highlighted the inefficiencies of the sectoral approach. In Kinshasa, the buses cannot run where the streets are blocked by garbage; in Nigeria, the waterworks shuts down because there is no electricity; in Dar es Salaam, refuse cannot be removed where the roads are not maintained, and industries have to shut down because the water supply is inadequate. To clear the garbage from the streets in Ibadan, in 1983 the new government drafted all the staff and vehicles from the River Clearance Division. Garbage then went back into the river beds, increasing the dangers of loss of life and property from flooding in the next rainy season.

It might seem idealistic to promote "management by objectives" in such a desperate situation, but nothing short of a new approach to urban management can meet the scale of the present problems. The old structure is simply inadequate.

The Decentralization of Urban Administration Should Be Made Effective

Notable attempts have been made to devolve power from the central government to local authorities, for example, in Côte d'Ivoire, Senegal, Zaire, and Tanzania. In the Anglophone countries local authorities have a long history, although it has not always been one of effective government. The reasons for this are analyzed in detail in the chapter on Tanzania. In Nigeria, the local government areas (LGAs) are simply too small to provide the basis for government for the large cities. So, the need there is more for aggregation of several LGAs to form coherent urban governments.

In the Francophone countries, as in the cases of Senegal and Côte d'Ivoire, a serious effort to decentralize urban administration began as early as 1978. Results, while more encouraging in the case of Côte d'Ivoire than in Senegal, are not yet fully satisfactory for two main reasons. First, the financial means have not been provided; the new governments depend on central government allocations which have often not been forthcoming. (In Nigeria, a similar problem is reported except that the funds were passed from the Federal Government to the States, which in turn did not always pass them on to the LGAs. In Kenya, by the mid-1980s parastatals and the central government owed an amount to the Nairobi City Commission equal to close to one year's operating revenue.) The second problem – more noticeable again in Senegal than in Côte d'Ivoire – is the weakness of local representation; too few of the new local government councillors are elected by the local people. Instead, they tend to be appointed by the central government or nominated to a party list within a one-party system. So, the new councillors may find themselves with few resources and little sense of accountability to the community. Obviously, this will not develop overnight; but it should remain a key objective in trying to develop a working relationship between the community and the government.

The Use and Ownership of Urban Land Must Be Modernized To Suit the Realities of Urban Life

For a number of reasons, most African governments nationalized urban land soon after independence. Generally, this was seen as a way of preventing speculation in urban land by foreigners as well as by local élites. It was also seen as a natural continuation with the traditional system, according to which land belonged to the local community which in turn allocated its use according to traditional rights and current needs. This reasoning was sound, but only up to a point. Land in big cities is put to completely different kinds of use than land in small scale agricultural societies. Specifically, in cities, people build villas, apartments, factories and office blocks – structures which cost far more than the land itself, however that may be valued.

When a highway is built through agricultural land in Nigeria, compensation to the occupant of the land is worked out on the basis of the annual value of the crop (in the case of annuals) or five times the annual value if the land is planted with fruiting trees. Such a basis for compensation is irrelevant in the city where each lot (whether built upon or not) has a certain "economic rent," whatever the government or the society may believe. The implications of this fact are discussed in detail in the chapter on Zaire, where this officially uncaptured rent has become very important. In Kinshasa, the result of an inadequate formal structure to allocate nationalized land and a strong commercial and residential competition for the land is land-use anarchy. Other cities may not be in such an extreme situation, although the same problem can clearly be seen in Nigeria, Senegal, and Tanzania. The "irregular" land situation becomes the norm. What happens is that those who are rich and powerful are in a better position to intercede in the official bureaucratic allocation process; thus, they seize the "economic rent," sharing little with the poor majority and depriving the government of a large part of a most important source of urban revenue – the property tax.

We are not advocating the adoption of western-style private ownership of land. But what is clear from the studies is that the land question is fundamental to any improvement in the standard of urban management. Perhaps what is needed is a system whereby the government (in the name of the people) retains the ownership of the land and allocates the use of the land based on a one hundred year leasehold. More attention in any case must be given to the organization of the process of allocation, as the tax resources that can be recaptured from proper registration of use would more than compensate for the administrative reforms necessary to rationalize the system.

A Final Word

It has not been the intention of this study to produce a formula for the solution of Africa's urban management problem. There is no formula, no simple cliché like "good government." On the other hand, as this study illustrates, a great deal is known about what has been attempted and what has happened in the name of "urban reform" in Africa. The clichés have been abandoned because the problems are complex and no simple solution exists. What is required is a long term commitment to understand the past, to determine why the experiments have failed, and to look for new variants of the experiments that will take root in the soil of a particular country and a particular city.

As many of the research teams found in this study, sometimes the most basic information is missing. In Nigeria, planners still must plan without a census. In Dakar, a city that has been very heavily researched over the years, an accurate map of the neighborhoods did not exist before this study was undertaken. There was no inventory of infrastructure in Dakar, nor in Khartoum. Both have now been made and mapped.

In the discussions that took place while this work was being carried out, it was often said that the planners needed more information, especially on the ownership and occupation of property, as the basis for an equitable property tax system. Yet we are not so naive as to believe that everyone in these large cities would welcome such a proposal. Would anyone volunteer to pay higher property taxes? Obviously, such an innovation would be opposed by powerful people. Even so, we are convinced that some systematic form of property tax would be useful as a means for financing the infrastructural work that is long overdue in these overgrown settlements. Central governments do not have this money, nor should they try to extract more from the rural population who have born the urban burden long enough.

So, we should cry "more information," by all means; but the collection of such information and the establishment of a proper data base and the resulting property taxes that pay for some urban services will entail a long and bitter struggle. In this struggle, we might hope that the international and bilateral agencies which lend money and offer advice will be prepared to go the distance. "Development" is not an easy path, except perhaps for the foreign "experts" who can retreat from their failures to the capitals of the industrial world and search again for the solution. Solutions lie in hard bargaining and long experience in the field where the struggle is taking place. These studies suggest that some partial solutions are already known, if the people and institutions with leverage will apply them. We cannot expect management clichés or the IMF's "conditionality" to solve problems that are essentially the product of personal relations, a power struggle between people and institutions, and of many years of complex historical development. We are not dealing with two or three variables in a regression equation. Some of the facts are presented in this study; these, and many more are waiting to be acted upon.

Bibliography

Abu Sin, Mohamed el Hadi. 1985. "A Survey of Squatter Settlements in Khartoum." Department of Geography, University of Khartoum.
Adetoyi, Olawale Kayode. 1987. "Autonomy versus Control of Local Government in Nigeria: The Case of Oyo State, 1976-1983," Ph.D thesis, Carleton University.
Adu, A.L. 1969. *The Civil Service in Commonwealth Africa*. London: George Allen and Unwin.
Adamolekun, L. and L. Rowland, eds. 1979. *The New Local Government System in Nigeria: Problems and Prospects for Implementation*. Ibadan: Heinemann Educational Books.
"Africa's Reserves Go on Dwindling." *Africa Analysis*, No. 19 (3 April 1987), 1.
Agarwala, Ramgopal. 1983. *Planning in Developing Countries: Lessons of Experience*. World Bank Staff Working Papers No. 576. Washington: The World Bank.
Alderfer, Harold F. 1964. *Local Government in Developing Countries*. New York: McGraw-Hill.
Alexander, Linda. 1983. "European Planning Ideology in Tanzania." *Habitat International* 7, no. 1/2: 17-36.
Ahmed, Hassab El Rasoul Hussein. 1973. "Urban Growth in the Three Towns." *The People's Local Government Journal* 2, no. 1 (in Arabic).
Aliyu, A.Y. and Peter H. Koehn. 1982. *Local Autonomy and Inter-Governmental Relations in Nigeria: The Case of the Northern States in the Immediate Post Local Government Reform Period (1976-79)*. Zaria: Institute of Administration, Ahmadu Bello University.
Ascher, Kate. 1987. *The Politics of Privatisation: Contracting out Public Services*. Houndmills, U.K.: Macmillan Education.
Attahi, Koffi. 1984. "Planning New Capital Cities in Developing Nations: Some Aspects of the Experience of Ivory Coast in Connection with Yamoussoukro." Paper delivered at the Workshop on the Planning of New Capital Cities in Developing Countries, Abuja, Nigeria, 4-9 March 1984.
———. 1985a. *Quelques Aspects des Principaux Problèmes Posés par la Crise Urbaine en Côte d'Ivoire*. Abidjan: Centre de Recherches Architecturales et Urbaines.
———. 1985b. *Structures de Gestion et Moyens des Communes de Côte d'Ivoire*. Abidjan: Centre de Recherches Architecturales et Urbaines.
———. 1986. *Côte d'Ivoire: Une évaluation de la réforme de la gestion urbaine*. Abidjan: Centre de Recherches Architecturales et Urbaines.
Ba, Amadou Tidiane et al. 1983. *Le Lac de Guiers: Problématique d'Environnement et de Développement*. Dakar: Université de Dakar, Actes du Colloque de l'Institut des Sciences de l'Environnement.

Bahl, Roy, Jerry Miner and Larry Schroeder. 1984. "Mobilizing Local Resources in Developing Countries." *Public Administration and Development* 4.
Banyikwa, William F. 1985. "Urban Passenger Transport Services in Dar es Salaam." Paper prepared for workshop on The Management of Urban Services in Africa: Challenge of the 80's. Nairobi, 9-10 July.
Banyombo, François. 1983. *Identification des Structures et Fonctions du Service du Nettoiement à Abidjan: SITAF*. Université d'Abidjan, Institut d'Ethno-Sociologie; Mémoire de maîtrise.
Barwell, Ian. 1979. "The Matatu Public Transport Sector in Nairobi." Mission Report for Urban Projects Department, World Bank. London: Intermediate Technology Transport Ltd.
Belliot, M. 1984. *Rapport sur les conditions de mise en place de fonctionnement de l'Agence d'urbanisme d'Abidjan*. Abidjan: AUA.
"Bilan et Perspectives." 1980. *Equipement et Transports* (Cte d'Ivoire). Numéro spécial.
Bloomberg, Lawrence and Charles Abrams. 1964. *United Nations Mission to Kenya on Housing*. Nairobi: Government Printer.
Bouat, Marie-Claire et Jean-Louis Fouilland. 1983. *Les finances publiques des communes et des communautés rurales au Sénégal*. Dakar: Editions Clairafrique.
Bourdin, Joel. 1984. *Monnaie et Politique Monetaire dans les Pays Africains de la Zone Franc*. Dakar: Les Nouvelles Editions Africaines.
Camacho, Martine. 1986. *Les poubelles de la survie: La décharge municipale de Tananarive*. Paris: Karthala.
Campbell, M.J., T.G. Brierly and L.F. Blitz. 1965. *The Structure of Local Government in West Africa*. The Hague: Martinus Nijhoff for the International Union of Local Authorities.
Centre de Recherches Architecturales et Urbaines (CRAU). 1983. *Les logements économiques à Abidjan: Une politique d'habitat du grand nombre en Côte d'Ivoire*. Abidjan: Université d'Abidjan.
———. 1986. *Les Equipements Urbains à Dakar*. Dakar: Ministère de l'Urbanisme et de l'Habitat.
Cheema, G. Shabbir and Dennis Rondinelli. 1983. "Implementing Decentralization Policies: An Introduction." In *Decentralization and Development: Policy Implementation in Developing Countries*, edited by Cheema and Rondinelli, 9-34. Beverly Hills: Sage Publications.
Chomentowski, Victor. 1986. "La patente dans les pays d'Afrique de l'ouest." Abidjan / Paris: Bureau Régional d'Etudes Economiques et Financières.
Cohen, Michael. 1983. *Learning by Doing*. Washington: The World Bank.
Collignon, René. 1984. "La lutte des pouvoirs publics contre les 'encombrements humains' à Dakar." *Revue canadienne des études africaines* 18, no. 3: 573-82.
Conyers, Diana. 1981. "Decentralization for Regional Development: A Comparative Study of Tanzania, Zambia and Papua New Guinea." *Public Administration and Development* 1, no. 2: 107-20.
Coopers and Lybrand. 1980. "Report on Specifications for a Standard Matatu." Nairobi.
———. 1984. "SOGEFIHA: Diagnostic de restructuration." 27 avril. Abidjan: Pour l'Union des fédérations d'organismes d'habitations à loyer modéré.
Daily News (Tanzania). 8 November 1986; 17 March 1987; 8 April 1987.
Dieng, Isidore M'Baye. 1977. *Relogement de bidonvillois à la péripherie urbaine*. Dakar: ENDA.

Djamat-Dubois, Marcel, Kouamé N'Guessan, and Aloko N'Guessan. 1983. *Les Logements économiques à Abidjan*. Abidjan: Centre de Recherches Architecturales et Urbaines.

Dryden, Stanley. 1967. "Local Government in Tanzania: Parts I and II." *Journal of Administration Overseas*, April, 109-20 and July, 165-78.

———. 1968. *Local Administration in Tanzania*. Nairobi: East African Publishing House.

Dumont, René et Marie-France Mottin. 1982. *Le Défi sénégalais: reconstruire les terroirs, libérer les paysans*. Dakar: ENDA.

———. 1983. *Stranglehold on Africa*. London: André Deutsch.

Economist Intelligence Unit, 1985a. *Quarterly Economic Review of Ivory Coast, Annual Supplement, 1985*. London: The Economist Publications Ltd.

———. 1985b. *Quarterly Economic Review of Senegal, The Gambia, Guinea-Bissau, Cape Verde, Annual Supplement, 1985*. London: The Economist Publications Ltd.

———. 1985c. *Quarterly Economic Review of Sudan, Annual Supplement, 1985*. London: The Economist Publications Ltd.

———. 1985d. *Quarterly Economic Review of Kenya, Annual Supplement, 1985*. London: The Economist Publications Ltd.

———. 1985e. *Quarterly Economic Review of Tanzania, Mozambique, Annual Supplement, 1985*. London: The Economist Publications Ltd.

———. 1985f. *Quarterly Economic Review of Zaire, Rwanda, Burundi, Annual Supplement, 1985*. London: The Economist Publications Ltd.

———. 1985g. *Quarterly Economic Review of Nigeria, Annual Supplement, 1985*. London: The Economist Publications Ltd.

El Sammani, M.O., M.A. Abu Sin, M. Talha, B.M. El Hassan, and Ian Haywood. 1986. *Management Problems of Greater Khartoum*. Khartoum: Institute of Environmental Studies.

Faber, M. and Dudley Seers, eds. 1972. *The Crisis in Planning*. London: Chatto and Windus. 2 vols.

FAO and the World Food Programme. 1984. *Food and Agriculture Situation in African Countries Affected by Calamities in 1983-85*. Situation Report No. 6, FAO, Rome, 30 September.

Fetter, Bruce. 1983. *Colonial Rule and Regional Imbalance in Central Africa*. Boulder: Westview Press.

France, Republic of. 1982. *Manuel d'urbanisme pour les pays en développement*. Tome 4. *Les transports urbains*. Paris: Coopération et aménagement.

Friedmann, John. 1973. *Urbanization, Planning, and National Development*. Beverly Hills: Sage Publications.

Garcia, Rolando. 1982. *Nature Pleads Not Guilty – the 1972 Drought Case History*. Oxford: Pergamon Press.

Gboyega, Alex. 1983. "Local Government Reform in Nigeria." In *Local Government in the Third World: The Experience of Tropical Africa*, edited by Philip Mawhood, 225-47. Chichester: John Wiley.

Glantz, Michael and Robert. W. Katz. 1985. "Drought as a Constraint to Development in Sub-Saharan Africa." *AMBIO: A Journal of the Human Environment*, December, 1985.

Godard, Xavier. 1985. "Quel modèle de transports collectifs pour les villes africaines? Cas de Brazzaville et Kinshasa." *Politique Africaine*, no. 17 (mars): 41-57.

Greenwood, Alan and John Howell. 1980. "Urban Local Authorities." In *Administra-*

tion in Zambia, edited by William Tordoff, 162-84. Manchester: Manchester University Press.

Gwatkin, Davidson. 1984. *Mortality Reduction, Fertility Decline, and Population Growth: Toward a More Relevant Assessment of the Relationships among Them.* World Bank Staff Working Papers No. 686. Washington: The World Bank.

Haeringer, Philippe. 1985. "Vingt-cinq ans de politique urbaine à Abidjan, ou la tentation de l'urbanisme intégral." *Politique Africaine,* no. 17 (mars): 20-40.

Hake, Andrew. 1977. *African Metropolis.* Sussex: Sussex University Press.

Hamdan, G. 1960. "The Growth and Functional Structure of Khartoum." *The Geographical Review* 50, no. 1.

Hardoy, Jorge E. and David Satterthwaite, eds. 1981. *Shelter: Need and Response. Housing, Land and Settlement Policies in Seventeen Third World Nations.* Chichester: John Wiley.

Hayuma, A.M. 1983. "The Management and Implementation of Physical Infrastructures in Dar es Salaam City, Tanzania." *Journal of Environmental Management* 16: 321-34.

———. 1984. *Economic and Financial Constraints in the Implementation of the 1968 Dar es Salaam City Master Plan from 1969 to 1979.* Occasional Paper No. 3. Dar es Salaam: Ardhi Institute, Department of Urban and Regional Planning.

Haywood, Ian. 1985. "City Profile: Khartoum." *Cities* 2, no. 3: 186-97.

Haywood, Ian and Adil Mustafa Ahmad. 1986. "Sudan" In *International Handbook on Land Use Planning,* edited by Nicholas N. Patricios, 153-84. New York: Greenwood Press.

Hepworth, N.P. 1971. *The Finance of Local Government.* London: George Allen and Unwin Ltd.

Hicks, Ursula K. 1961. *Development from Below: Local Government and Finance in Developing Countries of the Commonwealth.* Oxford: Clarendon Press.

———. 1974. *The Large City: A World Problem.* Chichester: John Wiley.

Hirschman, Albert. 1970. *Exit, Voice and Loyalty.* Cambridge, Mass: Harvard University Press.

Humes, Samuel. 1973. "The Role of Local Government in Economic Development in Africa." *Journal of Administration Overseas* 12, no.1: 21-27.

Hutton, John, ed. 1972. *Urban Challenge in East Africa.* Nairobi: East African Publishing House.

International Labour Office. 1972. *Employment, Incomes and Equality: A Strategy for Increasing Productive Employment in Kenya.* Geneva: ILO.

———. 1981. *Zambia: Basic Needs in an Economy Under Pressure.* Addis Ababa: Jobs and Skills Programme for Africa.

International Monetary Fund. 1976. "An Analysis of Local Government Finances in Kenya with Proposals for Reform." Washington: IMF.

Joshi, Heather, Harold Lubell and Jean Mouly. 1976. *Abidjan: Urban Development and Employment on the Ivory Coast.* Geneva: ILO.

Kapila, Sunita, Mutsembi Manundu and Davinder Lamba. 1982. *The Matatu Mode of Public Transport in Metropolitan Nairobi.* Nairobi: Mazingira Institute.

Kenya, Republic of. 1966. *Sessional Paper No. 5 of 1966 / 67.* Nairobi: Government Printer.

———. 1974. *Development Plan 1974-78.* Nairobi: Government Printer.

———. 1983. *Report of the Controller and Auditor-General on Local Authorities for the Three Years Ended 31st December, 1981.* Nairobi: Government Printer.

———. 1985. *Economic Survey 1985.* Nairobi: Ministry of Finance and Planning, Central Bureau of Statistics.

Koehn, Peter. 1983. "State Land Allocation and Class Formation in Nigeria" *Journal of Modern African Studies* 21, no. 3: 461-81.
Kulaba, Saitiel. 1979. "Development and Human Settlements Development." Paper presented at Symposium on Human Settlements Development Organized by Centre for Housing Studies and Urban and Rural Planning Department, Ardhi Institute, Dar es Salaam.
———. 1981. *Housing, Socialism and National Development in Tanzania: A Policy Framework*. Rotterdam: Bouwcentrum Centre for Housing Studies.
———. 1985a. "Managing Rapid Urban Growth Through Sites and Services and Squatter Upgrading Housing in Tanzania: Lessons of Experience." Paper presented at International Conference on the Management of Sites and Services and Squatter Upgrading Housing Areas, 18-22 February, AICC, at Arusha, Tanzania, organized by the Centre for Housing Studies, Tanzania.
———. 1985b. "Shelter and Housing Problems in Africa," *Proceedings and Report of the African Union of Architects Regional Conference on Architecture and National Development*, 1-22. 16-19 June, Arusha, organized by The Architectural Association (Tanzania) and The African Union of Architects.
———. 1985c. "Urban Growth and the Management of Urban Reform in Tanzania." Dar es Salaam: Ardhi Institute.
———. 1986a. "Designing Appropriate Private-Public Sector Partnerships in Housing and Urban Development: The Case of Tanzania." Paper for the Tenth Conference on Housing and Urban Development in Sub-Saharan Africa, 25-28 February 1986, Harare, Zimbabwe organized by USAID Office of Housing and Urban Development and Government of Zimbabwe.
———. 1986b. *Urban Growth and the Management of Urban Reform, Finance, Services and Housing in Tanzania: Revised Final Summary Report*. Dar es Salaam: Ardhi Institute, Centre for Housing Studies.
———. 1986c. "Urban Growth and the Management of Urban Reform, Finance, Services and Housing in Tanzania." Dar es Salaam: Ardhi Institute.
Laquian, Aprodicio A. 1983. *Basic Housing: Policies for Urban Sites, Services, and Shelter in Developing Countries*. Ottawa: IDRC.
Lee, Eugene C. 1965. *Local Taxation in Tanzania*. Dar es Salaam: Institute of Public Administration, University College.
Leyla, M.E. 1986. "Socio-economic aspects of 'environmental refugees' in West Omdurman." M.Sc. thesis, Institute of Environmental Studies, University of Khartoum.
Linn, J.F. 1982. "The Costs of Urbanisation in Developing Countries." *Economic Development and Cultural Change* 30, no. 3: 625-48.
Lipton, M. 1977. *Why Poor People Stay Poor: Urban Bias in World Development*. Cambridge: Harvard University Press.
Marguerat, Yves. 1984. "Pratiques foncières à Lomé, Togo: Résultats d'une enquête." *Pratiques Urbaines* No. 1, "Terres des Uns et Villes des Autres." Paris: CNRS-CEGET. 21-41.
Marshall Macklin Monaghan Limited. 1979. *Dar es Salaam Master Plan. Technical Supplements 1-4*. Toronto and Dar es Salaam: Ministry of Lands, Housing and Urban Development.
Mascarenhas, Adolfo. 1966. "Urban Development in Dar es Salaam." M. A. thesis, University of Dar es Salaam.
Mawhood, Philip. 1983. "Decentralization: the Concept and the Practice" and "Applying the French Model in Cameroon." In *Local Government in the Third World: The Experience of Tropical Africa*, edited by Mawhood, 1-24, 177-200.

Mazurelle, Jean et Nicholas You. 1987. "L'Appauvrissement des grandes villes en Afrique francophone de l'ouest: Est-il inevitable?" Abidjan: World Bank and UN Habitat.

Mbuyi, Kankondé. 1985. "Programme de Recherche. Croissance Urbaine et Gestion des Villes. Rapport d'Analyse Général." Kinshasa: BEAU.

Médard, Jean-François. 1987. "Charles Njonjo: Portrait d'un 'Big Man' au Kenya." In *L'Etat contemporain en Afrique*, sous la direction de Emmanuel Terray, 49-87. Paris: L'Harmattan.

Miti, Katabaro. 1985. "L'opération Nguvu Kazi à Dar es Salaam: Ardeur au travail et contrôle de l'espace urbain." *Politique Africaine*, no. 17: 88-104.

Mitullah, Winnie V. 1985. *Management of Urban Services in Nairobi: Focus on the Matatu Mode of Public Transport*. Project Ecoville Working Paper No. 26, Institute for Environmental Studies, University of Toronto.

Mutizwa-Mangiza, N.D. 1986. "Local Government and Planning in Zimbabwe: An Examination of Recent Changes With Special Reference to the Provincial / Regional Level." *Third World Planning Review* 8, no. 2: 153-75.

Nairobi City Council. Various years. *Abstracts of Accounts*. Nairobi.

Nairobi Urban Study Group. 1972. *Nairobi Metropolitan Growth Strategy*. Nairobi: Nairobi City Council.

Ndiaye, M. Malick Kamara. 1987. "L'Administration de la mobilisation des ressources: L'exemple des améliorations apportées au système fiscal dakarois." Abidjan: EDI Seminar.

"New Directions in Bank Urban Projects." *The Urban Edge* 9, no. 3 (1985): 1-5.

Newland, Kathleen. 1980. *City Limits: Emerging Constraints on Urban Growth*. Washington: Worldwatch Institute.

Nguessan-Zoukou, L. 1983. *Des Régions et de la Régionalisation en Côte d'Ivoire*. Abidjan: Ecole Normale Supérieure.

Nigeria, Federal Republic of. 1976. *Guidelines for Local Government Reform*. Kaduna: Government Printer.

Norris, Malcolm. 1983. "Sudan: Administrative versus Political Priorities." in Mawhood, 49-73.

Nyerere, Julius. 1967. *The Arusha Declaration*. Dar es Salaam: Government Printer.

———. 1968. *Socialism and Rural Development*. Dar es Salaam: Government Printer.

———. 1972. *Decentralisation*. Dar es Salaam: Government Printer.

Okpala, Donatus. 1984. "Urban Planning and the Control of Urban Physical Growth in Nigeria." *Habitat International* 8, no. 2: 73-94.

Oladosu, S.A. 1982. "Urbanization and Social Services Administration in Nigeria: The Case of Kaduna Township." In *The Administration of Social Services in Nigeria: The Challenge to Local Governments*, edited by Dele Olowu. Local Government Training Programme, University of Ife, Ile-Ife.

Olusanya, P.O. and D.E. Pursell. 1981. *The Prospects of Economic Development in Nigeria under the Conditions of Rapid Population Growth*. Ibadan: NISER.

Onibokun, Adepoju. 1973. "Forces Shaping the Physical Environment of Cities in the Developing Countries: The Ibadan Case." *Land Economics* 49, no. 4: 424-31.

———. 1985. *Urban Growth and Urban Management in Nigeria with Particular Reference to Public Utilities and Infrastructure: Interim Report*. Ibadan: Nigerian Institute of Social and Economic Research.

——— et al. 1986. *Urban Growth and Urban Management in Nigeria with Particular Reference to Public Utilities and Infrastructure: Final Report*. Ibadan: Nigerian Institute of Social and Economic Research.

Oyediran, Oyeleye and Alex Gboyega. 1979. "Local Government and Administration." In *Nigerian Government and Politics under Military Rule 1966-79*, edited by Oyeleye Oyediran, 169-91. London: Macmillan.
Pain, Marc. 1984. *Kinshasa: La ville et la cité*. Paris: ORSTOM.
Penner, R. 1970. *Financing Local Government in Tanzania*. Dar es Salaam: East African Publishing House.
Petit-Maire, N. and J. Riser, eds. 1983. *Sahara ou Sahel! Quaternaire Récent du Bassin de Taoudenni, Mali*. Marseille: Laboratoire du Quaternaire du Centre National de Recherche Scientifique.
Picard, L.A. 1979. "District Councils in Botswana – A Remnant of Local Autonomy." *Journal of Modern African Studies* 17, no. 2: 285-308.
Prats, Yves. 1979. "L'administration territoriale et les collectivités locales." In *Les institutions administratives des états francophones d'Afrique noire*, sous la direction de Gérard Conac, 133-44. Paris: Economica.
Project Planning Associates. 1968. *Dar es Salaam Master Plan* Toronto: Project Planning.
Ravenhill, John, ed. 1986. *Africa in Economic Crisis*. New York: Columbia University Press.
Reilly, Wyn. 1983. "Decentralization in Botswana – myth or reality?" In Mawhood, 141-76.
Renaud, Bertrand. 1981. *National Urbanization Policy in Developing Countries*. New York: Oxford University Press.
Rondinelli, Dennis A. 1983. "Decentralization of Development and Administration in East Africa." In Cheema and Rondinelli, 77-125.
Roth, Gabriel. 1987. *The Private Provision of Public Services in Developing Countries*. New York: Oxford University Press for the World Bank.
Rweyemamu, Anthony and Goran Hyden, eds. 1975. *A Decade of Public Administration in Africa*. Nairobi: East African Literature Bureau.
Saint-Vil, Jean. 1983. "L'eau chez soi et l'eau au coin de la rue: Les systèmes de distribution de l'eau à Abidjan." *Cahiers ORSTOM* (série Sciences Humaines) 19, no. 4: 471-89.
Salas, R. M. 1986. *The State of World Population 1986*. New York: UNFPA.
Schmetzer, Hartmut. 1982. "Housing in Dar-es-Salaam." *Habitat International* 6, no. 4: 497-511.
Sendaro, A.M. 1985. *The Management of Urban Development and Reform: The Case of Dar es Salaam City and Mbeya Municipal Councils*. Dar es Salaam: University of Dar es Salaam, Institute of Development Studies.
Sénégal, République du. 1984. "Décret fixant le régime des prix de certains produits et services." Ministère du Commerce, Dakar, No. 84-404.
Situma, Lan. 1977. "The Matatus: Public Transport in Nairobi." Nairobi: Nairobi City Council.
Sohair, L. 1986. "The 'Environmental Refugees' of Western Omdurman." M.Sc. thesis, University of Khartoum.
SONED Afrique et BCEOM. 1982. *Etude du Plan Directeur d'Urbanisme de Dakar: Livre Blanc*. Dakar: Ministère de l'Habitat, de l'Urbanisme et de l'Environnement.
Stamp, Patricia. 1980. "Appropriate Innovation in Third World Cities." In *Making Cities Work: The Dynamics of Urban Innovation*, edited by David Morley, Stuart Proudfoot and Thomas Burns, 245-56. London: Croom Helm.
———. 1981. "Governing Thika: Dilemmas of Municipal Politics in Kenya." Ph.D thesis, University of London.
Stren, Richard. 1975. *Urban Inequality and Housing Policy in Tanzania: The*

Problem of Squatting. Berkeley: Institute of International Studies, University of California.

——. 1978. *Housing the Urban Poor in Africa.* Berkeley: Institute of International Studies, University of California.

——. 1982. "Underdevelopment, Urban Squatting and the State Bureaucracy: A Case Study of Tanzania." *Canadian Journal of African Studies* 16, no. 1: 67-91.

——. 1984. "*Urban Policy.*" In Joel D. Barkan. ed. *Politics and Public Policy in Kenya and Tanzania,* edited by Joel D. Barkan, 233-64. New York: Praeger.

——. 1985. *Two Nigerian Towns in the Eighties: A Socio-Economic Survey of Idah and Makurdi, Benue State.* Project Ecoville Working Paper No. 21, Institute for Environmental Studies, University of Toronto.

——. 1986. "The Ruralization of African Cities: Learning to Live with Poverty." In *Coping with Rapid Urban Growth in Africa: An Annotated Bibliography,* edited by Richard Stren with Claire Letemendia, iii-xxi. Montreal: McGill University.

Tanzania, United Republic of. 1976. *Third Five Year Plan for Economic and Social Development 1st July 1976-30th June 1981, Volume I.* Dar es Salaam: Government Printer.

——. 1983. *The Human Resources Deployment Act, 1983.* Dar es Salaam: Government Printer.

——. 1984. *Report of a Technical Subcommittee on the Rationalisation of Urban Passenger Transport in Dar es Salaam.* Dar es Salaam: Research and Planning, Mawasiliano.

——. 1985. *Budget Speech of the Prime Minister Salim Ahmed Salim Presenting the 1985 / 86 Estimates to Parliament.* Dar es Salaam: Government Printer.

——. 1986. *Budget Speech of the Minister for Local Government and Cooperative Development Ndugu Kingunge Ngombale-Mwiru, MP, Presenting the 1986 / 87 Recurrent and Development Estimates of the Ministry of Local Government and Cooperative Development to Parliament.* Dar es Salaam. July.

Temple, Frederick and Nelle Temple. 1980. "The Politics of Public Housing in Nairobi." In *Politics and Policy Implementation in the Third World,* edited by Merilee S. Grindle, 224-49. Princeton: Princeton University Press.

Theunynck, Serge and Mamadou Dia. 1980. "The Young (and the Less Young) in Infra-urban Areas in Mauritania." *African Environment* 4: 2-4, 205-33.

Tibesar, A. and R.R. White. 1985. "An Analysis of Household Energy Use in Dakar, Senegal." Project Ecoville Working Paper Number 27, Institute for Environmental Studies, University of Toronto.

Todaro, M.P. 1976. *Internal Migration in Developing Countries.* Geneva: International Labour Office.

Wane, Oumar. 1983. "Utilisation urbaine de l'eau du Lac de Guiers et planification écologique intégrée de la ville." In Ba et al., 63- 75.

Warrell-Bowring, W.J. 1963. "The Reorganization of the Administration in Tanzania." *Journal of Local Administration Overseas* 2, no.4: 188-94.

Weekly Review (Nairobi). 16 August 1976; 11 March 1983; 25 March 1983; 8 April 1983; 21 December 1984; 25 January 1985; 28 March 1986.

Werlin, Herbert H. 1974. *Governing an African City: A Study of Nairobi.* New York and London: Africana.

White, Rodney and Ian Burton, eds. 1983. *Approaches to the Study of the Environmental Implications of Contemporary Urbanization: MAB Technical Notes 14.* Paris: UNESCO.

World Bank. 1972. *Urbanization: Sector Working Paper.* Washington D.C.: The World Bank.

---. 1977. *Tanzania: The Second National Sites and Services Project, Report No. 1513a-TA.* Washington, D.C.: The World Bank.

---. 1979. *The Economic Trends and Prospects of Senegal. Report No. 1720a-SE, Volume 11, The Agricultural Sector.* Washington D.C.

---. 1983. *World Development Report 1983.* New York: Oxford University Press.

---. 1984a. *Towards Sustained Development in Sub-Saharan Africa: A Joint Program of Action.* Washington: The World Bank.

---. 1984b. *World Tables. Volume II. Social Data.* [Third Edition] Baltimore: Johns Hopkins University Press.

---. 1985. *World Development Report 1985.* New York: Oxford University Press.

---. 1986a. *World Development Report 1986.* New York: Oxford University Press.

---. 1986b. *Population Growth and Policies in Subsaharan Africa: A World Bank Policy Study.* Washington: The World Bank.

---. 1986c. *Urban Transport: A World Bank Policy Study.* Washington: The World Bank.

Contributors

Koffi Attahi, an Ivorian planner, has a doctorate from the University of Montreal. He is a lecturer in the Department of Geography and the Director of the Centre de recherches architecturales et urbaines, University of Abidjan.

Saitiel Kulaba is a Tanzanian urban planner and the Director of the Centre for Housing Studies, Ardhi Institute, Dar es Salaam. Professor Kulaba has written *Housing, Socialism and National Development in Tanzania* (Rotterdam: Centre for Housing Studies, 1981) and numerous other articles on housing and planning in Tanzania.

Diana Lee-Smith is a British architect who has lived and worked in Kenya since 1975. She is a founding member of Mazingira Institute in Nairobi, a non-profit research institute, and the editor of Settlements Information Network Africa (SINA). She has worked as a consultant for the United Nations, the World Bank, USAID, IDRC, and the Kenya Government. In addition, she has held academic appointments in Kenya, Canada, and the United States, and has worked as an architect in three European countries.

Kankondé Mbuyi is a Zairian sociologist, trained at Louvanium University, Kinshasa. He is one of the co-authors of the *Atlas de Kinshasa* (1975), and presently the Director of the Bureau d'études d'aménagements urbaines, under the Ministry of Public Works, Kinshasa.

Thiécouta Ngom is a Senegalese urban planner with a master's degree from the Free University of Brussels and a further specialist diploma from the University of Dakar. At the time of writing the article in this volume, he was Director of the Centre de recherches pour l'habitat, l'urbanisme et l'architecture, under the Ministry of Urban Planning, Dakar. He is presently a technical adviser in the same Ministry.

Adepoju Onibokun is a Nigerian geographer and planner with a doctorate from the University of Waterloo, Canada. He has written numerous articles on urban and rural planning in Nigeria in both Nigerian and major international journals. He is Professor and Director of the Physical Planning Department, Nigerian Institute of Social and Economic Research, Ibadan.

Mohamed el Sammani is a Sudanese geographer, trained in Athens, the UK, and the University of Khartoum, where he obtained his doctorate. He is a lecturer in the Department of Geography and a staff member of the Institute of Environmental Studies, University of Khartoum. He has extensive experience as a researcher and consultant in problems of rural development in the Sudan.

Richard Stren is a Canadian political scientist with a doctorate from the University of California, Berkeley. Professor Stren holds appointments with the Department of Political Science and the Institute for Environmental Studies, University of Toronto. Among his publications are *Housing the Urban Poor in Africa* (University of California, 1978) and numerous journal articles on urban planning and local politics in Africa.

Rodney White is a Canadian geographer with a doctorate from Bristol University. He holds a teaching appointment in the Department of Geography and is the Associate Director of the Institute for Environmental Studies at the University of Toronto. Professor White has carried out extensive research on rural and environmental problems in West Africa and is the co-author of *Mental Maps* (Allen & Unwin), and the co-editor (with Ian Burton) of *Approaches to the Study of the Environmental Implications of Contemporary Urbanization* (UNESCO).

IFIAS Research Series

This book is also part of the IFIAS Research Series, which includes the volumes listed below. The books are available from the publishers cited.

VOLUME ONE
G. Hallsworth, *The Anatomy, Physiology and Psychology of Erosion.* Chichester: John Wiley and Sons Ltd., 1987.

VOLUME TWO
Rob Koudstaal, *Water Quality Management Plan, North Sea: Framework for Analysis.* Rotterdam: A. A. Balkema, 1987. Coastal Waters No. 1.

VOLUME THREE
Lies Dekker, Blair T. Bower and Rob Koudstaal, *Management of Toxic Materials in an International Setting: A Case Study of Cadmium in the North Sea.* Rotterdam: A. A. Balkema, 1987. Coastal Waters No. 2.

VOLUME FOUR
Thorkil Kristensen and Johan Peter Paludan, *The Earth's Fragile Systems: Perspectives on Global Change.* Boulder: Westview Press, 1988.

VOLUME FIVE
Richard E. Stren and Rodney R. White, eds. *African Cities in Crisis: Managing Rapid Urban Growth.* Boulder: Westview Press, 1988.

VOLUME SIX
G. Dosi, C. Freeman, R. Nelson, G. Silverberg, and L. Soete, eds., *Technical Change and Economic Thought.* London: Francis Pinter, 1988.

VOLUME SEVEN
N.K. Ståhle, S. Nilsson, and P. Lundblom. *From Vision to Action: Science and Global Development.* Toronto: IFIAS, 1988.

About the IFIAS

The International Federation of Institutes for Advanced Study is an association of thirty-five leading research institutes which collaborate to address major global problems of long-term importance in environment, economy, and science and technology. IFIAS research programs are interdisciplinary, seeking to advance understanding of complex systems for the improved management of a rapidly changing world with an uncertain future. IFIAS stands for the more effective and consistent use of scientific understanding in world councils and for the adoption of long-term strategic thinking.

IFIAS *Executive Committee Members*

Sir Hermann Bondi (Chairman)
Master, Churchill College
Cambridge, England

Prof. Darcy F. de Almeida (Vice Chairman)
Instituto de Biofisica
Rio de Janeiro, Brazil

Dr. Thomas R. Odhiambo
International Centre of Insect Physiology & Ecology
Nairobi, Kenya

Prof. C. H. Geoff Oldham
Science Policy Research Unit
Brighton, England

Mr. J. Egbert Prins
Delft Hydraulics
Delft, The Netherlands

Dr. Ian Burton (Director, IFIAS)
IFIAS Secretariat
Toronto, Ontario, Canada

IFIAS *Member Institutes*

Athens Center of Ekistics
Athens 10210, Greece

Center for Remote Sensing, Boston University
Boston, Mass. 02215, USA

Centro de Investigacion y de Estudios Avanzados del IPN (CINVESTAV)
07000 Mexico DF, Mexico

El Colegio de Mexico AC
01000 Mexico DF, Mexico

Delft Hydraulics
2600 MH Delft, The Netherlands

Food Research Institute, Stanford University
Stanford, CA 94305, USA

About the IFIAS   325

Global Studies Center
Arlington, VA 22209, USA

Graduate Institute of International
    Studies
CH-1211 Geneva 21, Switzerland

Institut National de la Recherche
    Scientifique, University of Quebec
Sainte-Foy, Quebec G1V 4C7, Canada

Institute for Environmental Studies,
    University of Toronto
Toronto, Ontario M5S 1A4, Canada

Institute for European Environmental
    Policy
D-5300 Bonn 1, West Germany

Institute for Futures Studies
DK-1468 Copenhagen K, Denmark

Institute for Studies on Research and
    Scientific Documentation
00100 Rome, Italy

Institute for World Economics of the
    Hungarian Academy of Sciences
    (IWEHAS)
H-1531 Budapest, Hungary

Instituto de Biofisica, UFRJ – CCS –
    Cidade Universitaria
21941 – Rio de Janeiro – RJ, Brazil

Instituto Brasileiro de Economia
20.000 – Rio de Janeiro – RJ, Brazil

Instituto de Ciencias del Hombre (ICH)
28001 Madrid, Spain

Instituts Internationaux de Physique et
    de Chimie (Solvay Institute)
B-1050 Brussels, Belgium

International Centre of Insect
    Physiology and Ecology (ICIPE)
Nairobi, Kenya

International Centre for Theoretical
    Physics (ICTP)
34100 Trieste, Italy

The Jacob Blaustein Institute for Desert
    Research, Ben-Gurion University of
    the Negev
Israel 84990

The Japan Economic Research Center
    (JERC)
Tokyo 100, Japan

Kernforschungsanlage Jülich GmbH
D-5170 Jülich, West Germany

Marga Institute
Colombo 5, Sri Lanka

National Institute for Research
    Advancement (NIRA)
Tokyo 160, Japan

National Research Center for Science
    and Technology for Development
    (NRCSTD)
Beijing, People's Republic of China

National Research Centre
Dokki-Cairo, Egypt

Niels Bohr Institute
2100 Copenhagen, Denmark

Research Institute, King Fahd
    University of Petroleum and Minerals
Dhahran 31261, Saudi Arabia

Research Policy Institute, University of
    Lund
S-220 02 Lund, Sweden

Royal Scientific Society
Amman, Jordan

Science Policy Research Unit (SPRU),
    University of Sussex
Brighton BN1 9RF, England

Tata Institute of Fundamental Research
Bombay 400 005, India

University Corporation for Atmospheric
 Research (UCAR)
Boulder, Col. 80307-3000, USA

The Weizmann Institute of Science
Rehovot 76100, Israel

Winrock International Institute for
 Agricultural Development
Morrilton, Ark. 72110, USA

Woods Hole Oceanographic Institution
 (WHOI)
Woods Hole, Mass. 02543, USA

World Resources Institute
Washington, DC 20006, USA

IFIAS *Corporate Affiliates*

AKZO NV
Arnhem, The Netherlands

ATLAS COPCO AB
Stockholm, Sweden

DSM CORPORATE PLANNING
AND DEVELOPMENT
Heerlen, The Netherlands

ENEA
Rome, Italy

GIST-BROCADES
Delft, The Netherlands

OCE-VAN DER GRINTEN
Venlo, The Netherlands

PHILLIPS INTERNATIONAL
Eindhoven, The Netherlands

SHELL INTERNATIONAL PETROLEUM MIJ.
Den Haag, The Netherlands

SKANDINAVISKA ENSKILDA BANKEN
Stockholm, Sweden

UNILEVER RESEARCH LABORATORIUM
Vlaardingen, The Netherlands

VBB AB
Stockholm, Sweden

VOLKER STEVIN WEGEN EN ASFALT
Utrecht, The Netherlands

Index

Abidjan, City of, 113-15
  budget and accounts of (with the ten communes), 136-40
  commune system of, 113-17, 142-44
  Council of, 26-27, 117-19, 126-27, 145-46
  decentralization of administration in, 65
  deficit of, 30
  destruction of squatter areas in (1969-73), 63
  financial resources of, 120, 131-36
  functions and powers of, 125-26
  health facilities in, 231
  housing in, 55-56
  material resources of, 121-23, 130-31
  Mayor, role of, 117-19, 126-27, 145-46
  municipal employees of, 119-20, 121-23, 129-30
  political and administrative structure of, 126-29
  spontaneous housing around, 56
  waste disposal in, 45-6, 130, 139
  water supply in, 40-41
aquifer, shrinkage of, 7
Adjamé, 115
AFECOZA. See women
African Estates, Ministry of (OCA, Zaire), 162
African Industrial Transport Company (SITAF, Côte d'Ivoire), 46, 130. See also waste disposal (Côte d'Ivoire)
agricultural production, decline in, 15-16
aid, 245 n.3. See also International Monetary Fund, USAID, World Bank
Anambra State Water Corporation (1976), 79
Angle-Mousse (Dakar), destruction of, 63

Arusha, refuse removal in, 44
Arusha Declaration (1967), 59, 203
AUA (formerly AURA). See Town Planning Agency of Abidjan
AURA. See Urban Planning Workshop for the Abidjan Area

Bauchi State
  land allocation in, 61
  les baux administratifs (administrative leases, Côte d'Ivoire), 55
BHS. See Housing Bank of Senegal
Bobodioulasso, tax returns of, 29
Bouaké
  communal status of, 114
  waste disposal in, 45-46
Brazzaville, transport in, 49-51
Brazzaville Transport Company (STB), 50
BCET. See Central Office for Technical Studies
BEAU. See Office for the Study of Urban Planning
BNETD. See National Office for Technical Studies of Development
BSIE. See Special Budget for Investment and Facilities

Canadian International Development Agency, master plan for Dar es Salaam (1968), 59
Cap-Vert Building Society (SICAP), 178
Central Bank of Nigeria, 308
Central Office for Technical Studies (BCET), 130
centralization of administration
  influence of, 30-32
  Francophone vs Anglophone countries, 21-22
Center for Architectural and Urban

Research (CRAU), study on public housing agencies, 55-56
Chama cha Mapinduzi (CCM), 206, practice on urban illegalities, 228
Chania II Scheme (Kenya), 39
chefs des quartiers (Department Heads of Dakar region), 181, 183
colonial government, structural influence of, 21, 279. *See also* urban history
Commissioner of Lands (Kenya), 34
Commissioner of Land Titles (Zaire), 155-56
commodity prices, government policy on, 15
commune system (Dakar), 195-20
 by "special statute," 195
 by "common law," 195
 (Côte d'Ivoire), 26-28, 113-17
 evaluation of management, 142-44
 "full exercise communes," 114-15
 "mixed communes," 114
 "normal exercise communes," 114-15
Company for the Financial Management of Housing (SOGEFIHA, Côte d'Ivoire), 55
Company for Lands and Urban Infrastructure (Côte d'Ivoire), 56, 131
CNECI. *See* National Housing Bank
la conjoncture (economic downturn), 41
Construction and Housing Company of Côte d'Ivoire (SICOGI), 55
Construction and Town Planning, Ministry of (Côte d'Ivoire), 116
coopérants (Francophone expatriates), 31
corruption
 in housing services, 62-63 (Greater Khartoum)
 in land allocation, 268 (Greater Khartoum), 34-35 (Kenya)
 of municipal employees, 224 (Dar es Salaam), 295 (Nairobi), 29 (Nigeria)
Council of Ministers (Côte d'Ivoire), 117
CRAU. *See* Center for Architectural and Urban Research
Crossroad Company (Kinshasa), 161

Dakar, city of, 177-202
 Urban Community of (CUD), 30, 195-200, 311
 decentralization of administration in, 65
 Department of (First Department), 181, 184-85, 307
 education in, 180, 189-90
 health facilities in, 179-80, 187-89
 regional primacy of, 180-81
 squatter areas of, 63
 tax returns of, 29-30
 waste disposal in, 8, 179, 191-95
 water supply in, 179, 190-91, 308
dala-dala (Tanzania), 52-53, 241. *See also* transport (Tanzania)
Dar es Salaam, city of, 203, 206
 City Council of, 43-44, 52-53, 63, 223, 224, 226, 240
 decentralization of administration in, 220
 finances of, 233
 health facilities in, 231
 housing in, 57-58, 213, 226
 income distribution in, 212
 local government structure, 230
 master plan for (1949), 58-59
 master plan for, (1968), 59
 sites and services schemes in, 225-26
 squatter settlements of, 57-58, 61
 transport in, 51-53
 University of, 242
 waste disposal of, 43-44, 223-24, 239, 308, 312
 water supply in, 42, 242-43, 308
Dar es Salaam Motor Transport (DMT), 51
debt
 effects of crisis on, 306
 servicing of, 13
Decentralisation (1972), 22-23
decentralization
 of administration, 22-25
 Anglophone vs Francophone countries, 309-10
 in Dakar, 65
 in Tanzania, 214-16, 219-21, 223, 227
decision-makers (Pikine Department), 185
deforestation, 8, 106
DMT. *See* Dar es Salaam Motor Transport, 51
Dodoma, 59-60, 206

Doxiadis Master Plan (1959), 256
drought, effects of, 9, 248-49, 306

Ecochard Master Plan (Dakar), 307
ENA. *See* National School of Administration
ENSTP. *See* National Upper School of Public Works
economic crisis, effects of, 1, 27-29, 133, 306
economic overview (general, by country), 11, 17-19
ecosystem, pressures on, 265, 270-71
education
  in Côte d'Ivoire, 116, 128
  in Greater Khartoum, 261
  in Kinshasa, 165
  in Nigeria, 73
  in Senegal, 180, 189-90
  in Tanzania, 207, 211, 229
ECZ. *See* Zaire, Christian Church of
Electric Energy Company of Côte d'Ivoire (EECI), 130
emigration, 249-51
energy supply, for domestic purposes, 8
  in Côte d'Ivoire, 116, 128, 130
  in Greater Khartoum, 264-65, 269, 273
  in Kinshasa, 161-62
  in Nigeria, 96-106
  in Senegal, 179
Enugu
  demography of, 72-73
  education in, 73
  energy supply in, 96-105
  health facilities in, 79
  urban management structure of, 109-10
  waste disposal in, 44-5, 85-95
  water supply in, 39, 79-85
environmental stress, 2, 7-11, 265, 270-71
exchange rates, 5, 13, 15

Family Planning National Committee (Greater Khartoum), 270
Federal Housing Authority (Nigeria, 1973), 57
food supply
  through aid, 11
  crop types, 8, 16
  cultivation in urban areas, 22-28
  "food gap," 8, 16-18
  in Kinshasa, 167-71, 308. *See also* markets
foula-foula (Brazzaville), 50. *See also* transport (Zaire)
fula-fula (Kinshasa), 50, 164-65

General Secretariat of Administrative Reform (Côte d'Ivoire), 115
Gibb, Sir Alexander, 58-59
Guidelines for Local Government Reform (Nigeria, 1976), 24

Hawkers and Vendors Association (Nairobi), 296
health facilities, 9, 231
  in Côte d'Ivoire, 116
  in Greater Khartoum, 266-7, 269-70, 273-74
  in Kinshasa, 165-67
  in Nigeria, 79
  in Senegal, 178-80, 187-89, 188-89
  in Tanzania, 231. *See also under separately listed cities and towns.*
housing, low-cost
  in Côte d'Ivoire, 55-56
  in Greater Khartoum, 256-57
  in Kenya, 34-35, 54-55, 281, 283, 284, 294-95
  in Nigeria, 57, 71
  in Senegal, 178-79
  in Tanzania, 57-58, 213, 224-27
  in Zaire, 57, 162-64. *See also* squatter settlements, sites and services schemes
Housing Bank of Senegal (BHS), 179
Housing Development Department (Nairobi), 284, 294-95
Human Resources Deployment Act (Tanzania, 1983), 63, 229

Ibadan, 8
  demography of, 73
  education in, 73
  energy supply in, 96-105
  health facilities in, 79
  urban management structure, 109-10
  waste disposal in, 44-45, 85-95, 312
  water supply in, 39, 79-85, 308
Idah, 39
industrialization, 11

informal sector
  in Dar es Salaam, 52-53, 212-13
  in Greater Khartoum, 64, 256-57
  in Kinshasa, 164-65
  in Nairobi, 276-77, 281, 283, 290, 297, 303
  in Nigeria, 63
  recycling of refuse in, 48-49
  in Senegal, 63
  taxation of, 29. See also private sector, matatu
import substitution, 2
Infrastructure Company of Côte d'Ivoire (SECI), 128, 130-31
integrated rural development, 1-2
International Development Association (IDA), 225
International Labour Association (ILO), 28
International Monetary Fund (IMF), 306, 312
Ivory Coast "miracle," 17, 19

JMPR. See Popular Revolutionary Youth Movement
job absenteeism, 48
jua kali ("hot sun") workshops, 290, 297

Kaduna
  demography of, 73
  education in, 73
  energy supply in, 96-105
  health facilities in, 79
  urban management structure, 109-110
  waste disposal in, 44-45,
  water supply in, 39, 79-85
Kaduna State Water Board (1971), 79
Kahara, Nathan, 32-33
KAMATA. See National Bus Company of Tanzania, 51-52
Kaolack, 178-79
Kenya Bus Service (KBS), 279, 286, 289
  fare structure, 291, 298, 299
  matatus, 53-54, 277, 283
Kenya Local Government Workers Union, 48
Kenyatta, Jomo, 276, 283, 297
Khartoum, Greater (the Three Towns), 253, 258-59
  building by-laws, 62

  energy supply in, 246;
  finances of, 260-61
  health services in, 266-67, 269-70, 273-74
  historical background, 253-55
  infrastructure of, 311
  land use in, 255-56
  population growth of, 267-68
  ruralization of, 254
  squatter self-help in, 64, 256-57
  urban planning and management of, 62-63, 257-58
  waste disposal in, 48, 262-64
  water supply in, 261-62, 269
Khartoum North, 258
  urban development of, 253-54
  waste disposal in 263
Khartoum Water Corporation (KWC), 261-62
Kilimanjaro Textile Mills (KILTEX), 242
kimalu-malu (Kinshasa), 50, 164-65
Kinshasa, city of, 149-75, 308
  education in, 165
  energy supply in, 161-62
  geography of, 153-54
  health facilities in, 165-67
  history of, 154
  informal sector in, 164-65
  land management in, 61, 154-58
  transport in, 49-51
  waste disposal in, 159-61
  water supply in, 159-61
Kisumu, 33, 295
kombi (Kinshasa), 164-65
Korhogo, 118, 120
  municipal employees in, 122
  municipal equipment in, 123
  taxes in, 136

Lagos, city of, 571
land
  irregular use of, 310-11
  equipment of, 56, 131 (Côte d'Ivoire)
  management of, 154-58, 173 (Kinshasa), 61 (Nigeria), 155-58 (Zaire)
  nationalization of, 310-11, 61 (Nigeria), 179 (Senegal), 154-58 (Zaire)
  speculation on, 197 (Dakar), 157-58, 173 (Kinshasa), 268 (Greater Khartoum)

mechanisms to control use, 255-56. *See also* housing, squatter settlements
Land Use Decree (Nigeria, 1978), 61
Lands, Housing and Urban Development, Ministry of (Tanzania), 225
"local democracy" (Tanzania), 23
local government
  agencies of, 20-21
  Anglophone, 27-29, 31-35, 207-08
  central government control over, 31-35, 230
  conflict in, 32-36
  finances of, 30-32, 120, 131-36 (Abidjan), 25-36 (Anglophone vs Francophone countries), 260-61 (Greater Khartoum), 107-09 (Nigeria), 30-31 (Senegal), 231-33, 234-35 (Tanzania)
  francophone, 29-31
  history of, 21-25 (Anglophone vs. Francophone countries), 214, 217-21 (Tanzania)
  reform of, 22-25, 107
  representative council system of, 25-28
  role in mobilizing resources, 214-15 (Tanzania)
  structure of, 117-21 (Abidjan), 258-59 (Greater Khartoum), 228-30 (Tanzania)
  virtues of, 216-17. *See also under cities and towns listed separately and commune system*
Local Government Edict (Nigeria, 1976), 107
Local Government Finances Act (Tanzania, 1982), 231
Local Government (Urban Authorities) Act (Tanzania, 1982), 229, 230
Lomé, 61
Low-Cost Housing Board (OHLM, Senegal), 178, 193
lower income groups, discrimination against, 34-35, 46, 61, 162
Lessor's Book (Zaire), 156-57

Man, 115
  municipal employees of, 122
  municipal equipment of, 123
  tax collection in, 135

Makurdi, 39
markets, 171-72, 308
matatu(s), 53-54, 276, 277-78
  assistance for, 287, 298
  associations, 292
  clientele of, 289-90
  financing and insurance, 300-02
  history and status, 283, 285-86
  operators of, 291-92, 302
  ownership of, 290
  profitability of, 292
  planning response to, 298
  policy options for, 299-303
  servicing of, 290-91, 297
  studies on, 286, 287
Matatu Act. *See* Traffic (Amendment) Act
Matatu Association of Kenya (1985), 293, 300
Matatu Vehicle Owners Association (1979), 277, 288, 293, 296, 300
Maternal and Infant Health Centre (PMI), 187, 188
Mauritania, 42
Mazingira Institute, 53, 277-78, 287-88
Mbeya, 203, 206
  master plan for, 59
  municipal decentralization of, 220
  sites and services schemes in, 225
  waste disposal in, 44, 239
Mefit Consulting Group Master Plan (1977), 256
migration, 9-10
  control of, 111
  rationality of, 2, 5-6
  rural to urban, 307-08 (general), 281 (Kenya), 151, 153 (Kinshasa), 69-72 (Nigeria), 249, 274-75 (Sudan), 208-09, 227 (Tanzania)
Miller Commission Report, 35
Moi, Daniel arap, 297
Mombasa, local government of, 33, 35, 295
Morogoro, 203, 207
  sites and services schemes in, 226
  waste disposal in, 239
Moshi, 203, 207
  master plan for, 59
  waste disposal in, 239
  water supply in, 241

Mtwara, master plan for, 58-59
municipal government. *See* local government
Mwanza, 225
Mwiru, Kingunge Ngombale, 36, n.4

Nairobi, city of
 historical development of, 278-85
 transport in, 53-54
 waste disposal in, 46-48
 water supply in, 38-39. *See* Nairobi City Council
Nairobi City Council (Nairobi City Commission, 1983-88), 278, 283, 293-4
 conflict with central government, 296-97
 finances of, 26-27, 32, 284, 285, 296-97, 310
 history of, 32-33, 35, 36 n.8
 reform of, 294-96
 in transport services, 53, 298, 299-300, 303
 in waste disposal, 46-48
 in water provision, 38-39
 World Bank and, 65
Nairobi Urban Study Group, 283
National Board for Water Supply of Senegal (SONEES), 179
National Bus Company of Tanzania (KAMATZ), 51-52
National Capital Commission Act (Greater Khartoum, 1983), 266
National Electric Power Authority (NEPA, Nigeria), 40
National Electricity Administration (NEA, Greater Khartoum), 265
National Electricity Company (SNEL, Zaire), 161
National Housing Bank (CNECI, Zaire, 1971), 163
National Housing Corporation (Kenya, 1967), 54-55, 281
National Housing Corporation (Tanzania, 1962), 57, 223
National Housing Office (ONL, Zaire, 1965), 163
National Office for Technical Studies of Development (Côte d'Ivoire), 130

National School of Administration (ENA, Côte d'Ivoire), 122, 143
National Upper School of Public Works (ENSTP, Côte d'Ivoire), 122
Nigerian Institute of Social and Economic Research (NISER), 39, 71
Nimzatt (Dakar), destruction of, 63
Njonjo, Charles, 35
Nyerere, Julius
 on decentralization of administration, 22-23, 36 n.4, 214
 on Dodoma Master Plan (1976), 60

OCA. *See* Ministry of African Estates
Office for the Study of Urban Planning (BEAU, Zaire), 167, 174
OHLM. *See* Low-Cost Housing Board
oil
 exploration for, 13
 importing of, 11
 price of, 11, 13, 306
 production of 11, 13
Omdurman, 253, 285
ONL. *See* National Housing Office
ordonnateur (authorisor of payments), 30-31. *See also* local government (Senegal)
Ouagadougou, 29
Oyo State Environmental Task Force, 45
Oyo State Water Corporation (1976), 79

parastatal corporations, 21, 26, 310
 Côte d'Ivoire, 40-41, 55-56, 164
 Nigeria, 38, 39-40, 79
 Tanzania, 51-52, 241
 Zaire, 161
Parti Socialiste Senegalais (PSS), 63
la patente (business tax), 29-30, 132, 135
payments, balance of, 11, 306
pendulum model, of administrative centralization / decentralization, 24
Pikine, Department of (Second Department of the Dakar region), 181-82, 184-85, 307
PMI. *See* Maternal and Infant Health Centre
Plot Identification Card (Zaire), 156-57
pollution, 71-72

of groundwater, 7-8
industrial 263
by sewage, 263
urban exposure to, 9
Popular Revolutionary Youth Movement (Zaire), 171
population growth, urban, 2-7, 113-114 (Côte d'Ivoire), 281 (Kenya), 69-72 (Nigeria), 178 (Senegal), 248, 253, 267-8, 274 (Sudan), 207-11 (Tanzania), 149, 151, 153, 308 (Zaire)
Port Bouet, 115, 135
price controls, 5
private sector, 37-39, 151, 197-98, 297-98
  in education, 180, 189 (Dakar), 165 (Kinshasa)
  in health facilities, 188-89 (Dakar), 267, 269-70, 273 (Greater Khartoum), 165, 167 (Kinshasa), 79 (Nigeria)
  in housing, 256-57 (Greater Khartoum), 54 (Kenya), 57-58 (Tanzania)
  in transport, 51-53, 241 (Dar es Salaam), 53-54, 276, 283, 285-93 (Kenya), 180 (Senegal), 49-51, 164-65 (Zaire)
  in waste disposal, 45-46 (Côte d'Ivoire), 161 (Kinshasa), 44-45 (Nigeria)
  in water supply, 40-41 (Côte d'Ivoire), 191 (Dakar), 262 (Greater Khartoum), 42 (Mauritania), 85 (Nigeria), 242 (Tanzania)
Public Transport Company (SOTRAC, Senegal), 180

receveur (receiver of cash payments), 30-31. *See also* local government (Senegal)
research methodology
  Dakar study, 181-85
  Nairobi study, 277-78
  Tanzania study, 211-12, 244-45
Revenue Allocation Act (Nigeria, 1981), 107
Revenue Sharing Formula, 106-08. *See also* urban management (Nigeria)
roads. *See* transport and roads
Rubia, Charles, 279, 297
rural bias, 220, 221
rural sector, 2, 6
ruralization. *See* Khartoum, Greater

SAUR. *See* Urban and Rural Planning Company
scavenging, of refuse dumps, 48-49
SECI. *See* Infrastructure Company of Côte d'Ivoire
SETU. *See* Company for Urban Lands and Infrastructure (Côte d'Ivoire)
Sewerage and Refuse Matters Department (Nigeria, 1984), 45
SIAS. *See* Waste Disposal Company of Senegal
SICAP. *See* Cap-Vert Building Society
SITAF. *See* African Industrial Truck Company
sites and services schemes 277, 284 (Nairobi), 224-27 (Tanzania), 34 (Thika), by World Bank, 64-65. *See also* World Bank
SNEL. *See* National Electricity Company (Zaire)
SOADIP. *See* Waste Management Agency for the Dakar Commune
"Socialism and Self-Reliance" (Tanzania), 203, 219
SODECI. *See* Water Supply Agency for Côte d'Ivoire
SOGEFIHA. *See* Company for the Financial Management of Housing (Côte d'Ivoire)
soil, salinization of, 8-9
Sokoine, Edward, 52
SONEES. *See* National Board for Water Supply of Senegal
SOTRAC. *See* Public Transport Company (Senegal)
SOTRAZ. *See* Transport Company of Zaire
squatter settlements, 63-64
  around Abidjan, 56
  in Dakar, 63
  in Dar es Salaam, 61, 224, 225-7
  in Greater Khartoum, 64, 255, 257, 262
  in Tanzania, 209
  in Zaire, 157
Special Budget for Investment and Facilities (BSIE, Côte d'Ivoire), 114

STB. *See* Brazzaville Transport Company
SUNGURATEX. *See* Tanganyika Dyeing and Weaving Mills

Tabora, 203, 206
  master plan for, 59
  sites and services scheme in, 226
  waste disposal in, 239
  water supply in, 241
Tananarive, waste disposal in, 48-49
Tanga, 203, 206
  master plan for, 59
  sites and services scheme in, 226
  waste disposal in, 44, 239
Tanganyika Dyeing and Weaving Mills (SUNGURATEX), 242
Tanzania Electricity Supply Company (TANESCO), 223
Tanzanian Housing Bank (THB, 1973), 57-58, 213, 225
Tanzanian People's Defence Forces, 223
Thiès, housing in, 178-79
Thika, 34
Toumodi, 115
  municipal employees of, 122
  municipal equipment of, 123
  tax recovery of, 134
tourism, effects of, 2
Town Planning Agency of the City of Abidjan (AUA), 130-31
Traffic (Amendment) Act (Matatu Act, 1984), 53-54, 278, 288
transport and roads
  in Côte d'Ivoire, 116, 128, 139, 140
  in Greater Khartoum, 255, 256
  in Kenya, 53-54, 285-303
  in Senegal, 180
  in Tanzania, 52-53, 238-41
  in Zaire, 49-51, 158, 164-65. *See also dala-dala, foula-foula, fula-fula, kimalu-malu, kombi, matatu*
Transport Company of Zaire (SOTRAZ), 51
tribal boundaries, 216

UDA. *See* Usafiri Dar es Salaam
Uganda, housing in, 57
ujamaa (Tanzania), 60
underemployment, 71
unemployment, 71

unicité de caisse (single account system), 31. *See* local government, Francophone
USAID, 276-77, 284
United Transport Overseas (UTO), 53, 279
Universal Primary Education (UPE, Nigeria, 1976-77), 73
Urafiki Textile Mills, 242
Urban and Rural Planning Company (SAUR), 41
urban bias, 1, 5, 11, 19, 296
urban crime, 71
urban crisis, international response to, 20
urban history
  of Côte d'Ivoire, 114-15
  of Greater Khartoum, 247-48, 253-56
  of Nairobi, 278-79, 281
urban management, 66, 305-07
  crisis in, 1, 65-66
  government policy on, 15
  policy recommendations for, 307-12
  in Côte d'Ivoire, 113-14, 142-44, 145-46
  in Dakar and Pikine Departments (CUD), 185-87
  in Kenya, 276, 281, 283
  in Greater Khartoum, 257-60, 268, 270-74
  in Nigeria, 106-111
  in Tanzania, 207-08, 243-44
  in Zaire, 151, 172-75. *See also* land (management of), local government, urban planning, urban services
urban planning, 58, 60-63
  response to, 63-65
  "basic needs" strategy, 284
  "management approach," 20
  "management by objectives," 309
  "master plan" strategy, 58-60, 256, 307
  Metropolitan Growth Strategy, 283
Urban Planning Workshop for the Abidjan Area (AURA), 130-31
urban services
  buying out of, 40
  contracting out of, 37-39, 43, 161, 197-98
  privatization of, 37-38, 48; provision of, 64, 256-57, 261, 262, 268-69, 273 (Greater Khartoum), 178-80, 221-23

(Tanzania), 149, 151, 167, 173-75 (Zaire). *See also* education, food supply, health facilities, housing, private sector, transport, waste disposal, water supply
Usafiri Dar es Salaam (UDA), 241

waste disposal, 7-8, 27, 43-49
 in Côte d'Ivoire, 45-46, 130, 139
 in Greater Khartoum, 262-64, 269, 272-73
 in Kinshasa, 159-61
 in Nairobi, 46-48
 in Nigeria, 39-40, 44-45, 85-95
 in Senegal, 173, 191-95
 in Tanzania, 43-44, 223-24, 236-37, 239, 245 n.3. *See also separately listed cities and towns*
Waste Disposal Company of Senegal (SIAS), 192-93
Waste Management Agency for the Dakar Commune (SOADIP), 192
water supply, 7, 13, 27, 38-42, 308
 in Côte d'Ivoire, 40-41
 in the Dakar region, 190-91
 in Greater Khartoum, 261-62, 269
 in Kinshasa, 158-59
 in Nairobi, 284
 in Nigeria, 79-85
 in Tanzania, 42, 241-43, 308. *See also separately listed cities and towns*
Water Supply Agency for Côte d'Ivoire (SODECI), 40-1
The Weekly Review, on Nairobi waste disposal, 46-7
"witnesses" (Pikine Department), 185
women, 153, business organization of (AFECOZA, Zaire), 171-72
World Bank
 evaluation of SODECI, 41
 loans, 38-39, 284, 294
 on local government, 29
 on population, 6
 on urban transport, 49
 urban projects, 20, 57, 59, 64-65, 225-26, 276-77

Youpougon, 135

Zaire, Christian Church of (ECZ), 164
Zambia, 28